K'ung-tzu or Confucius?

Paul A Rule

K'ung-tzu or Confucius?

The Jesuit interpretation of Confucianism

Paul A Rule

Asia
2021

First published in 1986 by Allen & Unwin Australia Pty Ltd 8 Napier Street, North Sydney, NSW 2060 Australia in association with Department of Far Eastern History Australian National University and Asian Studies Association of Australia.

Republished in 2021 by ATF Press Publishing Group, with a new introduction by Paul A Rule

Copy editor and Index by Gabriel Bueno Siqueira

ISBN:	978-1-922582-08-9	soft
	978-1-922582-09-6	hard
	978-1-922582-10-2	epub
	978-1-922582-11-9	pdf

Published by:

Asia

An imprint of the ATF Press Publishing
Group owned by ATF (Australia) Ltd.
PO Box 234
Brompton, SA 5007
Australia
ABN 90 116 359 963
www.atfpress.com
Making a lasting impact

Table of Contents

Acknowledgments

The author's indebtedness to a legion of people is obvious on every page of this work. During the years of its gestation I have received constant encouragement and good advice from historians, sinologists, librarians and members of the Society of Jesus, in Australia, Asia and Europe. May I tender the work itself as thanks, inadequate though it be, as the most appropriate way of expressing my gratitude for the interest they have taken in the subject and in my stumbling pursuit of understanding. I must, however, acknowledge my special debt to those without whose assistance the work could have been completed. To the late Otto van der Sprenkel for inspiration, criticism, and access to his enormous store of knowledge of men and books, Chinese and European; to Igor de Rachewiltz and Julia Ching for lighting dark places; to Professor AL Basham for smoothing my way in numerous directions; to Father Edmond Lamalle, Jesuit Archivist, for unfailing kindness and help; and to Mr JM Braga for sharing his enthusiasm for, and knowledge of, the Portuguese pioneers in Asia: to all these, heartfelt thanks and the hope that my work will repay to some extent their time and interest.

Finally, thanks are due to the Myer Foundation and to La Trobe University for enabling me to pursue further investigations in Rome in 1975 and 1979, and to La Trobe University's Publications Committee for a generous publishing subsidy.

Abbreviations

As far as possible, the form of abbreviation used for manuscripts follows the now standard forms in Joseph Dehergne SJ, *Répertoire des Jesuites de Chine de 1552* à *1800*, Roma/Paris 1973, XXXI–XXXVI.

The most important are as follows:

ARSJ:	Archivum Romanum Societatis Jesu—the Archives of the Society of Jesus, located at Borgo Santo Spirito 5, Roma, Italy
ARSJ:	FG The Fondo Gesuitico of the above
ARSJ:	JS The Japonica-Sinica section of the above
ASJP:	Archives of the Paris Province (the old 'Province de France') of the Society of Jesus
ASV:	Archivo Segreto Vaticano-Vatican Archive
BL:	British Library (formerly British Museum)
BN:	Bibliothèque Nationale, Paris
B Vat:	Biblioteca Apostolica Vaticana
B Vat:	Borg Cin. The Borgia Cinese collection of the above
B Vat:	Borg Lat. The Borgia Latino collection of the above
BVE:	Bibliotheca Vittorio Emmanuele (now Biblioteca Nazionale Centrale di Roma)
BVE:	FG The Fondo Gesuitico of the above
PRO:	Public Records Office, London

All references to manuscripts are to folio numbers unless otherwise specified, with 'r' and 'v' used to specify *recto* and *verso*, and the number in italics, the volume or box numbers.

All references to printed works in Western languages are to page numbers unless otherwise specified.

All references to Chinese works, printed or manuscript, are to the traditional folio numbers, with *recto* and *verso* indicated by 'a' and 'b', except where paginated Western-style, in which case 'p' for 'page' is used. When two or three *chuan* are numbered traditionally 上 or 下 or 上中下 this is indicated by A and B or A, B, C.

Chinese words are romanised in the text according to the Wade-Giles system. Readers are referred to the Character Index for Chinese characters, both for names of people and places and words. For titles of Chinese works see Bibliography.

Preface

Confucius is, in a sense, a Jesuit invention. It is one of the aims of study to establish what that sense is. It is not just a question of Latinised 'Confucius', although it is significant that he was introduced to Europe in the language of Rome. The crucial problem is to establish to what extent the 'Confucius' of the Jesuit letters, travel reports, treatises and translations, corresponds to the Chinese Confucius. We are not so much concerned here with Confucius the man, the K'ung Ch'iu of history, as with the myth, the K'ung-tzu of Chinese tradition.[1] To what extent was the 'Confucius' introduced to Europe by the Jesuits, a Jesuit creation, and to what extent an accurate representation of the view held by the Chinese themselves of the man and his ideas?

The process by which the Jesuits of the Old China mission[2] developed their image of Confucius is a fascinating subject of study for its own sake. It also provides us with an amply documented case of cultural confrontation. Two great cultures had developed in ignorance of each other and were now suddenly brought into contact. The Jesuits were the first intermediaries in that confrontation and since they quickly appreciated the dominant role of the Confucian value-system in Chinese society and government, their interpretation of Confucianism was the point of cultural shock. The political clash was delayed till the nineteenth century although the Jesuits played a role in the earliest diplomatic exchanges between China

1. I borrow this convenient distinction from HG Creel, *Confucius, the Man and the Myth,* New York, 1949.
2. That is from about 1580 to after the suppression of the Society of Jesus in 1773.

and Portugal, Holland, France, Russia and England.[3] Chinese, and especially Confucian, ideas . . . as interpreted by the Jesuits, also played an important role in the intellectual ferment of European Enlightenment. The enigmatic figure labelled 'Confucius' who gazes out at us from the pages of seventeenth and eighteenth-century Jesuit books is the key to many otherwise puzzling directions in European thought.

The abundance of the material, printed and manuscript, the problems of documents in several languages and variant copies, the inadequate bibliography of the subject, the physical dispersion of Jesuit libraries and archives,[4] make an exhaustive study impossible in the scope of a single volume. Moreover, early in my research it became clear that there are a number of areas closely related to the 'Jesuit interpretation of Confucianism' which demand extended treatment in their own right. Among these are the extent of Jesuit influence on late Ming-early Ch'ing intellectual trends, the peculiar activities of the group of French Jesuits in Peking known as 'Figurists', and above all the Chinese Rites controversy which in itself would require a multivolume study. However, a beginning has to be made somewhere, and I am convinced that at this stage in research into the role of the Jesuit mission in Chinese and European intellectual history, there is a place for a general survey covering the whole period of the mission of the late sixteenth to late eighteenth centuries, and concentrating on the central issue of the Jesuit response to Confucianism.

It may seem arrogant to speak of a 'beginning' since so much has been written of the Jesuit mission in China. A glance at the columns of Cordier's *Bibliotheca Sinica* or the relevant volumes of the Streit/Dindinger *Bibliotheca Missionum* is enough to show that the subject is one that has been much studied. However, a closer examination of this overwhelming mass of literature, or at least that part accessible to the scholar based in Australia, reveals that much remains to be done. A great deal of writing on the mission is popular in nature and based

3. In all cases they acted as interpreters, and often played a more active role. See, for example, J Sebes, *The Jesuits and the Sino-Russian Treaty of Nerchinsk (1689)*, Rome, 1961; and frequent comments in the *Journals* of Lord Macartney (JL, Cranmer-Byng, *An Embassy to China* [London, 1963], 100, 151 etc).
4. For a discussion of these problems see PA Rule, 'Jesuit Sources' in *Essays on the Sources for Chinese History*, DD Leslie, C Mackerras and Wang Gungwu, editors (Canberra, 1973), 176–87.

on a few standard printed sources. Most of the serious work falls into the special category of 'mission history', a genre which lends itself to distortion and special pleading. I would like to acknowledge my debt to the Jesuit historians of the China mission, to Henri Bernard-Maître, Joseph Dehergne, Pasquale M D'Elia, Francis Rouleau and Joseph Schütte, who are in general, and quite appropriately, primarily concerned with the 'mission history' aspects of the question. While a comprehensive history of the Jesuit mission in China remains to be written, the groundwork has been done and the collection and publication of the major documents has begun. We have reason to hope that the *esprit de corps* of the Society of Jesus and the revolution in missiology and the theology of Christian missions of the last half century will lead to much further work in mission history which will make the task of the historian of China and the historian of ideas much easier.

The present work, however, is not 'mission history' in the normal sense. I am concerned with the complex interaction of two cultures, the attempt of European scholars to understand the value-system and beliefs of a totally different culture. If America was the first 'new world', China was to prove a 'new world' in an even more fundamental sense. There was a mutual recognition, not only of high material culture, but of ideas, standards of behaviour and political systems which were worthy of respect and investigation. The glowing Jesuit accounts of Chinese society were matched by the exclamation of the late Ming scholar, Hsieh Chao-chih, 'Thus in foreign countries there are also real gentlemen'.[5] This rapport was not altogether typical, nor did it survive the tensions introduced by the European maritime encroachment of the nineteenth century. But, for a while, a serious attempt was made at understanding and interpreting China to the West and vice versa.

I shall be primarily concerned with the Jesuit interpretation of Chinese thought and religion to Europeans, rather than their contribution to the Chinese view of Europe. This weighting of the subject is partly due again to the limits of time and space, partly also to the difficulties posed by the Ch'ing dynasty suppression of

5. Quoted in SY Teng and JK Fairbank, *China's Response to the West* (New York: Atheneum, 1963), 13.

'unorthodox' literature.[6] I have tried to examine as much as possible of the Jesuit writings in Chinese and the more important recent studies by Chinese scholars. I can only hope that those Chinese, Japanese and Western scholars more competent than myself in the field of late Ming-early Ch'ing history will be able to exploit more fully what insights I may have gained in placing the Jesuits within the complex intellectual currents of the period.

Holmes Welch in *The Practice of Chinese Buddhism*[7] makes what I feel is a valid and pertinent distinction between the main sources in both Chinese and Western languages which must be consulted by all serious scholars of Chinese history, and 'the low-grade ore' in each. The latter should, he claims, be left each to its own, Chinese to Chinese scholars, Western language material to Western scholars. In this spirit, I have attempted as exhaustive a scrutiny as possible of material, printed and manuscript, in Western languages, relating to the Jesuit mission. The bibliography will, I hope, enable the critical reader to assess the extent of my success in this. Many of the items have been examined only cursorily in the light of my central concern with the Jesuit interpretation of Confucianism. I have not attempted to embrace in this study such questions as the Jesuit contribution to Chinese science or art which have been treated adequately by specialists; and I am only too aware of the superficiality of treatment of 'Figurism' and the Chinese Rites question, both of which I intend to pursue at proper length elsewhere. However, I have come to see that a critical chronological survey of the developing Jesuit interpretation of Confucianism over the whole period of the old Jesuit mission is the indispensable prelude to serious study of the last two subjects.[8]

When reading many of the accounts of the Jesuits' attitude towards Confucianism, I am reminded of Dickens' reviewer for the Eatanswill Gazette who wrote 'a copious review of a work on Chinese metaphysics' by combining, the articles on 'China' and 'Metaphysics'

6. See LC Goodrich, *The Literary Inquisition of Ch'ien Lung* (Baltimore: Waverly Press Inc, 1935).
7. Holmes Welch, *The Practice of Chinese Buddhism, 1900–1950* (Cambridge, Mass: Harvard University Press, 1967), vii.
8. For example, Joseph Needham and Wang Ling in *Science and Civilization in China*, especially volumes 2 and 3, and articles and books on the Jesuit artists, by Paul Pelliot, PM D'Elia and George Loehr.

in the Encyclopaedia Britannica.[9] Too often it is assumed that 'Jesuit' and 'Confucian' are static and self-explanatory terms. Even when the Jesuits are not seen in the lurid light of a Fulop-Miller.[10] they are assumed to be men formed in a rigid mould whose motivation, objectives and behaviour are fully predictable. The modern Jesuits I have known are a living refutation of this, and the Jesuits of the China mission display the same individuality and variety as their successors. Certainly they were products of a particular style of spiritual formation and their behaviour was regulated by the Constitutions and the distinctive forms of organisation of the Society of Jesus. But they were also men of their time, who had received the best education available and absorbed the latest developments in science, letters and theology. Over the two centuries of the mission one finds considerable change and development in ideas and attitudes. The eighteenth-century French Jesuit, formed by the religious and intellectual debates of the France of Louis XIV, was in his scholarly and missionary style completely different from the seventeenth century Portuguese Jesuit. At the same time, the experience of the earlier missionaries which had moulded the customs and practices of the China mission, was handed on to the later Jesuits. Nationality, training, personality and experience—all must be assessed as factors in the Jesuit interpretation of Confucianism.

Nor can the 'Confucianism' of the late Ming and early Ch'ing be regarded as a static monolithic orthodoxy. It was a living tradition, as Joseph Levenson demonstrated in *Confucian China and Its Modern Fate*. The late Ming period in particular saw an extraordinary range of divergent opinions within the ambit of Confucian literati society.[11] The Jesuit interpretation of Confucianism can be seen as but one of a range of contemporary 'revisionist' interpretations.

---

9. *The Posthumous Papers of the Pickwick Club,* chapter LI.
10. René Fülop-Miller, in the preface of his widely circulated *The Power and Secret of the Jesuits,* boasts that he has rejected 'impartial dryness and objectivity' to allow his imagination and the critics of the Society full play. For a more balanced assessment, and an examination of Jesuit stereotypes, see A Lynn Martin, *Henry III and the Jesuit Politicians,* Geneva, 1973, chapter l, and 'The Jesuit Mystique' in *The Sixteenth Century Journal,* IV/1 (1973): 31–40.
11. v WT de Bary editor, *Self and Society in Ming Thought* (New York: Columbia University Press, 1970), especially Professor de Bary's own contribution, 'Individualism and Humanitarianism in Late Ming Thought'.

The view of Confucianism that grew out of the meeting of Jesuit missionary and Chinese scholar was not, of course, an academic exercise. The Jesuits were primarily missionaries and the risks they took in getting to China, their tenacity in the face of obstacles and dangers, their single-mindedness, are only intelligible if this is taken into account. There was always in their lives some degree of tension between the scholar, the scientist or sinologist, and the missionary. But this was a tension that the Jesuit scholar faced in Europe too, and his whole training was directed towards harnessing scholarly work to the primary aim of 'the greater glory of God'. My impression is that the degree of bias that resulted is no greater than that in most other interpretations of Confucianism, Chinese or Western, positivist or Marxist. It was overt, consciously and explicitly present in all they wrote. On the other hand, the changes in emphasis, the qualifications and hesitations that are to be found especially in the private correspondence among Jesuits, the differences between views expressed in popular and propagandist works and scholarly works, suggest that most Jesuits possessed a scholarly conscience. The views that most shocked their European readers were often a simple presentation of Chinese realities.

It is impossible to write about the Jesuit mission in China without to some extent rehearsing old controversies. Under the stress of the Rites Controversy the Jesuit literature on China became increasingly polemical and a 'party line' emerged, partly imposed by the European Jesuit editors of the reports from China. There is a danger that concentration on these issues will produce a subtle foreshortening effect and that we will fail to see the Jesuits as mainly engaged in the prosaic daily work of the mission. They were not preoccupied with interpreting Chinese beliefs and customs, except in so far as circumstances forced them to be. Nor was the Jesuit interpretation of Confucianism a continuous conscious development. It is quite clear from the documents that many issues were forgotten only to be revived later, many methods discovered anew by later generations of missionaries. Most Jesuits did not have access to the mission archives and in any case were too busy and concerned with immediate practical issues to see the mission in historical perspective. The isolation of certain ideas, of certain controversial issues, from their context is always dangerous and misleading.

However, justification for this procedure may be found in the importance of the ideas and issues thus isolated. The controversies are not dead, the ideas and issues are still important. For the sociologist seeking to establish the parameters or conditions of cultural change, the Jesuit experiment in China should be of great interest. The theological issues raised by a wider ecumenism and the reassessment of the relations between Christianity and non-Christian religion are well exemplified in this case. For the historian or phenomenologist of religion, Confucianism presents a kind of extreme or limiting case in which the religious or sacred elements are elusive and challenge many of the accepted generalisations.[12] The Jesuits' apprehension of the religious value of Confucianism seems to me a first and faltering step towards the reappreciation of the nature of 'religion' and its relationship to the 'secular'. It was no accident that the philosophers of the Enlightenment took such an interest in the 'news from China'.[13] China was both a source and a test case for the new ideas about religion and its social role. Pascal was an implacable enemy of the Jesuits, but he perceived the crucial importance of their revelations about China, which, by enlarging the Christian world-view, simultaneously complicated and clarified the main issues.[14] It is my hope that this study of the Jesuit interpretation of Confucianism will shed some light on the issues that confronted Pascal and still confront us today.

---

12. See PA Rule, 'Sacred and Secular in China', in *Australian Essays in World Religions*, edited by VC Hayes (Adelaide: Australian Association for the Study of Religions, 1977), 83–95.
13. *Novissima Sinica,* the title of Leibniz's collection of Jesuit letters and treatises, first published in 1697.
14. See Blaise Pascal, *Pensées*, trans. M. Turnell, London, 1962, 229; Fragment 533 of the Brunschwig-Boutroux edition of Pascal's *Oeuvres*, Paris, 1904–14.

Introduction to the Re-Edition

This early (1968) work of mine has long been out of print and I have frequently received inquiries about its availability. When thinking of a re-edition I found that there was very little I would want to retract or substantially change in the text. There is much more I could say on many of the questions discussed and, in fact, have said in many later publications including those in progress. But as a general introduction to a very large subject I think it still has some value. And I have not changed my mind on major issues of interpretation. Hence I decided to let it stand even as a historical document in itself.

I have resisted the temptation to update the bibliography, to add to the references to include the enormous amount of archival material now accessible on-line as well as newly discovered: bibliographical resources are now so ample and search engines so refined as to make this much less necessary. I also decided not to convert the old Wade-Giles romanisation of the Chinese to Pinyin. It is a marker of an older state of play and also the primacy of the Chinese characters which all romanizations inadequately represent.

The cover illustration from the famous Jesuit work *Confucius Sinarum Philosophus* (Paris 1687) sums up the transition of the historical Chinese sage, known in China as K'ung-tzu or K'ung Fu-tzu (*Kongzi/Kong Fuzi* in Pinyin) to the Western Confucius. While it purports to represent the sage, or perhaps an image of the sage, with the National Academy in Beijing in the background with its tablets of the Master's disciples and library of Confucian books, and was presumably based on one or more Chinese illustrations, it is still the work of a French illustrator with accommmodations to European tastes. It is at one and the same time *chinoiserie* and a serious attempt to introduce Chinese ideas to a European public.

Thanks and gratitude is due to the Charles Strong Trust which provided a grant to enable this re-edition to proceed. My heartfelt thanks to them, to Hilary D Regan of ATF Press for his persistence and help with this project and to Gabriel Bueno Siqueira (also of ATF Press), for his checking of the proofs and for the new index.

1
Matteo Ricci and the Jesuit Interpretation of Confucianism

I make every effort to turn our way the ideas of the leader of the sect of the literati, Confucius, by interpreting in our favour things which he left ambiguous in his writings. In this way our Fathers gain great favour with the literati who do not adore the idols.

Matteo Ricci[1]

The Jesuit interpretation of Confucianism was not an abstract intellectual exercise, but the direct result of experience, of creative confrontation with and involvement in Chinese life. In this chapter, as in the rest of this study, I shall be obliged to isolate the Jesuits' confrontation with Confucianism from their total missionary concern and activities, a procedure that involves danger of distortion and misinterpretation. It would be less dangerous if there existed an adequate history of the Jesuit mission in China to which the reader could be referred to correct the imbalance of concentration on the issue of the Jesuits and Confucianism. But such a history does not yet exist,[2] and it would be distracting for the author to attempt to fill many of the lacunae himself. All I can do is to draw attention in a general way to the peculiar circumstances of each period of the development of the mission and to correct any major efforts or misunderstandings in the standard accounts that are relevant to the central theme.

Fortunately, the first period of the mission, the era of Matteo Ricci, is one of the best documented. Ricci's life has been treated by several

1. Translated from *Fonti Ricciane,* N709, II, 296.
2. One has, however, been promised as the joint work of two Jesuit sinologists, Francis Rouleau and Joseph Sebes *(NJ News,* December 1977, 17).

competent biographers[3] drawing on Ricci's own account of his mission[4] and his letters,[5] as well as his Chinese works. Ricci's predecessor and companion, Michele Ruggieri, has received less attention although he appears at least marginally in all the Ricci studies and has been the subject of a dissertation by Joseph Shih SJ.[6] The lesser figures of the period, Francesco Pasio, Antonio d'Almeida, Eduardo de Sande, Francisco de Petris, Didaco Pantoja, Emanuel Diaz, etc. are known only through a few published letters. One would like to know much more about the practice and views of Ricci's companions and fellow missionaries in order to speak confidently of the Jesuit interpretation of Confucianism in this period rather than Ricci's interpretation. However, for most of his time in China, Ricci was the superior of the mission, and for all of that period the dominant figure of the mission. Divisions do not seem to have appeared in the Jesuit ranks, at least such as to attract public notice, till after his death. As far as Confucianism is concerned, the personal history of Ricci is the history of the developing Jesuit interpretation of Confucianism in its first stages.

In this chapter, then, I shall concentrate on Ricci, on his discovery of Confucianism, his reaction to it, and the development by him of a distinctive interpretation of Confucianism that became normative for the mission. I shall also deal with Ricci's relations with individual Confucian scholars, but in outline only, reserving a fuller analytical

3. Notably by Henry Bernard [-Maître] in *Le Pere Matthieu Ricci et la Sociétee Chinoise de Son Temps, 2* volumes, Tientsin, 1937; O Gentili, *L'Apostolo delta Cina: P Matteo Ricci SJ*, Rome, 1953; Vincent Cronin, *The Wise Man from the West* (London: Penguin Books, 1955); and F Bortone, *P Matteo Ricci SJ: II 'Saggio d'Occidente'*, 2nd edition (Rome: Desclée & C, 1965). In Chinese, see especially Lo Kuang, *Li Ma-tou chuan,* 2nd edition (Taipei, 1972), and the collection, *Li Ma-tou yen-chiu lun-chi* (Hong Kong: Chung-wen. Bookstore, 1971). Mention should also be made of the treatment of Ricci in GF Dunne, *Generation of Giants: The Story of the Jesuits in China in the Last Decades of the Ming Dynasty* (London: Kessinger Publishing, 1962).
4. Published in the original form for the first time by P Tacchi Venturi in volume I of his *Opere Storiche del P. Matteo Ricci S.J.*, Macerata, 1911, and in a revised edition by PM D'Elia in the *Fonti Ricciane,* 3 volumes, Rome, 1942–49.
5. Published in Tacchi Venturi, *Opere Storiche*, II, Macerata, 1913.
6. *Le père Ruggieri et le problème de l'evangèlisation en Chine* (Rome: Pontificiae Universitatis Gregorianae, 1964).

treatment for another time.[7] The debate amongst Confucian scholars, both friends and opponents, largely centred upon Ricci's writings, even though it did not come to a head till sometime after his death and hence belongs to later chapters. On the other hand, I will discuss here Ricci's views on the Chinese Rites question which did not really become an issue till after his time. Ricci's successor as superior of the mission, Nicolò Longobardo, precipitated the controversy amongst the Jesuits themselves, and the influx of other religious orders exacerbated it. As for the influence on Europe of these early Jesuit contacts, until Nicholas Trigault published his version of Ricci's journals in 1615, there was hardly any knowledge of, not to say debate about, Confucianism, so the question of the Jesuits' role in introducing Confucianism to Europe must also wait till a later chapter.

The theme of this chapter is well summed up in the quotation from Ricci's journals with which I began it. The Jesuits were virtually the first Europeans to discover Confucius and Confucianism, 'the sect of the literati' as they not inaccurately called it.[8] They recognised the dominance of Chinese society, government and scholarship exercised by the Confucian literati and sought to make contact with them by allying themselves with the Confucians against the Buddhists. In the process they developed an interpretation of Confucianism that took advantage of the ambiguities of the Confucian tradition, interpreting it in a sense favourable to Christianity. The sources of that interpretation, its motivation and articulation, are the subject of this first stage of our investigation.

Michele Ruggieri and the Establishment of the Mission

The priority in the establishment of the Jesuit mission in China certainly belongs to Michele Ruggieri. In a sense he was also the discoverer of Confucianism, the first Westerner to study the Confucian

7. Two very recent publications on the subject are JD Young, *Confucianism and Christianity: The First Encounter* (Hong Kong: Hong Kong University Press, 1983); and J Gernet, *La Chine et Christianisme: Action et réaction* (Paris: Gallimard, 1982). I have taken Young's work into account in what follows, but Gernet's book was not available at the time of writing. I have however, seen some of Gernet's recent articles *v* Bibliography.
8. 'La setta de' letterati' is in fact a fairly literal and exact translation of the term they applied to themselves, *ju-chiao.*

books and to report on them to Westerners outside China. However, his account of Confucianism is so incomplete and his appreciation of its importance to the mission apparently so slight, that it is probably more appropriate to credit Ricci with its discovery. Pasquale M D'Elia characterises the relationship succinctly if rather blasphemously when he describes Ruggieri as playing John the Baptist to Ricci.[9]

Ruggieri was the first Jesuit to learn Chinese, and the first to implement the 'accommodation policy' drawn up by the Jesuit Visitor to the Indies, Alessandro Valignano.[10] How detailed were the instructions left behind in Macao by Valignano in July 1579 we do not know. Ruggieri describes them in terms that suggest they extended only to learning Chinese. We do have a later letter of Valignano which outlines his plans for the mission and stresses contact with the *letrados* as the key aim, but this postdates the crucial discovery of the significance of the Confucian literati and may not, I think, be used uncritically as evidence for Valignano's intentions in 1579 or 1582. Valignano wrote to the Bishop of Evora, Dom Theotonio de Braganca, from Goa, on 23 December 1585:

> When I was on the way to Japan, I decided that two fathers should be stationed in Amacao, the Portuguese port of China, and that they should be engaged in no other work than learning the language and letters of China, and be given masters and everything else necessary. They made such great progress in the language that when I returned from Japan I determined to try them out in this business of entering China. Giving them orders which appeared to me convenient for the task, I instructed them to introduce themselves in China as men of letters (*homes letrados*) who had come from far-off lands because of the fame of the wisdom and writings (*letras*) of China. To this end, they first wrote a treatise in the form of a dialogue in the language and letters of China, in which were presented all the substance of our holy faith, proving that the soul is immortal, that there is another life and one sole God

9. 'Quadro Storico-Sinologico del Primo Libro di Dottrina Cristiana in Cinese', in *Archivum Historicum Societatis Jesu*, III (1934): 222.
10. On Valignano, see PM D'Elia, 7 *Grandi Missionari* (Rome, 1940), II 119–70; JM Schütte, *Introductio ad Historiam Societatis Jesu in Japonia* (Rome: Apud Institutum Historicum Soc Jesu, 1968), 46–61; and JM Braga, 'The Paregyric of Alexander Valignano SJ', in *Monumenta Nipponica*, V (1942): 523–35.

> who must be adored, and finally dealing with the creation, the manner of our redemption, and all the most important things one has to do and believe in order to arrive at the other life. They joined to this a clock, a sphere, and a map of the world, which they also brought with them and adorned with Chinese letters. They dressed in the Chinese fashion, in capes with long sleeves and four-cornered hats, in the same way as some of their literati (*letrados*).[11]

This letter has many points of interest. it was written almost exactly three years after Valignano had left Macao for India and the section immediately following on the one quoted here shows that he had received some news of the initial successes of the mission. The stress on the *letrados* may then have been due to the information he had received from Ruggieri and Ricci in Chao-ch'ing, but I think it more likely that it represents his own intentions and instructions based on Ruggieri's early contacts with Chinese officials in Canton. Ruggieri and Pasio had left for Chao-ch'ing to establish a permanent mission residence a few days before Valignano departed from Macao and this letter may well indicate Valignano's thinking at that time. It stresses the necessity for gaining the approval of the '*grandes letrados*', especially the 'supreme Mandarin, and Viceroy of the Province of Canton'.[12]

What Valignano does not seem to have been aware of, is that Ruggieri and Pasio had not in fact established themselves in Chao-ch'ing in the guise of literati, but rather as Buddhist monks. This false step, as it later appeared to Ricci,[13] was, it would seem, undertaken at the request of Chinese officials. A letter of Ruggieri from Chao-ch'ing of 12 February 1583 describes an interview with the Military Commander (*tsung-ping*) of Kwangtung, an old acquaintance from Canton,[14] who was paying his respects to the visiting Censor in the viceregal seat of Chao-ch'ing.

---

11. *Cartas que os Padres e Irmaos da Companhia de Jesus escreverao dos Reynos de Japao e China . . .* (Evora, 1598), II, f 170,
12. *Cartas,* II, f 170v.
13. v *Fonti Ricciane,* N429, I, 335–7, for Ricci's arguments against the Buddhist role and Valignano's permission for Ricci and his companions to change to that of Confucian scholars (1593–94).
14. v *Fonti Ricciane,* N210, I, 156. This man is identified by D'Elia as Huang Ying-chia.

> We went to see him two days ago and he received us very well, giving us a tael of silver as alms. When he spoke about our dress, he designed a hat for us himself, saying that the Viceroy and everyone else wished us to wear the dress of their *padres* of Peking . . . who are highly respected and esteemed.[15]

What exactly this curious dress was like I have been unable to establish in detail. The hat was described as 'a beretta square in memory of the cross', and as standing 'a quarter [of a yard?] high'.[16] This may be the hat described by Valignano, or he may simply have been referring to the hat normally worn by Jesuit missionaries in the East.

In other respects, the Jesuits adopted the appearance of Buddhists. Ruggieri had at his first interview with the Viceroy in Chao-ch'ing sported a luxuriant beard which had been fingered and admired by the Viceroy.[17] When he and Ricci returned to Chaoch'ing late in 1583, on the advice of Wang P'an, the Prefect of the city, they cut off their beards, shaved their heads, and dressed as bonzes.[18]

Whatever the reasons, and whatever the dress Valignano described in his letter to the Bishop of Evora, it is clear that the Jesuits were being assimilated by the officials of Chao-ch'ing to Buddhist monks. Valignano's plan of gaining acceptance as scholars or *literati* was abandoned from the outset. It was only much later when Ricci had come to appreciate the social disadvantages of this, that the Jesuits once more grew their beards and hair and changed to the silk gowns of the Confucian scholars.

Joseph Shih SJ suggests in his study of Ruggieri that the latter had no objections to being regarded as a Christian bonze, as a monk and religious teacher. He sees Ruggieri and Ricci differing not only on the tactical question of the actual influence and social rank of the

---

15. Quoted in Bernard (-Maître), *Ricci,* 88–9. Jacques Gernet ('Sur les différentes versions du premier catéchisme en chinois de 1584', 410) identifies this costume as Taoist, and refers to 'les mémoires de Ricci' as authority. But Ricci's description of their new dress is as that 'of the more respectable people of that nation' which D'Elia identifies, curiously in the light of Ricci's anti-Buddhist prejudices, as Buddhist (*Fonti Ricciane,* N245, 192 and n 3). My view is that it was most likely simply the general long gown of the scholar. Their hairstyle, however, was clearly Buddhist.
16. v D'Elia's note in *Fonti Ricciane,* I, 167 n 3.
17. *Fonti Ricciane,* I, 162 n 6.
18. *Fonti Ricciane,* I, 337 n l.

Buddhists, but on the theoretical issue of missionary priorities: 'On the theoretical level, their differences may be reduced in essence to the conflict between the two fundamental desires of missionaries of all periods: that of retaining the religious character of the missionary, and that of becoming integrated with the society that they wish to evangelize.'[19] Ruggieri appears to have had a narrower view than Ricci as to the nature and scope of 'the religious', as I think an examination of his comparatively brief career in China attests. It should be pointed out, however, that it is only in comparison with Ricci that Ruggieri can be accused of narrowness. As a pioneer struggling with the language and customs of China, making contact with Chinese scholars and officials, producing Christian books in Chinese with no known precedents to guide him, his work was courageous and imaginative. It was his misfortune—and only unfortunate from a standpoint he himself would certainly not have approved of—to be overshadowed by his friend and companion Matteo Ricci.[20]

Ruggieri came from a background very similar to that of Valignano.[21] He was a native of Spinazzola in the Kingdom of Naples, a bachelor *in utroque jure*, and had served in the Spanish administration of Naples. He was born in 1543 which means that he was nearly forty when he began the study of Chinese, thus adding age to his other disadvantages.[22] When one considers the methods by which he learnt Chinese it is surprising that he made any progress at all. Ruggieri describes these methods in his letter to the Jesuit General, Mercurian, of 12 November 1581. The interpreters employed by the Portuguese were useless since they were barely literate.[23] So a Chinese painter was engaged who, since he knew little Portuguese,[24] would draw a picture

19. J Shih, *Le Pere Ruggieri*, 7.
20. It is noteworthy that in early accounts of the mission such as Luis de Guzman's *Historia de las Misiones de la Compania de Jesus en la India Oriental*, Libro Cuarto, 'El P Miguel Rogerio' looms much larger than 'El P Matteo Ricci'.
21. v The biographical sketch in D'Elia's introduction to the *Fonti Ricciane*, I, XCVIII-C.
22. A comment in his own account of his mission suggests that we should add corpulence to his missionary disabilities. He tells us that he required double the normal number of bearers when being carried in a litter, *perche era grande di* corpo (*Fonti Ricciane*, I, 228 n 3).
23. Ricci says they knew no written Chinese (*niente della lettera sinica*) and little Portuguese (*Fonti Ricciane*, N207, 1, 155.)
24. *Fonti Ricciane*, N207, 1, 155.

of the object corresponding to the Chinese character, then teach Ruggieri the pronunciation. 'He had to teach me the Chinese letters', wrote Ruggieri, 'by drawing a picture, as well as the pronunciation; when, for example, he wanted to teach me to read and write the word for "horse", he painted a horse and above it painted the character that signified "horse", which was pronounced *ma*.'[25]

In this way Ruggieri claimed to have learnt 15,000 characters between July 1580 and November 1581, a figure which in the light of experience as well as later evidence of his accomplishments[26] seems incredible. He even boasted that he was so proficient in Chinese after less than a year and a half that he was hailed by the Chinese as *Sifu*[27] or 'Gran Maestro'.[28] One suspects a certain irony in this comment, although by comparison with other Europeans he was no doubt a 'Great Master'. At least he had learnt enough Chinese to accompany the merchants to Canton, and to make the first contacts with Chinese officials. Ricci tells us that Ruggieri was treated with special honour because of his knowledge of Chinese and that during his four visits in 1580–1582, he managed to become friends with the Zumpino (*tsung-ping* or General), Huang Ying-chia, and the *haitao* or Marine Superintendent.[29]

In June 1582 the opportunity he had been waiting for finally arrived. The Viceroy, Ch'en Jui, called the Bishop and the Captain Major of Macao to Chao-ch'ing, Ricci suggests in order to extort whatever he could from the Macao merchants.[30] Ruggieri who was at the time on his fourth visit to Canton was sent as representative of the Bishop, with additional instructions from Valignano to try to secure permission to remain. Eventually, by means of a judicious bribe of a clock, Ruggieri was granted a patent for the Jesuits to remain in China and he and Francesco Pasio established themselves in December 1582 in a temple in Chao-ch'ing. In March 1583, when the Viceroy

25. Quoted in *Fonti Ricciane,* I, XCIX.
26. See, for example, Valignano's comments on his knowledge of Chinese in *Fonti Ricciane,* I, 43 n 2 and 250 n l.
27. Probably *shih-fu,* a 'teacher', the term found in Ruggieri's notes on common conversational phrases (ARSJ: JS *1.198,* 3–7).
28. Letter to Mercurian, 12 November 1581, in Tacchi Venturi, *Opere Storiche,* II, 402.
29. *Fonti Ricciane,* NN 209–10, I, 156.
30. *Fonti Ricciane,* NN 214, I, 161.

fell into disfavour, they were obliged to return to Macao, and Pasio was sent on to Japan by previous arrangement of Valignano. But by this time Matteo Ricci had learnt some Chinese and when, in August 1583, Ruggieri was granted permission by the new Viceroy to return to Chao-ch'ing, Ricci accompanied him. On 10 September, they arrived in Chao-ch'ing, thus beginning in definitive fashion the Jesuit mission in China.

This achievement of Ruggieri's, the establishment of the mission in the face of so many obstacles, had been accomplished by a combination of tact, knowledge of Chinese, and cultivation of Chinese officials. He had reached a practical accommodation with Chinese society. But there is little in his letters and writings either before 1583, or from the remainder of his period in China (till November 1588), that suggests he grasped the importance of Confucianism to the future of the mission. He had begun very early to translate Chinese books, enclosing a translation of *un libro molto piccolo* on the moral virtues 'transcribed hastily in bad Latin' while in Canton, with his letter to Mercurian of 12 November 1581. Whatever this work was—Father Henri Bernard-Maître plausibly suggests the *San-tzu-ching*[31]—it was almost certainly Confucian. However, the same letter reflects very unfavourably on Confucianism and on Chinese learning generally. 'They have no philosophy, but proceed by way of sentences and conclusions as their reason dictates. Although they are compelled to live morally, they have no knowledge of God, and they cannot be excused for not knowing.'[32] He interprets the Confucian 'Heaven' (*t'ien*) in material terms and concludes that the key to the conversion of China lies with the mandarins, who are 'adored' by the people.[33] Luis de Guzman was merely echoing the opinion of Ruggieri when he wrote in his *Historia* (1601)[34] that 'the principal idols of China are the mandarins'.

I have found no evidence that Ruggieri himself ever changed his low opinion of Confucianism. He must certainly have continued to study Confucian texts, because on his return to Europe he produced a

31. *Aux Portes de la Chine,* 155 n 50.
32. Tacchi Venturi, *Opere Storiche,* II, 402.
33. Tacchi Venturi, *Opere Storiche,* II 402–3.
34. *Historia de las Misiones de la Compania de Jesus en la India Oriental,* Bilboa, 1891, 184.

Latin translation of the Confucian Four Books.[35] He was not allowed to publish this translation or a Latin catechism for the China mission because of the opposition of Valignano, who wrote to the General in December 1596 that the translations 'could not be well made since Father Michele Ruggieri knows very little of the Chinese letters and language'.[36] Valignano must have been influenced in this judgement by the opinions of the men of the China mission itself, principally Matteo Ricci, and it is at least possible that Ruggieri's recall to Europe was due to conflict with Ricci over method, and particularly over the attitude of the missionaries to Confucianism.

There is little in Ruggieri's major work in Chinese, the *T'ien-chu shih-lu*, published in 1584, that enables us to assess Ruggieri's views on Confucianism. It is probably unfair to compare this work with Ricci's famous *T'ien-chu shih-i* when one considers its date and its intentions. Both have been described as 'catechisms' but if one accepts Humbertclaude's distinction between a *catechism*, a work of apologetics, defending Christian teaching against objections, and a *doctrina*, a positive and systematic exposition of doctrine, the *T'ien-chu shih-lu* is clearly a *doctrina* and Ricci's work a *catechism*.[37] Yet even in its exposition of doctrine, in its terminology and general method, Ruggieri's book appears to ignore almost completely the existence of Confucianism.

I have examined the *T'ien-chu shih-lu* both in the original edition of 1584[38] and in a later revised edition.[39] One major difference between the original and later editions seems to be the substitution of the description 'man of the Far West' (*yüan-hsi-jen*) for his original self-description as a 'monk from India' (*t'ien-chu-kuo seng*) but apart from some suppressions, and a revised account of hell, in substance they are the same. Basically the work is an exposition of Christian doctrine addressed not to a specific Chinese audience but to the common man. In Chapter 3, for example, we find an explanation of God's nature

35. Now in the Biblioteca Vittorio Emanuele in Rome (Fondo Gesuitico, 1195) and dated 1591–92 v Note in *Fonti Ricciane*, I, 43 n 2.
36. Goa, 16 December 1596 (ARSJ: JS *13.1*, 46r).
37. P Humbertclaude, 'La Littérature Chrétienne au Japon il y a trois cent ans', in *Bulletin de la Maison Franco-Japonaise*, VII (1936): 167 and 178–79.
38. There are two copies in the Jesuit Archives in Rome (ARSJ: JS 1. 189 and 190).
39. Published under the title of *Tien-chu sheng-chiao shih-lu* in the *T'ien-chu-chiao tung-ch'uan wen-hsien hsu-pien* (Taipei, 1966), II. 755–838.

for the 'ordinary man'[40] who knows black from white, but does not understand the nature of a spirit. The creation is described, as are the histories of Adam and Jesus Christ, and the ten commandments listed. The whole concludes with a chapter on baptism.

Of necessity, there are many Christian coinings in the terminology of the *T'ien-chu shih-lu*. Names are put into Chinese syllables—for example, Jesus Christ becomes *Yeh-su ch'i-li-ssu-tu*, and the Trinity is represented by an attempt to put the Portuguese Padre, Filho, Espirito Santo into Chinese.[41] The most important of the new terms, however, and one that was to become characteristic of the Catholic Church in China and to give it its Chinese name,[42] was *t'ien-chu*, 'Lord of Heaven'. Its first appearance in print was in Ruggieri's translation of the Ten Commandments, *Tsu-ch'uan t'ien-chu shih-ch'eng*, published in late 1583 or 1584. The origin of the use of this term is ascribed in Ricci's memoirs to one of the first converts 'Cim Nicò' (Ch'en?)[43] who during Ruggieri's absence from Chaoch'ing in mid-1583 had looked after the missionaries' altar. 'When at the time of our return we went to visit him, we found that he had placed the altar in a little room in his house, and, having no other image, had written on a tablet in the middle of the wall, two huge Chinese letters that said 'to the Lord of Heaven'.[44] The Jesuits, ignorant of other usages of this term in Chinese religious works,[45] enthusiastically adopted it. Despite the objections raised by critics of the use of the term it remains standard Catholic usage to the present day. However, Ricci himself, as we shall see, did not scruple to use other terms including *t'ien*, in his apologetic treatises, while retaining *t'ien-chu* as the normal name for the Christian God.

The only characteristically Confucian traits I have found in the *T'ien-chu shih-lu* are a few uncomplimentary remarks about Buddhism,[46] and a considerable development of the fourth commandment in terms of the Confucian five relationships.

40. *Shih-jen.* I presume Ruggieri is using the term in a sense uncommon in Chinese as equivalent to the Christian 'worldly'.
41. *Pa-ti-le, Fei-lüeh* (or *Fei-lioh),* and *Ssû-pi-li-to san-to.*
42. *Tien-chu-chiao.*
43. v *Fonti Ricciane,* I, 185–6, n 10, on the identification of 'Cim Nico'.
44. *Fonti Ricciane,* N236, I, 186.
45. *v Fonti Ricciane,* I, 186 n l, and H Havret, *T'ien-tch'ou 'Seigneur du Ciel'.*
46. *T'ien-chu shih-lu (Tien-chu-chiao tung-ch'uan wen-hsien hsü-pien* editor), 779.

Confucianism itself is not mentioned but it is stressed that children must obey their parents, servants their masters, students their teachers, and so on.[47] On the other hand, there is no attempt to conceal the 'stumbling blocks' of Christianity. Jesus is plainly stated to have died on a cross[48] and it is emphasised that Christianity allows for only one wife or one husband.[49]

On the evidence of Ruggieri's Chinese works alone we could not conclude to any major difference of opinion between Ruggieri and Ricci. Yet there are reasons for thinking that some divergence of views lay behind Ruggieri's departure for Europe in 1588. The account of Ruggieri's return to Europe given in Ricci's *Storia* is that Valignano was planning an embassy from the Pope to the Emperor of China and Ruggieri was sent back to arrange it. However, on the reasons for choosing Ruggieri, Ricci remarks that,

> Because Father Ruggieri was already old, and unable to learn the language, [Valignano] took the opportunity to send him to Europe; and also because after so many years in these parts, besides what was written in the letters to the Pope, to the Father General and others to promote this work, he could bear testimony to what he had seen, and recount other things that might be *à propos*.[50]

This is not altogether satisfactory as an account of the reasons for choosing Ruggieri, the most senior and experienced of the missionaries, for the task. Ruggieri was hardly 'old' at forty-five, and he himself claimed to be expert in Chinese. One suspects a deeper reason, an alliance of Valignano with Ricci against Ruggieri.

This suspicion is confirmed by a letter of Valignano to the General written at the time of Ruggieri's recall. He writes:

> Father Michele Ruggieri has laboured much in this mission, and sending him now to Rome seems reason enough to give him some repose; he is already much burdened with old age, and this journey is so long, that there is all the more reason to let him rest. Add to this that he does not pronounce the language well, and so it seems that Your Paternity should

47. *T'ien-chu shih-lu (Tien-chu-chiao tung-ch'uan wen-hsien hsü-pien* editor), 819.
48. *T'ien-chu shih-lu (Tien-chu-chiao tung-ch'uan wen-hsien hsü-pien* editor), 819.
49. *T'ien-chu shih-lu (Tien-chu-chiao tung-ch'uan wen-hsien hsü-pien* editor), 833.
50. *Fonti Ricciane*, N303, I, 249–50.

> excuse him from returning here, since this mission is not for men who are old and worn out, and he has done enough for the good of this mission by taking on the legation.[51]

The strong impression is that Valignano was trying to let down Ruggieri gently, to make sure that he did not return but to give him an honourable and dignified retirement.

Some clues to the reasons for this attitude on the part of Valignano are to be found in Ruggieri's Latin works preserved in the Jesuit Archives and elsewhere in Rome. We have already seen that Valignano objected to the publication of Ruggieri's translations from the Confucian books, and of his Latin Catechism; to the former on the grounds that his Chinese was imperfect, and to the latter because Ricci was producing a much better catechism.[52] In addition to these works in the Biblioteca Vittorio Emanuele,[53] there is in the Jesuit Archives in Rome[54] an incomplete manuscript ascribed to 'P. Mich. Roggeri', entitled *Commentarii*, and presumably dating from the period between his return to Europe in 1589 and his death in 1607. These fragments suggest that Ruggieri to the end thought of Buddhism rather than Confucianism as the most promising point of contact with Chinese culture. In the section entitled 'On the cultivation of the mind and the best disposition for receiving the gospel', he equates Chinese 'theology' with 'astrology'[55] in a way that suggests he still believed *t'ien* to refer exclusively to the physical heavens. He does, however, praise the Chinese teaching on virtue which he regards as favourable to the preaching of the Gospel. He lists the Confucian virtues[56] without, here or elsewhere, referring explicitly to Confucius or Confucianism.

51. Quoted from ARSJ: JS *11,29*\, in *Fonti Ricciane,* I, 250 n 2. The 1588 Goa Catalogue, probably reflecting Valignano's opinions, adds to age and 'mediocre ability', that Ruggieri suffered from a stomach complaint and headaches v JF Schütte, editor, *Monumenta Historica Japonica,* I, (Rome, 1975): Document 26, 217.
52. Valignano to the General, Goa, 16 December 1596, cited in *Fonti Ricciane,* I, 43 n 2.
53. The translation of the Four Books is in Fondo Gesuitico 1195.
54. ARSJ: JS *101, II,* 296–315.
55. 300r.
56. He lists these as *gin, universalis amor* (somewhat misleading in view of the contrast between the Confucian *jen* and the Mohist *chien ai); gni* or 'grati animi virtus' *(=i); li* or 'urbanitas'; *ci* or 'prudentia' *(=chih);* and *sin* 'veritas seu simplicitas' *(=hsin)* 300r–301r.

He is more explicit on Buddhism, listing the names and attributes of the principal Buddhist deities. Some are described under the heading, 'On the Adoration of False Gods and the Superstition of the Chinese'. Others, however, are significantly listed in the section on the 'Prophecies and Oracles of the Chinese' where he makes a clear attempt to interpret Buddhism as related in some way to Christianity:

> The Chinese have veiled and, in my opinion, prophetic intimations of the Christian religion, and first of all the chief object of their religious cult, *scie chia*,[57] the wisest and most intelligent of beings, whom they believe to have brought down from heaven the most holy law.[58]

This god is depicted under three different forms, *nan vu*,[59] *0-Mi-to-fe*,[60] and *scie-chia*, 'as if to signify in some way the most august mystery of the divine Trinity'.[61] He then tells the story of the dream of the Emperor Ming of Han in which the Emperor saw a golden youth who told him to seek truth in the West. This was really an angel announcing the birth of Christ to the Chinese, but the devil succeeded in preventing the legates sent by Ming Ti from reaching Judea, and diverted them to the land of idols.[62]

Ruggieri's thoughts, in exile from the mission he had founded, were turning on the apologetic uses of Buddhism for Christian propaganda in China. He had pioneered the process of accommodation, but diverted it into the natural channel of Chinese popular religion. The Jesuits were 'bonzes from the West', religious men preaching religious truth, a purified Buddhism. This role had been in the first place imposed by Chinese officials,[63] but there is no evidence that he

57. *shih-chia*, Sakya or Sakyamuni, the Buddha.
58. 310v.
59. Probable *nan-wu*, also pronounced *na-mo*, Sanskrit *namah*, 'to trust in (the Buddha)'. Ruggieri seems to have mistaken the Buddhist formula for the name of a manifestation of the Buddha.
60. *A-mi-to-fo*, or Am id a Buddha.
61. 310v.
62. 310v–311r.
63. See, for example, the inscriptions by the Prefect Wang P'an placed on the doors of the residence and chapel in Chao-ch'ing, both of them specifically Buddhist in tone (reproduced in Bortone, *P Matteo Ricci SI*, 202 & 203, and *Fonti Ricciane*, Tavola XII, opposite page 200).

questioned it. His companion and friend, Matteo Ricci, with a far greater command of Chinese, was already, by the time of Ruggieri's departure from China moving towards the adoption of a new role, that of a Christian Confucian scholar.

Matteo Ricci and the discovery of Confucianism

Ricci's mature views on Confucianism are presented to us in his *Storia dell' Introduzione del Cristianesimo in Cina,* written at the very end of his life. Much of the *Storia* is in the form of a historical narrative, although it is clearly not to be regarded as *Journals* in the sense of a diary or contemporary record. Rather it is, as Tacchi Venturi called it, *Commentarii,* recollections, memoirs, the record of a life's work. Yet even the *Storia* itself stresses the tentative trial and-error approach taken by Ricci, and this is confirmed by his letters. He set out with no preconceptions about Confucianism; nothing but Valignano's general directions to come into contact with 'men of letters' and to penetrate Chinese culture from within. In the process he may be said to have discovered Confucianism.

The discovery began, as in the case of Ruggieri, with his Chinese language studies. No doubt he proceeded from one of the standard Chinese primers to the study of the Confucian Four books-the *Analects* of Confucius, the *Mencius,* the *Doctrine of the Mean* and the *Great Learning;* the classics; and the dynastic histories.[64] Like Ruggieri, Ricci too eventually translated the Four Books into Latin.[65] This translation has not, unfortunately, been preserved, but we know from several references in his letters that it was finished before November 1593 and that he hoped to send it to Europe.[66] Giulio Aleni

64. Giulio Aleni's description of Ricci's Chinese studies in his Chinese life of Ricci is, no doubt, drawn from his own experiences, and not necessarily those of Ricci himself. But his description of the order of studies as 'classics, philosophers, histories' (*ching, tzu, shih)* is probably accurate (v passage cited in Chang Weihua, *Ming-shih,* 165).
65. This work was described by Ricci himself as a 'paraphrase . . . in Latin with many annotations' (*Fonti Ricciane,* N527, II, 33), which has led some authorities to regard it as something other than a true translation. But other references in his letters and Aleni's description of the work suggest that it was in fact a complete translation and that Ricci's title of *Parafrasi* was due to modesty, a praiseworthy restraint in view of his mere ten years' acquaintance with the language.
66. *Fonti Ricciane,* II, 33 n 5; Tacchi Venturi, *Opere Storiche,* II, 117–18, 125.

in his 1620 Chinese Life of Ricci, claimed that it had, in fact, been sent home[67] but no trace has been found in European archives. It would be extremely informative to have access to Ricci's reading of the Four Books after ten years of Chinese studies. What we do know is that Ricci used this translation to teach the language to newly arrived missionaries and that as well as the Four Books he used 'one of the Five Classics'.[68] The multiplicity of citations from both the Four Books and the Five Classics, as well as commentaries, in Ricci's Chinese works suggests that his initiation into Confucianism followed the conventional course of Confucian books and classics in editions with the commentaries of Chu Hsi, although one may not deduce too much from such citations. Ricci's Chinese collaborators rather than himself may be the source for particular references. However it seems reasonable to assume that he was well acquainted with both texts and standard commentaries and imbued the basic doctrines of Confucianism in the traditional Chinese way, by reading and memorising the texts under the guidance of a teacher. It seems that in this respect Ricci's acquaintance with Confucianism was similar to Ruggieri's with the crucial difference that Ricci's initiation was more intensive, more prolonged and clearly more successful.

One most interesting relic of this period is a manuscript dictionary, or rather vocabulary, now in the Jesuit archives in Rome.[69] The work probably dates from the early years in Chao-ch'ing. Ricci states in the introduction that he has been three years in the city, thus indicating 1585 or 1586, but the list was probably added to throughout the period. From the indications of date and authorship, it seems to me likely that it was taken to Rome by Ruggieri himself in 1588. It is incomplete and should not be confused with the later dictionary compiled by Ricci in 1599–1600 in which, with the aid of the musical Cattaneo, he indicated the five 'tones' of Chinese.[70] The

67. Jules Aleni, '*Ta-Hsi Li Hsien-sheng Ma-tou chuan*', translated by Léon Desbuquois, in *Revue d'Histoire des Missions,* I (1924): 56.

68. *Fonti Ricciane,* NN424, 494, II, 330 and 380.

69. ARSJ: JS *1.198.* For an account of its contents see PM D'Elia, 'II Domma Cattolico integralmente presentato de Matteo Ricci ai Letterati della Cina; secondo un documento cinese inedito di 350 anni fa', in *Civilta Cattolica,* 86/2 (1935): 35–53; and *Fonti Ricciane,* II, 32 n l. There are reproductions of pages of this manuscript in the *Fonti Ricciane,* II, Tavola V (of f 33 v) and in Bortone, *P Matteo Ricci SI,* 270 (of f 33r).

70. *Fonti Ricciane,* N526, II, 32–3.

vocabulary proper is in four columns. The first contains Portuguese words, arranged alphabetically, the second an Italian romanisation in Ricci's hand, the third Chinese characters, and the fourth (completed for the first eight pages only) an Italian translation in Ruggieri's hand. Even more valuable than this evidence of their struggles with the language are some notes which indicate their method of approach to Chinese scholars: remarks in Chinese characters on geographical and astronomical subjects (ff 17–27, 170–71); some conversational phrases in romanisation in the hand of Ruggieri (ff 3–7); and what D'Elia describes as *conversazioni catechetiche* by Ricci in Chinese characters (ff 13–16). The latter, apart from their linguistic interest, show Ricci already developing a catechetical. method based on Confucianism. He alludes to Confucian teaching on, for example, the five relationships, and he carefully distinguishes his doctrine from Buddhism. Ricci's pro-Confucian bias is clear in this earliest Chinese work from his pen.

Some clues to Ricci's later development may be found in his history before coming to China. He was younger than Ruggieri, only thirty years old when he arrived in Macao in 1582. He came from Macerata in the Papal States, had been a student of the Jesuit College there, and was studying law in Rome when he decided to join the Society of Jesus. He followed courses in rhetoric, philosophy and mathematics at the Roman College, the last under the famous Christopher Clavius, noted as astronomer and author of the Gregorian calendar reform. It would seem that his education up to this point was in the best Jesuit humanist tradition.[71] His theological studies were cut short by his call to the China mission from Goa but his deficiencies as a theologian have been exaggerated by opponents of the Jesuits' methods in China.[72] He spent the best part of three years studying theology in Goa (1578–1581) after preparatory studies in Coimbra, and his critics are clearly in disagreement more with his conclusions than with his competence in theology. One might agree to some extent with the author of the *Anecdotes sur l'état de la religion de la Chine* that he was *plus Politique que Théologien,*[73] but only in the sense that he was

71. On Jesuit education of the period, see RG Villoslada, *Storia del Collegio Romano* (Rome, 1954); F de Dainville, *La Naissance de l'humanisme moderne* (Paris: Beauchesne, 1940 (Paris Editions Slatkine, 2011); and F Rodrigues, *A Formacao Intellectual do Jesuita* (Porto: Livraria Magalhaes & Moniz, 1917).

72. See the citations in Bernard-Maître, *Le Père Matthieu Ricci,* II 350–51.

73. Quoted from t 3, page VIII, in Bernard-Maître, *Le Père Matthieu Ricci,* II, 350.

not primarily a scholar but a missionary, and more a humanist than a dogmatic theologian.

What is more striking is that even before he came to China the young Ricci had already made his mark with the Superiors of the Society. Valignano who had known him as a novice in Rome had personally selected him for the new mission, at the urgent request of Ruggieri[74] who had been his companion on the voyage out to Goa. Ricci had been chosen by his former teacher, the official historian of the Jesuit missions, Giovanni-Pietro Maffei SJ, as his correspondent and informant, and in a letter of 30 November 1580 from Cochin, he makes some caustic comments on the standard of previous reports from the Indies and promises a much greater reliability in his own contributions than in previous reports.[75] Even more significant is a most outspoken letter that the young priest wrote to the Jesuit General, Claudio Acquaviva, from Goa on 25 November 1581. Ricci is objecting to the policy beginning to be implemented in India of providing a second-rate education for native candidates for the priesthood. He sees this as demeaning, short-sighted and, in the long term, disastrous.

> This year the course of philosophy begins, and a quite new policy has been decreed which not everyone agrees with; namely, that no student from this land, that is, sons of natives of India, should follow the courses of philosophy and theology in our classes, but only Latin and cases of conscience. And this has been put into practice. Since this seems to me a matter of some importance I want to put it down here. I do not consider the reasons which are advanced for it very strong. They say that study makes them proud and that they will not want to minister in poor parishes; and that they will hold in low esteem the many Jesuits who are frequently heard of in these parts, who make little progress in philosophy and theology. But all this, and perhaps with even better reason, could be said of those who study in our schools elsewhere than in India, even in Europe; and we do not refuse, for that reason, to teach all comers. All the more reason, then, in the case of natives of this land who, however much they know, very rarely receive much credit from white men. On the other hand there is a

74. See Ruggieri's letter to the General, 8 November 1580 from ARSJ: JS *8, II,* 303, quoted in Bortone, *P Matteo Ricci SI,* 191.

75. Tacchi Venturi, *Opere Storiche,* II, 16–24. One of the first fruits of this collaboration is the *Relatione* of 1584 found in ARSJ: JS *123,* 43–48.

> universal custom in the whole Society to make no distinction between classes of people, and even here in India, there are so many Fathers, old, holy and experienced, who open schools and are favourably disposed to all who come there. Second, in this way we encourage ignorance in the ministers of the church in a place where learning is so necessary. These men have to be prepared in every way to be priests and to care for souls, and it is not a good thing if, with so many kinds of infidels, priests are so ignorant that they do not know how to answer an argument or to confirm themselves or others in our faith. We should not demand miracles where they are not necessary, and a simple. casuist cannot match up to these demands. Third, and this is the thing that most disturbs me, in my opinion they have none who show kindness to them except our people, and for this reason they have a special affection for us. If they come to learn that our Fathers are opposed to them and do not want to allow them to lift up their heads and obtain advantages and office equal to others, they will come to hate us, and thus will be impeded the principal goal of the Society in India, the conversion of the infidels and their conservation in our holy faith.[76]

I find this letter remarkably frank for so young and inexperienced a missionary, and a striking indication of the spirit in which he approached his future work. Just as Valignano in Japan was opposing the racially discriminatory policies of Cabral, Ricci in India was attacking the same tendencies. For Ricci, the fullest collaboration with native Christians, and concentration on the intellectual apostolate were axioms of missionary method.

Ricci's introduction to China was undertaken under the auspices of Ruggieri. He arrived in Macao on 7 August 1582 and immediately began to study Chinese. When Ruggieri set out with Francesco Pasio for Chao-ch'ing in December, Ricci was left in charge of the House of St Martin, the centre for the mission to the Chinese of Macao. In February Ruggieri obtained permission from the Viceroy, Ch'en Jui, for Ricci to join him, but the Viceroy was deposed from office shortly afterwards, and Ruggieri and Pasio returned to Macao. When Ruggieri finally returned to Chao-ch'ing in September 1583, he brought Ricci with him as his companion.

76. Translated from Tacchi Venturi, *Opere Storiche*, II, 20–1.

Ruggieri was, of course, Ricci's senior both in years and experience, and Ricci seems to have deferred to his views at least at first. The young mission was dependent in theory on the Jesuit Superiors in Macao but in practice most decisions had to be made independently and Ruggieri acted as de facto superior. It was he who gave the mission its initial Buddhist orientation and it is quite probable that Ricci at first agreed with this policy. Francisco Cabral, who had been replaced by Valignano as Superior of the Japanese mission, was now Rector of the College of Macao and seems to have been uneasy about Ruggieri's direction of the mission. He wrote to the General on 20 November 1583 that Ruggieri was unsuitable to control the mission. For all his virtues, he was 'too ingenuous and not a little timid'.[77]

The General in reply instructed Valignano to appoint 'a man of greater prudence' to the post of Superior of the mission.[78] Duarte de Sande was chosen for the job and arrived in Macao from Goa in May 1585. Despite two attempts, in 1587 and 1588, he failed to establish himself in Chao-ch'ing, and to the end of his term of office in 1597 he ruled the mission from Macao.[79] On de Sande's retirement from office Ricci was named Superior of the China mission. In practice, however, Ricci had been directing the mission for a long time before, with de Sande in Macao, and Valignano providing general guidance from outside. From at least November 1588, when Ruggieri set out for Europe, we may confidently regard Ricci as the policy-maker and leading spirit of the mission.

The decisive change from the dress and role of Buddhist monks to those of Confucian literati was accomplished in May 1595 when Ricci left Shao-chou for Nanking, but it had been in preparation for a considerable time. As early as 1585 the Jesuits had begun to perceive the inconveniences of their identification as 'bonzes'. In a letter of 20 October of that year Ricci told the General that the Emperor had ordered the destruction of Buddhist temples throughout China

77. ARSJ: JS *9,11*, 186 *cf. Fonti Ricciane*, I, 222 n l.

78. *Fonti Ricciane*, I, 222 n l.

79. He did manage to spend three months with Ricci in Shao-chou in 1591 *(Fonti Ricciane*, NN383–4, I, 307–308) but by this time he had also been given charge of the Macao mission and was obliged to return. In Macao de Sande was responsible for the Latin work, *De Missione Legatorum—Japanensium ad Romanam Curiam*, 1590, often, but erroneously, called 'the first book printed by Europeans in China' (*v Fonti Ricciane*, I, 223–4 n).

because of the involvement of some Buddhist monks in a seditious movement. Wang P'an, Prefect of Chao-ch'ing, who had earlier recommended that the Jesuits dress as bonzes, took fright. He felt compromised by the fact that he had lent his name to the first edition of Ricci's *Map of the World* (*Shan-hai yü-ti ch'uan-t'u*) and ordered it to be erased. He had, even more dangerously in view of the proscription of the temples, presented the Jesuits with an inscription for their church, reading 'Temple of the Flower of Saints', and another for their residence, 'Men who have come from the Pure Land of the West'.[80] He was persuaded to allow the inscriptions to stand and defended his actions to the Imperial Commissioner entrusted with investigating Buddhist establishments by explaining that the Jesuits were not 'bonzes' but 'literati' and 'teachers' (*maestri di dottrina*). Ruggieri, who records this contretemps[81] does not seem to have drawn the obvious conclusion that it would be more expedient to appear in public as 'literati' rather than 'bonzes'.

Ruggieri's reluctance to change may have been due to a genuine attachment to the role of religious ascetic and devotee. But even in the period of his direction of the mission the Jesuits were moving beyond this. As the process of accommodation to Chinese culture continued, they increasingly moved over to the role of teachers not only of an esoteric new doctrine but of secular wisdom as well. The secular learning was often used as a vehicle for first attracting, then propagating their religious message. There is, unfortunately, no surviving example of the first (1584) edition of Ricci's *Map of the World* but Ricci's Preface to the third, Peking edition of 1602, suggests the way in which the display of new scientific ideas was linked with the exposition of the new religion. He writes:

> I have heard it said that only the true gentleman can read in the one great book of heaven and earth and perfect his knowledge. He who has exhausted the mysteries of heaven and earth is absolutely good, absolutely great, and absolutely one. The ignorant reject heaven but learning that does not get back in the end to the original Emperor of Heaven (*t'ien-ti*) is no true learning.[82]

80. v *Fonti Ricciane,* N254, 1, 199–200.
81. v *Fonti Ricciane,* I, 234 n 9.
82. Translated from the text in Tavola XVIII of PM D'Elia, *// Mappo-mondo Cinese del P Matteo Ricci SI* (Vatican City: Biblioteca Apostolica Vaticana, 1938).

Whatever their ultimate aims and the use made of their learning, it is clear that long before 1595 the Jesuits were cultivating the public image of scholars and gentlemen. In European terms, they were 'clerks' not monks, an identification which was perfectly in accord both with the Constitutions of the Society of Jesus and the activities of the Society throughout the world in education and scholarship.

From the beginning the missionaries sought respect for their learning and secular accomplishments. One of their first public activities in Chao-ch'ing had been a display of Western goods which included prisms, clocks, maps and astronomical instruments as well as religious objects.[83] In the *Storia*, Ricci stresses their scholarly activities during the early days in Chao-ch'ing:

> No little credit in the eyes of the Chinese did the Fathers, and consequently the Christian religion receive, through the many books we had, containing the sciences and laws of our lands. Some of these books were large, such as our Bibles, and others were gilded and sumptuously bound. Even to those who could not read them nor understand what they contained within, purely from the delicacy of their exterior and the fineness of their printing, all were easily persuaded that these books treated of important matters since in our kingdom we made so much of them. In this matter of books, our nation excelled not only all the other nations the Chinese had heard of, but even China itself, which up till now they thought to be superior in letters to all the kingdoms of the world. Added to this, they saw that the Fathers always kept someone learned in Chinese studies in the house, that they applied themselves with great diligence day and night to the study of letters, and to this end had bought many of their books which already filled the whole study.[84]

The effect of this activity, or at least as Ricci recalled it over twenty years later, was to distinguish the Jesuits from the Buddhist bonzes.

> From this they came to understand both that letters and sciences were esteemed in our land and that the Fathers were, as they had declared, *literati* in their own land and in their own sciences, which is the only kind of nobility recognized

83. *Fonti Ricciane*, NN239, 240, 1, 188–89; N262, 1, 207–11; N310, 1, 253–599.
84. *Fonti Ricciane*, N252, 1, 196.

> in China. Hence, by comparing our priests with those of their sects in which ignorance reigned, they easily concluded how much more reasonable must be the law that our (Fathers) professed than that which the ministers of the idols [the Buddhists] taught.[85]

After Ruggieri's departure for Europe and the move of the mission to Shao-chou (1589), we find Ricci's lifestyle falling more clearly into the literati pattern. Early in the Shao-chou period (late 1590), Ricci acquired his first important disciple, Ch'ü Ju-k'uei,[86] of Soochow, whose father had been a scholar of some renown and held high office including that of President of the Board of Rites. The son, although intelligent, had dissipated his patrimony and travelled the country living off friends and acquaintances, 'a way of life amongst these people'.[87] He was interested in alchemy, and seems to have been attracted to Ricci through the reputation the Fathers had acquired in this respect, a reputation based partly on their display of science and partly on the fact that they appeared to have no source of income.[88] Ch'ü had first met Ricci in Chao-ch'ing in 1589, and the next year he followed him to Shao-chou. To Ricci's astonishment,

> One morning (Ch'ü) came with great solemnity, in the Chinese fashion, with a large present of lengths of silk and other precious things, made three prostrations before Father Matteo, and took him as his master.[89]

Ricci soon disabused Ch'ii of his belief that the Jesuits possessed the art of turning mercury into silver. But Ch'ü remained as his student in mathematics and science, and Ricci began to appreciate the advantages

85. *Fonti Ricciane,* N252, I, 196–197.
86. Ricci refers to him as 'Chiutaisu' after his *tzu,* T'ai-su. v Biographical note in *Fonti Ricciane,* I, 295–296, n l.
87. *Un modo di vita in questa gentilita—Fonti Ricciane,* N359, 1, 296.
88. The Jesuits were always careful to conceal the fact that they received income from outside China, which might have left them open to charges of subversion. Hsu Kuang-ch'i in his *Apologia* of 1616, insisted that the Jesuits received an allowance, not from subversive foreign merchants but directly from Europe, and suggested that this be checked at the Canton customs house so that 'all communication (with Europe) will be cut off, and every suspicion removed' ('Paul Sü's Apology addressed to the Emperor Wanlih', in *The Chinese* Repository, XIX [1850]: 124).
89. *Fonti Ricciane,* N361, I, 297.

of having influential friends in the world of scholar-officials. Through Ch'ü Ju-k'uei he was introduced to a number of influential people, all friends, acquaintances and relatives of the Ch'ü family.[90] If Ricci had not up to this time appreciated the nature of Chinese gentry society, the system in which power and influence flowed from a combination of family and scholarship,[91] he must certainly have learned a great deal from his friendship with Ch'ü.

Ricci learned other lessons, too, from his relationship with Ch'ü Ju-k'uei. He soon succeeded in interesting Ch'ü in his religious ideas as well as his mathematics. Ch'ü listened and compiled a list of difficulties which he found in the Catholic faith as presented to him. Ricci was surprised by the subtlety of Ch'ü's objections which he found to be 'the most difficult that are treated in all theology'.[92] The task of converting a Chinese scholar was to be no easy one. When, eventually, he convinced Ch'ü and resolved his doubts, he found another difficulty. Ch'ü declared himself a Christian but had to be refused baptism because of his attachment to a concubine. Although his first wife was dead, the concubine was of too low birth to become his principal wife, and he had no son or heir. Ch'ü remained a close friend and associate of Ricci in his literary work, but it was not until 1605 that he finally married the concubine and received Baptism.[93]

The whole experience with Ch'ü Ju-k'uei must have been of decisive importance in the development of Ricci's missionary methods. He learned the value of a sympathetic Chinese collaborator, the difficulties involved in persuading even a friendly Chinese scholar to accept Christianity, both in theory and in practice, and the importance of social role in Chinese eyes. It seems to have been Ch'ü Ju-k'uei who finally persuaded him to abandon the dress of the Buddhist monks. Li Chih-tsao, who did not come to know Ricci till later, but who was in a position to know the facts, appears to attribute the change to Ch'ü's influence. In his commentary on the Nestorian Monument he notes that the Nestorian monks wore their hair long and adds:

---

90. *Fonti Ricciane,* N367, 1, 299–300.
91. v Ho Ping-ti, *The Ladder of Success in Imperial China,* New York, 1962; O.B. van der Sprenkel, 'High Officials in the Ming', in *Bulletin of the School of Oriental and African Studies,* XIV (1952): 87–114.
92. *Fonti Ricciane,* N366, 1, 299.
93. *Fonti Ricciane,* N755, II, 342.

> When Ricci first entered Canton for some years he was feeling his way. Then he met Ch'ü T'ai-su and found it inconvenient to behave like a bonze. Later he let his hair grow and described himself as a scholar (*ju*) who had come to our country to admire our ways.[94]

Ch'ü Ju-k'uei may have explicitly advised a change of dress during his first contact with Ricci in 1589–90, but it was some time before action was taken. It seems more likely that Ricci was inspired by his experience with Ch'ü to rethink the whole basis of his mission. He visited Macao in late 1592 or early 1593 to consult with Valignano[95] but amongst the 'many matters which were conducive to the promotion of our affairs in China',[96] curiously enough, the change of dress does not seem to have figured. Perhaps Ricci feared that Valignano, whose recent Japanese experience had led him to a policy of accommodation with Buddhism, would not approve. Or perhaps he was still uncertain what the best course of action would be. According to his own account,[97] the missionaries were following a halfway policy of denying they were *osciani* (*ho-shang*, Buddhist monks), wearing their hair short and shaving their beards in the normal fashion of priests and religious in Portugal. Whatever the reasons, it was not Ricci himself, but Lazzaro Cattaneo, a newcomer to the mission, who raised the question with Valignano. Before setting out from Macao for Shao-chou he asked Valignano for permission for the Jesuits of the China mission 'to grow their beards and hair, like our Fathers in Germany, and to use formal dress, namely of silk, when paying courtesy calls, especially on mandarins'. Cattaneo adds to his account a curious remark that might be interpreted as meaning that the suggestion really came from Ricci. 'Father (Valignano) gave the permission, since Father Matteo Ricci also thought it necessary, and had never thought otherwise, but he had not wanted to be the first to permit it.'[98] Whether Ricci indirectly inspired the approach to Valignano, or merely approved the suggestion when his opinion

94. *Tu Ching-chiao pei-shu hou, Tien-hsüeh ch'u-han* (Taipei, 1965), I. 85, *cf* translation and text in *Fonti Ricciane,* I, 336 n l.
95. *Fonti Ricciane,* N410, I, 323.
96. *Fonti Ricciane,* N411, I, 323.
97. *Fonti Ricciane,* N429, I, 335.
98. Letter of 12 October 1599 to the General describing the events of 'five years ago'; ARSJ: JS *13,* 319r, quoted in *Fonti Ricciane,* I, 336 n l.

was asked, Valignano agreed to the request. When he departed for India in November 1594 he left the Superior, de Sande, instructions that the missionaries were, in future, to call themselves *letrados* not *bonsos*, were to wear beards and hair down to their ears, and to use silk garments for formal occasions.[99] The Church authorities in Rome in turn gave their approval for the innovation.

Ricci seems to have immediately begun to grow his beard, because by August 1595 he could write that both he and Cattaneo had beards down to their waists. He left the change of dress till his departure for Shao-chou in April 1595 and, according to a letter of 29 August 1595 to de Sande, appeared for the first time in his new garments in Chi-shui in Kiangsi Province in May 1595. From this time on, as is attested both in written accounts and in drawings and paintings the Jesuits dressed like Confucian scholars in a long silk outer garment and a hat, playfully described by Ricci as 'an extravagant cap as steep as a Bishop's mitre'.[100]

Even before the change of dress, however, the new policy began to bear fruit. Ricci's memoirs describe the delight of their friends in Shao-chou at their new identification:

> The Fathers of Shao-chou began little by little to put (the new policy) into execution. Our friends were very pleased with this, seeing that they could use many more signs of respect to us than they used to their bonzes. Although from the first we were regarded very differently from the ministers of the idols, in view of the great difference in virtue between them and the Fathers, nevertheless the ordinary people made little distinction between us and the bonzes, and the upper class could not pass the barriers that we had set up by our name, our dress and our appearance.[101]

Ricci goes on to describe their assumption of the rank of *hsiu-tsai*, or 'bachelors', and their acceptance as such by the mandarins and scholars.

Some difficulties remained, however, due to their long identification as Buddhists. In Kwangtung the Jesuits continued to be called *seng*, 'bonzes', and their churches *ssu* or *miao*, 'temples',[102]

99. ARSJ: JS *14*, 230, quoted in *Fonti Ricciane,* I, 336 n l.
100. Letter to G Benci, Nanchang, 7 October 1595, cited in *Fonti Ricciane,* I, 337 n 4.
101. *Fonti Ricciane,* N430, 1, 338.
102. v Chang Ju-lin & Yin Kuang-jen, *Ao-men chi-lueh,* (Taipei, 1968 edition), 28–29.

despite the efforts of the Jesuits to change these titles. Elsewhere the Jesuits became known as *tao-jen*, or 'preachers of the Way',[103] and their churches were called *t'ang* or 'halls'. The latter title avoided the difficulties experienced in Chao-ch'ing and elsewhere from the Chinese custom of using temples as places of public recreation.[104]

Ricci had been thinking for some time of moving the mission both because of the unhealthy climate of Shaochou[105] and as part of a more general long-term plan to reach Peking and obtain imperial approval for the preaching of Christianity. The first attempt in 1595 proved fruitless due to a spy scare arising from the current war with Japan in Korea. He was forced to leave Nanking after only two weeks in June 1595, but instead of returning to Shao-chou he established himself in Nan-ch'ang and in Kiangsi province, where he found his reputation had preceded him. Here, Ricci extended his policy of accommodation to gentry society. He began the exhausting and often frustrating round of banquets and learned conversations, visiting and being visited, that was to occupy much of his time. He wrote to a friend in October 1595 that he often had no time to eat till at least one o'clock in the afternoon, and that sometimes he had to attend two dinners in the one day.[106] All this required a quite different lifestyle to the old mission-church centred approach practised at Chao-ch'ing and Shao-chou. When he acquired a permanent residence in Nan-ch'ang he decided to have no public church but a reception hall, 'because one preaches more effectively and with greater fruit here through conversations than through formal sermons'.[107] The missionary 'monk from the West' had become a Confucian scholar.

It was in Nan-ch'ang that Ricci first established himself as a member of the world of Chinese scholars. By now he had twelve years of Chinese studies behind him and was able to carry off the role successfully. He became acquainted with two princes residing in Nan-ch'ang, and became quite friendly with one of them, the Prince

103. Ricci translates this as *predicatori letterati* (*Fonti Ricciane,* N431, I, 338) which does capture the ambiguities of *tao* with its overtones of teaching and of Confucianism, v D'Elia's note (*Fonti Ricciane,* I, 338 n 3) and also his note (335 n 2) on the later, more common, usage of *shen-fu,* 'spiritual father'.

104. v Dunne, *Generation of Giants,* 46–47.

105. v *Fonti Ricciane,* N429, 1, 337.

106. Tacchi Venturi, *Opere Storiche,* II, 186.

107. Letter to Giulio Fuligatti, Nan-ch'ang, 12 October 1596, Tacchi Venturi, *Opere Storiche,* II, 215, translated in part in Dunne, *Generation of Giants,* 46.

of Chien-an.[108] If he hoped to gain help from him in approaching the throne, he had seriously misunderstood the position of distant relatives of the Emperor.[109] However, I think it would be wrong to assign such calculated motives to Ricci's relations with the Prince. It was for this man that Ricci produced his first Chinese work, entitled 'A Treatise on Friendship' (*Chiao-yu lun*), sometime in the year 1595. It is a collection of maxims translated or paraphrased from European sources, mainly from Andreas d'Evora, *Sententiae et Exempla*. The original work appears to have been in Chinese and some form of transliteration,[110] but only the Chinese text was published. Actually, the publication was not the responsibility of Ricci himself. A friend published it in Ningtu in 1595 or 1596 without authorisation, thus circumventing Ricci's scruples about 'publication without an ecclesiastical imprimatur'.[111] Later editions by Ch'ü Ju-k'uei (1599), Feng Ying-ching (1601) and Li Chih-tsao',[112] were considerably enlarged by the addition of some maxims of Ricci's own. It seems to have been immensely popular. Ricci himself claimed, in a letter of 14 August 1599,[113] that it 'gave more credit to me and to Europe than anything we have done', and ten years later he noted that 'even now it continues to astonish this kingdom'.[114] Confirmation of this may be found in the fact that it went through many editions and was eventually included in the great Ch'ing encyclopedic compilation, the *Ku-chin t'u-shu chi-ch'eng*.[115]

108. *Fonti Ricciane,* NN478–483, 1, 365–71.
109. He was disabused in 1597. v *Fonti Ricciane,* N503, II, 17.
110. v *Fonti Ricciane,* I, 369 n l.
111. D'Elia, 'II Trattato sull'Amicizia . . .', 455. *cf* Tacchi Venturi, *Opere Storiche,* II, 250, letter of 14 August 1599 to Girolamo Costa: 'I cannot publish it (the *Chiao-yu lün),* because in order to publish anything I have to get permission from so many of our people that I cannot do anything. Men who are not in China, and cannot read Chinese, insist upon passing judgement.' (translated in Dunne, *Generation of Giants,* 44.)
112. Included in his *Tien-hsüeh ch'u-han,* 1629.
113. To Girolamo Costa, cited in *Fonti Ricciane,* I, 369 n.
114. *Fonti Ricciane,* N482, I, 369.
115. In the section entitled *Ming lun-hui-pien chiao-i tien,* chapter 12, ff 12–52. The editors appended a note pointing out that its style was Western and many of the passages unintelligible, which may be no more than a device on their part to avoid charges of unorthodoxy. v G Gné & J Dehergne, 'Le "Traité de l'Amitié" de Matthieu Ricci', in *Bulletin de l'Université L'Aurore,* 3s/VIII (1947): 586.

It is significant and appropriate that Ricci's first work, and the first fruit of his Nan-ch'ang period, should be a treatise on friendship. He was beginning to achieve real intimacy with a number of Chinese scholars, who returned his regard. Feng Ying-ching begins his *Preface* to the 1601 edition by claiming that 'Ricci endured the discomfort of travelling 80,000 *li* in an easterly direction to China for the sake of friendship. He understands the ways of friendship'.[116] No doubt Ricci saw his own motives differently, but there is an element of truth in the comment. What he was doing was establishing a link between the European humanist tradition and the Confucian humanist tradition.[117] He wanted to be received not just as a pedlar of novelties but as a scholar and a friend. 'The other things', he wrote, 'give us the reputation of possessing ingenuity in the construction of mechanical artefacts and instruments; but this treatise has established our reputation as scholars of talent and virtue'.[118]

Ricci attracted attention as much by his personality, as by his status as cultural intermediary. Shên Tê-fu, who makes a number of comments on the Jesuits, not all of them favourable, in his *Yeh-huo pien* of 1606, remarks that Ricci had 'a strange power to move men'[119] and describes his attractive qualities as follows:

> Li Hsi-t'ai [Ricci] took a vow to try to use his own religion to entice the Chinese to be converted . . . He is of attractive disposition, adaptable to all circumstances, and everybody appreciates his sincerity and generosity and the fact that he doesn't make himself a burden to anybody. He has a healthy appetite for food and drink, and is very clever in what he makes. He does not make money by lending at interest, and he is continually generous to others, yet he is not poor, so he is suspected of practising alchemy, but I don't believe this is so.[120]

116. *T'ien-hsüeh ch'u-han* (Taipei, 1965 edition), I, 291.
117. v Bernard (-Maître), *Le Père Matthieu Ricci,* I, 248.
118. Translated from Tacchi Venturi, *Opere Storiche,* II, 243, in G Dunne, *Generation of Giants,* 44.
119. Chapter 30, cited in Chang Wei-hua, *Ming-shih Fo-lang-chi, Lu-sung, Ho-lan, I-ta-li-ya, ssd-chuan chu-shih* (Peiping, 1934), 167.
120. *Yeh-huo pien,* chapter 30, in Chang Wei-hua, *Ming-shih,* 111.

This description actually comes from a slightly later period in Peking where Shen was a neighbour of Ricci,[121] but it seems to apply equally well to Ricci's years in Nan-ch'ang. He appeared as a scholar with an open and generous character yet something mysterious about him.

The mystery was increased by Ricci's reputation for a prodigious memory.[122] At a banquet early in his stay in Nan-ch'ang he repeated after one reading a random list of some hundreds of characters[123] and this seems to have become a regular 'party trick'.[124] Ricci's interest in memory training went back to his student days in Rome when he had written a short treatise on the subject for his friend Lelio Passionei. He had brought this with him to China[125] and he made good use of it in 1596 when the Governor of Nan-ch'ang, Wang Tso, fearful of getting into trouble over Ricci's presence in the city, tried to force him to live in a temple outside the walls. Ricci had no desire to revive the old identification as a bonze, and he appealed to the Viceroy, whom he had met earlier, accompanying the request with a copy of a work in Chinese, the *Hsi-kuo chi-fa*, on memory training.[126] The Viceroy accepted this on behalf of his sons, appreciating the value of a good memory in the competitive examinations which led to office, and gave Ricci permission to reside where he wished.[127]

In Nan-ch'ang Ricci made contact with many scholars whose friendship was to prove of great value. In December 1597 the triennial provincial examinations were held in Nan-ch'ang and Ricci was overwhelmed with visitors.[128] In Nan-ch'ang too, he was introduced to the less official aspects of Confucianism, the world of academies and discussion circles. He was beginning to appreciate that Confucianism

121. *Fonti Ricciane,* II, 73 n l. For details of Shen's life and career and further references see TH Yang, 'Three Ming Officials: Biographical Sketches', in *Journal of Oriental Studies,* VIII/2 (July 1970): 385–86.
122. Ricci's interest in memory was one shared by many of his contemporaries (v F Yates, *The Art of Memory* [London, 1966]) and indicates a common concern of Confucians and European classical humanists—the memorising of and commenting on texts.
123. *Fonti Ricciane,* I, 360 n l.
124. v *Fonti Ricciane,* N469, I, 359–60; N475, I, 363.
125. See his letter to Passionei, 25 December 1597, cited in *Fonti Ricciane,* I, 376 n 6.
126. The *Hsi-kuo chi-fa* is reprinted in the *T'ien-chu-chiao tung-ch'uan wen-hsien* (Taipei, 1965), 1–70.
127. *Fonti Ricciane,* N475, 1, 363.
128. Tacchi Venturi, *Opere Storiche,* II, 242.

was not a monolithic orthodoxy but a living doctrine with a variety of conflicting tendencies. And he was beginning to feel his way towards establishing a place for Christianity within these movements. In his *Storia* he describes these first encounters:

> The Father gained even more authority from his friendship with another sort of scholar, the satraps of this country, who profess to preach in their confraternities the true law which must be followed. The head of them all at the time was an old man of seventy whose surname was Chang and personal name Tou-chin.[129] This man and his companions had heard much about the Father from our friend Chü T'ai-su, who had stayed for a long time in that place and had spread the fame of the learning and sanctity of our men, so much so that the Father was very much afraid of not being able to fulfil the expectations they had about him. And so these men, who are accustomed to treat everybody with great haughtiness, treated the Father with great humility and courtesy, and were even more pleased when they perceived that the Father was well versed in their books, and could adduce and prove the things that he said about our holy law on the authority of their ancient books.[130]

From the last remark it would appear that it was in this period and on the basis of these contacts that Ricci developed his interpretation of Confucianism. We know from his letters that he worked on his definitive book, the *T'ien-chu shih-i*, during these years. It had been begun in 1594 as a revision and amplification of Ruggieri's *T'ien-chu shih-lu*, put aside during 1595 due to his busy round of engagements, and taken up again in 1596 when it was sufficiently advanced for friends to urge him to publish it.[131] Although not printed till 1603, it was the fruit of the Nan-ch'ang years.

Ricci's mature policy may be regarded as a logical extension of the methods evolved during the formative years in Chao-ch'ing, Shao-

---

129. Chang Tou-chin, or Chang Huang, was President of the Academy of the White Deer Cave *(Pai-lu-tung shu-yuan)* to which the great Sung Neo-Confucian philosopher, Chu Hsi, once belonged. For biographical details see *Fonti Ricciane,* I, 371 n 5.
130. *Fonti Ricciane,* N484, I, 371–2.
131. See the note, including references to Ricci's letters, in *Fonti Ricciane,* I, 379–80.

chou and Nan-ch'ang. New men arrived on the mission and were trained in the language and customs of polite Chinese society. From Ricci's pen there flowed a stream of books on scientific and religious subjects.[132] The conversations with Chinese scholars continued, new friends were made, collaborators and converts secured; but the basic method of working through Confucianism was followed everywhere.

The main change in Ricci's life was the shift to the north, to Nanking and on to Peking. In August 1597, Valignano, back in Macao once more, decided that the time had come for changes in the mission. Ricci was named Superior and ordered to attempt once more to establish himself in Peking. Just at this time Wang Hung-hui, President of the *Li Pu* (Board of Rites) in Nanking, whom Ricci had met in Shao-chou,[133] passed through Nanch'ang on his way to take up his office. Since he intended to travel to Peking, for the Emperor's birthday celebrations on 17 September 1598, he offered to take Ricci with him.[134] His motives were not altogether disinterested since the *Li Pu* had responsibility for the mathematical bureau which compiled the imperial calendar. At this time the old Chinese calendar was badly out of adjustment[135] and Wang seems to have hoped to gain credit, and perhaps the senior presidency in Peking, by introducing Ricci there.[136]

It was a bad time to travel since hostilities had broken out again in Korea. Despite Wang's patronage, Ricci was distrusted in Nanking, and when he finally arrived in Peking he found doors closed against him. He returned via Soochow to Nanking where, with the news of peace with Japan, he was able to set up a mission residence. In this metropolis he acquired a new group of friends and students. He visited the astronomical observatory, and became acquainted with the royal astronomers and their methods. It was here also that for the first time he came into contact with sophisticated exponents of Buddhist philosophy such as the syncretist Li Chih,[137] Li Pen-ku,[138] and the

132. See the list of Ricci's works in *Fonti Ricciane,* I, CXXVII–CXXVIII, and the bibliography of this work.
133. *Fonti Ricciane,* N417, 1, 326.
134. *Fonti Ricciane,* N505, II, 9.
135. An error of four and a half hours according to D'Elia's note, *Fonti Ricciane,* II, 8 n 5.
136. *Fonti Ricciane,* N504, II, 8.
137. *Fonti Ricciane,* N551, II, 66–9.
138. *Fonti Ricciane,* N556, II, 73–4.

monk San-hui.[139] Ricci recognised in San-hui a serious opponent, 'quite different from the other bonzes, being a great poet, intelligent and learned in all matters of his sect, and an adept in their practices',[140] and accepted an invitation to debate with him. The debate was, of course, inconclusive, and it is clear from Ricci's own account[141] that they were literally speaking different languages. It was a confrontation rather than a true exchange of views; but it did cause Ricci to take Buddhism more seriously and resulted in the composition of a treatise on the virtues called the *Twenty-five Sentences* (*êrh-shih-wu yen*), conceived as a counter to the Buddhist *Forty-two Paragraphs* sutra (*ssû-shih-êrh chang ching*).[142]

It was in Nanking in early 1600 that Ricci met for the first time the man who was to become the most illustrious of all Chinese Christians, Hsü Kuang-ch'i, or 'Doctor Paul'. This first brief meeting led to a friendship, cemented later in Peking, and to a collaboration on scientific and religious writings with Ricci and other Jesuits that proved enormously fruitful. As holder of several high offices, eventually the highest of all, *ko-lao*, or Grand Secretary, he was protector of the mission during the crucial period of its establishment and early growth. Without Hsü Kuang-ch'i, Li Chih-tsao and Yang T'ing-yün, the 'three great pillars'[143] of the Church in China, the mission might well have been destroyed quite early. For our purposes, however, the importance of these three men lies more in the insight they gave Ricci and his successors into the potentialities of a rapprochement between Confucianism and Christianity. The 'Christian Confucian' was a living reality, not an abstract concept.

In May 1600, with the arrival of reinforcements for the Nanking mission, and of some valuable objects suitable as gifts to be offered

139. *Fonti Ricciane,* N558, II, 75–7.
140. *Fonti Ricciane,* N558, II, 75.
141. *Fonti Ricciane,* NN558-9, II, 75–80.
142. Ricci first mentions this in the *Storia* in his account of the Nanking mission (*Fonti Ricciane,* II, 97). Later he cancelled the passage and included a paragraph on the subject in a later chapter in which he describes its publication in Peking in 1604 *(Fonti Ricciane,* N707, II, 286–8). The Epilogue to the work, by Hsu Kuang-ch'i, attributes it to this period in Nanking (v *Fonti Ricciane,* II, 289 n). On the Stoic sources for the *Twenty-five Sentences,* see CA Spalatin, *Matteo Ricci's Use of Epictetus* (Waegwan: University of Gregoriana Press, 1975).
143. *San ta chu-shih.* See, for example, the preface to Yang Ch'en-o, *Yang Ch'i-yiian hsien-sheng nien-p'u* (Shanghai, 1946), 1.

to the Emperor, Ricci set out once more for Peking. This time he was successful both in having an audience with the Emperor and in establishing the mission in the capital itself. The details of Ricci's reception in Peking need not delay us here.[144] For a time he found himself unwittingly caught up in the power struggle between the court eunuchs and the official bureaucracy. Ricci and his gifts were taken over on the way by the powerful eunuch Ma T'ang and the whole enterprise was almost lost through the opposition of the Board of Rites to this irregular procedure. The 'audience', on which Ricci had placed his hopes for so long, was an anti-climax. Despite later claims by Aleni in his life of Ricci[145] that the Emperor observed proceedings from behind the screen, Ricci's own account makes it clear that it was merely a formal presentation before the empty throne. Matteo Ricci's entry to Peking was simultaneously an initiation into the enormous gap between Confucian theory and the practice of government in the late Ming.[146]

The last ten years of Ricci's life were richer and more fruitful than the long years of preparation that preceded them, but I can detect no major changes in his methods. It was a period of development and refining of the basic approach; a time of harvesting. His major works in Chinese belong to this period—the third and fullest edition of his *World Map* in 1602; the publication of the *Tien-chu shih-i* (1603) and the *Twenty-five Sentences* (1605); the *Ten Paradoxes* (*Chi-jen shih-p'ien*) in 1608. In the last years of his life he worked on his *Storia del Cristianesimo in Cina* which was completed shortly before his death but not published in its original form till 1911 (a Latin version by Nicholas Trigault was published in 1615). He conducted an extensive correspondence in Chinese and, by this time at least, seems to have written his letters without the aid of a Chinese secretary.[147]

144. For Ricci's own account, see *Fonti Ricciane*, NN581ff, II, 107 ff; and for Chinese sources on the same events, Chang wei-hua, *Ming shih*, 171 ff.

145. *Ta-hsi Li hsien-sheng Ma-tou chuan*, translated by L Desbuquois, *Revue d'Histoire des Missions*, 1 (1924): 61. D'Elia gives an account of the origin of this error in *Fonti Ricciane*, II, 160 n l.

146. v *Fonti Ricciane*, N609, II, 144; (reiterated in N622, II, 160) for details of Ricci's reception. Ray Huang, *1587: A Year of No Significance* (New Haven, 1981), is the best introduction to late Ming politics; see especially 113–14 and 117 on Wan-Li's reluctance to hold audiences.

147. v *Fonti Ricciane*, II, 531–32.

We even find him sending an example of his calligraphy together with a complimentary essay to the ink-merchant and connoisseur, Ch'eng Ta-yüeh.[148] Some new and important friends and allies were gained, among them Feng Ying-ching, courageous critic of corrupt government;[149] Li Chih-tsao, who was to collect many of Ricci's works in his *T'ien-hsüeh ch'u-han* of 1629 and to produce a number of scientific works in collaboration with the missionaries; and Li T'ai-tsai, President of the Board of Civil Office. The encounters with leading Buddhists continued, mainly centred now around Ricci's arguments in the *T'ien-chu shih-I*,[150] and touching on substantial points such as reincarnation and monism.

On the pretext of regulating the clocks presented to the Emperor, Ricci and his companions gained access to the Forbidden City and, through the eunuchs, answered the Emperor's queries about Europe.[151] Ricci did not succeed in obtaining formal permission to reside in Peking or to preach his religion but the Emperor, by his refusal to reply to the complaints of the Board of Rites against Ricci, indicated his wishes. The eunuchs privately informed Ricci that the Emperor favoured him and that he should regard the official silence as permission to stay.[152] The *Ming History* represents Ricci's *de facto* position accurately when it says: 'The Emperor commended him for coming from so far, granted him food and lodging, and a generous allowance. The nobles, officials and common people respected, appreciated and welcomed him. [Li] Ma-tou settled down [in Peking] and remained there for the rest of his life. He died in the capital on May [10th] 1610 and was buried outside the western suburb.'[153]

148. See '"The Transmission by Writing", presented to Master Ch'eng Yu-po', translated by JJ L Duyvendak in *T'oung Pao*, XXXV (1940): 394–97.
149. v *Fonti Ricciane*, NN624–7, II, 162–68, *Ming shih*, chapter 237, 7a–10b; Huang Tsung-hsi, *Ming Ju Hsüeh-an*, chapter 24,17a in the *Ssu-pu pei-yao* edn.
150. See *Fonti Ricciane*, NN633–64, II, 180–82, for Ricci's exchanges with Huang-hui; and the *Pien-hsueh i-tu*, an account of a debate between Ricci and the monk Shen Chu-hung (Shen Lien-chih) c1608, probably recorded by Hsu Kuang-ch'i and published by Li Chih-tsao (*T'ien-hsüeh ch'u-han* (Taipei, 1965 edition), I, 637–88). See also, Chun-fang Yu, *The Renewal of Buddhism in China* (New York; Columbia University Press, 1981), especially chapter 4.
151. *Fonti Ricciane*, N595, II, 127. Ricci also prepared a special edition of his map for the Emperor with notes which he hoped would interest him in Christianity (*Fonti Ricciane*, N893, II, 474).
152. *Fonti Ricciane*, N617, II, 153.
153. Chang Wei-hua, *Ming shih*, 177–78.

In a strange way it was Ricci's death itself that confirmed his status and ratified the position of the mission. Important people came in large numbers to express their condolences, and a curious but appropriate combination of Christian and traditional Chinese ceremonies was observed.[154] Li Chih-tsao prepared a memorial in the name of the Peking Jesuits requesting a fitting burial ground for the great man. The memorial stressed his virtue and his devotion to Chinese culture:

> Your servant, Li Ma-tou, from the time he entered your court, began to absorb your brilliant culture, to read [Chinese] books and penetrate their meaning. Morning and evening, reverently and respectfully he burnt incense and prayed to Heaven, reciting your praises in poor return for your kindness. The loyalty of his heart is known to everybody, high or low, in the city, and we would not dare to embellish it. While he was yet alive he was reputed to be a lover of scholarship and a writer of no mean ability. In his earlier days across the seas he was known as a famous scholar, and when he came to this country he was praised by high officials who did not fear to liken him to the hermits who withdraw to lonely places.[155]

Wu Tao-nan, acting Minister of Rites, passed on the memorial, again stressing Ricci's devotion to Chinese culture:

> [Li] Ma-tou gradually absorbed the teaching of China, and diligently studied our important doctrines, and achieved fame as a writer. One day without warning he died. He has no family within 10 000 *li* and it is impossible to send his coffin home. The situation is extremely unfortunate.[156]

With the support of Yeh Hsiang-kao, the Grand Secretary, another old friend of Ricci, the request was approved and a villa confiscated from one of the eunuchs granted to the Jesuits. Ricci's body was transferred to this site where some years later the tomb was adorned with a long inscription in his praise by Wang Ying-lin, Governor of Peking.[157]

---

154. *Fonti Ricciane,* N967, II, 547–79. The account of Ricci's death and its aftermath in the *Fonti* comes from Trigault's *De Christiana Expeditione* which in turn draws on the Annual Letter for 1610 written by Ferreira.
155. *Fonti Ricciane,* III, 5, for Chinese text and D'Elia's translation.
156. *Fonti Ricciane,* III, 7.
157. v *Fonti Ricciane,* III, Appendix II, 9 ff.

Through his death Ricci, and by association the other Jesuits, had received official recognition of their presence in Peking. The posthumous honours paid to him culminating in an entry in the *Ming shih*, the eulogies of friends and acquaintances, all combined to identify him as a scholar and a gentleman in the Confucian sense. The Jesuits had found a definitive place in the Chinese world, as Western scholars and assimilated Confucians. Ricci was perfectly aware of the ambiguities of that position and its dangers but he had discovered a way of accommodation to Chinese culture. His deathbed remarks were a perfect summing up of his achievement: 'I leave you at a door opened up to great rewards, but fraught with peril and labour.'[158]

Ricci's Interpretation of Confucianism

We have seen how Matteo Ricci first discovered then adapted himself to Confucianism in the course of his thirty-odd years in China, thus setting a pattern for the Jesuits of the China mission. In practical terms this meant an accommodation to the social role of Confucian scholars, extending to title, dress, language and, in general, way of life. In intellectual terms, it involved the presentation of Christianity in Confucian language, and the placing of the *T'ien-chu-chiao* in relation to the Confucian tradition. It is this intellectual accommodation to which I now turn.

In delineating Ricci's interpretation of Confucianism there are two kinds of sources we may draw on: his writings in European languages, addressed primarily to his Jesuit colleagues and through them to a European public; and his writings in Chinese. As for the former, we have in his letters an indication of his developing views on Confucianism, and in the *Storia dell 'Introduzione del Cristianesimo in Cina,* a full statement of his mature position. However, in some respects, the *Storia* is of less value for a systematic overview of the Jesuit interpretation of Confucianism than it might seem. It was, I presume, intended for publication in Europe, or at least Ricci foresaw this as a strong possibility.[159] Apart from the general practice of publication

158. *Fonti Ricciane,* N962, II, 540.

159. Trigault, in his preliminary remarks 'To the Reader', suggests that Ricci left the manuscript 'to furnish some future writer with material prepared for the Mission annals' (*China in the Sixteenth Century,* translated by LJ Gallagher [New York, 1953, xiii]). But this misrepresents the quality of the original manuscript which,

of mission reports for propaganda purposes—using 'propaganda' in its primary and neutral sense of spreading and advancing a cause—a practice to which Ricci had contributed from the beginning in his correspondence with Maffei and others, Ricci seems to have regarded the *Storia* as an exercise in keeping the record straight, presumably publicly.[160]

The manuscript was taken to Europe by Nicholas Trigault in 1613, no copy to my knowledge remaining in the mission, and published in a Latin version by Trigault in 1615. It is this Trigault version, which went through many editions in at least six European languages, which was taken in Europe to represent Ricci's view of Confucianism. In fact, however, it shows considerable modification and simplification, especially in the passages referring to Confucianism. It plays a considerable role in the Jesuit interpretation of Confucianism, but it is not reliable as evidence for Ricci's own view.

The earliest reference to Confucianism in the *Storia* occurs in a passage dealing with the moral philosophy of the Chinese. Ricci's original text begins by noting that Chinese philosophers are accustomed to present their views in dialogue form, not according to any system of logic. Trigault's additions are censorious and pedantically 'scholastic':

> They seem to have obscured matters by the introduction of error rather than enlightened them. They have no conception of the rules of logic, and consequently treat the precepts of the science of ethics without any regard to the intrinsic co-ordination of the various divisions of this subject.[161]

Then follows in both the original Italian and Trigault's Latin version a brief account of the life of Confucius, his reputation and influence. Most of Ricci's conclusion to the paragraph, however, has been omitted by Trigault. It has been scored out in the manuscript either

---

apart from some *lacunae* deliberately left to be filled by reference to records not at hand, was complete and polished. It was only Ricci's death which prevented it being sent on to Rome by the author-himself.

160. See his letter to the Portuguese Assistant, Alvarez, 17 February 1609, quoted in part in *Fonti Ricciane,* I, CLXVII.

161. Gallagher, *China in the Sixteenth Century,* 30 *cf. Fonti Ricciane,* N55, 1, 39.

by Trigault, or possibly by the superior of the mission, Longobardo,[162] quite clearly because of its embarrassingly frank description of Confucian rites. Ricci wrote that:

> Besides these [honours paid to Confucius and his descendants], in every city and school where the literati congregate, according to an ancient law, there is a very sumptuous temple of Confucius, in which there stands his statue with his name and title; and every new moon and full moon, and four times in the year, the literati offer to him a certain kind of sacrifice with incense and dead animals which they offer up, although they acknowledge no divinity in him and ask nothing of him. And so it cannot be called a true sacrifice.[163]

Trigault has reduced this careful description with its qualifications to a flat statement: 'He was never venerated with religious rites, however, as they venerate a god'.[164]

The context of this subtle but crucial shift from qualified description to assertion was the bitter debate about the nature of Confucian rites which, as we shall see later, was beginning in the period immediately after Ricci's death. Trigault wished to avoid any possibility of Ricci's authority being invoked by the opponents of the practices of the China mission. But he betrayed one of Ricci's own vital principles in the process. Even after nearly thirty years' experience of China, Matteo Ricci was well aware of his outsider's point of view and of the complexity of the Confucian tradition itself, not to mention the diversity of practice in so huge a country. He proclaimed his hermeneutical principles clearly and unequivocally in the passage I have already cited at the beginning of this chapter, one significatly altered by Trigault.[165] For tactical purposes Ricci wished

162. v *Fonti Ricciane,* I, 40 n 3, and facsimile of the page of the manuscript in Tavola III, opposite page 40.
163. *Fonti Ricciane,* N55, I, 40.
164. Gallagher, *China in the Sixteenth Century,* 30.
165. The corresponding passage in Trigault (Gallagher, *China in the Sixteenth Century,* 448 *cf* Riquebourg-Trigault, *Histoire,* 419) is not only misleadingly abbreviated, but qualified by an assertion that is complete nonsense: 'The Fathers were accustomed to use the authority of this sect to their own advantage, by commenting only on what had happened since the time of Confucius, who lived some five hundred years before the coming of Christ.' Not only did Ricci and others in their Chinese writings make numerous references to the mythical

an alliance with the Confucians against the Buddhists. He recognised that many aspects of Confucianism were ambiguous; that they could be, and were, interpreted in various ways, some perfectly compatible with basic Christian doctrines, others less so. So the Jesuits in seeking to identify their teachings with Confucianism, were obliged to 'interpret in [their] favour things which [Confucius] left ambiguous in his writings'.

That this alliance with and assimilation to Confucianism was tactical in origin can hardly be denied. My examination of Ricci's formative experiences in Chao-ch'ing, Shao-chou and Nan-ch'ang has abundantly demonstrated the pressures which led Ricci to this position. But I do not see it as purely tactical. Ricci's letters show how the development of his understanding of Confucianism led him to an increasingly favourable judgement on it, a genuine intellectual rapport and not just 'a tactic . . . born of a sound instinct that some sort of tactic was necessary'.[166]

In his earliest surviving letter from China, to the Spanish official Román, written on 13 September 1584, Ricci gives his assessment of the major 'religions or sects' of China. He thinks that in China there is really no 'religion' worth speaking of, but of the 'sects' he prefers 'the sect of the literati'. Although 'commonly they do not believe in the immortality of the soul' they reject the superstitions of the others, and practise an austere cult of heaven and earth.[167] A year later, writing to Claudio Acquaviva, the Jesuit General, he again compares favourably the Confucians, whom he describes as 'a sect of Epicureans, not in name, but in their laws and opinions', with the Buddhists who are 'Pythagoreans' and devil-worshippers.[168] By 1593, again writing to Acquaviva, and describing his translation of the Confucian Four Books, he finds a more favourable comparison for Confucius. The Sage is now *un altro Seneca* and the Four Books are *buoni documenti*

Golden Age of China, but the *Storia*, even in Trigault's version, refers frequently to early Chinese history, the Sage Kings, to Five Classics etc. See, for example, Gallagher, *China in the Sixteenth Century*, 30, 55, 93.

166. J Levenson, *Confucian China and Its Modern Fate*, I (London: Routledge and Kegan Paul, 1958), 119; *cf* JD Young, *Confucianism and Christianity*, 25, 'a calculated Jesuit strategy'.

167. Tacchi Venturi, *Opere Storiche*, II, 48–49.

168. Chao-ch'ing, 20 October 1585, in Tacchi Venturi, *Opere Storiche*, II, 57.

morali.[169] In other words, Ricci was attracted to Confucianism in the first place not by the religious values he saw in it, but by what he saw as its non-religious nature, its ethical and social values.

As he systematically extended his studies beyond what he calls the 'Tetrabiblion' (the 'Four Books') to the six classics (*sei dottrine antiche*)[170] he became more convinced of the compatibility of Christianity with Confucianism. 'During these last years', he writes in 1595, '1 have interpreted with the aid of good masters, not only the Four Books but also all Six Classics, and I have noted many passages in all of them which favour the teachings of our faith, such as the unity of God, the immortality of the soul, the glory of the blessed etc'.[171] This was not, perhaps, the method of pure disinterested scholarship but neither was it dishonest. Ricci's commitment to Confucianism was confirmed by study of the sources.

The next, and crucial, stage in the development of his interpretation of Confucianism was his realisation of the divergencies between the commentaries and the basic sources of Confuciansim. To his old friend, Lelio Passionei, he wrote in 1597:

> At the very time when, if I calculate correctly, Plato and Aristotle flourished amongst us, there also flourished amongst [the Chinese] certain literati of good life who produced books dealing with moral matters, not in a scientific way, but in the form of maxims. The chief of these wrote four books which are most highly esteemed, and read day and night. In volume they do not exceed the size of the letters of Marcus Tullius, but the commentaries and glosses, and the commentaries on the commentaries, and further treatises and discourses upon them by this time are infinite.[172]

169. Shao-chou, 10 December 1593, in Tacchi Venturi, *Opere Storiche,* II, 117–18. This conviction of an affinity between Confucius and the Stoics seems to be the impulse for Ricci's *Erh-shih-wu-yen,* begun a little later *cf* C Spalatin, *Matteo Ricci's Use of Epictetus* (Waegwan: Gregoriana University Press, 1975).

170. Actually there were five not six classics since the *Music Classic (Yueh ching)* was reputedly lost. But the *Yueh chi* or 'Record of Music', a section of the *Li chi,* was often counted separately to restore the ancient 'six'.

171. To Acquaviva, Nan-ch'ang, 4 November 1595, in Tacchi Venturi, *Opere Storiche,* II, 207.

172. Letter from Nan-ch'ang, 9 September 1597, in Tacchi Venturi, *Opere Storiche,* II, 237.

It was from an appreciation of the variety of alternative interpretations of Confucianism that Ricci began to develop a distinctively Christian interpretation, which he based on a return to the texts themselves. Ricci placed himself and Christianity firmly on the side of those urging a return to the purity of primitive Confucianism.

Ricci spelled out his hopes for the success of this accommodation to Confucianism in a long letter to the Vice-Provincial, Francesco Pasio, written in Peking, 15 February 1609.[173] He describes his hopes for the mission as *grandissima* and gives a number of reasons for his optimism. Firstly, the high reputation of the Jesuits both as 'virtuous men' and as 'literati'—'the two things most highly regarded' in China. Secondly, he mentions the Chinese openness to reasoned argument. The third reason is the Chinese love of books and their response to Christian literature; and the fourth their natural intelligence. All these are themes which could be paralleled in his earliest letters from China, the appeal of Christian humanism to Chinese humanism. In the fifth reason, however, he breaks new ground and outlines his final position *vis-à-vis* Confucianism:

> Fifth, they are also inclined to religion (*pietà*), as I am little by little coming to perceive, although it will seem the contrary to others. To begin with the beginning, in ancient times they followed the natural law as faithfully as in our lands; and for 1500 years this people was little given to idols and those they adored were not such a wretched crowd as our Egyptians, Greeks and Romans adored, but a lot who were very virtuous and to whom were attributed very good deeds. In fact, in the books of the literati which are those most ancient and of greatest authority, they give no other adoration than to heaven and earth and the Lord of them. When we examine closely all these books we discover in them very few things contrary to the light of reason and very many in conformity with it, and their natural philosophers need yield to none. We may hope, in the divine mercy, that many of their ancestors were saved by the observance of the natural law with the help that God in his goodness gave them. Neither should we be so silent about the fact that after the entry of the idols into this kingdom they made so little or even nothing at all of them, but rather praise them for not wanting to give them more faith than such a law

173. Tacchi Venturi, *Opere Storiche,* II, N 42, 375 ff.

> merited, since it was not well founded and worthy of belief. We can hope that the contrary will occur with regard to the truth of the Catholic faith. Neither, on the other hand, do they make so little of the idols which have very elaborate temples in which are so many thousands of priests, maintained by rents or alms, and in every case with gods of wood, bronze or other material, well made, and greatly revered by the women and common people, that we need fear for the Christians in their cult of the true God.[174]

I find this passage peculiarly significant for a number of reasons. Clearly, it gives the main lines of Ricci's interpretation of the historical development of Confucianism, from a pure theism to an ethically orientated polytheism to an austere rationalism. Buddhism he sees as the foreign intrusive element, rightly rejected by some, and by others accepted, but in that very acceptance showing the Chinese openness to religious devotion. But there are also serious and unresolved ambiguities in the account. Ricci acknowledges a class-based divergence between 'religious' and 'non-religious' Chinese. He sees the majority of Chinese as 'religious' in an overt but not acceptable form. On the other hand, he seems to imply that the apparently non-religious literati are not really so, yet he fails to indicate in precisely what sense they are 'religious'. I suspect that Ricci was confronted with a situation in which the classical Western dichotomies of religious/secular, sacred/profane, simply did not apply; that he intuitively grasped this, but was unable to resolve it on the theoretical plane. This passage is, to me, evidence of a wrestling with the paradox of Confucianism as a secular religion, this-worldly in emphasis yet appealing to transcendent values embodied in the concept of 'heaven'. Contemporary historians and phenomenologists of religion have not yet satisfactorily resolved the dilemma.[175]

Ricci's sixth reason, in his letter to Pasio, is an appeal to the Christian teaching on peace between nations. If, he says, the Chinese, so peaceable by disposition, became Christians, how much more

174. Tacchi Venturi, *Opere Storiche,* II, 385.

175. v H Smith, 'Transcendence in Traditional China', in *Religious Studies,* II. 2 (1967) 185–96; P Rule, 'Sacred and Secular in China', in V Hayes, editor, *Australian Essays in World Religions* (Adelaide: Australian Association for the Study of Religions, 1977), 83–95; and H Fingarette, *Confucius—the Secular as Sacred* (New York: Waveland Press, 1972).

peaceable they would be. This is ironic in view of the record of 'peace-loving' Christians in the Far East. Even Ricci's own Jesuit confreres were currently plotting in the Philippines the conquest of China, and would soon become cannon-founders for the Chinese government. It would be unfair, however, to associate Ricci himself with such actions. He, at least, had faith in persuasion by reason alone. And the seventh point which he proceeds to make, confirms this. Pasio should take care that all members of the mission be thoroughly grounded not only in theology but in 'the letters of China'. What is at stake is not the conversion of 10,000 or so Christians, but 'the universal conversion of the whole kingdom'. Ricci aimed at the conversion of a culture, the Christianising of Confucian China.

In the eighth and last point, Ricci presents his whole programme vis-à-vis Confucianism in terms that sum up neatly the fuller treatment he was currently recording in his *Storia*.

> The eighth point, in which I wish to finish this discussion of the aid we find in the books of the literati of China in matters of our faith. Your Reverence will have understood that in this kingdom there are three sects. One, the most ancient, is that of the literati who now as always have governed China; the other two are idolaters, although there are differences between them, who are continually under attack from the literati. Even though the literati do not set out to speak of supernatural things, in morals they are almost completely in accord with us. And so I commenced in the books I wrote to praise them and to make use of them to confute the others, not directly refuting but interpreting the places in which they are contrary to our faith. In this way I have gained so much credit that not only are the literati not my enemies, but they are friends; so much so that a very distinguished person who is a follower of the sect of the idols has called me in a letter he wrote to me, an adulator of the literati, because, he said, I would place some of the ancient literati in Paradise. And I take care that others see me in this light since we would have much more to do if we had to fight against all three sects. Nevertheless, I do not leave off attacking certain new opinions of the literati of this age who do not wish to follow the ancients. And in this way many of them become Christians, confessing and communicating

> and striving themselves, in so far as their talents allow, to spread our holy faith.[176]

And so, by 1609, we have the Jesuit approach to Confucianism fully evolved—alliance with Confucians against Buddhists, and within Confuciansim, against the Neo-Confucians in support of a return to the sources.

The detailed workings out of the consequences of this basic stance are found in the *Storia* and the *T'ien-chu shih-i* with some particular applications in Ricci's other writings in Chinese. Since I have elsewhere[177] examined the view presented in the *Storia* I will here draw mainly on the *T'ien-chu shih-i* for illustrations of Ricci's positions. In many ways these two major works are complementary. To a Western audience Ricci stressed the unfamiliar aspects of Confucianism which are implicit in the *T'ien-chu shih-i*, while in the Chinese work he comes into more direct engagement with specific problems of textual interpretation. From the two combined emerges the full range of Ricci's interpretation of Confucianism.

The *T'ien-chu shih-i* ('The True Idea of the Lord of Heaven') was not published till 1603 but it is the fruit of many years of effort on Ricci's part. Its dialogue form suggests direct descent from the earliest of Ricci's writings in Chinese that we possess, the *conversazioni catechetiche* appended to the Portuguese-Chinese vocabulary produced during the Chao-ch'ing period. More directly it seems to have been inspired by Valignano. The Visitor had been dissatisfied with Ruggieri's *T'ien-chu shih-lu*, not only because of its language (the references to the Jesuits as 'bonzes') and its stylistic defects, but also because of its narrow range.[178] It was, as we have seen, a *doctrina* rather than a 'catechism', a simple exposition of Christian teaching rather than a work of apologetics, and the latter was seen to be necessary as work amongst the literati grew. PM D'Elia has traced[179] Ricci's references to work on the 'Catechism' back to 1594 when he

176. Tacchi Venturi, *Opere Storiche,* II, 386–87.

177. 'Jesuit and Confucian? Chinese Religion in the *Journals* of Matteo Ricci S.J., 1583–1610', in *Journal of Religious History,* V/2 (December 1968): 105–24.

178. *Fonti Ricciane*, I, 379 nn 3&4.

179. 'Prima Introduzione della Filosofia Scolastica in Cina (1584, 1603)', in 'Studies presented to Dr Hu Shih on his 65th birthday', in *Bulletin of the Institute of History and Philology,* Academia Sinica, XXVIII (1956): 141–96.

wrote about preparing 'a book on the matters of our faith, completely based on natural reason'.[180] It seems to have been largely completed by 1596 but publication was delayed while it was censored by Superiors who could not read Chinese. Ricci waxed eloquent on this subject in a letter to the Jesuit General in 1606, insisting on the absurdity of his having to prepare a Latin translation for the 'revisors' of the work.[181] The anomaly was corrected later, but in this case publication was delayed for several years while Ricci awaited the imprimatur from the Goa Inquisition. The work must have circulated in manuscript, however, because Feng Ying-ching's preface is dated 3 February 1601, and the first printed edition did not appear till late 1603[182] (Ricci's own preface is dated 22 August 1603).

The term *Catechism* when applied to the *T'ien-chu shih-i* has caused a good deal of confusion and misunderstanding. Strictly speaking it refers to a work in question and answer form, and this is an accurate if inadequate description of Ricci's book. Ricci himself calls it a 'catechism', but his Latin translation of the title, *De Deo Verax Disputatio,*[183] indicates better its nature, a 'disputation' or argument about matters of religion. Later critics of Ricci have looked in the work, failed to discover what they regard as the essential tenets of Christianity, and concluded that he was preaching an adulterated faith.[184] It should be considered not in isolation but together with works such as his *Dottrina Christiana* (*T'ien-chu-chiao yao*)[185] which are 'catechisms' in the modern sense of basic expositions of doctrine. Ricci carefully explains at the beginning of the first chapter that he is concerned only with 'the general meaning of the Lord of Heaven Religion' and establishing that it is the 'true religion', but not with

180. Ricci to Costa, 12 October 1594, in Tacchi Venturi, *Opere Storiche,* II, 122.

181. Ricci to Acquaviva, Peking, 15 August 1606, in Tacchi Venturi, *Opere Storiche,* II, No 37.

182. *Fonti Ricciane,* II, 293 n *cf* II, 301 where Ricci points out that Feng first saw it *scritto di mano*, and undertook to print it at his own expense.

183. In a letter accompanying the first edition sent to Rome in 1604. See *Fonti Ricciane,* II, 293 n.

184. Bernard-Maître, *Ricci,* II, 123 gives examples of this kind of criticism.

185. See *Fonti Ricciane,* N708, II, 289–91. I have not seen the edition in 14ff described by D'Elia (II, 290 n) but the copy in ARSJ: JS *I. 57a* (33 ff) may be of the time of Ricci.

expounding its beliefs and practices, nor its scriptures and traditions.[186] The *T'ien-chu shih-i* is primarily aimed at convincing the non-Christian, hence its form of a dialogue between a Western scholar and a Chinese scholar.

To the modern reader much of the argument in the *T'ien-chu shih-i* has a heavy scholastic flavour. I find it difficult to imagine what impact arguments based on the Aristotelian distinction between four kinds of causes, between substance and accidents etc., all couched in newly invented terminology, would have had on a Ming scholar. Yet it does seem to have impressed many. Most notable of these was the official Feng Ying-ching, referred to by Ricci as 'Fummocam' (Feng Mu-kang), the very model of uprightness and Confucian orthodoxy.[187] He was strongly anti-Buddhist, and in politics an opponent of the eunuchs, for which he was deprived of office and imprisoned. In fact he undertook the printing of the *T'ien-chu shih-i* while still in prison. It is clear that, to Feng, Ricci was not preaching an unorthodox teaching, but rather a return to early Confucian orthodoxy. The key to this interpretation of the work lies at the very beginning of his preface where he equates Ricci's 'Lord of Heaven' (*T'ien-chu*) with the *Shang-ti* of the classics: 'Who is the Lord of Heaven? He is *Shang-ti*!'[188] And he continues:

> Truly what [Ricci] says is to the point. The six classics and four philosophers of our land are sacred and honoured. He says to revere *Shang-ti*, to assist *Shang-ti*, to serve *Shang-ti*, to investigate *Shang-ti*. Who would consider this empty talk?[189]

Feng Ying-ching had grasped the central thrust of Ricci's argument very well. The whole appeal to Chinese tradition rested on a certain view of early Confucianism. Ricci claimed that this was a pure form of natural religion underpinning a social and ethical philosophy. In the *T'ien-chu shih-i* he does not develop this explicitly, nor at length, but allows it to emerge from his critical remarks on Buddhism and Neo-Confucianism, usually placed in the mouth of the Chinese scholar

186. *T'ien-chu shih-i,* A.2a. I have cited throughout the Taipei 1967 edition, a reprint of the Ming edition, which is also that used in the *T'ien-hsueh ch'u-han,* comparing my translation in each case with the modem Chinese version by Liu Shun-te (Taichung, 1966).
187. For a sketch of his career see *Fonti Ricciane,* II, 162, n l.
188. *T'ien-chu ho? Shang-ti yeh!*
189. *Tien-chu shih-i,* Preface la.

rather than the Westerner. Selective quotations from the classics are used to demonstrate that many doctrines of Christianity about God, man and a future life, are not innovations but were held in an inchoate way by the ancient Confucians. These views were misinterpreted or ignored by later Confucians, partly through the pernicious influence of Buddhism, and partly in justifiable reaction to Buddhist excesses. But the main points are still taught by the Confucian school, and the texts in which they are expressed are still revered by all Confucians.

In the *Storia* Ricci presents his conclusions about the nature of early Confucianism in a more systematic way. He begins his chapter on the religions of China by remarking that the ancient Chinese had less erroneous views on religion than any other people known to Europe.[190] They adored a Supreme God whom they called the 'King of Heaven' or 'Heaven and Earth', 'perhaps in the belief that heaven and earth were animated to make one living body by the supreme god, as if he were their soul'.[191] He adds that various subsidiary spirits were also worshipped, but these were not as powerful as the 'Lord of Heaven' himself.[192] Note that Ricci scrupulously presents the complexity of Chinese beliefs as found in the classics. Trigault, while translating most of this accurately enough, oversimplifies one key passage to the bald assertion: 'They do not believe in idol worship. In fact they have no idols. They do, however, believe in one deity who preserves and governs all things on earth.'[193] Ricci certainly implies this, and argues for it in many passages of the *T'ien-chu shih-i*, but as an interpretation of complex phenomenon, not as a self-evident

190. *Fonti Ricciane,* N170, 1, 108.

191. *Fonti Ricciane,* N170, 1, 108–9. Gernet, basing his argument partly on this passage, attributes to Ricci the mistaken belief that the Chinese are pantheists ('Christian and Chinese Visions of the World in the Seventeenth Century', in *Chinese Science* 4 [1980]: 8). However the position presented here preserves the ontological distinction between God and the world, hence cannot be called 'Pantheism' in the strict sense. Furthermore, Ricci is referring to the ancient Chinese, his early Confucians, not to the contemporary Chinese whom he regards as monists *(Fonti Ricciane,* N176, I. 116—the other passage cited by Gernet, ('Christian and Chinese Visions of the World in the Seventeenth Century', n 21).

192. *Fonti Ricciane,* NN170 & 176, 1, 109, 115.

193. Gallagher, *China in the Sixteenth Century,* 94; Riquebourg-Trigault, *Histoire,* 86 *cf* the original which explicitly refers to the more nuanced picture of the first paragraph of the chapter (*Fonti Ricciane,* N176, 1, 115).

proposition. His position would be fairly represented as an assertion that there is some notion of a supreme God in the earliest Chinese texts, associated especially with the terms *t'ien* and *shang-ti*; and that reason, by logical deduction, can establish that he must be the sole preserver and governor of all things.

Confucius himself is presented in the *Storia* as 'the author, restorer and head' of 'the sect of the literati',[194] responsible for the collection and transmission of the teaching of the ancients.[195] The Chinese regard him 'as the most holy man who ever existed in the world, and, in truth, in what he said and in his good manner of living in conformity with nature, he is not inferior to our ancient philosophers, and superior to many'.[196] This cautious conclusion shows that whatever later Jesuits may have contributed to the cult of Confucius in the West, its excesses should not be attributed to Ricci.

Later Confucians, according to Ricci, may be divided into two groups: those who remained faithful to the views of Confucius and the classics, and those who invented new doctrines. The 'true literati' have nothing to say about the time and manner of the creation of the world, but commentators 'of little authority' have expressed opinions quite frivolous and ill-founded' on the subject.[197] Similarly, the ancient literati seem to have been uncertain about the immortality of the soul, and about its fate after death. It is only the recent Confucians who teach that the soul dies with the body and explicitly deny the existence of a heaven and a hell.[198]

In the *T'ien-chu shih-i* Ricci has a passage on this subject, in which he not only defends the doctrine of heaven and hell from the classics, but makes some illuminating comments on the Confucian tradition itself. The Chinese scholar has raised the obvious objection that Confucians follow the religion of the sages, and the classics in which their teachings are transmitted say nothing about heaven and hell. Ricci's Western scholar replies:

> Can the instructions which the sages transmitted be examined by later generations? There are some traditions

194. *Fonti Ricciane,* N176, 1, 115.
195. *Fonti Ricciane,* N61, 1, 42–43.
196. *Fonti Ricciane,* N55, I, 39.
197. *Fonti Ricciane,* N176, 1, 115.
198. *Fonti Ricciane,* N176, 1, 115–16.

> which are incomplete. Either they were delivered orally and not completely recorded in writing; or they were recorded but later lost; or later, stupid scribes did not believe they were authentic and obliterated them. Furthermore the wording of texts is sometimes altered and we cannot be certain whether or not a particular text really read as it now does. Modern scholars make mistakes in interpreting ancient books, and cannot master the meaning. They are quick to quote the text, but slow to interpret it. And so, while modern scholarship flourishes, modern manners are in decline.[199]

After this attempted demolition of the argument from the silence of the classics, Ricci proceeds to quote from the *Songs*[200] and the *Book of History*[201] passages which place famous ancient kings 'on high' or 'in heaven'. When the Chinese scholar accepts these passages as evidence for an ancient belief in heaven, Ricci argues that if the good kings go to heaven, there must be a hell for bad kings.

The last stage in this key example of Ricci's method is his redefinition of the true Confucian 'gentleman' (*chün-tzu*). Ricci is well aware that his arguments up to this point may simply strengthen the Confucian prejudices of his reader and he makes his Chinese scholar say:

> Now I get the idea. I see that this is what the books of the ancient sages say. But why must one believe in heaven and hell? If there is a heaven the gentleman must get there, and if there is a hell the small-minded man (*hsiao jen*) must go there. I only have to act like a gentleman and everything is alright. That's the point you're getting at, isn't it?

The Western scholar replies:

> You have missed the point completely. Why do I think this? If there is a heaven the gentleman must necessarily get there. But if you do not believe in the doctrine of heaven and hell you are certainly not a gentleman.
>
> The dialogue continues:

199. *T'ien-chu shih-i*, B.31a.
200. *Ta ya*, I. i (Mao 235) and I. ix (Mao 243).
201. *Chou shu* XII, 'The Announcement of the Duke of Shao'.

> CHINESE SCHOLAR: Why is that?
> WESTERN SCHOLAR: Just now I asked you whether or not a man who does not believe in Shang-ti is a gentleman.
> CHINESE SCHOLAR: Of course not. The *Shih Ching* says: 'Now this King Wen was careful and reverent, and openly served *Shang-ti*' [*Ta ya* 1. ii, Mao 236]. Who can call himself a 'gentleman' and not believe in Shang-ti?
> WESTERN SCHOLAR: A man who does not believe that *Shang-ti* is perfectly good and perfectly just—is he a gentleman or not?
> CHINESE SCHOLAR: No. *Shang-ti* is the source of goodness and the just lord of all that is. Who can call himself a 'gentleman' and not believe that *Shang-ti* is perfectly good and perfectly just?
> WESTERN SCHOLAR: Goodness consists in the ability to love men and the ability to hate men. If *Shang-ti* does not allow the good to ascend to heaven, how can he be said to love men? And if he does not condemn the evil to hell how can he be said to hate men? This world's rewards are usually not completely just. If heaven and hell do not exist after death for each according to his merits it is grossly unfair. If you do not believe this, how can you believe that *Shang-ti* is good and just? As for the retribution of heaven and hell, in China the Buddhists and Taoists believe it, and wise Confucians also follow it. All the great nations of East and West have no doubts about it. The Holy Scriptures of the Lord of Heaven refer to it. I myself on previous occasions have revealed this doctrine and proved it. So, he who persists in denying it cannot be a gentleman.
> CHINESE SCHOLAR: After that, I certainly believe it. But I would still like to hear more about it.
> WESTERN SCHOLAR: These things are difficult to explain. The Scriptures mention them in a general way but do not explain them in detail. However, the punishments of hell can be compared to the calamities of this world. Let me give a few examples . . .[202]

I have cited this passage at length because it is typical of Ricci's method of working and reveals his approach to the Confucian tradition in all its complexity. He both accepts and reinterprets the tradition, commits himself to its basic concepts and redefines their context. Joseph Levenson points out that one of the implications of this tactic is that 'in effect, it authorized the potential convert to see in the

202. *T'ien-chu shih-i*, B.33a–34a.

foreign church-organization, and in its foreign composed Scriptures, at best vessels of the truth which must also exist in his own historical inheritance'.[203] Ricci, in the passage just examined, seems to me to have been aware of the dilemma. He wished to relate his teaching to Confucianism both for reasons of expediency and from predilection for some of the intellectual options of the Confucian tradition. He implies, however, that the ideas of the ancient Confucians have been forgotten and distorted by later Confucians and that they need complementing by Christian revelation.

The *T'ien-chu shih-i* itself is primarily concerned with the restoration of the pristine doctrines of Confucianism rather than the complementary truths of Christianity, although this subject is cautiously raised in the last section, entitled 'A General View of the Customs of the West . . . and how the Lord of Heaven descended to be born in the West'. The *Catechism*, as we have seen, was intended as a *preparatio evangelica*, a preparation for receiving the full message, which was elaborated elsewhere. He himself described his work as neither harvesting, nor even sowing, but clearing the forests.[204] The *T'ien-chu shih-i* was a major part of that clearing operation, addressed to the 'many people desirous of knowing the truth' and aimed at convincing them 'that we Europeans are not an ignorant people who do not understand things or cannot develop a rational argument'.[205]

The theme of the complementarity of Confucianism and Christianity is implicit in the whole of Ricci's writings. It is the note struck in the prelude to the *T'ien-chu shih-i* where the Chinese scholar declares himself dissatisfied with his way of life, virtuous though it is.

> Our way of self-cultivation-where will it end up? Although our plan is clear as far as this life is concerned, we know nothing about what happens after death. I have found that you, sir, have travelled throughout the whole world to transmit the scriptures and commands of the Lord of Heaven and induce men to do good. I wish to receive this great teaching.[206]

---

203. *Confucian China and Its Modern Fate,* I, 119.
204. Letter to Costa, Nan-ch'ang, 14 August 1599, in Tacchi Venturi, *Opere Storiche,* II, 246–47.
205. *Fonti Ricciane,* N710, II, 300.
206. *T'ien-chu shih-i,* A.Ia–b.

And, again and again, we find the Chinese scholar concluding that the Christian view is a logical extension of his Confucian premises. I know of no place in Ricci's own writings in which he speaks specifically of complementarity. There is, however, a passage in Trigault's version of Ricci's memoirs which develops this idea in the sort of theological language that Ricci himself eschewed, and in this case I think it is a fair representation of his practice.

> What the Fathers continually endeavoured to emphasize . . . was the fact that the Christian law was in perfect accord with the innate light of conscience. It was, as they maintained, by this same light of conscience that the most ancient of the Chinese scholars had approached to this same doctrine of Christianity in their writings, centuries before the appearance of the idols. They explained, also, that they themselves were not abolishing the natural law, rather they were adding to it what was lacking, namely the supernatural as taught by God who Himself had become a man.[207]

Ricci's careful avoidance of the natural/supernatural dichotomy was, I believe, deliberate. But whatever his reservations about the exact theological status of Confucianism, he undoubtedly saw it as lacking something. In this, as in so many respects, his best interpreter was Hsü Kuang-ch'i, who remarked succinctly that Christianity 'does away with the idols and completes the law of the literati'.[208]

'Doing away with the idols' meant more than an attack on Buddhism. It also involved a rejection of Neo-Confucianism which Ricci regarded as the product of Buddhist influence. The basic error of the Neo-Confucians, as Ricci saw it, was their monism, their reduction of all things, including God, to one substance.

> The opinion that is most commonly followed here appears to me to be taken over from the sect of the idols five hundred years ago. It is that the whole of this world is composed of one substance only, and that its creator, together with heaven and earth, men and animals, trees and plants, and the four

207. Gallagher, *China in the Sixteenth Century*, 156.

208. Gallagher, *China in the Sixteenth Century*, 448. The Chinese phrase is given as 'Ciue Fo pu Giu', presumably *ch'üeh-Fo pu-Ju*. The passage is an interpolation by Trigault, not found in the original text of the *Storia*.

> elements, all make up one continuous body, and all are members of this body. And from this unity of substance they derive the love which we ought have one for the other. In this way all men can come to be like God through being of one and the same substance with him. This we endeavour to refute not only by reason, but even more by the authority of their ancient (philosophers) who quite clearly teach a very different doctrine.[209]

I do not intend to pursue here the vexed question of the interpretation of Neo-Confucian metaphysics. It seems clear to me that Ricci's view derives from a translation of the Chinese term *t'i* as 'substance' (*substantia*), and his subsequent conclusion that when the Neo-Confucians speak of all things being one *t'i* they are alleging identity of 'substance' in the Western sense. *T'i*, however, is a far wider term than 'substance', both less precise and carrying an enormous weight of associations to the educated Chinese that may even seem mutually incompatible to the Western mind.[210] Certainly Neo-Confucianism stresses the unity of all things, but whether in terms of 'substance' or 'monism' in the Western sense, we may leave aside.

On the level of exegesis of Ricci's text, however, it is clear that Ricci's interpretation is far more tentative than that of most later Jesuits. As we shall see, most of Ricci's successors alleged that the Neo-Confucians were atheists or pantheists, or curiously, even both at once. And they could cite the authority of Ricci on both counts. Ricci does describe the modern Confucians as atheists,[211] even asserting that 'the majority of this people end up in profound atheism'.[212] And he does, in the passage just cited, and elsewhere,[213] claim that the Chinese believe that God is identical with the universe. However, on

209. *Fonti Ricciane,* NI76, 1, 116.
210. See W Liebenthal, *The Book of Chao* (Peiping: Monumenta Serica Monographs, 1948), XIII, 19–20, for comments on the impossibility of translating *t'i,* and examples of its use. Julia Ching in her study of Wang Yang-ming *To Acquire Wisdom: The 'Way' of Wang Yang-ming,* uses 'reality' for *t'i,* perhaps the best that can be done in English. I am indebted to Professor Ching for some stimulating conversations on the subject of Neo-Confucian concepts which have left their mark on many places in this work which touch on Neo-Confucianism.
211. *Fonti Ricciane,* N170, I, 110.
212. *Fonti Ricciane,* N199, I, 132.
213. *Fonti Ricciane,* N170, I, 109.

closer examination, it is seen that the passages about Chinese 'atheism' refer to practical attitudes to life and in each case describe a reaction against Buddhist 'idolatry' and superstition. Where Ricci appears to describe Chinese pantheism, one finds that he avoids the term itself and its equivalents, and hedges his description with 'perhaps', 'as if' etc. Even in the account of the Chinese belief that all things make up one substance the conclusion of monism is not explicitly drawn. Where modern Jesuits, including the editor of the *Storia*,[214] do not hesitate to speak of the 'materialism', 'pantheism' and 'atheism' of Neo-Confucianism, Ricci, wisely, confined himself to simple and cautious statement.

Ricci's caution is even more marked when writing, in the *T'ienchu shih-i*, for a Chinese audience. In the second chapter, 'Explanation of the Misconceptions held by previous generations about the Lord of Heaven', he tentatively raises the question of the basic conceptions of reality in Chinese thought.

> CHINESE SCHOLAR: . . . In our country there are three sects each with its own adherents. The Taoists say that things are produced from Nothing (*wu*) and that Nothing is their chief principle (*tao*). The Buddhists say that the world of appearance comes out of the Void (*k'ung*) and they regard the Void as fundamental. The Confucians say that change in being comes from the Supreme Ultimate (*t'ai-chi*) and hence only Being (*yu*) should be honoured and Sincerity (*ch'eng*) the object of study. I do not know whom you consider to be right.

The Western scholar is sure about Taoism and Buddhism, but he is much more tentative about Confucianism.

> The two sects that talk of 'Nothing' and the 'Void' are completely different in their teaching from the doctrine of the Lord of Heaven, and it is clear that they are not worthy of respect. As for the Confucians who talk of 'Being' and

214. *Fonti Ricciane*, I, 116 n 3—*questa nuova scuola di letterati panteisti e materialisti cf* S Le Gall, *Le Philosophe Tchou Hi, Sa Doctrine, Son Influence*, Shanghai, (*Variétés* Sinologiques No 6) 1923, especially 15–16, 23; and H Bernard-Maître, *Sagesse Chinoise et Philosophie Chrétienne* (Tientsin: école des hautes-études, 1935), Iere partie, Leçon VIII and IX.

> 'Sincerity', I have not thoroughly examined their explanations but they seem to be nearly identical (with ours).[215]

Note that Ricci, at this point, evades the question that he himself has raised about the interpretation of *t'ai-chi*, the Supreme Ultimate, and restricts his comments to the basic metaphysical and ethical positions of Confucianism. And even within this restricted area his comments are cautious.

Later in this chapter, Ricci returns to the question of *t'ai-chi*, having disposed of the Buddhists and Taoists in a fairly summary way.

> CHINESE SCHOLAR: What do you think of this Supreme Ultimate that our Confucian scholars speak of?
>
> WESTERN SCHOLAR: Although I have only recently entered China I have thoroughly and diligently studied the ancient classics; I have heard that the gentlemen of ancient times paid their respects to the High Lord of Heaven and Earth (*T'ien-ti chih shang-ti*), but I have never heard that they reverenced the Supreme Ultimate. If the Supreme Ultimate was the begetter (*tsu*) of the High Lord of all things, why didn't the ancient sages say so openly?[216]

When the Chinese scholar advances the usual explanation, that the doctrine is implicit in early Confucianism and is based on ancient cosmological diagrams, Ricci replies that the diagrams are nothing but 'weird designs', and, in any case, don't show *t'ai-chi* producing heaven and earth.[217] Furthermore, he goes on to argue, the Supreme Ultimate and Principle (*1i*) with which the Neo-Confucians equate it, cannot be the causes of all things, because they are not 'substances' but 'accidents'. The *li* of a thing does not produce the thing itself, but merely determines what sort of thing it will be. A Creator is still necessary.[218]

Ricci's objections to the Neo-Confucian theory of *t'ai-chi* are, then, twofold. On the one hand he pre-empts the Confucians' own ground by an appeal to the true ancient teaching before the accretion of metaphysical commentary; and on the other, he invokes his own

215. *T'ien-chu shih-i*, A.12a–b.
216. *T'ien-chu shih-i*, A.14b.
217. *T'ien-chu shih-i*, A. 15a. On this question, see Chow Yih-ching, *La Philosophie Morale dans le Neo-Confucianisme* (Paris: Presses universitaires de France, 1954).
218. *T'ien-chu shih-i*, A.16a–18b.

metaphysical system to criticise that of the Neo-Confucians. The former argument is historically well founded but rather specious in its interpretation of Confucian 'tradition' and Confucian 'orthodoxy'. Both of these are assumed to be static, or fixed in basic content. I suspect that, unconsciously at least, Ricci was invoking the model of a Catholic view of the development of Christian tradition: from initial revelation in Christ, through theological elaboration by the Fathers, to radical perversion by the Protestants and counter-renewal by the Catholic reformers. If this is so, one might object that Ricci is the Protestant in this case, advocating return to the roots and abandonment of a corrupt 'tradition'. As for his own metaphysical arguments, they are based once more on a false, or at least dubious, equation, that of the Neo-Confucian *li* with the scholastic concept of 'form'. We do not possess Ricci's Latin version of the *T'ien-chu shih-i* prepared for the censors, and it is not certain that he would have translated li as 'form', but it does seem to be implied in his treatment of the relationship between existing things and their li. What is certain from his diagram of the 'Porphyrean tree' in Chapter 4 is that he uses *tzu-li* and *i-la*i as strict equivalents of 'substance' and 'accident'.[219] Non-Chinese categories are being employed to locate and then refute Chinese conceptions. To assert that *li* is an 'accident', while excusable in the pioneer Western exponent of Chinese philosophy, was a very dangerous procedure.

In a note which Ricci wrote to the Jesuit General to accompany a copy of the first edition of his *Catechism,*[220] he makes another essay in the comparative interpretation of *t'ai-chi*. He explains that he decided to attack the identification of *t'ai-chi* with *li* for tactical reasons, 'lest we appear rather to follow the Chinese theory, than to interpret and make Chinese authors follow our own teaching'. In fact, he says, although many Chinese interpret *t'ai-ch*i as the 'reason of things' [*1i*], it seems to be 'nothing else than that which our philosophers call "prime matter."'[221] However, this is a controversial matter, and one

219. *T'ien-chu shih-i*, A.43b *cf* notes, on pages 68 and 70 to the modern Chinese version.

220. The Latin text of this passage is given in *Fonti Ricciane,* II, 297–98 n.

221. I know of only one other case of a Jesuit taking up this line of interpretation of *t'ai-chi.* Andreas Lubelli in his *Chen-fu chieh-chih,* c 1670, equates *t'ai-chi* with *yuan-chih.* See Chu Ch'ien-chih, 'Ye-su-hui tui-yu Sung-Ju li-hsueh chih fan-ying', in *Ming shih lun-ts'ung,* X (Taipei, 1968), 152.

likely to arouse the ire of 'the literati who govern China . . . unless we attack the explanation of this principle rather than the principle itself.' He insists that what he is concerned about is not terminology, but substance of teaching. 'If', he says, 'they would understand *t'ai-chi* as the first principle, substantial, intelligent and infinite, we would assert that it is indeed God and nothing else'.

Once more we are reminded that this first Jesuit essay in the interpretation of Confucianism was a work of apologetics, seeking to use and interpret whatever presented itself in the Chinese tradition as amenable to interpretation in a Christian sense. The attitude to Neo-Confucianism and Buddhist adopted in the *T'ien-chu shih-i* was primarily due to Ricci's judgement that the basis of Neo-Confucian and Buddhist metaphysics was monistic, and therefore incompatible with Christianity. The Buddhists would make God one substance with all things, and confuse his nature.[222] The Neo-Confucians would make man one substance with all things and destroy all sense of moral discrimination. The truth, as taught by the ancient Confucians and the *T'ien-chu-chiao*, is that God is distinct from both man and other things.[223]

Ricci's attitude towards Buddhism was more hostile than that towards Neo-Confucianism. He regarded the most objectionable feature of Neo-Confucian philosophy, its monism, as derived from Buddhism, and he attempted to discredit it by stressing its Buddhist origin. He knew that any attack on Buddhism would be favourably received by many contemporary Confucians. Feng Ying-ching's Preface to the *T'ien-chu shih-i* strongly approves of this attack. Ricci, he says, has proved that the Emperor Ming of Han, was deceived by the envoys sent to the West to inquire about the 'sage from the West' he saw in his dream. They stopped short of the real West (*Ta-Hsi*, 'the great West') and brought back from India the teachings of Buddha.[224]

> In the old days scholars acknowledged Heaven and obeyed Heaven, but today they recite the name of Buddha and follow the way of Buddha.[225]

222. *T'ien-chu shih-i*, A.47a-49a.
223. *T'ien-chu shih-i*, A.54b-57b.
224. *T'ien-chu shih-I*, Preface, Ia-b.
225. *T'ien-chu shih-I*, Preface, 2a.

And now a man from the Great West itself has come to set the record straight. Although a foreigner, he teaches the doctrines of the ancient sages of China, the Three Emperors, the Five Rulers, the Three Kings, Duke Chou and Confucius, and attacks those of the Indian Prince, Buddha.[226]

Recent studies of the Jesuits' early conflicts with Buddhism have demonstrated that there were substantial issues at stake.[227] Ricci was not simply taking advantage of Confucian hostility to Buddhism but attacking what he saw as fundamental errors about God, man and the world. Besides the monism of Buddhism he attacked their cosmology, their theory of the soul, their superstition and idolatry. I will not pursue here the question of the basis and accuracy of Ricci's critique of Buddhism. I have elsewhere[228] examined the view of Buddhism that appears in the *Storia*, and more work needs to be done on Ricci's contacts with Buddhists in Nanking and Peking.[229]

However, my theme here is the Jesuits and Confucianism, not the Jesuits and Buddhism. There are a few passages in the *T'ien-chu shih-i* dealing with Buddhism which are also of crucial importance for understanding Ricci's interpretation of Confucianism. Most of these deal with his view of Buddhism as a late intrusion into China. He does not state clearly in the *T'ien-chu shih-i*, as he does in the *Storia*, that the modern Confucians have adopted Buddhist doctrines or are excessively influenced by Buddhism, although it is implied in many places, and Feng Ying-ching certainly read the *T'ienchu shih-i*

226. *T'ien-chu shih-I,* Preface, 2a.

227. See, for example, D Lancashire, 'Anti-Christian Polemics in Seventeenth Century China', in *Church History,* XXXVIII (1969): 218–41; Y Raguin, 'Father Ricci's Presentation of some Fundamental Theories of Buddhism', in *Chinese Culture,* x (1969): 37–43; and R Etiemble 'Le boudhisme chinois vu par les jésuites confuciens', in L Lanciotti, editodor *Sviluppi scientifici, prospettive religiose, movimenti rivoluzionari in Cina* (Firenze: Olschki, 1975), 103–14.

228. *Journal of Religious History,* V (1968): 117–22.

229. Hung Ming-shui claims that Ricci's hostility to Buddhism was due to 'ignorance of the changing intellectual trends' of the time ('Yuan Hung-tao and the late Ming Literary and Intellectual Movement', unpublished PhD thesis University of Wisconsin, 1974, 225); yet the section of his thesis on 'Yuan's Group viewed by Matteo Ricci and other European Jesuits' ('Yuan Hung-tao and the late Ming Literary and Intellectual Movement', chapter V A, 213–27) demonstrates the extent and depth of Ricci's engagement with the leading figures of his day. See also W Franke 'Matteo Ricci in den Augen eines Chinesischer Zeit-genossen', in *Studia Sino-Altaica: Festschrift fur Erich Haonisch* (Wiesbaden, 1961), 72–5.

this way. Rather, he concentrates on the return to the pure teaching of the ancients, Western as well as Chinese. India is the source of the corruption of these ideas. At the time when China got the doctrines of Sakyamuni from India, the latter was 'a small country, not to be compared with the great nations, uncultured, barbarous in its morals, even its existence unknown to many countries'.[230] Many of the ideas of Sakyamuni were, in fact, borrowed from the West. Transmigration[231] was borrowed from Pythagoras, and whatever truth there is in Buddhism comes from the West.[232] When, for example, the Chinese scholar objects to Ricci that only Buddhists speak of heaven and hell, Ricci's alter ego replies that Confucians are not Buddhists because they forbid murder, just as insects are not birds merely because they fly.

> Christianity is an ancient religion. The Buddhists must have stolen these ideas from Westerners. Generally speaking, if you wish to impart your own teaching, don't you use three or four orthodox sayings mixed in with what you yourself believe? The Buddhists have used the Christian teachings about Heaven and Hell in order to impart their own private views and heterodox doctrines. We teach an orthodox doctrine; should we reject it because the Buddhists also talk about it? Before the Buddha was born there were Christians. Those who speak of cultivating the Way, must bear witness to later

230. *Tien-chu shih-i,* B.2a.
231. Throughout chapter 5 of the *Tien-chu shih-i* Ricci uses the Buddhist term *hui-liu-tao,* the 'six ways of return'. Although in primitive Buddhism there seems to have been no 'soul' to 'transmigrate' (the doctrine of *anatta),* the 'six ways of return' of Chinese Buddhism—as deva, man, asura, beast, hungry ghost or in hell—are usually presented in terms of the Chinese notion of 'soul'. Ricci's own translation of the title of this chapter in the copy of the *Tien-chu shih-i* preserved in ARSJ: JS /, 45, uses the term 'transmigration' (*de transmigration animarum; v* facsimile in *Fonti Ricciane,* II, Tavola XVIII, opp page 292.
232. This point is developed by Yang T'ing-yun in his *T'ien Shih ming-pien* (*Tien-chu-chiao tung-ch'uan wen-hsien hsü-pien* [Taipei, 1966], I, 229–417), especially in the first section on 'origins' (241–46). I have not, however, found in any of the Jesuit anti-Buddhist writings in Chinese the argument commonly used elsewhere that the Buddhists were aping Christian rituals which they had borrowed in India from the converts of St. Thomas. See, for example, Daniello Bartoli, *La Cina,* Lib. I, cap. CXXVI, 279–81 in volume I of the Ancona, 1843 edition.

> generations that there is a Heaven of everlasting pleasure to be gained, and a Hell of inexhaustible punishment to be avoided.[233]

Needless to say, the Chinese scholar does not make the obvious retort that Ricci is treating Confucianism in the same way that he accuses the Buddhists of treating Christianity—using 'three or four orthodox sayings mixed in with what you yourself believe'. Nor does he object, as a modern scholar would, to Ricci's chronology. Ricci appears to believe that the Buddha was a contemporary of Han Ming Ti, although it is possible that he thought of the *T'ien-chu-chiao* as embracing the Old Testament as well as the New. Once more, however, we find the attempt to conflate early Confucianism with the *T'ien-chu-chiao* to form one all-embracing orthodox Way (*cheng-tao*).

Ricci's attitude to Buddhism is one of uncompromising opposition. They are 'the sect of the idols', corrupters of the ancient Chinese theism and purveyors of superstition to the masses. It would not be fair to Ricci, however, to accuse him of pandering to Confucian prejudices. The Chinese scholar remarks, in one place, that the 'gentlemen' of China oppose and 'have a deep hatred' for Buddhists and Taoists. Ricci replies:

> It is better to argue against them than to hate them, and better to convince them by reasoning than to argue against them. The followers of the two sects are all made by the Father of the Lord of Heaven, and so are our brothers. If my younger brother goes mad and is led astray by wild stories would I act as a brother ought and show him sympathy, or would I hate him? Wouldn't I use reasoning to persuade him? In my extensive reading of Confucian books I have frequently come across expressions of hatred for the two sects, ranking them with barbarians, and accusing them of heresy, but I have not seen the application of first principles in order to refute them. We say they are wrong, and they in turn say we are wrong, and so our disputation is confused, and neither is convinced. This has gone on for more than 1,500 years and there can be no agreement. But if we both use reasoning in conducting our argument, then without harsh words the right and the wrong will appear, and the three schools will return to unity.[234]

233. *Tien-chu shih-i*, A.26b-27a.
234. *Tien-chu shih-i*, A.12b-13a.

Matteo Ricci and the Chinese Rites question

Matteo Ricci's faith in sweet reasonableness is touching, and in the light of the later history of the mission rather ironic. There was to be a great deal of hating and arguing against, rather than convincing by reasoning in the matter of 'Chinese Rites'. It is to this question that we must turn to conclude our conspectus of Ricci's interpretation of Confucianism. The Chinese Rites controversy as it developed after Ricci's death was really over two separate issues which are often confused. From the beginning I wish to distinguish them, because, although they take root in the same basic attitudes, and in practice those who take a stand on one tend to take a similar stand on the other, they are logically distinct. In several crucial instances we shall find the expected pattern does not hold.

The first issue is more properly called the 'Terms' rather than the 'Chinese Rites' controversy. It is not primarily concerned with the permission or prohibition of private and public rituals, but with the use of Chinese terms to denote the Christian God. Ricci's position on this is unequivocal. He early adopted the use of *t'ien-chu*, 'Lord of Heaven', as the usual name for God, but in his Chinese and Western writings he does not hesitate to equate the ancient Chinese terms, *t'ien* or 'Heaven', and *shang-ti* or 'Lord on High', with the Christian 'God'. In the second chapter of the *T'ien-chu shih-i* he examines several passages from the classics and concludes that '*Shang-ti* and *t'ien-chu* differ in name only'.[235] As for *t'ien*, sometimes it is used to mean the physical heavens, the sky, and in this sense, of course, cannot be equated with the 'Lord of Heaven', *t'ien-chu.*[236] But frequently it is used synonymously with shang-ti[237] and in this sense is quite acceptable. As Ricci explained in the *Storia*, *t'ien-chu* was adopted very early and more or less by chance, but he came to see its advantages. It was both similar to and distinct from the terminology of the Chinese classics, and avoided the ambiguities of *t'ien* used alone.

> It fitted well with our intentions since the Chinese adore 'Heaven' as their supreme God [*suppremo nume*] and some

235. *Tien-chu shih-i*, A.20b.
236. *Tien-chu shih-i*, A.11a, 21a.
237. *Tien-chu shih-i*, A.21a: 'If *t'ien* is used to explain *shang-ti* it is acceptable'. This usage corresponds to the second of the five meanings of *t'ien* distinguished by Fung Yu-lan, *A History of Chinese Philosophy* (Princeton, 1952), 1, 30–31.

> even think that this Heaven is the material sky. By this name we have given to God, we clearly declare how much greater our God is than that which they hold as their supreme God, because He is the Lord of their Heaven.[238]

By its use in the *T'ien-chu shih-lu* and the *T'ien-chu shih*-i, the term *t'ien-chu* became the identification mark of Christianity, or more correctly, of Catholic Christianity, since the nineteenth century Protestant missionaries adopted a different terminology.[239] Once adopted as the name for God and employed in liturgical and apologetic works, the question of its origins and suitability became largely academic. The debate after Ricci was over the use in Christian works of *t'ien*, *shang-ti* and other Chinese terms.

Pasquale M D'Elia has tabulated Ricci's use of these terms in his Chinese works[240] and he finds a predominance of *t'ien-chu*, with *shang-ti* and *t'ien* or combinations used occasionally as synonyms. It is typical of Ricci's method that in his 'Eight Songs for the Western Lute' (*Hsi-ch'in chü-i pa-chang*) composed for the court, he uses only *shang-ti*, the term consecrated by ancient ritual use;[241] while in liturgical texts and works exclusively for Christians, such as the *T'ien-chu-chiao yao*, he employs *t'ien-chu* throughout. For him, the terms question was essentially a practical one. *T'ien-chu* was an appropriate name for the Christian God who, once named, could be described in orthodox theological fashion. Where Chinese works ascribe to *t'ien*, *shang-ti*, or even *t'ai-chi*, attributes of the Christian God, one need not hesitate to employ these terms. Later missionaries were hesitant to use them and we find an attempt to revise Ricci's works, eliminating

---

238. *Fonti Ricciane*, N246, I, 193 *cf T'ien-chu shih-i*, A. 3a, where Ricci argues that by simply looking at the heavens *(t'ien)* one can see the need for a Lord of Heaven *(t'ien-chu)* to govern them. This, he says, is he who is called in the West *tou-ssu (Deus)*.
239. Some characteristic contributions to the nineteenth century debate on the 'Terms Controversy' are WH Medhurst, *A Dissertation on the Theology of the Chinese* (Shanghai, 1847); WJ Boone, *Some Thoughts on the Proper Term to be employed to translate Elohim and Theos into Chinese*, Shanghai, 1850; J Legge, *Notions of the Chinese concerning God and Spirits* (Hongkong, 1852).
240. 'Prima Introduzione della Filosofia Scolastica in Cina', in *Li-shih yü-yen yen-chiu-so chi-k'an* (Bulletin of the Institute of History and Philology, Academia Sinica), XXVIII (1956): 166–67.
241. *T'ien-hsueh ch'u-han*, I, 283–90.

the suspect terms.[242] Ricci could not afford to be a purist. He was concerned with convincing the Chinese that early Chinese beliefs and Christianity were in fact reconcilable, and that *t'ien-chu* was not just another foreign deity competing with the native ones. His approach was a practical one, well expressed in the opening exchange of the *T'ien-chu shih*-i, where he asserts that 'the Way of the Lord of Heaven is not the Way of any one person, any one school, any one country'.[243]

The heart of the Chinese Rites Controversy lay not in the debate about the appropriateness or inappropriateness of using certain terms for 'God'. This was always a secondary issue, although it serves as a convenient touchstone for judging the openness of any individual missionary to accommodation to Chinese culture. Once a Chinese became a Christian in practice he acknowledged, believed in, prayed to *t'ien-chu*; and *t'ien-chu* acquired for him specifically Christian connotations. He was not required to abandon his cultural heritage; to redefine it, perhaps, but not to reject it. And in public he could continue to behave as before. His monogamy might be regarded as eccentric, and his moral code excessively strict, but in essentials he remained a *ju*, a Confucian scholar.

The matter of Confucian rites was more delicate. This was public, and affected his social standing and career prospects. The rites in question were the following: the public rites directed to Confucius himself together with certain rituals incumbent on a scholar in his official capacity; ancestor rites held within and on behalf of the family or lineage; and funeral rites. There were, of course, many other customary domestic rituals associated with festivals and family events but if judged superstitious these could be dropped without too much public notice. It was the rites that defined and confirmed social status, those held to embody the Confucian code of right behaviour, or *li*, that were important. If Christianity meant abandoning these rituals, it in effect demanded a de-classing, a drastic break with family, career prospects and, in a fundamental sense, culture.

Matteo Ricci approached the rites question, as he approached other aspects of Chinese culture, cautiously. I have found nothing substantial on the subject in his Chinese writings although his silence

242. v Fang Hao, 'T'ien-chu shih-i chih kai-ts'uan', in *Fang Hao liu-shih tzu-ting kao*, II, 1593–1603.

243. *T'ien-chu shih-i*, A. lb.

together with his general approbation of Confucianism may be read as approval of the status quo. There are, however, several passages in his *Storia* which give us clues as to his interpretation of Confucian rites, domestic and public. And the general assumption by later writers, supporters and opponents of the rites, that Ricci allowed Chinese Christians to practise Confucian rites, may be taken as evidence in itself.

Ricci's starting point is a functional interpretation of the role of the Confucian literati in Chinese society. He sees Confucianism in practice as primarily a system of ethics, a social philosophy.

> The aim of this law of the literati is the peace and quiet of the kingdom and the good government of households and their individual members. In these matters they give very good advice, completely in conformity with the light of nature and Catholic truth.[244]

Confucianism is not really a 'sect' in the strict sense (*una legge formata*) but a learned society, an 'academy' which exists for the good of society, and, as such, Christians may freely belong to it.[245] It is on this foundation that Ricci builds his interpretation of Confucian rites as social customs designed to promote good order in society and the state by recalling the teaching and example of the great men of the past. Note, however, that he does not say that they are purely secular or 'political'[246] in nature as many later Jesuits interpreted them. To deny that Confucianism is *una legge formata* is not, I think, to deny that it has any 'religious' aspects. Such a position would make nonsense of Ricci's stress elsewhere in the *Storia* on the pure theism of

244. *Fonti Ricciane,* N180, I, 120.

245. *Fonti Ricciane,* N181, I, 120. The corresponding passage in Trigault contains some significant alterations. Where Ricci states the view that Confucianism is not a sect as his conclusion, Trigault makes it their own claim, which is strictly untrue, since the Confucians did not disclaim the title of *chiao.* Ricci again says there is nothing essential *(nel suo essentiale . . . niente)* contrary to Catholic faith in their teaching, while Trigault qualifies this somewhat and changes the emphasis from the obligation of Catholics to support this 'academy' to the need for it to be 'developed and perfected' by Christianity, v Gallagher, *China in the Sixteenth Century,* 97–98, and Riquebourg-Trigault, *Histoire,* 89.

246. The term 'political', somewhat wider in its Latin than its modern English sense, was first used by Trigault in his account of Ricci's funeral, v *Fonti Ricciane,* N998, II, 628.

early Confucianism. It was rather a system of 'natural religion' which was not overtly religious in the way that Buddhism and Taoism were. Unlike them it had no temples, no priests, no commandments, no religious leaders.[247] And its rituals were not acts of worship of specific gods of the sect but celebrations of the natural and moral order of the universe.

To consider first the rites to Confucius. In every city, says Ricci, there is a 'temple' of Confucius, attached to the Confucian 'school'. In it there is a statue of Confucius or a tablet containing his name, and on either side the statues or names of his principal disciples who are held to be 'saints'.[248] Here, every new moon and full moon the officials (*magistrati*) and scholars (*graduati*) of the city come to pay reverence to him by genuflexions and by burning candles and incense. On his birthday and at certain times of the year they offer dead animals and food. The purpose of these exercises is 'to praise him for the good teaching he left in his books, by means of which they have obtained their posts and degrees, without however reciting any prayer nor asking any favour'.[249]

Ricci seems to have had no objections to these ceremonies which involved, as he saw it, no false worship. Confucius, by this account, is clearly not a god.[250] In another passage, however, Ricci gives a more compromising account of the solemn sacrifice to Confucius in the 'Hall or Temple of Heaven' in Nanking. He witnesses a dress rehearsal for this ceremony and describes the temple itself, the dress of the Taoist priests who provided the music, and the musical instruments employed.[251] This appears an exception to Ricci's general conclusion that the rituals in honour of Confucius are not religious rites. He calls the ceremony

247. *Fonti Ricciane,* N176, 1, 116. Note that almost immediately afterwards, Ricci ascribes a 'temple' to Confucius.
248. *Saint,* clearly a rendering of the Chinese *sheng-jen,* perhaps better translated as 'sage' since the stress is on the wisdom and teaching rather than the asceticism of the alleged *sheng-jen.*
249. *Fonti Ricciane,* N178, I, 118–119.
250. D'Elia has demonstrated (*Fonti Ricciane,* I, 119 n 2; and 'Ermeneutica Ricciana', *Gregorianum,* XXIV [1953]: 671–72) how this very passage 'orribilmente transformato' by a later French translator of Athanasius Kircher's reproduction of Trigault's Latin, has served as ammunition for anti-Jesuit commentators. In this version Confucius and his disciples become 'gods' making nonsense of the rest of the passage. Trigault himself is partly to blame in describing the disciples as 'gods, but of an inferior order', a gloss quite unwarranted on the basis of the original text.
251. *Fonti Ricciane,* NN553-4, II, 70–71.

tout court a 'sacrifice'. Certainly Trigault was somewhat scandalised by this account and adds a number of glosses to the passage stressing that Ricci attended the ceremony because it was a mere rehearsal not the actual ceremony, and that 'the Chinese honour the great philosopher as a master, and not as a deity, and they are accustomed to use the word "sacrifice" in a broad and indefinite sense'.[252] But Trigault has also misread the original. Ricci specifically points out that the priests present were Taoist priests (*tausu*) and that they were there because they were members of the royal orchestra. In Trigault they have become 'priests of the literary class',[253] a contradiction in terms, and are described as priests of the Temple itself.[254] Finally, where Ricci is content merely to describe the temple in detail, listing the altars outside dedicated to the sun, moon, stars and mountains, Trigault adds: 'They say that the God who is worshipped in the temple is the creator of all that is outside of the temple and that these things are not to be worshipped as deities.'[255] No doubt Trigault when editing Ricci's manuscript was aware of what appeared to be dangerous inconsistencies between Ricci's generalisations about the rites to Confucius and this description of the Nanking temple and the ceremonies performed there. However, I question whether he was true to Ricci's mind on the matter. Ricci seems to me to be justly non-committal. He leaves open the question of the status of the Temple-calling it in one place simply 'Temple' and in another 'Hall or Temple' (later Jesuits were careful to translate the terms applied to Confucian 'temples' as 'hall', giving it a strictly secular connotation). He makes no bones about it being a sacrifice, but neither does he make any comments on its nature. Later missionaries who examined these ceremonies in detail decided that the solemn sacrifices to Confucius were superstitious in nature and should be forbidden. All we can say about Ricci's attitude to them is that he enjoyed the visit if not the music.[256]

---

252. Gallagher, *China in the Sixteenth Century*, 335, *cf* Riquebourg-Trigault, *Histoire*, 314.
253. Gallagher, *China in the Sixteenth Century*, 336; Riquebourg-Trigault, *Histoire*, 314.
254. Riquebourg-Trigault, 315, has 'Templiers', and Gallagher, 336, has 'priests'.
255. Gallagher, 337 *cf* Riquebourg-Trigault, 315.
256. *Fonti Ricciane*, N553, II, 71—'all sounded at once with the greatest noise possible, and, to tell the truth, they appeared to be completely out of tune'.

There is another piece of evidence in relation to Ricci's views on Confucian rites which should be mentioned. In Ch'ü T'ai-su's preface to the 1599 edition of Ricci's *Treatise on Friendship*, written at about the time of Ricci's visit to the Temple of Heaven,[257] Chü describes 'Mr Li' (Ricci) as attracted to China by its glorious culture. He has become a true Confucian scholar:

> He recites the texts of the Sages, and observes the laws of the kingdom. He wears a scholar's cap and belt, and he offers the spring and autumn sacrifices. He is chaste in his behaviour and walks in the paths of virtue. He respects and serves the commands of Heaven and promotes orthodoxy. Neither (Yeh-lü) Ch'u-ts'ai nor (Lien) Hsi-hsien could match the conversation of Mr. Li.[258]

I doubt very much that this passage may be invoked to prove that Ricci actually offered the spring and autumn sacrifices to Confucius. The language is too stereotyped and the context clearly an assertion that Ricci despite his foreign origin is an orthodox Confucian in his behaviour. It does, however, indicate that Ricci was not known to be opposed to these ceremonies.

Other sacrifices are mentioned in the *Storia*—the annual sacrifices offered by the Emperor to Heaven and Earth,[259] the sacrifices offered by high officials to the spirits of the mountains and rivers,[260] and those offered by magistrates to the local 'protector spirits'.[261] Ricci makes no comment on the first two but in the last case he remarks that they do attribute power to reward and punish to these spirits, perhaps implying by this that the rite is superstitious. He is careful, however, to avoid labelling these spirits as 'gods' which is what Trigault in his version does.[262] This question of sacrifices to the 'city god' (*ch'êng-huang*) was to loom large in the later development of the rites controversy. Being a part of the ceremonies associated with the

257. v *Fonti Ricciane*, II, 70, n 5.
258. *Tien-hsüeh ch'u-han*, 1, 295–96, translated in PM D'Elia, 'Il Trattato sull 'Amicizia . . .', *Studia Missionalia*, VII (1952): 457–78. Yeh-lü Ch'u-ts'ai and Lien Hsi-hsien were famous examples of Sinicised 'barbarians'.
259. *Fonti Ricciane*, N176, 1, 117.
260. *Fonti Ricciane*, N176, I, 117.
261. *Fonti Ricciane*, N179, I, 119-20.
262. Gallagher, *China in the Sixteenth Century*, 97; Riquebourg-Trigault, *Histoire*, 88.

assumption of office, it affected the eligibility of Christian scholars for office. Some Jesuits, taking a clue from Ricci's 'protector spirits' argued that the ch'êng-huang were the 'guardian angels' of Christian tradition, and so could legitimately be honoured. Others substituted a Christian rite, or insisted on a modification of the ceremony. There is no real evidence, however, as to Ricci's opinion on the matter, and I know of no instance during his lifetime when he might have been asked to give a decision about the practices.

From his commentary in the *Tien-chu shih*-i on selected passages from the classics dealing with sacrifices, it would seem to have been Ricci's general view that the multitude of sacrifices described were ultimately directed to God, to *shang-ti*.[263] For example, in commenting on the *Doctrine of the Mean*, XIX.6, 'the ceremonies of the altar of the god of the soil are directed to the service of *shang-ti*', he rejects on good grounds[264] Chu Hsi's gloss attributing it to Hou-t'u, the God of the Earth. One sacrifice can be offered to one god only.[265] The principle of 'interpreting in our favour things left ambiguous' in the classics apparently extended to sacrificial rites.

Ricci is much more explicit in his treatment of ancestor rites. In a passage in the *Storia*[266] he describes the offering of food, incense and silk or paper, to the dead ancestors, and goes on:

> The reason they give for this observance on behalf of their ancestors is this, 'to serve the dead as if they were living'.[267] Nor do they think that the dead come to eat these things, or have need of them; but they say they do it because they know of no other way of showing the love and gratitude they have for them. Some say that this ceremony was instituted more for the living than the dead, that is to teach the children and ignorant to know and serve their parents while alive, seeing that important people, once they are dead, perform for them the services they were accustomed to perform when they were alive. And since they neither recognize any divinity in

263. See *Tien-chu shih-i,* A.20a-b.
264. See Legge, *Chinese Classics,* I, 404.
265. *Tien-chu shih-i,* A.20a.
266. *Fonti Ricciane,* N177, 1, 117–18.
267. A reference to *The Doctrine of the Mean,* XIX, 5. Ricci also quotes this passage in the *Tien-chu shih-i,* A.33a, in another context—to demonstrate an ancient Chinese belief in the immortality of the soul.

> these dead, nor ask anything of them, nor hope for anything from them, the practice is completely free from any idolatry, and perhaps could even be said to involve no superstition. Nevertheless, it would be better to replace this custom with giving alms to the poor for the souls of these dead, when they become Christians.

This passage has been subjected to a great deal of critical examination[268] although I fail to see how it could be clearer. Ricci concludes that they do not believe that the dead are actually present,[269], nor that they are divine. The practice is certainly not idolatrous (*sta tutto questo fuori di ogni idolatria*) and perhaps (*forse*) not superstitious. His caution in the last instance is, I imagine, due to a reluctance to generalise about the actual beliefs of all Chinese. Ricci saw that the orthodox Confucian view of such ceremonies, as presented in the *Four Books*, was not necessarily what people actually thought. Because of the danger of superstition, it was better to aim at eventually eradicating or rather replacing such customs. He was no casuist, but a missionary with a practical pastoral concern.

The last area about which controversy raged in later times was Chinese funerary rites. Ricci describes these in Book 1, Chapter 7 of the *Storia*, 'On the Courtesy and Other Rites of China'.[270] Again it is a simple description with no attempt to minimise the religious aspects of the ceremonies, the customary participation of 'many priests of the idols', the offerings of food and clothing. He points out that the offerings are made 'as if' (*come*) the dead needed food and clothing, but makes no further comment. His position on these matters was presumably identical with that on ancestor rites. They must be purged of any overt superstition and may otherwise be tolerated, but gradually specifically Christian rituals should be introduced.

In a work dating from 1680, Giovanni Gabiani's *De Ritibus Ecclesiae Sinicae permissis Apologetica Dissertatio*, we find listed

268. See, for example, Bernard (-Maître), *Ricci,* Part Ill, chapter 6, and D'Elia, 'Ermeneutica Ricciana', 669–79.

269. He argues in the *Tien-chu shih-i,* A.40b–41b, after demonstrating at length the immortality of the soul, that the souls of the dead do not remain in their original home after death, because it is not the will of heaven.

270. *Fonti Ricciane,* NN132-3, I, 83–85.

some documents then extant containing Ricci's instructions on the rites and other matters which were approved by Valignano in 1603. I have been unable to find any trace of these documents but I doubt if they would add anything to the picture that emerges from the *Storia*. Gabiani notes that 'the cult of Confucius and of the dead' was approved by Valignano 'after deep inquiry and careful examination of each and every relevant particular, not only through the faithful account of Father Matteo (Ricci) and other of his companions, but by special confirmation of Father Emanuel Diaz Senior, delegated by the same Father Visitor to investigate the matter'.[271] In other words, this first generation of missionaries was well aware of the issues raised by the Chinese rites, had discussed them at length and arrived at a policy of general approval. There was bound to be controversy over the details as the mission expanded and knowledge of the enormous variety of Chinese customs and rituals grew. The ambiguities latent in the view that Confucians were both proponents of an ethical theism, and utilitarian and secular in their ceremonial, were sure to create difficulties in minds less open and more theologically rigid than Ricci's. Yet, to the modern student of Chinese religion, Ricci's simple description of Chinese practices and hesitant judgements usually get closer to the Chinese reality than the endless theologising and hair-splitting of many of his successors. He was fortunate to be able to interpret Chinese rites before they became 'Chinese Rites', a subject of controversy rather than the practices of actual living people.

Ricci and Confucianism: syncretism, accommodation, encounter?

I have attempted to describe Matteo Ricci's involvement with Confucianism in all its complexity, with all its nuances, and, so far as possible, in his own words. It might appear superfluous to add a postscript on the labels one should apply to those thirty years of active life. Yet labels are instructive, as much by their inappropriateness, the contents that do not match, as by their appropriateness. And in this case a number of contradictory labels have been applied. Confucius and Confucians have always insisted on the Importance of labels, of 'names'. It is in the spirit of the Confucian rectification of names' that I approach this question.

271. See *Fonti Ricciane,* II, 273–4, n l.

Perhaps the least happy 'name' applied to Ricci's life's work is 'syncretism'. It is used, for example, by Joseph Levenson in his work on Liang Ch'i-ch'ao. I do not wish to set Levenson up as a chopping-block. I am too indebted to him in so many ways, and I have rarely felt impelled flatly to reject his ideas. It may be that 'syncretism', for Levenson, did not imply that reductionism. or the blunting of claims to truth that I associate with the term.[272] But his strictures on the Jesuits' methods, and the language he employs, suggest that he saw their attempt as, in some sense, dishonest or at least intrinsically contradictory. The Jesuits, he writes, attempted 'to syncretize Confucianism with a European tradition', 'to make a Western idea seem properly Chinese'.[273] And a similar view underlies the more extended treatment given to the Jesuits in Levenson's *Confucian China and Its Modern Fate*. I think that Levenson has been unduly influenced by Liang's treatment of the Jesuits in his *Chung-kuo chin san-pai nien hsüeh-shu shih*.[274] Liang saw the Jesuits as deliberately fostering the attitude of 'public Christians, private Confucians'.[275] He writes that:

> The earliest missionaries of the Society [of Jesus] used extremely clever methods in propagating their teachings; they penetrated deeply into the mentality of the Chinese. They realized that the Chinese are not fond of excessively

272. Franz Schurmann, in his moving tribute to Levenson 'In memory of a Friend', prefacing Levenson's and his *China: An Interpretative History* (Berkeley, 1969), writes of Levenson's life-work as the progressive unfolding of 'he spirit of syncretism'. He sees this as a harmony within opposites, not a blunting of conflict and honesty, but a tolerance of difference. In this sense, I have no quarrel with the use of the term 'syncretism' as applied to the Jesuits. I cannot, however, reconcile this usage with Levenson's own use of the term in his *Liang Ch'i-ch'ao* and *Confucian China and Its Modern Fate,* nor does it represent common usage which stresses the attempted reconciliation of objectively contradictory elements. In the debate on this topic between Robert Baird and Judith Berling, I am with Baird (v RD Baird, *Category Formation and the History of Religions* [The Hague, 1971], 142–52 *cf* JA Berling, *The Syncretic Religion of Lin Chao-en* [New York: Columbia University Press, 1980], chapter l.)
273. *Liang Ch'i-ch'ao and the Mind of Modern China* (Berkeley: University of California Press, 1967), 84.
274. See Liang's Collected Works, *Yin-ping-shih ho-chi, chuan-chi* XVII (Shanghai, 1936), especially chapters 1–4.
275. *Chung-kuo chin san-pai nien hsüeh-shu shih (Yin-ping-shih ho-chi* editor), 18.

> superstitious religions, and so they confined themselves to introducing the Chinese to scientific knowledge where they were very conscious of their deficiencies, and to outward appearances they seemed to have turned from being missionaries to sundry other pursuits. Those who believed in their religion were permitted as before to worship 'the Chinese Heaven' and their ancestors. These methods were pursued for some decades and would have been outstandingly successful if the Pope in Rome, not understanding the circumstances, had not suddenly issued what is called 'the 1704 decree' and enforced its provisions.[276]

We have already seen enough of Ricci's methods to realise the falsity of the claim that for Ricci his religious mission took second place, and that nothing further was demanded of converts than a continuance of their Confucian beliefs. As for the use of Western science, certainly it was employed as a bait, but there is no evidence that conversion was a precondition for learning it. As Ch'en Shou-i demonstrates in his critical analysis of Liang's charge,[277] Ricci and his successors at no time concealed their missionary aims, and there is no strict correlation between their teaching of science and their teaching of Christianity; some became Christians who were not interested in science, and many learnt Western science without become Christians. Li Chih-tsao studied science with Ricci for a considerable time before becoming interested in Christianity, while Hsü Kuang-chi's interest in science followed his conversion.

Western science was important to the Jesuits in gaining an audience and winning respect, but it was not central or indispensable. Certainly it could not be regarded as an element in a new syncretism. Western science plus Confucian ethics, or even a reinterpreted Confucian theism, do not add up to the *T'ien-chu-chiao*. All contemporary accounts agree that Ricci's most influential works were his treatise on friendship, his *T'ien-chu shih-i* and *Chi-jen shih-p'ien*. None of these so much as mentions science. The stress is rather on humanism, Confucian and European, and philosophical reasoning. Levenson rightly describes Ricci as 'vaunting the western arts and sciences, (to shake) the Chinese bias against anything foreign and

276. *Chung-kuo chin san-pai nien hsüeh-shu shih (Yin-ping-shih ho-chi* editor), 18.
277. 'Ming-mo Yeh-su-hui-shih . . .', 70–72.

(make) it possible for Christianity not to be pre-judged'.[278] However, he seriously misquotes the *Storia* in this context, implying that Ricci was discounting Chinese ideas generally by his scientific revelations. In fact the original passage quite clearly deals specifically with Buddhist cosmological speculations, and recounts the advice of a friendly scholar that they should use mathematics to explore 'the falsity of the books of the idols'.[279] Ricci continues:

> And in truth it thus happened that many, having learnt our mathematical sciences, laughed at the law and doctrine of the idols, saying that if they taught so much error in natural matters and those of this life, there is no reason to give them credit in supernatural matters and those of the other life.[280]

This is not, I think, to argue that the science is somehow part and parcel of the new religion. Joseph Needham in *Science and Civilization in China*[281] sees the 'implicit logic' of the Jesuits' presentation of Western science as the claim that only Christendom could have produced it. 'Every correct eclipse prediction was thus an indirect demonstration of the truth of Christian theology.' Needham credits the Chinese with too much intelligence to be taken in by this line of argument, but he might also have credited the Jesuits with sufficient intelligence not to have attempted to argue this way. The only evidence that can be adduced for Needham's point of view is the indiscriminate use by some Jesuits after Ricci of *t'ien hsüeh*, as a general term applied to both the study of the Christian religion and astronomy. In practice, however, they were distinguished; and in the *T'ien-hsüeh ch'u han* of 1629 a strict division is made between the sections dealing with doctrine (*li-pien*) and those dealing with science (*ch'i-pien*).

The most convincing rebuttal of this whole interpretation is to be found in the profession of faith made by Ch'ü Ju-k'uei in 1605. Ch'ü is a striking case of a man who was attracted to the Jesuits by their science and later accepted their religion. In his profession he emphasises that he is turning away from Buddhism because it is 'a sect contrary to reason and false', and that reason has led him to a

278. *Confucian China and Its Modern Fate,* I, 121.
279. *Fonti Ricciane,* N540, II, 54–55.
280. *Fonti Ricciane,* N540, II, 55.
281. Volume Ill, 449.

belief in the God who governs heaven, earth and men. It is, he says in the text translated in the *Storia*, 'the things of God' which he has learnt from Ricci, Cattaneo and the other Jesuits.

> I, having this day received the water of holy baptism that washes and cleanses me of all my past uncleanness, promise that the sect of the idols and words contrary to reason will be extirpated from my heart . . . I will obey the heavenly Father, and will be converted, following in all things the right path and controlling my senses so that I may perfect in myself the natural light of reason (*il lume naturale*) which was infused in me by God, who exists by himself and extends his goodness to others.
>
> As for the articles of the Christian faith, although I cannot penetrate the depths of every mystery, with all my heart I submit and believe what is contained in it, and I pray to the Holy Spirit to enlighten me. Now I am beginning anew to believe and my heart is like a weak and tender reed. I beg the Holy Mother of the Lord of Heaven to deign to inspire and strengthen me and to pray to Him that my will may be firm, my mind strengthened and my spirit pure and clear; so that, with heart thus illuminated, I may adhere to truth and reason, and with mouth thus opened to the holy word, I may spread it through all China, so that all may come to know the holy law of God and be subjected to it.[282]

Unless this whole passage is a pious forgery, which is most unlikely given the circumstances and the language, it seems to me sufficient refutation of any charge of syncretism. Ch'ü is no syncretist creating a new hybrid scientistic religion, nor is he a 'public Christian private Confucian'. The only connection between science and his religious faith lies in his conviction that they have a common base in *il lume naturale*, the light of reason.

This is not to dispose completely of the question of syncretism. It was always a problem to the Jesuits. Trigault writing about the Shao-chou missions complains that it was much easier to get the Chinese to accept the Lord of Heaven than to get them to reject their other gods.[283]

282. *Fonti Ricciane, N756*, 11, 344–45.

283. *Fonti Ricciane,* N658, II, 217–78 (passage added in Portuguese by Trigault, possibly based on Longobardo's account).

The cultural instinct to absorb and assimilate was so strong as to be at times overwhelming. Even Ricci himself was transmogrified into *Li Ma-tou p'u-sa*, the Bodhisattva Li Ma-tou, patron of clockmakers.[284] There are no ready yardsticks for judging the real beliefs of men, and dogmatic formulae do not always (perhaps never) measure the dimensions of the human spirit. What we can be sure of, however, is that syncretism was not the intention of Ricci and his successors. To call him, as Levenson does, 'pioneer spokesman for a Christian-Confucian syncretism'[285] is to accuse him of deliberately fostering ambiguity and confusion. His strictures on syncretism in the *T'ien-chu shih-i*[286] are so strong as to leave no doubt as to his intentions. When the Chinese scholar suggests that there might be something to be gained from worshipping the Buddhas, Ricci launches into a diatribe on behalf of orthodoxy.

> In the case of heterodox doctrines, the more you reverence and respect them, the more serious is the crime. There is only one head in each family, and to have two is a crime. There is only one ruler to each state, and to have two is a crime. Heaven and earth are governed by one lord. How could it not be the greatest crime in the world to have two of them?[287]

To show that he was not intentionally syncretistic does not, of course, exclude the possibility that the end product was a syncretism, an unsuccessful harmonising of de facto opposites. Ultimately this depends on the validity of Ricci's interpretation of Confucianism, a question I do not intend to pursue in this study. Even if this were to prove the case, however, I would hesitate to use the term. If the interpretation of a particular tradition leaves no doubt that it is the partial, fragmentary truth to be subsumed within the wider truth; and if that wider truth is explicitly related to a revelation superseding all others; then 'syncretism' seems inappropriate. Was St Paul a syncretist when he appealed in the Epistle to the Romans[288] to the

---

284. v. O. Titner, 'II P. Matteo Ricci, Genio Tutelare degli Orologiai di Cina (II Buddha-Ricci)', in *Atti e Memorie del Convegno di Geografi-Orientalisti,* (Macerata, 1911), 166.
285. *Confucian China and its Modern Fate,* I, 120.
286. B.51b–56b.
287. *T'ien-chu shih-i,* B.51b.
288. Romans, 1:18–23.

revelation of God in the natural world? Or when he used their beliefs, and the literature of their poets to persuade the Athenians to worship his God?[289] Even with reference to the Buddhist tradition, where deliberate syncretism has certainly occurred, I think the term has been overused. As Alicia Matsunaga demonstrates in *The Buddhist Philosophy of Assimilation*,[290] as well as the usual combining or juxtaposition of new and old, Buddhism developed a philosophical justification for the assimilation of the older gods of India, China and Japan. In terms of this theory, the process could be reduced to a systematic unity in which Buddhism predominated. The Buddha was all in all. It is where the disparate elements are left unresolved, or opposites held to be equally true, that syncretism reigns. In this sense the Jesuits were not syncretists.

The term most commonly applied to Ricci's approach is 'accommodation'. Johannes Bettray SVD has analysed Ricci's whole career in terms of his 'accommodation method',[291] external and intellectual. This is a convenient approach and it seems to correspond to a large extent to his own view of what he was doing. It preserves Ricci's sense of the centrality of Christianity—the missionaries accommodate or adapt themselves to all aspects of Chinese culture in order, as it were, to clothe the naked truth of the Christian message in Chinese dress. But it is more enlightening as a metaphor when applied to externals than to 'inner' processes. Language is culturally determined. Specific traditions are irrevocably conditioned by history. When an attempt is made to express one religion in the language and through the historical traditions of another, is there any true meeting of minds?

It is here that Levenson's critique becomes disturbingly relevant. During the several years I have been reflecting upon the Jesuit experience in China I have again and again found myself reverting to Levenson's gnomic phrases:

289. Acts 17:22–34.

290. Subtitled, 'The Historical Development of the *Honji-Suijaku* Theory' (Tokyo [Monumenta Nipponica Monographs] 1969).

291. *Die Akkommodationsmethode des P. Matteo Ricci S.I. in China* (Rome [Analecta Gregoriana, LXXVI] 1955).

> Revelation, the emphasis on what was *sui generis* to the religion, was deliberately shadowed in mysticism, in the insistence that truth is free of temporal, historical context.
>
> And so the Christians insist that western history, though in some sense, clearly, a Christian history, is just an embodiment (not the embodiment) of a supra-historical value.
>
> Christian cultural relativism is a poor servant, in the last analysis, to the Christian religious absolute.[292]

I would like to claim that these pieces of grit working away in my mind have been coated with pearls of wisdom. Alas, I am still uncertain what to make of them as general propositions. They presuppose a whole philosophy of religion-and, for that matter, a general philosophical position—the examination of which is quite beyond the scope of this study. I could point out that Levenson's notion of 'the Christian religious absolute' is one that few contemporary theologians would accept. I could add that there have been and still are non-Western Christian churches, and that in its origins Christianity is non-Western, or at least, non-European. In so far as his remarks are meant to describe the Jesuit approach to China I might object to 'deliberately shadowed in mysticism' since, as we have seen, it is rather an interpretation of Chinese intellectual history than an appeal to the unknowable that lies at the heart of Ricci's work. I could also refer, as Henri Bernard-Maître does,[293], to the scholastic distinction between philosophy and theology, Ricci's *lume naturale* and revelation. On this reading, which receives much backing from Ricci's writings cited above, a refined Confucian philosophy was to serve as the starting point for a Chinese theology, in much the same way as Thomas Aquinas employed Greek philosophy in his theological *Summa*.

In the last analysis, however, I think Levenson has hit upon an important weakness in the Jesuits' position. I doubt whether it was a fatal flaw in the logic of their position. Rather I see it, as Levenson also does to a large extent, as a flaw in the psychology of the method. The more they accommodated, the greater the Confucian wrapping they placed on the Christian core, the less distinct became their message and the greater the possibility of misunderstanding. Many Confucians would not have been as impressed as the Chinese Scholar

292. *Confucian China and its Modern Fate*, I, 119, 120.
293. *Sagesse Chinoise et Philosophie Chrétienne*, Part II, Leçon II.

of the *T'ien-chu shih-i* with the necessity for going further, and would find their sense of cultural superiority merely confirmed from this unexpected source.

The 'accommodation' model is radically deficient in another way. Ultimately it rests on just one of those sets of false dichotomies that Levenson mercilessly exposes in his celebrated treatment of the use of *t'i* and *yung* by the late nineteenth century Chinese reformers.[294] When Christianity, or any other religion for that matter, is considered as an actual living religion and not as an abstract system, it becomes impossible to separate substance and function, inner reality and external appearance, revealed core and cultural expression. A revelation without words and concepts can be found only in the awful reality of a living God himself. To name Him is not only to claim control over Him as primitive men thought, but also to limit and denature Him. Yet we do name Him as men have always named Him. As Langdon Gilkey has demonstrated in Naming the Whirlwind,[295] the very universality of the attempt to name God points to a common basis in human experience. The plurality of language and the variety of cultural expressions of human experience does not necessarily invalidate a belief in the universality of that experience. Language, however, enters so immediately into the rendering intelligible of our experience, even to ourselves, that the notion of pure religious experience is chimerical. Part of our religious experience itself is the language through which it is mediated. One religion cannot accommodate itself to the language of another without betraying something of itself. At best, it can offer an invitation to share its insights and encounter the same reality.

Where I part company with Levenson is over the excesses of his cultural relativism. If taken literally, his rejection of 'supra-historical values' would deny the very possibility of communication and understanding between cultures not only in religion but in all respects. His own work in elucidating Chinese culture in general, and Confucianism in particular, to a Western audience, is a refutation of this scepticism. Cross-cultural understanding itself has a history which transcends cultural particularities, and the Jesuit mission in China is a prime example of such understanding.

294. *Confucian China and its Modern Fate,* I, chapter IV.

295. *Naming the Whirlwind: The Renewal of God-Language* (Indianapolis: The Bobbs-Merrill Company, 1969).

How, then, to characterise Ricci's engagement with Confucianism? Not 'syncretism' which implies a conscious combining of diverse elements into a new synthesis in which all the disparate parts have equal status. Not 'accommodation' which assumes a relationship between the core and cultural wrapping which grossly oversimplifies the reality of religious experience. If we must use a general term to describe his method I would suggest 'encounter'. Jacques Kamstra, in a study on the introduction of Buddhism to Japan,[296] poses the alternatives in cultural intercourse as 'encounter or syncretism'. Where there is no real existential encounter, where neither side attempts sympathetically to engage with the personal and systematic beliefs of the other, syncretism is the only possible alternative to outright rejection. In encounter, on the other hand, of necessity something new comes into being, born of the exchange at the personal level between individuals, and at the systematic level between cultures.[297] There is a sharing of experience in so far as cultural barriers permit, and the development of a new language drawing from both cultures to express this common experience.

There can be no questioning, I think, of the personal encounter, in the case of Ricci. His gift for friendship, his involvement with so many Chinese of talent and influence who reciprocated his regard, the reputation he acquired, all attest to the reality of the encounter. He appeared to them as one both familiar and strange, familiar in his knowledge of and facility within the Confucian tradition, strange in his beliefs and inner life. Many who were attracted by the familiar aspects and the new avenues in science opened up by Ricci came in time to appreciate and share his religious views. Christianity was presented to them not in the first place as a system, but as the deeply held values of a man who attracted and fascinated them as a person.

This is not to deny that there was also an encounter on the systematic level. Here there was a tentative process, a feeling of the way. It was a true encounter in so far as it was two-way, with each side attempting to grasp the other in its otherness. Ricci does, of course, attempt to translate Chinese reality into familiar terms, but he is notably wary, particularly in comparison with some of his

296. Jacques Kamstra, *Encounter or Syncretism? The Initial Growth of Japanese Buddhism* (Leiden: Brill, 1967).

297. Kamstra, *Encounter or Syncretism?*, 5–9.

confreres; and even in the *Storia* addressed to a European audience with no experience of China, he always prefers description to explicit comparison. In his Chinese works he shows an ever-deepening grasp of the language and value system of Confucianism, and the approach to Confucianism which began as a tactic became, I believe, something much deeper.

The reality of Ricci's encounter with Confucianism is best tested by looking at the impact of Ricci and his colleagues on Confucian scholars, both those who became Confucian Christians and those who rejected the new religion. Did the Chinese see Ricci's *T'ien-chu shih-i* in the same terms as Ricci himself? Were they attracted, or alternatively repelled, by Christianity itself or by an ersatz Confucianism confected by Ricci? What better witnesses could we call for the genuineness of the Jesuits' encounter with Confucianism than Confucians themselves? So, from the Jesuit interpretation of Confucianism let us turn to the Confucian interpretation of the Jesuits.

The Confucian interpretation of the Jesuits

The question of what we might call the Confucian interpretation of the Jesuits is a complex one which cannot be thoroughly canvassed here.[298] The complexity arises as much from what we now see to be the highly fluid intellectual climate of the late Ming, as from the variety of personal response. However, a few tentative generalisations seem possible.

For what was essentially a marginal intellectual movement in China (certainly in the late Ming), Christianity is mentioned surprisingly frequently in contemporary writings. Partly this was due to the Christians' role as new and unexpected allies of the anti-Buddhist Confucian reactionaries.[299] But less orthodox thinkers, such as Li Chih, expressed great interest in Ricci's ideas.

298. I have already published a preliminary statement, 'The Confucian Interpretation of the Jesuits', in *Papers on Far Eastern History* (Canberra) No 6, September 1972, 1–61.

299. See, for example, the passage on the *T'ien-chu-chiao* in Hsieh Chao-chih's *Wu-tsa-tsu,* chapter 4, *Ti-pu 2* (Shanghai) 1935 edition, 1, 171–72.

> Of all the people I have known there is none who can compare with him . . . However, I do not know why he has come here . . . I think it would be stupid of him to want to use his studies to change the teachings of our [sages, the Duke of] Chou and Confucius, so I suspect this is not the reason.[300]

The note of ambiguity in Li's comment, acknowledgement of Ricci's overt Confucianism, but suspicion as to his intentions is probably a representative view.

Others wrote glowingly of the Jesuit's orthodoxy, but writing in Prefaces to Jesuit writings,[301] may be seen as responding to the personalities and exotic qualities of the early missionaries, rather than through any deeper engagement with the Jesuits' ideas.

The most common hostile reaction was, as might be expected, on Neo-Confucian grounds. What was objectionable in Christianity was not its appeal to the ancient texts; nor the attempt to interpret and apply them; but that the interpretation should move so far beyond the traditional bounds of Confucian discourse. One of the leaders of the late Ming orthodox reaction known as the Tung-lin movement, Feng Ts'ung-wu, expressed his disapproval in his *Discussions in the Capital* (*Tu-men yü-lu*):

> Of course we consider Heaven as Lord. But, on the other hand, we never talk exclusively of Heaven, without accepting and developing the heritage of Yao and Shun, because we want to follow in the footsteps of Confucius. To accept and develop the heritage of Yao and Shun and to want to follow Confucius-that is precisely the way to know Heaven. These people, however, put aside Yao and Shun, Confucius and Mencius, and talk exclusively of the Lord of Heaven . . . Master Chang says: 'Our way is by itself sufficient; what business do we have to search elsewhere?' I also say: 'Our way is by itself perfect; what business do we have to search elsewhere?'[302]

---

300. *Hsü fen-shu*, Peking, 1959 edition, 26.
301. For example those collected in *Hsi-ch'ao ch'ung-cheng chi (T'ien-chu-chiao wen-hsien*, (Taipei, 1965), 633–91.
302. Translated from the *Feng Shao-hsü chi*, chapter 15, lla-b, in H Busch, 'The Tung-lin Academy and its Political and Philosophical Significance', in *Monumenta Serica*, XIV (1949–55): 160–61.

Feng recognised the Jesuit interpretation of Confucianism for what it is, a highly selective use of the classics, combined with a totally new non-Chinese doctrine.

So, I believe, did the 'Christian Confucians', those Chinese scholars and officials who accepted baptism and became the disciples of Ricci and his successors. Much further study is required before a final verdict can be reached as to the objective orthodoxy (in both Christian and Confucian senses) of their views.[303] Subjectively, however, they seem to have been convinced that their twin allegiances were neither antagonistic nor completely identical. Rather, to use the language of the most important of them, Hsü Kuang-ch'i, they were 'complementary'.[304]

Why should some literati of the period find Confucianism in need of complementing by a foreign creed? If we examine the spiritual biographies of the three most important Confucian converts, Hsü Kuang-ch'i, Li Chih-tsao and Yang T'ing-yün we find many common elements including a general despair at the decadence of morals and public life, and a search for alternatives leading eventually to Christianity. But none of them seems to have seen his endpoint as a repudiation of the Confucian heritage. On the contrary, they saw it as a return to the original values of the Confucian tradition.

Hsü Kuang-ch'i

Hsü Kuang-ch'i (1562–1633), known to the Jesuits as 'Doctor Paul', was certainly the most illustrious of the Chinese Christians. He held many high offices including those of head of the Calendrical Bureau,

303. I have begun such an investigation on the basis of the published and especially manuscript works by Chinese Christians. What is sorely lacking in the literature is an approach from the point of view of the Chinese Christians themselves rather than the missionaries; or to use the jargon of missiology, of 'indigenisation' as opposed to 'accommodation'. John D Young's work is a useful beginning, but is vitiated by an implicit assumption that Confucian and Christian 'orthodoxies' are fixed and easily applied categories. My own tentative position on this question is close to that of Julia Ching, *Confucianism and Christianity* (Tokyo, 1977).

304. Nicholas Trigault, in a passage interpolated into Ricci's memoirs, quotes Hsü as asserting that Christianity 'complemented Confucianism' *(puJu)* v L Gallagher, translator, *China in the Sixteenth Century,* 448.

President of the Board of Rites, and Grand Secretary.[305] His biography in the *Ming shih*[306] mentions his connections with the Jesuits, and his writings on Western scientific methods, but not his adherence to Christianity. However, even a recent Chinese mainland publication, which in general avoids the issue by concentrating on his scientific works and especially his treatise on agricultural methods, admits that he was 'completely sincere in his belief in Christianity'.[307]

His own account of his conversion to Christianity may be found in a Preface that he wrote for Ricci's *Twenty-five Sentences* of 1605, some two years after his baptism. He states that he first became aware of the missionaries through a picture of the Lord of Heaven, and later, Ricci's map of the world. Then in 1600 he met Ricci himself in Nanking and 'decided that he was the most learned and accomplished gentleman in the whole world'. Ricci's whole life was given over to the worship of Shangti. He was a paragon of virtue, practising purity, loyalty and filial piety. Kuang-ch'i describes his reaction to the meeting with Ricci as like the dissipation of clouds. 'I, who was always subject to doubt . . . found that I need no longer remain in uncertainty.'[308]

Further details are supplied by Matteo Ricci in the *Storia dell'Introduzione del Cristianesimo in Cina*. After brilliant early successes in the examinations, Hsü failed the doctoral examination in 1598 and was classed seventh in the 1601 examination only to be eliminated by lot from the final list when the examiners discovered they had accidentally classed one more than the regular three hundred candidates. Ricci claims that Hsü saw this as the hand of divine providence because, despite his initial attraction to Christianity, he would probably at that period have taken a second wife in order to

305. For details of his career see JC Yang's biography in Hummel, *Eminent Chinese of the Ch'ing Period*, 316–19; *Fonti Ricciane*, II, 250–511, n 3; Juan Yuan, *Ch'ou-jen chuan*, chapter 32; *Ming shih*, chapter 251; *Tseng-ting Hsü wen-ting kung-chi*, edited by Hsü Mao-hsi, (Taipei, 1962); *Hsü Kuang-ch'i chi*, editred by Wang Chung-min (Peking, 1963), II, 549–80; Monika Übelhor, 'Hsü Kuang-ch'I', in *Oriens Extremus*, XV/2 (1968): 217–30; *Hsü Kuang-ch'i Nien-p'u*, edited by Liang Chia-mien (Shanghai, 1981); Wang Chung-min (revision Ho Chao-wu), *Hsü K'uang-ch'i* (Shanghai, 1981); Lo Kuang, *Hsü Kuang-ch'i chuan* (Taipei, 1970).

306. Chapter 251 v *Hsu Kuang-ch'i chi*, II, 550–51.

307. Po Shu-jen's article on 'Hsü Kuang-ch'I's Works on Astronomy', in Chu K'o-chen editor, *Hsü Kuang-ch'i chi-nien lun-wen chi* (Peking, 1963), 128.

308. v *T'ien-hsüeh ch'u-han*, 327; translated in *Fonti Ricciane*, II, 288–89, n 3.

ensure the continuance of the family line[309] if his career had prospered. This would, of course, have been an obstacle to his conversion.

It seems that this disappointment, however interpreted, was crucial in Hsü's conversion. Ricci describes him as 'very upset' on his departure from Peking after his first failure,[310] and it was during this period that he began seriously to investigate Christianity, finally asking for baptism in 1603 in Nanking. By this time Ricci was in Peking, but Father Giovanni de Rocha gave Hsü Kuang-ch'i the manuscript of Ricci's *Dottrina Christiana* (*T'ien-chu chiao-yao*) and of the *T'ien-chu shih-i*, which apparently completed the process of conversion.[311]

The *Storia* attributes some role in Hsü Kuang-ch'I's conversion to a dream he had after meeting Ricci in Nanking in 1601, which he later interpreted as a revelation of the Trinity.[312] It appears that the Jesuits played down the significance of the dream[313] and it does not seem to have been decisive for Hsü. Rather it indicates the state of indecision and spiritual crisis he was undergoing, graphically described by him as 'a state of constant doubt' (*p'ing-shan-i*).[314] This seems to have been more than a temporary phase, a mere reaction to his examination failure. The *Storia*, having praised Hsü Kuang-ch'I's virtue and learning, describes him as having tried many schools in search of spiritual peace.

> Seeing that in the sect of the literati little was spoken about the other life and the salvation of souls, he had taken up many masters of the sect of the idols and other sects which

309. *Fonti Ricciane,* N680, II, 252–23. Ricci points out that Kuang-ch'i had only one son, Hsu Chi (Lung-yü), who was at that time childless. Later Hsü Chi, who was himself baptised in 1608, had ten children, including five sons. Many of the Hsü family are mentioned in the mission's records, but perhaps the most famous was Kuang-ch'I's grand-daughter, Candida. The case of Chü Ju-k'uei, discussed in the previous chapter, illustrates well the obstacle that polygamy posed to conversion.
310. *Fonti Ricciane,* N681, II, 253.
311. *Fonti Ricciane,* N682, II, 254.
312. *Fonti Ricciane,* N681, II, 253–54.
313. *Fonti Ricciane,* N681, II, 254. Hsü is alleged to have said nothing of it in 1603 because 'he had heard from the Fathers that it was not good to believe in dreams', but later he was pleased to find that Ricci thought God sometimes revealed himself in dreams.
314. Preface to Ricci's *Erh-shih-wu yen, T'ien-hsüeh ch'u-han,* I, 327. See also *Fonti Ricciane,* II, 252, n 5.

> promised paradise after death, but with none of them did he remain satisfied.[315]

This spiritual quest is described in more detailed by Aleni in his life of Ricci.

> The *ta-tsung-po* Hsü Hsüan-hu,[316] erudite and talented, was desirous of penetrating the mysteries of life and death but found the Confucians unable to explain their significance. He went thoroughly into the teachings of the Profound Learning School (*hsüan-hsüeh*) and the Ch'an Buddhists, and there was no famous teacher he did not seek out, but still he saw no solution to the mysteries of life and death, and his mind was not at rest. In the 28th year of Wan-li (AD 1600) he came to Nanking, met Ricci, and absorbed his ideas.[317]

Such an intellectual biography does not seem to have been as uncommon as it might appear from some accounts,[318] and we can establish at least one source for such interest on the part of Paul Hsü. Hsü Kuang-ch'i's examiner in the 1597 Peking examinations was Chiao Hung,[319] whom Ricci had met in Nanking in 1599. Chiao was a friend and associate of Li Chih, interested in Ch'an Buddhism and in the 'Three Teachings' movement,[320] and Hsü Kuang-ch'i seems to have been for a time a disciple of his.[321] Certainly, the account of their

---

315. *Fonti Ricciane,* N680, II, 252.
316. *Ta-tsung-po* was the title of a Senior Vice-President of the Board of Rites *(Li pu),* an office to which Hü Kuang-ch'i was appointed in 1629. Hsüan-hu was Hsü Kuang-ch'i's *hao* or courtesy title.
317. Aleni's *Ta-hsi Li hsien-sheng hsing-chi,* quoted in Chang Wei-hua, *Ming shih,* 178.
318. See de Bary's remarks on the Ming quest for 'enlightenment' and its depreciation by recent historians in the Introduction to *Self and Society in Ming Thought,* 13.
319. *Fonti Ricciane,* II, 250, n 3.
320. *Fonti Ricciane,* N550, II, 65–66, and especially 66, n l; See also *Ming shih,* chapter 288, 7b–10a; Huang Tsung-hsi, *Ming Ju hsüeh-an,* chapter 35, 8b–12a; Jung Chao-tsu, 'Chiao Hung chi ch'i ssu-hsiang', in *Yen-ching hsüeh-pao,* 23 June 1938, 1–45.
321. The *Storia* describes Chiao Hung as Hsü Kuang-ch'i's 'master' *(Fonti Ricciane,* N912, II, 489). This may be simply a way of describing the traditional relationship between examiner and successful candidate, but Chiao's praise of Hsü (quoted in *Fonti Ricciane,* II, 250, n 3) as a 'famous scholar and great Confucian' and their later meeting (described in *Fonti Ricciane,* N912) suggests a closer bond between them.

meeting in Nanking in 1609 suggests a master-disciple relationship, or rather the rupture of such a relationship.

> (Hsü Kuang-ch'i) came there (to Nanking) to visit and to console[322] one of the most famous literati of this kingdom, his master, by name of Chiao, who since he was an extreme partisan of the sect of the idols, reproved our Paul for having embraced a foreign teaching, and exhorted him to abandon it. However, knowing that it was useless to try to convince him, Doctor Paul did not wish to argue with him and politely changed the subject.[323]

We may, then, regard Hsü Kuang-ch'i's history as a sort of pilgrim's progress, differing from that of many of his contemporaries only in its end, Christianity.

What was it in Christianity that attracted him and made it seem the answer both to his personal problems and the political crisis of the times?[324] On the personal level Hsü seems to have found in Christianity a way of reconciling the Chinese past with the present, of satisfying the pull of tradition and the needs of his soul. In a brief note entitled *Jottings on the True Religion (Chêng-tao t'i-kang)* he describes the development of Chinese culture as a heroic venture, but one which wandered from the truth, from the Author and Cause of all. In the teachings of Confucius and Mencius there was some sketchy knowledge of him, but in the magical practices of the Taoists and the empty ceremonies of the Buddhists, mere deceit. What is needed is a return to the Source.[325]

In Christianity, or to be more precise, in the Christians—for in typical Chinese fashion Hsü looks to the lives of the Jesuits for confirmation of the teaching—he found the combination of high morality and religious absolutes, orthodox tradition and universal truth, that he had been looking for. In his *Apologia* of 1616, he gives the reasons why he and other 'gentlemen and scholars' have accepted Christianity.

322. Chiao Hung was in mourning for his wife and son (*Fonti Ricciane,* II, 489, n 7).
323. *Fonti Ricciane,* N912, II, 489.
324. I agree with Monika Übelhor's judgement that the Jesuits merely provided answers to questions which Hsü had independently been asking ('Hsü Kuang Ch'i', in *Oriens Extremus,* XV/2, 194).
325. Quoted in *Fonti Ricciane,* II, 252, n 4.

> Truly they are all followers of the holy sages. Their way is completely orthodox, their conduct very strict, their learning very extensive, their associations very refined, their hearts quite pure, their views quite definite. In their own country they are all outstanding men. They have travelled from the West several thousand miles for this reason. In their country everybody devotes themselves to self cultivation by serving the Lord of Heaven. They had heard of the teaching of the Chinese sages and that everybody (in China) practises self-cultivation and serves Heaven. Their principles were in agreement. So they endured hardships and difficulties, underwent perils and disregarded dangers, and came (to China) to examine our orthodoxy. They wanted to make everybody good by declaring the meaning of the love of exalted Heaven for men.[326]

This account of Christianity might be discounted as self-defence and face-saving on the part of Hsü, and it certainly stresses the points of similarity between Christianity and orthodox Confucianism. It is, however, couched in quite general terms, and when he goes on to specify the teachings of the *t'ien-chu-chiao*, they do appear distinctively Christian in their totality and emphasis.

> According to them, the service of Shang-ti is fundamental, and the salvation of body and soul are essential. Sincerity, filial piety, compassion and love are to be practised. The first step is repentance and reform, and shame and purification are the beginning of virtue. The true happiness of life in Heaven is the reward for doing good, while the eternal misery of Hell is the punishment for doing evil. All their commandments and injunctions are congruent with the laws of Heaven and with human nature. Their precepts are capable of persuading men to do good invariably and avoid evil completely. What they say about the bounty of the Lord of Heaven producing, nourishing and preserving, and their teaching about rewarding good and punishing evil, is easy to understand and completely true, and sufficient to move the hearts of men and inspire in them the loving confidence and careful concern which flow from inner rectitude.[327]

---

326. Translated from the *P'ien-hsüeh shu-kao, T'ien-chu-chiao tung-ch'uan wen-hsien hsü-pien*, I, 22–23 *cf* the translation by EC Bridgman, and (a slightly different) text in *The Chinese Repository*, XX (1850): 119, and 127–28.
327. *P'ien-hsüeh shu-kao*, 23 *cf* Bridgman, 119.

What Hsü has done in this passage is to link Christian revelation and Confucian morality. The former becomes the foundation and motivation for the latter. Hsü Kuang-ch'i is not a private Christian and public Confucian, nor vice versa, but a public Christian and public Confucian. The two are complementary.

Nor, I believe, was Hsü a syncretist, consciously or unwittingly attempting to reconcile incompatible metaphysical systems and moral beliefs.[328] He seems to have accepted Ricci's reading of the development of Confucianism; to have assumed that it was the moral and self-cultivation aspects of Confucianism that mattered; and to have found nothing contradictory in a simultaneous commitment to the roles of Confucian reformer and Christian theist. The consistency and reiteration of that commitment places the onus on those who accuse him of bad faith to demonstrate wherein it lay.[329] Certainly, he had an eirenic disposition and an extraordinary range of interests: he wrote prefaces to collections of writings of both Chu Hsi and his rival Wang Yang-ming, and treatises on science, theology, history, classical studies, agriculture and military tactics as well as poetry and essays.[330] But, a man of many parts is not necessarily a divided man. Hsü seems to have found his point of rest in the Christian God.

Hsü Kuang-ch'I's programme of complementing Confucianism and opposing Buddhism is well illustrated in his 1616 *Apologia*. Buddhism is rejected as based on false teaching, incompatible with the ancient traditions of China, 'placing Buddha above Shang-ti, and opposing the commands of the ancient rulers and kings, sages and worthies'; while Christianity 'is truly able to implement good government, assist Confucianism and reform Buddhism'.[331] Buddhism and Taoism have corrupted good government and morals, and 1,800

328. This appears to be John Young's conclusion *(Confucianism and Christianity,* 57–58). Young is surprised that Hsü nowhere 'specifically attacked the Neo-Confucian cosmology of *li* and *ch'I*' and finds it 'indeed remarkable that Hsü's writings should show no tension between his Christian and Confucian moral beliefs'. Young's dilemma stems from his conviction that Hsü's God was 'anthropomorphic' and hence incompatible with the Confucian world-view.

329. Jacques Gernet, 'Christian and Chinese Visions of the World . . .', *Chinese Society,* 4 (1980): 14.

330. v *Hsü Kuang-ch'i nien-p'u,* edited by Liang Chia-mien, 229–39 for a chronological list of Hsü's writings.

331. *P'ien-hsüeh shu-kao,* 25; *cf* Bridgman, 120.

years[332] of Buddhism in the East have seen no improvement. On the contrary, 'where one law has been enacted, a hundred irregularities have resulted; the desire for good government has been frustrated, and schemes for reform of government have proved unavailing'.[333]

The last passage brings us to an important aspect of Hsü Kuang-ch'i's adherence to Christianity, its political implications. A contributor to a symposium to celebrate the fourth centenary of Hsü's birth, published in Peking in 1963, sees this as the prime aim of his life:

> When he saw the corruption of the government of the time, the conniving, the social unrest, and the extremely dangerous situation on the borders, he sought means of changing the condition of society. He aimed at a peaceful, prosperous society in which the state would be strong and the people happy. Consequently, he was deeply impressed by the teachings of the Wang Yang-ming school, because it was primarily concerned with political morality. He considered that religion could help people to be good, and could be of use to the government. Hence the hypocritical efforts of the Jesuits, their doctrines about what they called serving Heaven and loving men, and even more their useful scientific methods, persuaded Hsü Kuang-ch'i to spread their erroneous teachings.[334]

Leaving aside the imputation of deceit on the part of the Jesuits, I think this is a fair if incomplete statement of Hsu's position. It is clearly one-sided in ignoring the appeal to personal salvation in the teachings of both the Wang Yang-ming school and Christianity. But for the upright Confucian scholar-official, 'self-cultivation' and good government were not separable in theory or practice. It is the emphasis on this aspect of Hsü's life that makes Monika Übelhör's recent study of his career[335] so much more satisfactory than earlier treatments in Western sinological literature. He was not just a

332. The figure is interesting since, unlike Ricci's computation of the comparative chronology of Buddha and Christ, it appears to give Buddha precedence.

333. *P'ien-hsüeh shu-kao,* 24; *cf* Bridgman, 120.

334. Po Shu-jen, in *Hsü Kuang-ch'i chi-nien lun-wen chi,* 139.

335. Her two-part article in *Oriens Extremus,* XV/2, 1968, and XVI/1, 1969, is based on her Hamburg doctoral dissertation of 1967. The full title of the dissertation reveals the emphasis of her study: 'Hsu Kuang-ch'i (1562–1634) und seine Einstellung zum Christentum—Studie zur geistigen Haltung der chin. Beamtenschaft Ende der Ming Dynastie'.

Christian who happened to be an official and political reformer, but a Chinese scholar who found in Christianity confirmation and motivation for his political activities. In this, as in other respects, Hsü Kuang-ch'i appears the archetypal Confucian Christian.

Li Chih-tsao

Li Chih-tsao, like Hsü Kuang-ch'i, was an official. His political and scholarly allegiances were in many respects similar to Hsü Kuang-ch'i's but the offices he held were less exalted and mostly concerned with technical matter—waterways, animal breeding, the calendar.[336] The reasons for his initial attraction to the Jesuits seem to have been scientific and he is usually regarded as foremost in the introduction of Western science.[337] He became interested first in Ricci's map which contrasted so strongly with a *Map of the World* he himself had prepared as a young man.[338] Li collaborated with Ricci on the third edition of the map which appeared in 1602, and later on several scientific works. He also produced a second edition of Ricci's *T'ien-chu shih-i* with an adulatory preface by himself in 1607.

The reader of this preface would, I think, assume that Li Chih-tsao was by this time a Christian. In fact, he was not baptised till March 1610, a few months before Ricci's death. The reason for this delay is given by Ricci in the *Storia*.

> He is well instructed in the things of our Holy Faith, and decided to be baptized, but the Fathers discovered that there was an impediment in his polygamy. He has promised that he will get rid of it. However, he holds our Holy Religion to be true, and preaches it and exhorts others to it, as if he were a Christian. And already many of his household have received holy baptism and are amongst the best Christians of them all.[339]

336. For details of Li's career, see Hummel, *Eminent Chinese,* 452–54; *Fonti Ricciane,* N168, II, 168–71, n 3; Juan Yuan, *Ch'ou-jên chuan,* chapter 32 (387–90 of the Shanghai, 1955 edition); Fang Hao, *Li Chih-tsao yen-chiu* (Taipei, 1966); and L Van Hee, 'Grands Chrétiens de Chine', in *Xaveriava,* 140 (August 1930): 261–71.
337. Juan Yiian, the nineteenth century historian of Chinese science, in his biography of Li Chih-tsao, says 'Chih-tsao was the first to introduce to China the knowledge of Western books and instruments. Hsü Kuang-ch'i and Li T'ien-ching were later' *(Ch'ou-jên chuan,* 390).
338. *Fonti Ricciane,* N628, II, 169–70.
339. *Fonti Ricciane,* N632, II, 178–9.

It might appear from this account that Li Chih-tsao's approach to Christianity was independent of the Jesuit views on Confucianism. However, Li was as much of a Confucian scholar as Hsü Kuang-ch'i. Among his major works, besides the great collection of Western religious and scientific works, the *T'ien-hsüeh ch'u-han* of 1629, was a history in 10 chiian of the rites to Confucius (the *P'an-kung li-yüeh shu*)[340] which was included in the great Ch'ing *Ssü-k'u ch'uan-shu* collection; and a commentary on the Confucian Four Books.[341] There is no reason for regarding the constant references to Confucian teachings in his prefaces to Christian works as merely conventional, although we cannot document the precise role of the Jesuit interpretation of Confucianism in his conversion.

A most interesting statement of Li Chih-tsao's position vis-à-vis Confucianism is the preface he contributed to an account by his friend Yang T'ing-yün of the latter's conversion to Christianity, the *Record of the Holy Water (of Baptism)*:

> This teaching (Christianity) reveres the Lord of Heaven, while we Confucians speak of acknowledging Heaven, serving Heaven, serving *Shang-ti*. These phrases do not refer to *ti* but to a 'Lord' (*chu*). Chu Hsi says, '*Ti* is the lord and master (*chu tsai*) of Heaven', and so he who is said to give birth to heaven, to give birth to earth, and to give birth to all things is their lord, and the most accurate name for him is 'Lord' (*chu*) . . . There is a common saying that the main source of the Way is Heaven. If the Way of the Western sages is quite different from Buddhism and Taoism, it is rather similar to the precepts of Yao, Shun, (The Duke of) Chou and Confucius. Compared with the Buddhists and Taoists, it is contemporaneous with the Hundred Schools and the Nine Traditions, and does not contradict our great Chinese (thinkers); and compared with the teachings of Yao, Shun, (the Duke of) Chou and Confucius, there are not a few points of comparison with what the six classics say about Heaven and Shang-ti. What is there to be suspicious of here?[342]

340. See *Fonti Ricciane,* 170 n., and Hummel, *Eminent Chinese,* 454.
341. *Ssû-shu tsung-chu* v *Fonti Ricciane,* II, 170 n.
342. Preface to the *Shêng-shui chi-yen,* quoted in Ch'en Shou-i, 'Ming-mo Yeh-su-hui-shih . . .', 98.

The context of these remarks is avowedly apologetic but, however specious the textual arguments, the impression is one of a simultaneous commitment to Confucianism and Christianity. The two are not simply identified but related through their language and key concepts to a single truth; or, in Western terms, Li is expounding a theology drawing on two traditions. As Li said in his Preface to Ricci's *T'ien-chu shih-i*: 'In the East and the West minds and ideas are the same. Where there are differences, when you examine the contexts of the sayings and passages you find the differences come from the editors.'[343] Truth is one and indivisible, whether found in Confucius or Christ.

Yang T'ing-yün

Yang T'ing-yün, or 'Doctor Michael', provides yet a third variant on the theme of Confucian and Christian. He, too, was a *chin-shih* or holder of the highest degree, a scholar from a well-known scholar-official family, who filled many important offices including those of Viceroy of Szechwan and Kiangsi, and Vice-Governor of Peking.[344] His published writings included works on textual interpretation and the first collection of writings on Western science and religion, the *Chüeh-chiao t'ung-wen chi*, of 1615. It would appear, however, that Yang's approach to Christianity was neither through science nor a desire for political and social reform (although he was a Tung-lin Academy supporter). Yang was first and foremost a religious man, a seeker after truth.

In a work by the Jesuit Giulio Aleni, the Chinese title of which has been suggestively rendered as *The Spiritual Odyssey of Yang Ch'i-yüan*,[345] Yang's quest for religious enlightenment is described in detail. He had met Matteo Ricci in Peking, and discussed philosophical questions with him.[346] In 1609, after some seventeen years of distinguished government service, he retired to his native Hangchow,

343. *T'ien-chu shih-i*, Preface, 3b.

344. See the biography by Wang Chung-min in Hummel, *Eminent Chinese*, 894–45; *Fonti Ricciane*, III, 13–14, n 3; and Yang Ch'ên-o, *Yang Ch'i-yüan hsien-sheng nien-p'u* (Shanghai, 1946.

345. Dunne, *Generation of Giants*, 114. The work was entitled *Yang Ch'i-yüan hsien-sheng ch'ai-hsing shih-chi.*

346. See the extract from his Preface to Ricci's *Arithmetic* in *Fonti Ricciane*, III, 114n.

where, at the governor's invitation, he lectured on philosophy. He seems to have been deeply interested in Buddhism at this period, holding discussions with Ch'an Buddhist monks and contributing to their monasteries. He also founded a philosophical society which he called characteristically the Truth Society (*chên-shih shê*). In 1611, Li Chih-tsao, a relative of Yang's, returned to Hangchow to observe the period of formal mourning, on the death of his father. Li invited the Jesuits to Hangchow, and at his house Yang T'ing-yün met Iazzaro Cattaneo, Nicholas Trigault and the Chinese Jesuit brother, Sebastian Fernandez (Chung Ming-jen).

Aleni, whose account was drawn from Yang T'ing-yün himself, and put into Chinese by Ting Chih-lin, describes a series of discussions on Christianity held between Cattaneo and Yang at Yang's house, which lasted for nine days.[347] The issues which particularly bothered Yang are of great interest, since on the one hand, they show that the Jesuits made no attempt to water down the central dogmas of Christianity, and, on the other, they point to the areas where Chinese intellectuals found special difficulty. Yang's main problem was with the whole notion of the Incarnation, a God who became man, suffered and died. It is interesting to note that another friend of the Jesuits, Yeh Hsiang-kao, the Grand Secretary, who supported the Jesuits in many ways, encouraging their preaching, helping secure the Cha-la burial-ground for Ricci, praising Aleni as 'the Confucius of the West', found this an insuperable obstacle.[348] As he wrote in a poem in praise of Aleni,

> I believe that Heaven and Earth are infinite,
> This is enough to satisfy my weak intellect.[349]

Yang T'ing-yiin did not succumb to this Confucian agnosticism but his acceptance was only after a long struggle. He embraced Christianity despite rather than because of his Confucian instincts. Once convinced, however, he had no reservations. In his *Tai-i p'ien* there is a full exposition of the Christian doctrine of the Incarnation

347. Another account, presumably based on letters no longer extant, is given in Bartoli, *La Cina,* Lib. Ill, Cap. XVIII, volume Ill, 95–98 of the Ancona, 1843 edition.
348. See *Fonti Ricciane,* II, 42–43, n l.
349. Text and translation in *Fonti Ricciane,* II, 42, n l.

and an account of the crucifixion of Christ. He accepts the Trinity as a revealed mystery, commenting, 'If you ask how there can be three persons who are one, even the cleverest tongue cannot describe it'.[350] Yang, unlike Confucius, was prepared to speak about what he had not experienced.

Another question at issue was the status of the sages of China. In what sense could a Christian regard them as *sheng*, an ambiguous term used by Chinese Christians to translate the Western 'saint' but in Confucianism bearing more the sense of wise man, moral teacher, authoritative source of doctrine and model of behaviour? The difficulty here was that according to one, perhaps the dominant school of theological opinion at the time, they could not be regarded as saved, let alone in any sense models. The Jesuits generally tried to avoid the issue by concentrating on the value of the teaching of the 'sages', rather than on their personal salvation, and leaving the latter question open.[351] We do not know precisely how Cattaneo satisfied Yang T'ing-yün in this regard, but apparently he was successful.

Yang's other main problem was much more practical. He had a concubine as well as a principal wife, and if he were to become a Christian, he would have to send her away. At first Yang tried to evade this and Aleni reports that he thought it unfair that the Jesuits would not make an exception for him as his Buddhist monk friends would have done. Li Chih-tsao, who had, just previously to this, done the same, was not sympathetic. 'That just goes to show', he said, 'that these Western gentlemen are not like the bonzes'.[352] There is a notable

350. *Tai-i p'ien,* B.6a, 593 of the *T'ien-chu-chiao tung-ch'uan wen-hsien* edition (Taipei, 1965).

351. In the *Sheng-ch'ao p'o-hsieh chi,* Huang Chên records a conversation on this question with Aleni. When pressed about the fate of King Wen who, contrary to Christian teaching, had many wives, Aleni says hesitatingly, 'I fear that King Wen too has entered hell', but quickly adds, 'Let us talk about principles instead of personalities'. v D Lancashire, 'Anti-Christian Polemics in Seventeenth Century China', in *Church History,* XXXVIII/2 (1969): 23132. Daniello Bartoli in *La Cina,* originally published in 1663, asserts that the Jesuits refused to regard Confucius as irreparably damned 'because the Holy Spirit has not revealed the damnation of any man and, as is clear from his own writings, [Confucius] disapproved of idolatry and recognized one sole God'. (Lib. I, Cap. LXXII, Ancona, 1843 edition, I, 173). The date of this work, however, precludes its being taken as evidence for attitudes in the early part of the century.

352. Quoted in *Fonti Ricciane,* II, 178, n 3.

lack of sympathy in the Jesuit sources for the unfortunate wife or wives affected by these conversions, although they usually insisted that generous provision be made for them. Once more, however, it is clear that conversion to Christianity was not taken lightly. It involved not just a readjustment of ideas and beliefs but a serious change in lifestyle. The private Christian could not remain the private Confucian, at least in all respects.

Yang T'ing-yün was baptised on Easter Sunday 1613, and from this date till his death in 1627, spent most of his time in activities related to Christianity. He wrote several books on religious matters alone or in collaboration with the missionaries, as well as contributing prefaces or stylistic improvements to other writings of the Jesuits. His major religious work was the Seven Victories (*Ch'i kê*), in which, in collaboration with Diego de Pantoia, he discussed the seven deadly sins and the seven virtues.[353] He also wrote a series of polemical works against the Buddhists which display his knowledge of Buddhism as well as his antipathy to its tenets.[354] They show a considerable extension of Ricci's arguments and provided material for later Christian controversialists. It is to the former Buddhist devotee more than to any other that we owe the decisive anti-Buddhist stance of the Christian church in China, and its insistence that Buddhism and Christianity have nothing in common. The owl and the phoenix not only did not sing together,[355] they screeched at each other.

The spiritual histories of Hsü, Li and Yang, despite their individual variations, have enough in common to justify certain general conclusions. It seems to me perverse to argue, as Jacques Gernet has recently[356] that Christianity was fundamentally incompatible with sixteenth and seventeenth century Confucianism. He describes the

353. Published in Li Chih-tsao's *Tien-hsüeh ch'u-han,* Taipei, 1965 edition, II, 689–1126. Pantoia is described (717) as the 'compiler' and Yang T'ing-yiin as 'revisor'.

354. They include the *Tai-i p'ien* of 1621, republished in the *T'ien-chu-chiao tung-ch'uan wen-hsien* (Taipei, 1965), 471–631; the *Tien Shih ming-pien,* and the *Hsiao luan pu ping-ming shuo,* both included in the *Tien-chu-chiao tung-ch'uan wen-hsien hsü-pien* (Taipei, 1966), I, 229–417 and 39–47.

355. The title of the *Hsiao luan pu ping-ming shuo* may be translated as 'The Owl and the Phoenix do not sing together'.

356. Jacques Gernet, 'Philosophie Chinoise et Christianisme de la fin du XVIe au milieu du XVIe siècle', in *Actes du Colloque Internationale de Sinologie* (Paris: Les Belles Lettres, 1976), 13–25.

conversions of men like Hsü, Li and Yang as 'marginal and exceptional',[357] which in numerical terms they were. But, given the practical obstacles to conversion—family ties, polygamy, ritual obligations, political ambition—it seems to me altogether remarkable that a few Western missionaries could have made any conversions at all. The key, surely, lies in the very ambiguity of the term 'conversion'. For these men to embrace Christianity was not to 'turn away' from their own values, but to enlarge them to include the Christian revelation.[358] It was only when 'conversion' came to mean a radical rejection of all that they prized, in other words, when a Western model of belief and practice was enforced during the Chinese Rites controversy, that literati ceased almost entirely to become Christians.

One last argument sometimes invoked to question the genuineness of the Christianity of such Confucian converts is to point to their personal relations with Jesuit missionaries. They accepted, it is said, the men, not their message. If, however, we could find a case of a Confucian who accepted the whole Christian message, including the most difficult doctrines, without any direct contact with missionaries but from their books alone, this would go far to demonstrate that the personal factor was not necessarily crucial. If, further, such a convert were to remain a strong Confucian in his ethical system and to accept totally Ricci's interpretation of Confucianism, the case for Confucian Christian compatibility would be strengthened. Such cases may exist in China, and they certainly existed in Korea where a group of Confucians, led by Yi Piek, became Christians through

357. Gernet, 'Philosophie Chinoise et Christianisme', 18.

358. Gernet cites as evidence against the genuineness of Yang's conversion, tendentiously described as 'a complete change', Longobardo's strictures on Yang's opinions. But Longobardo's treatise (published in French as the *Traité sur quelques points de la religion des chinois*) was rejected and suppressed by his colleagues as holding an untenable view of Confucianism. Yang's major heresies, according to Longobardo, were to defend the Neo-Confucian concept of *li* and to cite as evidence for the rational possibility of the incarnation Yeh Hsiang-kao's argument that the sages were incarnations. However, these 'errors' are attributed to a work never published and no longer accessible, and neither appear to me to be *prima facie* heterodox. Longobardo, elsewhere in the same treatise (Dutens edition, 108) grossly misinterprets *li* as Aristotelean 'prime matter', and Yeh was himself not a Christian, v J Gernet, 'Christian and Chinese Visions of the World', 16 especially n 44. (See chapter 3 for more detailed comments).

reading Jesuit writings alone. Jean Sangbae Ri has shown through a study of Yi Piek's writings that, without any missionary help, and even before one of his group went to China to be baptised, Yi had committed himself completely, and independently developed a Confucian-Christian synthesis on the basis of Ricci's.[359] It is clear that the Jesuit interpretation of Confucianism appealed to something intrinsic to the Confucian system and met the spiritual needs of men who retained a total commitment to the socio-political doctrines of Confucius.

---

359. J Ri, *Confucius et Jésus Christ* (Paris: Beauchesne, 1979).

2
A Point of Fact: The Debate Over Terms and Rites (1610–1688)

The whole question boils down to a point of fact: to know what the Chinese think about their Confucius and their ancestors, and what they intend by the ceremonies with which they honour them.

> *Prejugez Legitimes en faveur du decret de N.S. Père le PapeAlexandre VII et de la Pratique des Jesuites au sujet des Honneurs que les Chinois rendent a Confucius et a ieurs ancestres . . .*[1]

The history of the Jesuit mission in China from the death of Ricci till the suppression of the Society of Jesus towards the end of the eighteenth century is complicated story of expansion, numerical and geographical, despite checks and setbacks. Some of these checks and setbacks were due to 'persecution', to officially or locally inspired attempts to suppress the growth of heterodoxy and foreign ideas. Others were due to internal strife within the mission and decisions imposed on the mission from Europe. The most important of these concerned the question of Chinese Rites, the continuing debate, growing increasingly acrimonious towards the end of the seventeenth century and culminating in a series of papal decrees in the first half of the eighteenth century, which definitively rejected the Jesuit interpretation of these rites. In the remaining chapters of this work I shall attempt to discuss the development of the Jesuit interpretation of Confucianism against this background of an expanding mission, and conflict with both Chinese and Western opponents. The background must, however, remain very sketchy indeed, and will be filled in only

1. (Paris, 1700), 2.

where absolutely necessary for the elucidation of some new turn or modulation of the Jesuit approach.

It may seem disproportionate to devote so much of this work to the first thirty-odd years of the mission, and the remainder to some century and a half. However, apart from the 'Figurists' of the early eighteenth century, who were, in any case, only marginally concerned with Confucianism, the interpretation of Confucianism adopted by the Jesuits in China right to the end of the eighteenth century remained essentially that of Matteo Ricci. As the Jesuits' knowledge of Confucianism grew in range and depth they were able to develop and modify the details of Ricci's basic orientation of the mission. Under pressure of circumstances, and criticism from outside the Society, an increasingly oversimplified and insufficiently qualified party-line emerged in publications intended for the European public; but what was being defended was always, in the last resort, Ricci's view. Even the decisions of Rome in the early eighteenth century which overturned Ricci's interpretation of Chinese rites were regarded by most of the Jesuits as affecting their public presentation of Christianity but not their private views. They preserved what they could of the Confucian—Christian alliance founded by Ricci, remained silent as far as possible on the specific questions raised by Rome—the significance of *tien* and *shang-ti*, the status of ancestor and funerary rites—and continued to present themselves as 'scholars' *(ju)* in the Confucian tradition.

Even before the final condemnation by Pope Benedict XIV in 1742, the accession of the Yung-cheng Emperor and subsequent expulsion of many of the missionaries had so limited the apostolic activities of the Jesuits that the interpretation of Confucianism was no longer an all-important issue to the mission. Work among the scholar—official class was restricted to scientific activities and the pockets of Christians who remained throughout the Empire were concerned with survival rather than expansion. Those Jesuits who remained in Peking had more leisure for scientific and sinological studies and their reports to Europe, both published and manuscript, served as the basis for the development of the scientific study of Chinese culture. These works had much to say about Confucius and Confucianism, but they were less concerned with interpreting Confucianism than with translating Confucian works and presenting the Chinese view of Confucius in its own terms. The tone was still one of admiration for the Confucian value-system but the concern was sinological rather than missiological.

In the present chapter I shall treat the development of the Jesuit interpretation of Confucianism from Ricci's death in 1610 to the arrival of the first members of the French mission in Peking in 1688. There had been Frenchmen, as well as many other nationalities, among the members of the mission before 1688, but they had all entered China under the auspices of the Portuguese, following the approved route from Lisbon to Goa and Macao, and accepting the Portuguese *padroado* or right of patronage and jurisdiction over the churches of the East. 1688 marks a new departure, a distinctive and would-be independent mission, preserving close links with France and bringing characteristically French attitudes to the encounter with Chinese civilisation. By drawing a line through the history of the mission in 1688 I do not intend to imply that the French made a new beginning. They clearly owed a great debt—often unacknowledged—to their predecessors going back to Ricci, and their writings which deal with Confucianism follow the well-worn track of the earlier Jesuit interpreters. Nor, certainly, do I wish to depreciate the achievement of non-French missionaries after 1688. The historian is, however, dependent on the availability of sources, and the French Jesuits were remarkably productive of letters, treatises, polemical works and massive compilations on China. Their arrival marks a new era in the documentation of the fortunes of the mission, and their relations with the intellectual capital of the world of the time, Paris, gave China an altogether new significance in the intellectual history of Europe.

Another reason for ending this chapter in 1688 is that this year marked the end as well as the beginning of an era. On 28 January 1688, a few days before the arrival of the French group in Peking, died the last of the great figures of the early history of the mission, Ferdinand Verbiest. Verbiest, as Adam Schall and Ricci before him, had exercised great influence over the fortunes of the mission from Peking and played a role in court affairs that gained him an honourable entry in the Ch'ing history.[2] After Verbiest no individual Jesuit was to loom so large nor play so crucial a role in protecting and fostering the nascent Chinese Christian Church.

---

2. *Ch'ing shih kao, lieh chüan* 59, which also contains a biography of Adam Schall.

In another respect too, this period marks the end of a stage in the development of the Jesuit interpretation of Confucianism. In 1687 in Paris appeared *Confucius Sinarum Philosophus,* the first full translation of any of the Confucian books[3] to be published in Europe. This was the culmination of a long process of translation beginning, as we have seen, with Ruggieri and Ricci. Ignacio da Costa and Prospero Intorcetta had published in China, in 1662, a Latin translation[4] of part of the *Analects* of Confucius and the *Great Learning,* and a translation of part of the *Doctrine of the Mean* by Intorcetta had appeared in 1667–1669.[5] The rarity of these works in European libraries demonstrates their limited circulation. *Confucius Sinarum Philosophus,* however, was widely circulated, translated and analysed. It was the basis of the popular image of 'Confucius, the Philosopher of China' which haunted European thought for a century or more. Even the portrait of Confucius was plagiarised by countless works of the late seventeenth and early eighteenth century. Its publication marks the beginning of the vogue for *chinoiserie* in art and literature as well as the serious impact of China on the intellectuals of Europe.

The most conspicuous feature of the fortunes of the Jesuit interpretation of Confucianism, 1610–1688, is the developing criticism of Matteo Ricci's position which eventually erupted at the end of the century in the Chinese Rites controversy. This criticism came, at first, from within the Society of Jesus, and was resolved at a conference of the missionaries held at Kiating[6] in 1628, which adopted a common policy, in essence that of Ricci himself. Then, in 1631 the Dominicans, and in 1633 the Franciscans, arrived, bringing with them attitudes and methods of evangelisation tried and successful in the New World and the Philippines. These attitudes

3. It included three of the Confucian Four Books—the *Analects (lun-yu), Doctrine of the Mean (chung-yung)* and *Great Learning (ta-hsueh).*
4. Entitled *Sapientia Sinica.*
5. *Sinarum Scientia Politico-Moralis a Prospero Intorcetta Siculo Societatis Jesu, in lucem edita.* It appears that part was printed in Canton in 1667 and a Preface and Life of Confucius added in Goa in 1669. This curious publication history was due to the difficulties of the mission in the late 1660s and Intorcetta's mission to Europe in 1668. It was reprinted in Thevenot's *Relations de Divers Voyages Curieux,* Part 4 (Paris, 1676).
6. Thus in most of the literature. *Chia-ting* is the more correct romanisation of the name of this town, situated near Shanghai, and a centre of Confucian scholarship, v J Dennerline, *The Chiating Loyalists: Confucian Leadership and Social Change in Seventeenth-Century China* (New Haven: Yale University Press, 1981).

and methods conflicted with those of the Jesuit mission, and so began the debate about the missionary approach to China which was soon referred to Rome for decision. Rome decided in 1645 in favour of the newcomers; on representation by the Jesuits, in 1656, in favour of their approach; and in 1669, in defiance of logic but not of commonsense, in favour of both. The compromise of 1669 was to last till the arrival of yet another group, the French missionary Vicars Apostolic, who were to upset the *status quo.* It would be misleading, however, to see this period in the history of the mission purely in the light of the debate on this subject. It was for most of the time, and certainly for most of the members of the China mission, marginal. Communications with Europe were poor, and the practical problems of dealing with local officials and providing pastoral care for an ever-expanding Christian flock were predominant. The seventeenth century was marked for the China mission more by steady growth in knowledge of, and adaptation to local conditions, the production of a substantial body of Chinese Christian literature, and development along the lines laid down by Ricci than by controversy. The debate began, but most of the missionaries were too preoccupied with making a practical accommodation to China, the China of peasants and merchants, as well as the Confucian China of the scholars and the court, to participate in it.

The Jesuit debate over terms

As long as Matteo Ricci lived, his personal qualities, as much as his position as Superior of the mission, guaranteed that his ideas prevailed in the mission. I have found no evidence of any dissent from his views, and the practice of the mission was a direct application of the positions Ricci took, namely accommodation to Chinese upper-class society, a cautious but positive attitude to Confucianism, and permission for Chinese converts to continue to perform public and private Confucian rites.

After Ricci's death, however, dissension arose from two sources. The Jesuits of the Japanese mission, which had a common base with the China mission in Macao, and which made use of some of the Chinese works of their colleagues in China, became disturbed at the policy of that mission. They felt that the use of Chinese terms for the Christian God was dangerous, and that the distinctiveness and integrity of the Christian message was compromised by an identification, even partial and critical, with Confucianism. At the same time, the man Ricci had designated as his successor as Superior of the mission, Nicolò Longobardo, began to have scruples about aspects of Ricci's interpretation of Confucianism. Since it is often alleged that Longobardo became an opponent of Ricci's position on Chinese Rites,[7] I think it is important to stress that his difficulties were not over the rites, in the strict sense, that is over ancestral and funeral ceremonies, or those in honour of Confucius; but over the terms used for 'God' and the dominance of Neo-Confucian interpretations of the classics. His views on the last point certainly, and to some extent his views on the terms question, made him an opponent of Ricci's interpretation of Confucianism. But I have found no indications either in his own writings, or other documents of the period, that he ever doubted either Ricci's general approach to Confucianism, or the permissibility of Confucian rites. In fact, his uncompromising assertion of the 'atheism' of the Confucian *literati* confirmed rather than destroyed the argument that these rituals were purely social in nature.

The objections of the Japanese mission to the policies of the China mission are well represented by a letter from João Rodrigues to the Jesuit General, Claudio Acquaviva, written from Macao on 22 January 1616.[8] Rodrigues, according to Pfister,[9] was primarily

7. See, for example, Pfister, *Notices,* 61, and the majority of anti-Jesuit writers on the Rites Controversy. Dunne, *Generation of Giants,* chapter XVII, 'A Question of Rites', more accurately links Longobardo's objections with the question of terminology.
8. Ms in ARSJ: JS *16, I,* 284–88.
9. See the brief biography in Pfister's *Notices,* No 71, 214–45, and also the 'Addenda and Corrigenda', 23–25, which correct Pfister's confusion of this João Rodrigues, known in Japan as *Tçuzzu,* 'the interpreter', with another João Rodrigues. (See also, G Schurhammer, 'Doppel-ganger in Portugiesisch-Asien', in his collected *Orientalia* [Lisbon-Rome, 1963], 124–7). The signature on the letter in question is identical with the quite distinctive signature of João Rodrigues Tçuzzu on the endpapers of Michael Cooper's *The Southern Barbarians* (Tokyo, 1971). For a brief biographical sketch of João Rodrigues and some comments on his contribution to Japanese linguistic studies, see CR Boxer, 'Padre João Rodriguez Tçuzzu SJ and his Japanese Grammars of 1604 and 1620', in *Miscelanea de Filologia, Literatura e Historia Cultural a Memoria de Francisco Adolfo Coelho (1847–2919),* II (Lisbon, 1950), 338–63. The only full-length biography is M Cooper, *Rodrigues, the Interpreter: An Early Jesuit in Japan and China* (New York/Tokyo: Weatherhill (John) Inc, US & Japan, 1974).

interested in polemics against the Japanese Buddhists.[10] He came to China from Japan in order to investigate the sources of Japanese Buddhism and from 1613 to 1615 pursued his studies of 'the sects of the philosophers which existed here in the Orient in ancient times'.[11] He adds, significantly, that he planned to prepare a common catechism for the missions of China, Japan and Cochinchina. While his remarks about the common use of Chinese characters in all three lands are accurate enough, he seems to be totally unaware of the divergent cultural and social contexts in each of them. Both his polemical intent and his lack of discrimination between the cultures of East Asia were an unfortunate basis for a serious investigation of Chinese religion.

Rodrigues tells the General that he has come to the conclusion that Ricci and the fathers of the China mission were deceived in adhering to the 'doutrina civil e fabulosa popular—a curious description which seems to confuse unnecessarily and misleadingly Confucianism and Chinese popular religions. The major reason why they are incompatible with Christianity is that 'in fact and in theory *(em seu e speculativo)* all the sects of China are atheistic'. They do not believe in the creation, but derive the Universe from 'external matter or Chaos'.[12] They seem to have borrowed their ideas from Plato—the idea of two souls, one good, one bad, and the Platonic 'world soul—and from Pythagoras—the concept of two principles, one good, one bad.'[13] This account is sufficiently garbled and dominated by Western preconceptions to be unrecognisable as a description of any Chinese philosophical or religious system. One is astonished, however, to find that it is intended as a description of Confucianism, because he goes on to distinguish from this 'civil and fabulous popular doctrine'

10. 'He came to China a first time in 1612, in order to study the secret doctrines of the bonzes in their own books' *(Notices,* 214). Pfister does not seem aware of the fact that his coming to China, or at least to Macao, was not voluntary, but due to his expulsion from Japan by Tokugawa Ieyasu. However his activities in Japan, and his own account in the letter, confirm the purpose of his tour of the China mission. His prejudices against China as the source of Japanese errors are frequently displayed in his *Historia da Igreja do Japao* (Macau, 1954; English translated by M Cooper, *This Island of Japan: João Rodrigues' Account of 16th-century Japan* [Tokyo: Kodansha International, 1973]).
11. ARSJ: JS *16.1,* 284r.
12. ARSJ: JS *16.1,* 284v.
13. ARSJ: JS *16.1,* 285r.

another sect, that of 'Xaca' or 'Xekia', in other words, Buddhism. This is 'very close' to the Gymnofistos' of India 'well known to our ancestors'.[14]

Confident that he has perceived the errors in the approach of Ricci and his colleagues, he then set himself 'to remedy the situation'.[15] He made a thorough examination of the works of Matteo Ricci and Alfonso Vagnoni and, with the permission of the Provincial in Macao, set out with Emanuel Diaz Junior on a tour of the mission. It might be noted that this tour by Diaz had as its prime aim the publication of a prohibition by Father Carvalho, the Provincial of the Japanese Province,[16] on the 'teaching of mathematics and science'.[17] Another pillar of Ricci's method was under attack from the unsympathetic Japanese missioners. Rodrigues claims to have consulted all the Jesuits 'well versed in the language', yet to have concluded that they were all wrong, a conclusion not at all surprising given the circumstances of his inquiry.

Rodrigues's recommendations to the General were that all the books produced by the members of the China mission should be revised and that their methods should be changed. The early fathers of the mission were well intentioned but they had been misled and in their ignorance allowed many customs that were 'scandalous to the natives'. They allowed ceremonies for the dead, including lighting candles, burning incense and 'coming before the dead to perform a certain adoration', which are certainly 'superstitious ceremonies'.[18] As for their Chinese books, they should be submitted to the Inquisition and corrected, not by Chinese *literati* like 'Doctor Paul' (Hsu Kuang-ch'i) or 'Doctor Michael' (Yang T'ing-yün) who are ignorant of these matters, but by 'Japanese clerics'.[19] His final recommendation is that 'the Italian fathers' of the China mission be brought firmly under the

14. ARSJ: JS *16.1,* 285v.
15. ARSJ: JS *16.1,* 285v.
16. Until the creation of the separate Vice-Province of China in 1618, the China mission was dependent upon the Province of Japan.
17. See Pfister, *Notices,* 106–107, and Bartoli, *La Cina,* Liv Ill, cap LXIII, expressively entitled 'Ordine d'un superiore poco savio, e molto dannosa alla Missione Cinese'. Bartoli notes that 'Father Valentin Carvalho had never entered China to see for himself what conditions were like' (III, 234).
18. Bartoli, *La Cina,* Liv Ill, 286r.
19. Bartoli, *La Cina,* Liv. Ill, 286v.

control of the Japanese mission and a Visitor be appointed, preferably Emanuel Diaz Jr to bring them into line with the practices of Japan.[20]

In many respects this letter needs no commentary. The bias, superficiality, and inter-mission jealousy is apparent in even a most cursory summary such as the above. The policy and methods which Rodrigues wishes to foist on the China mission are clearly those of the Japanese mission; direct and vigorous evangelisation with little concession to the indigenous religious traditions. These were, in the short run, extremely effective and the rate of conversion in Japan far outstripped that in China. Ironically, the very next year began the great persecution of Christianity in Japan which to some extent may be attributed to the aggressive methods of the mission.[21]

However, there was some substance in Rodrigues's criticisms. Even his labelling of Confucianism as the 'civil and fabulous popular doctrine' points to an unresolved ambiguity in Ricci's position. There was a 'popular' aspect to Confucianism which was effected more by the pressure of local customs and popular practices than by a conscious policy of syncretism. In so far as the rites were 'civil', that is public expressions of basic ideas about political and social relations, they necessarily embraced a variety of attitudes and beliefs. The repeated attempts by Emperors and their ministers to purify Confucian rituals from contamination by Buddhist and Taoist practices, demonstrate the persistence and strength of such popular syncretism.[22] Ricci had been more concerned with the intentions of Christians participating in domestic and public ceremonies, and with what he understood to be their inner meaning and purpose, than with the common understanding of them.

Moreover, in his remarks about what one assumes was Neo-Confucianism, misleading though the Platonic and Pythagorean analogies were, Rodrigues pointed to another ambiguity in Ricci's legacy to the mission. If the Confucians, that is the real Confucians and not some idealised type of the ancient 'pure' Confucian, were in fact 'atheists' or 'pantheists' (Rodrigues's comments on the doctrine of the

20. Bartoli, *La Cina,* Liv. Ill, 286v–287r.

21. See Boxer, *The Christian Century in Japan,* chapter VII, especially 323–24, 333, 337–79.

22. See, for example, JK Shryock, *The Origin and Development of the State Cult of Confucius,* on the practices of various dynasties, including the Ming (chapter XII), and the 'protestant' or reform movements they engendered.

'world soul' somewhat contradict his 'atheist' label) then a Christian-Confucian accommodation would be a reconciliation of opposites, an uneasy and ultimately unviable alliance.[23] We have already seen the grounds upon which Ricci sought to avoid this impasse—a return to the pure, uncontaminated doctrine of the classics and the four books. But it was very difficult in practice to achieve this *tour de force,* given the Chinese system of classical education, the editions of classical works used in the schools and the opacity of the texts themselves. The Chinese *ching,* like the sacred texts of any religion, were not easily detached from their traditional interpretation, and by the Ming period this tradition was unequivocally Neo-Confucian. Ricci sought to take advantage of the intellectual ferment of the period and to attract those already disenchanted by the sterile rationalism of some aspects of Neo-Confucianism. Moreover, his hesitations and cautious statements about Neo-Confucianism seem to indicate an awareness that it could not be dismissed simply as 'atheism'. However, he had used the term,[24] and those seeking to attack his method could turn his own statements back on his head. If Confucians were atheists, their terminology was unsuitable to convey the Christian mysteries. The fact that this strengthened the argument in favour of the 'civil' nature of Chinese rites and rendered unlikely, if not absurd, the charge that they were superstitious, does not seem to have bothered Rodrigues. Nicolò Longobarbo, for his part, was more consistent. His disagreement with Ricci's methods was purely over the interpretation of Confucianism. If the clear distinction between the text and the commentators could not be maintained, if Neo-Confucianism was unequivocally atheistic and materialistic, with no concept of 'spirit', then Confucian terms such as *shang-ti* and *lien* must be abandoned, and Confucianism in all its forms added to the list of false and pernicious doctrines to be attacked at all times.

---

23. Although my purpose here is exegesis not interpretation, and I must reluctantly leave to another place a discussion of the realities of Neo-Confucianism, let me note that, in my view, *li hsüeh* tends more towards the 'spiritualist' than the 'materialist' end of the scale, the 'mystical' rather than the 'prophetic' v J Ching, *Confucianism and Christianity,* 178.
24. *Fonti Ricciane,* NN170, 199, I, 110, 132.

It is possible to trace Longobardo's opposition to Ricci's methods back to the period before he became superior of the mission.[25] From his arrival in 1597 to 1611 when he came to Peking, he laboured in Shao-Chou. Shao-chou was hardly, as the title of Father Bernard-Maître's chapter on these years suggests, the backwoods of China,[26] but it was perhaps 'the bush' by comparison with the two metropolises of Nanking and Peking where so many of the Jesuits worked. A letter written shortly after his arrival shows traces of animus against the sophisticated techniques of the mission to the Chinese upper-class. All we need here, he wrote, are simple books and pious objects, not glass prisms and scientific instruments.[27] Another letter (18 October 1598) shows a greater appreciation of the peculiar conditions of the China mission. He repeated his objections to 'spheres, maps, visits and other human means' but he admits the necessity for studying and using Confucian books. Recently he had been congratulated by a Chinese scholar on his proficiency in the *Great Learning* and the *Doctrine of the Mean* and such studies were very profitable. But, he adds, significantly, although the scholars observe six commandments, they completely neglect the first since they are atheists.[28]

Longobardo's experiences in evangelising the villages around Shao-chou, as well as in the city itself, soon convinced him of the importance of the friendship of the mandarins. The *Annual Letter* for 1602 relates how some Christians were protected from their enemies by a friendly official,[29] and several other examples are given in the account of the Shao-chou mission in the *Storia* which, D'Elia argues plausibly, must be the work of Longobardo.[30] In 1604 he rehearses Ricci's apologetic arguments in the *T'ien-chu shih-i* which had just

25. For details of this career, see Pfister, *Notices,* No 17, 58–64; Bernard-Maître, *Ricci,* II, part 3, chapter 3; and *Fonti Ricciane,* NN641-73, II, 192–244 (the Shao-chou mission) and I, 358, n 5 (a general biographical note).
26. Bernard-Maître, *Ricci,* Part 3, chapter 3, 'L'Appel Irresistable de la Brousse'.
27. Letter of 4 November 1598 in Tacchi Venturi, *Opere Storiche,* II, 475 *cf* translation in Bernard-Maître, *Ricci,* II, 55.
28. Bernard-Maître, *Ricci,* II, 56–57. This letter was published in English translation in *Purchase His Pilgimes* (Glasgow, 1906 edition, XII, 314–18). The original is in ARSJ: JS *13, I,* 174–78, and shows Longobardo echoing Ricci's Language on rites and Confucianism, for example, 'riti puramente politici' (174), 'Xamti' *[Shang-ti]* for God (176), even an apparent reference to *t'ai-chi* as God (175).
29. Bernard-Maître, *Ricci,* II, 65.
30. *Fonti Ricciane,* II, 196, n 2.

been printed, and appears to be in complete agreement with his approach to Confucianism.[31] Up till the time that Longobardo became Superior, then, it would seem that he adhered to Ricci's methods, differing from him only in his preference for the direct apostolate amongst the lower classes to the long-term and indirect work amongst the *literati.* George Dunne argues that his experiences in the south had made Longobardo even more optimistic than Ricci about the future of the mission and the prospects of success along the lines laid down by the founders of the mission.[32] Ricci, for his part, although he appears never to have met Longobardo, thoroughly approved of his activities, and as early as 1606 recommended him to the General as the most suitable person to govern the mission.[33] The dying Ricci's nomination of Longobardo as his successor suggests that, up to that time, Longobardo had expressed no serious dissent from the agreed policy of the mission.

In 1613, when Nicholas Trigault was being sent to Europe as 'Procurator' to secure reinforcements and backing for the mission, Longobardo prepared some instructions for him, detailing the questions he was to raise with the church authorities in Rome.[34] These might be read as marking the beginning of the Rites Controversy but it should be noted that they merely pose problems without necessarily indicating Longobardo's own position, and that only one of the questions raised is concerned with the question of 'rites'. This is the second of the four 'cases' to be presented by the Procurator.[35] It concerns the obligation of mandarins to take part in ceremonies to the local god on taking office. Longobardo asks whether a Christian mandarin might place an image of the angel who is the guardian of the place, or of the Saviour, above the altar, and so fulfil his duty to the satisfaction of the people, while explaining to the Christians what

---

31. Letter of 13 November 1604, reprinted in F Guerreiro, *Relacao Anual da Coisas que fizeram os Padres da Companhia de Jesus nas suas Missoes do Japao, China, Cataio,* II (Lisbon, 1607) (Coimbra, 1931 edition, 125).
32. Dunne, *Generation of Giants,* 110–11.
33. Letter to Acquaviva, Peking, 15 August 1606, No 37 in Tacchi-Venturi, *Opere Storiche,* II.
34. 'Appontamentos a cerca da Ida do nosso P.^c Procurador a Roma', 'Nanhium' (Nanhsiung), 8 May 1613, in ARSJ: JS *113 (Annuae Sinar-um, 1595–1616),* 301–309.
35. See Nicolô Longobardo Cap 3, 'Dalgus casos e dispensaçoes q se hao detratar pollo P.e procurador'. The first deals with polygamy, the third with Christian participation in religious processions, and the fourth with the scandal to Chinese of uncovering the head at mass as provided in the Roman ritual.

he is doing, to avoid scandal. (This subterfuge was later frequently attributed to Christian mandarins by opponents of the Rites. I have not found any unequivocal evidence that it was the practice, and there are several denials that it was the case in Jesuit sources. It is possible that it was considered, but rejected, at this time, and that reports of the discussions on the subject gave rise to the idea that it was common practice.) What is most interesting about Longobardo's reference to this in the document, is a note in the margin which appears to indicate his mind on the subject: 'There is no question of Idolatry here since the Chinese acknowledge neither the true God, nor his angels. And so the statue is more likely to be that of a mandarin than a representation of a spirit.'[36] Once again, Longobardo appears on close scrutiny a defender rather than opponent of the Jesuit position on the Rites question.

Where Longobardo did differ from the majority of his colleagues was on the question of terminology, and soon after coming to office, he opened a war of words that was not resolved finally till after 1628. Of the several treatises he wrote on the subject, only one has survived, and that by a curious accident. According to the account of the history of the work given by JS Cummins in his edition of the *Travels and Controversies of Friar Domingo Navarrete*, the *Reposta breve sobre as controversias* was written in 1623–1624, and was ordered destroyed at a later date by the Vice-Provincial, Francisco Furtado; a single incomplete copy escaped destruction, and eventually came into the possession of the Dominican Navarrete who published it in his *Tratados historicos, politicos, ethicos y religiosos de Ia monarchia de China*, Madrid, 1676. A French translation was published in Paris[37] at the height of the Rites Controversy and a version annotated by Leibniz was included in the latter's works.[38] The original manuscript, deposited by Navarrete in the Archives of Propaganda Fide, still exists there.[39]

36. Longobardo Cap 3, 'Dalgus casos e dispensaçoes q se hao detratar pollo P.e procurador', 306v.

37. *Traité sur quelques points de la religion des Chinois*, published together with Antonio de Santa Maria's treatise on the rites under the general title, *Anciens Traitez de Divers auteurs sur les Ceremonies de la Chine* in 1701. It appears from Louis de Cicé's *Lettre . . . aux RR. PP. Jesuites . . .* (Paris, 1700), 27, that de Cicé, a MEP missionary and Vicar Apostolic of Siam, was the translator.

38. *Gothofredi Guillelmi Leibnitii Opera Omnia*, edited by L. Dutens (Geneva, 1768), IV, 89–144.

39. SRC I, 145–68, together with a Latin translation by Antonio de Santa Maria OFM, 171–97.

The full title of Longobardo's treatise indicates very well its scope—A *short Reply concerning the controversies about Shang-ti, T'ien-shên, and Ling-hun, and other Chinese Names and Terms; to determine which of them may or may not be used in this Christian community. Shang-ti,* as we have seen, was a term commonly employed in the classics, which Ricci argued was, in some respects at least, the equivalent of the Christian 'God'. *T'ien-shen,* 'heavenly spirits', was coming to be used as a translation of 'angel', and the Chinese *ling-hun* for 'soul'. Longobardo opposes all three terms on the same grounds—the Chinese are atheists and materialists; an examination of Neo-Confucian metaphysics reveals that they have no concept of 'spirit', hence such Confucian terms as *shang-ti, shen,* and *ling-hun* represent material beings, and may not be employed without serious misunderstanding as equivalents to the Christian concepts of spiritual beings.

The author explains in his Preface[40] that he had misgivings, from the very beginning of his mission in China about the use of *shang-ti* because of the divergence between the explanations of the commentators on the Four Books[41] and the Christian idea of the divine nature. But he deferred to the experienced fathers of the mission and thought that the problem must have arisen from the error of 'some of those expositors . . . being but particular authors who did not consent to the ancient doctrine'.[42] After assuming office in 1610, he received a letter from Father Francesco Pasio, the Visitor, about the doubts some of the Jesuits of the Japanese mission held on

40. *Traite,* 89. I refer throughout to the French text of the *Traité* in Dutens' edition of Leibniz's *Works,* volume IV, 89–144. On occasion I also refer to the English translation in Navarrete's *Account of the Empire of China,* BK V. I have used a rare edition, undated and without place of publication, formerly in the possession of Associate Professor OB van der Sprenkel, but the translation is that found in Churchill's *Collection of Voyages and Travels,* volume I (London, 1704), 1–424.
41. Longobardo specifically mentions the 'Four Books of Confucius', but according to Legge's Character Index to the Four Books in vols 1 and 2 of his *Chinese Classics,* there are only five references to *Shang-ti* in the whole of the Four Books, none at all in the only work probably emanating from Confucius himself, the *Analects.* Longobardo is more likely thinking of Classics such as the *Shu Ching* and *Shih Ching.*
42. Navarrete, *Account,* 165 *cf Traite,* 89.

the works in Chinese emanating from the mission.[43] Then began a major investigation in which the members of the mission took sides,[44] Longobardo, Sebastiano de Ursis and Camillo Constanzo agreeing with the Jesuits of Japan while Diego de Pantoia and Alfonso Vagnoni replied on behalf of the majority position. A conference at Macao in 1621 reaffirmed Ricci's position but Longobardo continued to press his point of view in writings such as this *Reposta breve.*

Longobardo makes some curious admissions in the course of his exposition of the debate. He states that all of the Chinese Christians consulted, including Hsu Kuang-ch'i and Yang T'ing-yun, urged adherence to the text, and ignoring the commentators. Longobardo and de Ursis were dissatisfied with this since 'the learned Chinese Christians generally suit their sentiments to ours, and explicate their doctrines according as they think corresponds with our holy faith, without regarding of how great consequence it is to have the truth of these controversies brought to light'.[45] I think that this comment is particularly revealing since it indicates the acceptance by the Chinese Christians of Ricci's principle of interpreting favourably Confucian texts, and its rejection by Longobardo. He admits that there was no difficulty in practice over a 'correct' theological understanding of the terms in question, but gives primacy to an abstract 'truth' unrelated to usage and context. As Leibniz noted in his copy[46] this is to create an artificial difficulty where none really exists.

Longobardo's exposition of Confucianism which opens his treatise contains many inaccuracies and tendentious comments which I shall not pause to discuss here. Some of his assumptions are, however, relevant and important. He claims that all the commentators on the Confucian books for 1,600 years, from the burning of the books in the Ch'in period to the compilation of the Ming editions of the

43. Longobardo's account (*Traité,* 90) implies that this letter was received some time between the death of Ricci and his own transfer to Peking from Shao-chou that is late 1610 or early 1611. The objections from the Japanese mission may, then, be connected with Rodrigues's arrival in 1610, and he may have been commissioned to conduct an investigation by his colleagues in Japan. Longobardo describes Rodrigues's arrival as providential, in the sense that it revived a debate already decided against him.

44. For details of the line-up of Jesuits on either side and a sketch of the discussions held from 1611 to the 1630s see Dunne, *Generation of Giants,* 284–5.

45. Navarrete, *Account,* 166 *cf Traité,* 91.

46. *Traité,* 91, n 2.

classics, are in complete agreement, 'not unlike our holy doctors in the exposition of scripture'[47] a grossly misleading claim in the light of the sort of fundamental reassessment of the Confucian tradition which was occurring as he wrote.[48] He adds an argument which he attributes to João Rodrigues, to the effect that Fo Hi', the originator of all Chinese philosophy,[49] must be Zoroaster, Head of the Chaldean Magis, and founder of all the erroneous sects of the West. Hence, he says, we should expect to find in the ancient books of China all the errors which the devil used to mislead the 'Gentiles of the West'.[50] Even making due allowance for the fact that Longobardo was hard pressed and on the defensive, it is difficult to sympathise with his debating tactics and impossible to accept his methodological assumptions.

It is ironical but, I think, true, that Longobardo's arguments on close examination appear to err in favour of, rather than against, the Jesuit position on the rites question. He notes the presence of an abundance of spirits—spirits of heaven and earth, mountains, rivers etc. in the ancient texts. Instead of arguing, as he might plausibly have done, that this evidence of animism and polytheism makes conclusions about ancient Chinese monotheism embodied in the concepts of *t'ien* and *shang-ti* untenable or at least dubious, he instead proposes that these texts should be read in the light of the commentators who universally agree that *t'ien, shang-ti* and the human soul are all one 'celestial substance'.[51] Where passages in the texts appear to indicate otherwise, we must, in the end, follow the commentators, since the Chinese agree that the commentators are never contrary to the text. If the Chinese follow the commentators when the text is obscure, so much the more should foreigners.[52]

To the obvious objection proposed by Pantoia and Vagnoni that the text is always more important than the commentator, Longobardo

---

47. Navarrete, *Account,* 169 *cf Traits,* 96.
48. See especially the recent collections edited by WT de Bary.
49. This 'fact', which Ricci wisely never mentioned in any of his works, was to play a central role in much later debate, not only about Confucianism, but also about Chinese chronology. Longobardo is also the first, to my knowledge, to point out that the Chinese version of their history appears to place the founding of the Empire before the Deluge, hence is contrary to the Bible account which appears to make the Deluge universal (v *Traite,* 96).
50. *Traité,* 96.
51. *Traité,* 97.
52. *Traité,* 99.

replies that this is to regard the text as infallible,[53] an argument which Leibniz neatly turns on its head by asking whether Longobardo thought that scholastic theologians should take precedence over the Bible.[54] However, Longobardo's main contention was not a trivial one. He rightly points out that everything in Confucianism difficult to reconcile with Christianity cannot be attributed to Buddhist influence, and that, even if it could, it is not easy to persuade Chinese scholars that what they regard as Confucianism is not really so.[55] The great weakness of Ricci's position was its failure to come to grips, except negatively, with the real Confucianism of the commentators. 'To rely on the texts expounded completely at variance from the commentaries, is to build upon sand.'[56]

It would be tedious, and beyond the scope of this study, to undertake a detailed exegesis of the interpretation of Neo-Confucianism proposed by Longobardo in the course of his treatise. As we would expect from the methodological assumptions propounded at the beginning, Longobardo frequently argues anachronistically, conflating Han and Sung commentators, the classical philosophy of the hundred schools and their Ming interpreters.[57] There is also a constant constriction of Chinese material within the strait-jacket of European philosophical terminology, and the attempt to identify an ancient system of materialism, common to China and Greece, and derived from a common source in Zoroaster,[58] which justifies the interpretation of the one in terms of the other. All points in one direction, the conclusion that 'the Chinese' are materialists[59] that the apparent multiplicity of the Gods and spirits is an illusion[60] that they have no notion of an immortal soul[61] and that 'the most able of the Chinese *literati* are atheists'.[62] He dismisses Ricci's basic argument that the 'moderns' are atheists, but the 'ancient philosophers' were not, with a bald assertion:

---

53. *Traité,* 101
54. *Traité,* 99, n 17.
55. *Traité,* 101.
56. *Traité,* 102.
57. An extreme example of this is the attribution to Confucius himself of the Neo-Confucian *li-hsüeh* v *Traité,* 117.
58. See, for example, *Traité,* 113.
59. *Traité,* 116 (Section 10).
60. *Traité,* 117–33 (Sections 11–14).
61. *Traité,* 133–35 (Section 15).
62. The title of Section 16 of the *Traité,* 135–36.

> To prove that the ancients were atheists, it is enough to say the modern Chinese are so, because these are but the mere echo of the ancients, on whom they build, and whom they quote in their discourses, as well relating to sciences as virtues, but chiefly in matters of religion.[63]

The last section of Longobardo's *Reposta breve* consists of the opinions of 'several learned men of note', both non-Christian and Christian, on the subject under discussion. The non-Christians' objections to Christianity are substantially based on the standard 'school' Confucianism of the time, and may be easily related either to orthodox Neo-Confucianism *(Shang-ti = t'ai-chi; tien = Ii* etc)[64] or to late Ming syncretism (the Confucian *Shang-ti* = the Taoist *Yu Huamg* and the Buddhist *Fo).*[65] Most of the 'Christian *literati*' according to Longobardo, follow Ricci in his distinction between the modern atheists and the true doctrine of Confucius. Some, however, when caught unawares, made what Longobardo regarded as damaging admissions.

Considerable space is devoted to an interrogation of Yang T'ing-yün, most of whose answers are again the pure Ricci line. Yang appears to identify the Sung commentators with 'the meaning of the Ancients' but in a context that strongly suggests he is expounding their position rather than accepting it as his own.[66] Longobardo concludes his account of Yang T'ing-yün's views with an allusion to 'several treatises on various matters', including an explanation of the ten commandments,[67] composed by Yang and shown by him to the Jesuits of Peking. The views attributed to Yang are so far from those of any of his extant works—at least of those I have seen—-that I suspect serious misrepresentation. Yang is claimed by Longobardo to have advocated an absolute monism, which leads logically to atheism, in which 'all things are really one substance'[68] and to hold that the ancient sages of China were 'Spirits or angels Incarnate' (Longobardo reconciles the apparent contradiction by noting that— 'according to

63. Navarrete, *Account,* 196 *cf Traité,* 136.
64. *Traite,* 136–40.
65. *Traite,* 138–39.
66. *Traite,* 141.
67. This seems to be the *Hsi-hsüeh shih-chieh ch'u chieh hsu* referred to by D'Elia (*Fonti Ricciane,* II, 42, n 1).
68. *Traite,* 142.

the sentiments of the Chinese—they were all expressions of the one *Ii* or principle).[69] As for the three sects of China:

> He endeavours in this treatise to speak well of them all, shewing that all of them have the same end and design, which is to assign a principle to the universe; and that therefore they border upon our holy faith, and come to be the same thing with it in essentials. And if any man should object the many errors there are in the sects, all of them very opposite to our holy law: He answers, there were not at the beginning, when the sects flourished in their pure and true doctrine, but that they crept In afterwards by means of the comments made by disciples, who did not reach the design of ancient authors; therefore he often advised us in explicating things, to use a two-fold, or amphibological method, which may be easily apply[70] to either part of the controversy; and thus, he says, we may please, and so gain all.

This representation of Yang's views is quite incredible. All three extant religious works written by Yang T'ing-yun are in fact devoted to an attack on just this sort of syncretism. Two, 'The Owl and the Phoenix do not sing Together' *(Hsiao tuan pu ping-ming shuo),* and 'Explanation of the Differences between Christianity and Buddhism' *(T'ien shth rning-pien)* were probably published after Longobardo's *Reposta breve* was written. But the *Tai-i pien* which was published two years before, in 1621, is equally outspoken in its anti-Buddhist line. If Yang ever held the views attributed to him by Longobardo, it was at a period long before Longobardo wrote his treatise.

The most damaging evidence cited by Longobardo is a preface written for the same work by 'Ie Ko Lao', presumably the Yeh Hsiang-kao whose relations with Ricci and the other missionaries have already been mentioned. Longobardo claims that Yeh's preface defended the Incarnation of Jesus by arguing that *Shang-ti* had become man several times—as the sage kings Yao and Shun, as Confucius, and as several other famous individuals in Chinese tradition. Hence, it was not surprising to find him becoming man as Jesus, sage of the West.[71] Longobardo then attempts to associate Yang T'ing-yun with

69. *Traite,* 142.
70. Navarrete, *Account,* 199, *cf Traité,* 143.
71. *Traite,* 142.

these ideas by claiming that 'complete Christian, as he is, he is still full of this Chinese idea, or to speak more accurately, of this idea which resembles the confusion of Babylon.'" He does not point out that Yeh Hsiang-kao was not a Christian despite personal sympathy with the Jesuits; and what is more, according to Bartoli, the obstacle to his conversion was precisely that he could not believe that it was worthy of God to become man.[72]

Once more we are faced with a curious discrepancy between the evidence we have from other sources for the views of Yang T'ingyun and Yeh Hsiang-kao. The only way of reconciling them is to assume that both Yang and Yeh had briefly flirted with these ideas and later rejected them. Some weight is given to this argument if, as seems to be the case, this particular work of Yang's was never published. On the other hand, Longobardo is rather vague in the whole of this passage about the nature of the 'incarnations' that Yeh directly, and Yang indirectly, are supposed to have expounded. If it is simply the belief that 'sages' are mouthpieces of the divine, or that they have 'sparks of the divine', 'divine illumination', etc, one could find many parallels in the orthodox theological and mystical literature of the West. Without an examination of the text of Yang T'ing-yun's 'Preface to the First Explanation of the Western Ten Commandments', and Yeh Hsiang-kao's preface to this work, the question must be left unresolved. What is perfectly clear, however, is that Longobardo is not attacking Yang T'ing-yun's defence of the sacrifices 'to Heaven, to earth, to Doctors, and to the dead', but the alleged doctrinal base for these practices, the belief 'that all things are one and the same substance'.[73]

The last, and perhaps most important, piece of evidence cited by Longobardo in favour of his view, is the testimony of 'Doctor Paul', Hsü Kuang-ch'i. I give this passage in full since, if true, it would throw considerable doubt on much I have said about Hsü in the previous chapter, and undermine his credibility, if not as a sincere Christian, at least as a sincere advocate of Ricci's interpretation of Confucianism:

> I put the same question to Doctor Paul, who answered very ingeniously, that he was of opinion, the king of the upper region could not be our God, and he believ'd neither the antient nor modem Chinese had any knowledge of God. But

72. *Fonti Ricciane,* II, 43, n.
73. *Traité,* 143.

> since the fathers upon good motives call that king God, that the learned Chinese might make no objections, and because this epithet was decent, he judged it good and requisite to give him the attributes we give to God. As for the soul, he said, he fancied the Chinese had some knowledge of it, but imperfect.[74]

If these were truly the opinions of Hsü Kuang-chi, one must impute to him constant and deliberate prevarication in all his religious writings. These equate the Christian *tien-chu* with *shang-ti,* describe the Jesuits as followers of *Shang-ti* and preachers of the way of ancient China, and proclaim Christianity as complementing Confucianism.[75] I hesitate however to give much weight to Longobardo's evidence over against the testimony of Hsü's own writings and his reputation for integrity. Longobardo gives just one side of a conversation where it is particularly important to know precisely what was the question asked. Ricci himself would have agreed that *Slung-ti* was not unequivocally the Christian God, and that the Chinese notion of the soul was 'imperfect' in relation to his theology. But he insisted that there was a historical and textual basis for his interpretation of Confucianism, as well as pressing practical reasons for an identification with Confucians rather than their rivals. He did not believe, and it is hard to imagine that Hsü did either, that one could convince Confucian scholars of the truth of an interpretation which had no historical foundation and went against the textual evidence.

It is ironical that the one Chinese work of Longobardo's I have examined apparently involves its author in just the position he attributed to Hsü Kuang-ch'i. Longobardo argues in his *Reposta breve* that the Chinese had no notion of an immortal, immaterial soul, and one of the avowed purposes of the work is to attack the use of the Chinese term *ling-hun* as equivalent to 'soul' in Catholic theology. Yet his most important work in Chinese uses the term in its title, *Ling-hun tao-ti shuo,* 'On the Substance of the Soul', and throughout, in precisely the sense attacked in the treatise. The edition I have seen[76] is undated, but it clearly postdates the *Reposta breve*

74. Navarrete, *Account,* 200; *Traité,* 144.

75. See the section on Hsü Kuang-ch'i in chapter 3.

76. In ARSJ: JS /, *115.*

by at least several years.[77] It is possible that it was amended[78] by the addition of the commonly used term *ling-hun,* but this could hardly have been done without Longobardo's knowledge, and it would have required major rewriting since the whole work is built around the usual Jesuit method of starting with a commonly accepted notion and demonstrating that its true nature must be interpreted in a Christian sense. By far the most economic explanation is that Longobardo had changed his adherence to this central premise of his objections to Ricci's methods—that the Chinese have no notion of a spiritual or immaterial substance.

The letters from this period of the mission's history and compilations based on them, such as that of Bartoli, all indicate that Longobardo was an opponent of Ricci's methods, but on the question of terms only. The *Reposta breve* should be seen in its context, the intra-mural dispute over 'terms'.[78] It was circulated and exploited much later by Navarrete and others in the context of a wider and different debate, thus giving rise to the notion that Longobardo was totally opposed to the methods of his colleagues, and that his dissent had been silenced and his views suppressed by the other members of the mission. He was not, however, opposed to the practical position adopted by the mission on the Chinese rites in the broad sense; and even if his ideas had been accepted, they would have strengthened, rather than weakened, the case for the licitness of Confucian funeral, ancestor and civic rituals.

Longobardo's treatise did, however, raise some fundamental questions about Ricci's basic method, by reappraising Neo-Confucianism and its *de facto* dominance of Chinese philosophy. He did not, in fact, differ from Ricci on the nature of Neo-Confucianism, but rather on his assessment of primitive Confucianism, and on the

77. It was edited by Adam Schall and Giacomo Rho, the former of whom entered China in 1622 and the latter in 1624. They had been together briefly in Macao where they jointly directed the defence against a Dutch invading force in June 1622, but their Chinese studies can hardly have been sufficiently advanced at that time for them to undertake this task. They were together after 1630 in Peking where they collaborated on the reform of the Chinese calendar, and this joint work of editing Longobardo's treatise probably dates between 1630 and 1638 when Rho died (v Pfister, *Notices,* 162–82 and 188–90).

78. A note on the title-page names T'ang Jo-wang (Schall) and Lo Ya-k'o (Rho) as 'censors' and 'editors' but the latter phrase *(kung ting)* is ambiguous and could mean anything from seeing the work through the press to totally rewriting it.

viability of Ricci's distinction between this primitive Confucianism and that of the modern Confucians. The former was open to controversy; the latter a matter of experience and practice. What must have told most strongly against Longobardo's reiterated objections was the practical success of Ricci's method, together with the increasingly dangerous attacks on the 'unorthodoxy' of Christianity.

We do not know for certain whether Longobardo ever came to accept either the validity or the expediency of the mission practice in regard to the use of Chinese terminology. As late as 1633 he was still attacking the use of *shang-ti* and even arguing that instead of *t'ien-chu* Chinese Christians should pray to *tou-ssû,* or *Deus.*[79] The use of *t'ien-chu* and *ling-hun* in the *Ling-hun tao-t'i shuo* may indicate a change of heart before his death. More likely, he simply accepted that he had lost his case and ceased to object to what had become the agreed policy of the mission. It should be noted moreover that Longobardo's treatise, and those of other Jesuits for and against his position, were all private documents, circulated only within the mission or, in some cases, sent to the Jesuit authorities in Rome, but never intended for publication. It is doubtful, even, if many of the Chinese Christians came to know of them.[80] There is considerable difference between such a 'position paper' and a published treatise, and the excesses of Longobardo's arguments, as those of his opponents, should be viewed in this light. The *Reposta breve* may not be used as unequivocal evidence for Longobardo's attitude, even in 1623, let alone up till his death in 1654.

The main effect of Longobardo's reiterated attacks was a series of discussions and conferences which decided against his views and confirmed Ricci's policies. The most important of these were conferences called by the Visitor, Jeronomo Rodrigues at Macao in 1621 and at Kiating in December-January 1627–1628. I have found no detailed report of the 1621 Conference, but there are many extant documents dealing with the circumstances of the Kiating Conference and its aftermath. It was apparently convened by Rodrigues as one

79. See Dunne, *Generation of Giants,* 285. In the *Ling-hun tao t'i shuo, t'ien-chu* is used throughout, although the author notes that 'in the West *t'ien-chu* is called *tou-ssû*'. (la).

80. One Chinese supporter of Longobardo, however, was Pascoal Mendes (Ch'iu Liang-hou) a Macaist Jesuit brother who as late as 1630 wrote to the Jesuit General in condemnation of the use of Chinese terms for God, even *t'ien-chu* (Letter to Vitelleschi, Peking, 1 June 1630, ARSJ: *FG* 730, 8–11).

of his last acts as Visitor, in an attempt to prevent further damaging disputes on the question of terms. The Conference concentrated on the use of *shang-ti* and *t'ien* in the Chinese classics and Chinese philosophy, and quickly became a dispute between Longobardo and his followers on the one hand, and Alfonso Vagnoni and the other defenders of Ricci such as Nicholas Trigault on the other. The Vice-Provincial, Emmanuel Diaz Jr presided.

Longobardo's case was presumably still that advanced in his *Reposta breve.* Alfonso Vagnoni, for his part, defended Ricci's position. A document in the Jesuit Archives in Rome,[81] probably dating from this period, gives Vagnoni's exposition of the case for the use of terms such as *tien* and *shang-ti.* It is basically the position developed over thirty years before by Ricci—the distinction between the ancient and modern Confucians, the appeal to 'the better part of the *Literati*', and the argument from expediency. There are, however, a few new twists to the argument. One seems to me a very strong point, the example of the early Church taking over words for 'God', 'spirit' etc. from their contemporaries, and transforming rather than abolishing pagan festivals and customs.[82] Another feature of Vagnoni's argument, however, is more disturbing. Again and again he begins points with the assertion, 'It is certain that . . .' In this controversy, as in the Chinese Rites controversy later, there was a tendency to convert cautious generalisations about Chinese beliefs and practices into flat unqualified general statements. If it was indeed 'certain' that *Shang-ti* implied a creator God, exercising providence over all, rewarding and punishing, then presumably the controversy would never have arisen. Ricci's argument for the probability of a Christian interpretation of the ancient texts, has become an appeal to the certainty of such a reading of them.

The conclusions of the Conference after a month's deliberations were in favour of Vagnoni. *Shang-ti* and *t'ien* might be used, as in the past, as an equivalent for 'God'. However, since these terms, and *t'ien-chu* itself, might be misunderstood by the uninstructed, they should be used cautiously and explained fully.[83] Ricci had been vindicated. But Longobardo was still not satisfied, and when a new Visitor,

81. 'Breve Informacao sobre o nome Xam ti, e Tien em lugar di Deos p.^{e} os Sup.^{res}' in ARSJ: JS *161, 11,* 225–56.
82. Jap Sin *161, 11,* 225v-226r.
83. Dunyn-Szpot, 'Historia Sinarum Imperii, Jap Sin *102,* 226v.

Palmeiro, was appointed, he once more reopened the question. Palmeiro went on an extensive tour of the mission during 1628–1629, and his reports to the General at the end of the visit show him on the whole satisfied with the progress made.[84]

He admits to having been disturbed at the beginning about the comparative lack of progress of the mission—only 6,000 converts at the most—and about the time spent on cultivating the mandarins, the use of fine clothes etc. But he is now satisfied that they are necessary in the peculiar conditions of the mission.[85] As for the disputes between the missionaries, he finds that they have not caused disunion but it is important to resolve them. He then gives an account of the teaching of the 'letrados' which clearly derives from Longobardo,[86] stressing their atheism and their corruption by the pernicious doctrine of the 'pagodes' (Buddhist bonzes).

In the light of this judgement, it is not surprising to find Palmeiro leaving instructions to the mission prohibiting the terms *shang-ti* and *t'ien*. Once again, the argument resumed. Vagnoni appealed to Rome pointing out the scandal to the Christians which would result if they were told that *Shang-ti* was not really the Christian God, that all the books used on the mission were incorrect, and that the founders of the mission had preached a false god.[87] The General, and Palmeiro's successor as Visitor, Emanuel Diaz the Elder, reversed the decision, and reaffirmed the established practice of the mission.

From this time on, the Jesuits closed ranks on the question. On the 'terms' as on the larger issue of Chinese Rites, they maintained a common policy, which became all the more rigid as, in the early l630s, outside criticism began. There are hints in many of the letters of the period before 1630 that the members of the China mission already felt themselves under fire.[88] As Franciscan and Dominican

84. Four letters dated Macao, 20 December 1629, are in ARSJ: JS *161, II,* 109–17. There are in addition a full report of the Visitation (Jap Sin 161, II, 118–33) and a copy of the Instructions *(Ordinationes)* he drew up, dated 15 August 1629 (Jap Sin *100,* 20–39).
85. Jap Sin *161, II,* 109 r-v.
86. Jap Sin *161, II,* 113r
87. Letter of 18 December 1629 to the General, Vitelleschi, in ARSJ: JS *161, II,* ff 107–108. Manoel Dias Jr appears to has sided with Palmeiro (letter to Vitelleschi, 18 November 1629, ARSJ: FG 730, 8.5).
88. See, for example, Vagnoni's reference in the letter cited above (108v) to the calumniators of the mission in Cochinchina, Manila

missionaries from the Philippines arrived on the scene the 'partyline' became firmer, leading to exasperation on the part of their opponents and to lack of flexibility and candour on their part. In a sense they were victims of their own success because, as Vagnoni pointed out, once Christianity was preached in Confucian guise and language, it could not be changed without grave damage to the nascent Church. What had begun as tentative guidelines for the encounter with Chinese culture had hardened into dogmatic and immutable rules.

The arrival of the friars and the beginning of the debate over Chinese Rites

In all the documents I have seen dealing with the discussions in the period between Ricci's death and the arrival in China of members of other religious orders, I have found no suggestion of disagreement on the part of Jesuits of the China mission with Ricci's basic accommodation policy. Even Longobardo, who challenged the basis of accommodation with Confucianism, did not deny the necessity for some sort of engagement with Chinese ideas and Chinese values, and for a practical accommodation to Chinese society. Nor have I found any evidence of concern about the question of Chinese Rites in the strict sense. It was only with the arrival of Dominicans and Franciscans that the accommodation policy itself was called into question, and that controversy about the participation of Chinese Christians in traditional ceremonies arose.

The reasons—theological, cultural and political—that brought about the clash between the orders, are questions that lie quite outside the scope of this study. By concentrating on the Jesuits, and avoiding as far as possible detailed evaluation of the views of their opponents, I do not wish to imply that the Jesuits were necessarily right or that their opponents were less experienced or less knowledgeable. These are questions, important in themselves, that demand much fuller treatment. I feel that it is less unfair to the opponents of the Jesuits to prescind altogether, except where absolutely necessary, from their arguments, rather than to discuss them only as foils to the Jesuits. I plead simply that my theme is the *Jesuit* interpretation of Confucianism, and that the views of those outside the Society of Jesus are only relevant to that theme in so far as they precipitated modifications or changes in the Jesuit approach.

The history of the entry of other orders into China and of their activities is likewise beyond the bounds of this work. It should be noted, however, that it was their activities rather than their ideas which made most impact on the Jesuits in the beginning. The Rites Controversy, like the Jesuit interpretation of Confucianism, arose directly out of practical decisions taken in regard to missionary activity. The divergence of interpretations of that missionary experience was the beginning of the controversy.

The difference of approach between the orders is reflected in a series of letters and reports to Rome written between 1636 and 1640 by the Superior of the Jesuit mission in China, the Vice-Provincial, Francesco Furtado. The first of these is a letter dated 10 November 1636. Although it was later published as part of the Jesuit defence in the Rites case,[89] it was originally written for the eyes of the General alone and not as a public apologia. The picture it gives of Jesuit practices in regard to the rites, as well as of the reaction of the Jesuits and the Chinese Christians to the methods of the mendicant friars, is all the more valuable because of this, and because of its early date. In the letter[90] he describes the activities of 'the religious of St Dominic and St Francis' in Fukien since their arrival from Manila, their initial setbacks and their agreement in 1635 to follow the Jesuits' methods. Now complaints are being received from the Christians in Fukien—perhaps unfounded, notes Furtado—that the friars are claiming that the Jesuits from the time of Ricci on have deceived the Christians, and that they have been sent by God and the pope to undeceive them. Furtado then lists the questions raised by the mendicants the previous year in Foochow, and his replies, which he had thought satisfied their scruples.

The first of these deals with the problem of the application of church law to China. The Jesuits frankly admit to not having promulgated the positive law of the church which they regard as premature and they have done so with permission from the appropriate church authorities. Similarly in answer to the sixth and last complaint, they admit to making special provision for women, omitting the ceremony of anointing the body at baptism, and not insisting on the women coming to church. The friars apparently thought that canon

89. In *Informatio Antiquissima de praxi missionariorum Sinensium Societatis Jesu* (Paris, 1700).

90. I have consulted both the Portuguese original in ARSJ: JS *161, II,* 164–65, and the Latin translation in *Informatio Antiquissima,* 8–18.

law should be applied in all its rigour from the beginning and that no concessions should be made to Chinese *mores.* The fifth charge, that the Jesuits concealed the crucifixion, is one we have already examined. Furtado answers simply that the crucifix is not displayed in public, but that the crucifixion of Christ is constantly preached, written about, and included in the devotional practices of the church.[91] Once again, we see a clash over the importation of European customs directly into China. Dunne gives several more examples of the 'Europeanism' of the friars—horror at a portrait of Christ wearing shoes[92] and at the presence in the Jesuit chapel of a tablet in honour of the Emperor;[93] public display of the crucifix,[94] and public preaching without permission of the magistrates.[95] All these are understandable as initial reactions of men whose previous experience of 'the Indies' was in the Philippines or Mexico. And there is abundant evidence of the way many of them learnt from their experiences and adapted themselves to the peculiar conditions of the China mission. But there remained an irreducible residue of difference between the Jesuits and the friars on matters of principle that prevented harmony on the mission. Dunne may be right in attributing it to national rather than to theological differences or inter-order rivalry[96] but, whatever the cause, it persisted and even intensified with the passage of time.

Three of the six charges made by the mendicants relate directly to the question of rites—funeral ceremonies, ancestor rites and rituals in honour of Confucius—the earliest mention to my knowledge, and apparently dating from some two years after the landing of the friars who made them.[97] Furtado's reply to the charge that these

91. See Dunne, *Generation of Giants,* 275–80, for evidence of the Jesuit practice.
92. *Generation of Giants,* 248. I suspect that the psychological importance of the old argument between 'calced' and 'discalced' friars was involved here.
93. *Generation of Giants,* 248–49
94. *Generation of Giants,* 250, 252, 257.
95. *Generation of Giants,* 257–58
96. *Generation of Giants,* 236.
97. Furtado does not identify the friars in question but they were probably the Franciscans, Antonio de Santa Maria and Francisco de la Madre de Dios, and the Dominicans, Antonio de Morales and Francisco Dias. These four drew up in late 1635–early1636 two *Informaciones* which Dias and Santa Maria carried to Manila in February 1636. Morales and Santa Maria had landed in June 1633, and Dias and Francisco de la Madre de Dios in November 1634. (See Dunne, *Generation of Giants,* 238, 245, 246, 269).

ceremonies were superstitious is the standard one which goes back to Ricci and was to continue to be the Jesuit answer. Funeral rites are purely 'political', showing respect for the dead; the use of incense and prostrations before the corpse are not *per se* religious; in Europe special reverence is shown to the dead, even to a heretical king.[98] On ancestor rites, Furtado gives the earliest statement I know regarding the Jesuit practices. All those signs of respect commonly given to the living may also be given to the dead. Offerings of food are probably not superstitious, but Christians are encouraged to abandon the custom. Anything resembling a sacrifice is never permitted.[99] As for the rites to 'Cum cu' (Confucius), 'he was a wise and prudent man so full of the moral virtues that the Chinese honour him as a Saint, and so learned in his writings that all the Kingdom take him as their master . . . and so the Kings laid down certain rites to honour him as Master of the Kingdom'. But 'since they seem to contain an element of superstition, we only permit the Christians to make the same reverence to him that they make before the dead, that is, as we have said, the same that they make to the living; and to light candles with the intention of thanking him as a disciple to his master, without making any prayer of petition'.[100]

Much of the same ground is covered in two later documents emanating from Furtado, a report to Pope Urban VIII, dated 5 November 1639,[101] and a detailed reply to twelve charges made by JB de Morales OP, dated 8 February 1640.[102] Furtado protests at the imprudence and hasty judgments about Chinese practices of the

98. Jap Sin *161, II,* 164v and *Informatio Antiquissima,* 12–13. Furtado's reply suggests that one of the arguments used by the friars was that a dead pagan must be in hell, and the case of the heretical king was brought in to answer it.
99. Jap Sin *161, II,* 164v; *Informatio Antiquissima,* 14.
100. Jap Sin *161, II,* 165r; *Informatio Antiquissima,* 15–16.
101. 'Informacao p. a Sua Santidade do estado desta Missam da China', in ARSJ: JS *161, II,* 221–23; another copy is in Jap Sin *123,* 75–78, together with a Latin translation, ff 69–74.
102. I have not located the original of this document which is claimed, in the Preface to the *Informatio Antiquissima,* to be found in the Jesuit Archives in Rome. A Latin translation, entitled 'Responsio . . . ad duodecim quaestiones a PF Joanne Baptista de Morales Ordinis S. Dominici Manilensi, propositas Patribus Societatis Jesu laborantibus in praedicatione Sancti Evangelii in Imperio Sinarum anno 1640', is given in the *Informatio Antiquissima* (separately paginated 1–52).

friars. They claim that Confucius is in Hell because he died before the coming of Christ, and that honours paid to him are therefore blasphemous as well as superstitious. But there is no idolatry in the ceremonies and, apart from the rashness of openly preaching that Confucius is in Hell, it is not necessarily so, since the evidence of his good life suggests that he lived according to the law of nature.[103] They are unnecessarily aggressive, publicly confronting the mandarins and courting martyrdom.[104] Two Spanish friars[105] have even boasted that 'the Catholic King' could conquer China with 4000 men. Furtado concedes that this is just loose talk but it could easily ruin Christianity in China and cause distrust in Macao, on whose merchants the mission depends for support.[106]

In his *Reply* to Morales, Furtado outlines the Jesuit policy regarding another disputed ceremony, that to the City God *(ch'ěng-huang)*. This ceremony has never been permitted by the Fathers, and if any Christian mandarin takes part in it, it is against the instructions of the Jesuits and on the conscience of the mandarin. In fact, he says, it is not difficult to avoid it, and he quotes the cases of 'Doctor Michael' (Yang T'ing-yün) and 'the licentiate Ignatius', both of whom in time of drought refused to offer sacrifices to the City God and successfully prayed for rain to the Christian God. There is, however, a rather defensive tone to Furtado's remarks which suggests that some Christian magistrates did in fact take part in this ceremony, arguing, with Yang T'ing-yün, that the City God was simply the guardian spirit of the place and thus equivalent to a 'guardian angel'.[107]

In his ninth and tenth replies Furtado gives some illuminating details on the ceremonies for the dead and ancestors, and the Jesuit attitude to them. Not only the Chinese Christians but the Jesuits themselves customarily perform the *tiao* or ceremony of condolence. Literally, says Furtado, *tiao* means 'to inquire about a death'[108] and is simply a matter of good manners *(urbanitas)* and custom, instituted for the consolation of the living rather than for any alleged benefit to

103. Jap Sin *161, II, 222r cf Informatio Antiquissima,* Q 11, 34.
104. Jap Sin *161, II,* 223v-r.
105. Gaspar Alendra and Francisco de la Madre de Dios.
106. Jap Sin.161, II, 222v.
107. *Informatio Antiquissima,* 9–13.
108. 'De morte interrogare' or 'ven chun'. *Wen chung* is the definition of *tiao* given in the *Shuo-wen* dictionary.

the dead. The Chinese do not believe that the souls of their ancestors reside in the ancestral tablets 'like worms in the wood or birds perched upon them', There follows an interesting excursus on Chinese ideas about the soul in which he distinguishes between the 'atheists' who do not believe in survival after death; the 'Pagodes' who believe that souls transmigrate after death or go to some 'Indian Elysian fields in the homeland of Buddha'; and the 'Literati' who believe that souls are dissipated. In all three cases, they cannot be said to believe the souls are actually present, but rather that they are revered 'as if they were present'.[109] And he concludes:

> From all that has been said, it appears that it is not a sin to possess nor to permit the tablets. Nevertheless, we desire and endeavour to see that these and like customs are dropped, so that there may be made one beautiful church, without any defect at all.[110]

The logic of the conclusion might be questioned, but it represents a simple application of Ricci's policy of gradually replacing indigenous ceremonies of doubtful antecedents, with specifically Christian rituals.

Furtado concludes his 1640 *Reply* with a point that sums up neatly the Jesuit attitude to the evangelisation of China and their sixty years' experience of Chinese conditions. The friars say they want harmony on the mission. So, he says, do we. We want charity and cooperation. But when they say we 'should join together with them in creating a single body or army to attack idolatry in order to convert this country' we must reject it. Our whole experience teaches that such aggressive methods do not work.

The first published comment relating to the Rites Controversy that I know of is a brief reference to the experiences of the Dominicans in China in Diego Aduarte's *Historia de Ia Provincia del Santo Rosario de ía Orden de Predicadores,* published in Manila in 1640.[111] The charges

---

109. He cites the Confucian explanation that they are 'ju cai' *(ju tsai).* This is a reference to *Analects,* III. 12, 'He sacrificed (to the dead), as if they were present. He sacrificed to the spirits, as if the spirits were present' (Legge, *Chinese Classics,* I, 159).

110. *Informatio Antiquissima,* 'Reponsio . . .', 33.

111. I have not seen the original work, but an English translation was published by EH Blair and JA Robertson in *The Philippine Islands 1493–1803,* volumes 30–32. Unfortunately the sections on the Rites question (Liv II, chapters LIII and LIV) in volume 32, 246–48, are given in synopsis rather than in translation.

it makes appear to have been general, and to specifically exonerate the Jesuits themselves from complicity in the practices described. But the publication of this work, together with the circulation of the charges of Antonio de Santa Maria OFM and JB de Morales OP, drew forth a *Reply* from the Jesuit Visitor, Antonio Rubino SJ. His *Riposta as Calumnias que os Padres de S. Domingo e de S. Francisco impoem aos padres de Companhia de Jesus, que se occupão na conversacão do reino da China*[112] is dated 1641, but it was not published till 1665 in an Italian translation by Giovanni Filippo de Marini SJ.[113] It was condemned in 1678 by the Congregation of Propaganda Fide and placed on the Index of Forbidden Books by the Holy Office in 1680.

What is most significant about Rubino's treatise is the evidence it provides of the increasing remoteness of the controversy from Chinese reality. Rubino had little, if any, first-hand experience of China. His purpose in writing was purely apologetic—to defend the practices of the mission, then under attack, by as many arguments as he could muster. Theological propositions, casuistry, historical analogies, are all invoked in such abundance that the facts of the case are often obscured. In this respect, his *Reply* is typical and symptomatic of the whole of the subsequent discussion of the Rites question on both sides.

In comparison with Furtado's reports, Rubino seems often to concede too much; to argue that the Jesuits do not allow certain practices, but that even if they did, they would be legitimate. I suspect that Rubino's work was a source for many of the later charges against the Jesuits, and that his ingenious defence later rebounded against the people he was defending. It is interesting to note that the *Metodo della Dottrina* was not condemned on its appearance in 1665, but several years later, after the publication of Navarrete's *Tratados,* and at a time when Navarrete's attacks on the Jesuits were being widely canvassed.

It would be tedious, and not at all germane to our understanding of the Jesuit interpretation of Confucianism, to rehearse all of Rubino's arguments. One example will suffice, both to illustrate Rubino's method and to demonstrate its dangers to the Jesuits on the mission. We have seen that Furtado, after nearly twenty years on the mission, emphatically denied that the Jesuits permitted their converts to participate in ceremonies to the City God. Rubino, too, supports this:

112. A manuscript, possibly the original, of the *Riposta* is in ARSJ: JS *155,* and another in BVE: FG *1249,* n 4.

113. *Metodo della Dottrina che i Padri della Compagnia di Giesu insegnano a' Neofiti, nelle Missioni nella Cina.*

> The Fathers of the Company do not consent to, nor approve, that (Christian) mandarins adore, nor offer sacrifice to, the Idol *Cim Hoam.*[114]

Furtado implied that Christian magistrates, against the instructions of the Jesuits, sometimes attended the temple. Rubino goes further and defends, on theological grounds, their right to do so. However, he confuses the issue considerably by failing to distinguish between the original charge—that Christians offered the sacrifice, having first concealed a crucifix among the flowers or engraved on a candlestick[115]—and the legitimacy of a Christian magistrate praying in a pagan temple to the Christian God.[116] Aduarte's *Historia* had explicitly dissociated the Jesuits from the practices described.[117] Rubino now appeared to repudiate this. It is legitimate, he says, for Christians to adore the Holy Cross and the Lord of Heaven in the Temple of the City God[118] and it is no disrespect for a Christian to place a cross on a table in the temple, and pray before it[119] It is clear from the context that he is not referring to the association of this with the regular ceremonies to the *cheng-huang*; nor does he claim that this was in fact done by Chinese Christians, and certainly not with the permission of the Jesuits. But it was not at all difficult for ill-disposed readers to read this defence in principle of the licitness of praying before a crucifix in the temple of the City God, as an admission that it was the approved practice, and to associate it with the description given by the Dominicans and Franciscans of such a custom.

On most of the disputed issues, however, Rubino's position is the standard Jesuit one, going back to Ricci. On ceremonies in honour of Confucius, he cites Trigault and Furtado[120] to demonstrate that Confucius is honoured as 'a Master'. Some Chinese even regard him as 'a Saint', and since it is not an article of faith that he died a gentile, nor that he is in Hell, it is not unreasonable to regard him as a saint. 'It could be that many through ignorance regard Confucius as an

114. *Metodo,* 22. *Cim Hoam* is, of course, *Ch'eng huang,* the City God.
115. Blair and Robertson, *The Philippine Islands,* volume 32, 248; Rubino, *Metodo,* 21.
116. *Metodo,* 24.
117. Blair and Robertson, *The Philippine Islands,* volume 32, 248.
118. *Metodo,* 27.
119. *Metodo,* 29–30.
120. *Metodo,* 38.

Idol, but that doesn't greatly matter, because something good is not vitiated by the bad use it is put to, as the law says . . .'[121] Again, on rites for the ancestors, while some Chinese believe the souls of the dead reside in the tablets, the Christians do not, and simply adapt the rites for Christian use.[122] In all things, we should follow the practice of the Roman church of allowing customs that are not openly superstitious.[123]

Rubino's treatise may be regarded in many respects as the archetype of Jesuit Rites Controversy literature. It presupposes and defends the Jesuit interpretation of Confucianism, but its main concern seems to lie more with the defence of the Jesuits against their opponents than with the facts of the case. Increasingly, the question of Chinese Rites became subordinate to ecclesiastical and theological politics. Two general theological issues raised by Rubino were to play an important part in the later history of the controversy. One was the use of 'mental reservation' which Rubino discusses in relation to the question of swearing by idols. He argues that it is licit to swear apparently by an idol but actually by the Holy Cross; and that this opinion was supported by many Jesuit theologians and approved by Pope Clement VIII.[124] It was 'mental reservation' which first brought the Jansenists into the controversy. The other—much more pertinent—was the doctrine of 'probabilism'. Rubino saw that it was impossible to say with certainty that many Chinese customs were completely free from superstition. It was sufficient to show that they were probably so. This was, of course, the position that Ricci had adopted, but on grounds of common-sense rather than theological principle. Rubino erects it into a principle; moral certainty is not required, merely probability, and one may always follow 'the most common opinion'.[125] Much later discussion of the rites question got lost in a wilderness of argument about opinions that were 'probable', 'more probable' and 'common',[126] and the tendency of later Jesuit authors to claim that

121. *Metodo,* 50.
122. *Metodo,* 57–65.
123. *Metodo,* 66.
124. *Metodo,* 28.
125. *Metodo,* 77. One might add that, for Rubino, the very fact that the Jesuits held a certain position, seems to have sufficed for him to regard it as 'probable'. See his remarks in *Metodo,* 75–76.
126. See the *New Catholic Encyclopedia,* volume, 9, 1133, for a discussion of 'probabilism', 'probabiliorism' etc.

their interpretation of Chinese customs was 'certain' should be seen as a counter to those who would deny that probability was enough. In Rubino's treatise of 1641 the process of 'theologisation' of what was essentially a dispute over facts rather than doctrine, had already begun.

The concerns expressed in Rubino's treatise were in most respects ahead of their time. Neither the Rites Controversy, nor even the dispute over Chinese terminology, were of central importance to the mission in the last few decades of the Ming dynasty. There was first of all the problem of survival and extension of the mission. The adjustment to an increasingly turbulent and fragmented political situation, and, after 1644 to the new Manchu rulers, required delicate and sustained effort, Adam Schall survived the Manchu conquest of Peking to be appointed Director of the Astronomical Bureau by the Regent, Dorgon. In the provinces many of the Jesuits were caught up in the death-throes of the dynasty. In Szechwan Luigi Buglio and Gabriel de Magalhaes became prisoners first of the bandit general Chang Hsien-chung, then of the Manchu Prince Haoge. Others became associated with the Ming loyalists in the South; several leading Christians, and some of the Jesuits were attached to the court of the Ming Pretender, the Prince of Kuei, who was pronounced Emperor at Chao-ch'ing in 1646. Michael Boym SJ in late 1650 was entrusted by the Dowager Empress, Helena, who with the mother and wife of the Pretender had become Christians, with a letter to Pope Innocent X asking for support for the Ming cause. His mission was a political failure but proved a boon to the nascent European science of sinology through his writings.

Most of the members of the mission were engaged in the less spectacular work of extension of the mission along the lines we have already examined. Some were prolific writers in Chinese on religion, science and mathematics. Giulio Aleni, for example, produced at least twenty-four works in Chinese'[127] ranging from an illustrated life of Christ to a complete world geography. He wrote a Christian primer, or 'Four Character Classic'[128] in imitation of the standard 'Three Character Classic' *(San-tzû-ching)*. Where the latter has the story of Mencius and his mother, the former begins with the three

127. See Pfister, *Notices,* 131–35.

128. *T'ien-chusheng-chiao ssu-tzu ching-wen* (Peking, 1642).

Magi visiting King Herod. He wrote a treatise on the six liberal arts of the West,[129] and a Chinese-style dialogue on the nature of God.[130] In all these works he shows himself a faithful adherent to the Ricci method, presenting the Western missionaries as scholars, in both the Chinese and Western sciences; and Christianity and Western culture as equivalent to, yet intriguingly different from, Chinese values. Mathematics and astronomy, he insists, are not the main purpose of the mission, but the study of the Way *(tao)* and the ultimate things.[131] And the Western *tao* is not substantially different from that of China.

> What (asks his interlocutor in the *Hsi-fang ta-wen*) are the ceremonies in sacrificing to the ancestors in your country? Ceremonies for the ancestors are very important in my native country. As for slaughtering animals for sacrifices, that was done in ancient times only in God's honour. Since God's reincarnation amongst men in this world, the sacrifice of the mass has been established, and animal sacrifices are no longer used. Whoever reveres his ancestors, has masses said for them, praying God to protect their souls and grant them rest. This is of real benefit to the ancestors and increases their happiness in the other world. Their portraits are also painted and hung up in the house to serve as examples to their descendants, so that by looking at them they may be induced to imitate their ancestors' virtues. Sometimes food and drink are placed on the ancestors' graves; when the ceremony is over, the offerings are given to the church for distribution among the poor.[132]

In other words, as presented by Aleni, Christianity preserves all that is best in Confucianism, while adding a new dimension. As another work of the period, João Monteiro's *tien-hsüeh lüeh*-i[133] puts it, in terms that echo many of his predecessors:

> When (modem Confucians) condemn the Lord of Heaven, still more do they turn their backs on the injunctions of

129. *Hsi-hsüeh fan,* in *Tien-hsüeh ch'u-han,* I, 9–59.
130. *San-shan lun hsüeh-chi,* in *Tien-chu-chiao tung-ch'uan wen-hsien,* I, 419–93.
131. See JL Mish's translation of Aleni's *Hsi-fang ta-wen,* in *Monumenta Serica,* XXIII (1964): 70.
132. JL Mish's translation of Aleni's *Hsi-fang ta-wen,* 61–62.
133. 'A Short Sketch of Christian Doctrine', published in the *Tien-chu-chiao tung-ch'uan wen-hsien hsü-pien,* II, 839–904.

> Confucius and Mencius. If you ask whether Christianity is the same or different from Confucianism, 1 say, examine the preceding work and judge for yourself. Hsü Wenting (i.e. Hsü Kuang-ch'i) of Wu-sung says, 'Christianity supersedes Buddhism and complements Confucianism' and Prime Minister Ch'ien Sai-an of Wu-t'ang also says: 'By replacing what our Confucians have lost, Christianity is unique, and conserves and reforms the other sects.'[134]

Monteiro's work, written about 1640, indicates that at the very end of the Ming and despite the controversies of the preceding years, the Jesuit interpretation of Confucianism was still substantially that of Matteo Ricci.

Moreover, there were signs at last of the emergence of what Ricci had hoped for forty years previously, new distinctively Christian rites. Again, it is Monteiro who tells us in his *Annua* for 1641–1642[135] of an adaptation of the Feast of Lanterris by the Christians of Soochow who spent the whole night in prayers and devotions before a candle-lit altar of Our Lady. These were the rites that the Jesuits favoured, at once Chinese and Christian, and the product of Christian community life.

Legitimate prejudices?

The compilers of the aptly named *Legitimate Prejudices in Favour of the Decree of Our Holy Father Pope Alexander VII and the Practice of the Jesuits* cited at the beginning of this chapter, maintained that the question of rites was simply a question of fact: what do the Chinese really believe about the ceremonies to Confucius and their ancestors? In a sense, of course, they were right. Yet 'facts' do not exist in a vacuum, but in human minds where they are filtered, interpreted and assembled into mental constructs labelled 'Confucianism', 'Chinese Rites' etc. Perhaps, if the Chinese Rites controversy had been thrashed out in China where statement and counter-statement could be assessed against experience and actual observation, it might have been possible to resolve the question definitively, at least in the form of a working compromise or common policy, although the actual course

134. *Tien-chu-chiao tung-ch'uan wen-hsien hsü-pien,* II, 899–900.

135. 'Annua della Viceprovincia della Cina dell anno 1641 sino a Settembre del 1642 . . .', ms in ARSJ: JS *118,* 1–34.

of the debate even within China makes one hesitate to claim this. But, once Chinese Rites had been claimed to be a theological question and referred to the supreme arbiter of all theological questions within the Catholic Church, the See of Rome and the Congregations and Offices of the Papal Curia, it was inevitable that prejudices and facts should come into conflict.

To disentangle the prejudices from the facts involved in the series of decisions emanating from Rome over nearly a century—the earliest in 1645, the last in 1742—is a task I leave to some future historian. Let it suffice to say that the mid-seventeenth century decrees, those of 12 September 1645 in favour of the arguments of JB de Morales OP, and of 23 March 1656 in favour of the representations of Martino Martini SJ, procurator of the Jesuit mission of China, left the main questions undecided. Morales had claimed that the Jesuits were not observing church laws regarding the administration of the sacraments; were allowing the Chinese to loan money at usurious rates of interest; and, above all, were permitting ancestral rites, funeral rites, and ceremonies to Confucius and the City God, that were idolatrous and superstitious. The resolutions of the Congregation of Propaganda Fide, approved by Pope Innocent X, were generally in his favour, but qualified 'until His Holiness or the Holy See will provide otherwise'.[136] The Jesuits' counter-claim was presented to the Congregation of the Inquisition by Martini in 1654–1656, and Pope Alexander VII approved his interpretation of the rites as purely civil, this time with the qualification that the decree was 'according to the facts as presented above'.[137] In other words, on the central issue of the Chinese Rites, the church authorities in Rome took the very sensible position that Rome was too far away from China for a definitive judgement about the facts of the case, differently presented by the two parties, to be pronounced.

The Dominicans were not satisfied with this compromise and demanded an interpretation of the status of the two decrees. On 13 November 1669, the Roman Inquisition gave its decision, which was confirmed by Pope Clement IX on 20 November.

136. Rosso, *Apostolic Legations to China the Eighteenth Century* (S Pasadena: PD and I Perkins, 1948), 113.

137. Rosso, *Apostolic Legations to China the Eighteenth Century*, 119; Navarrete, *Account*, 340.

> The most eminent fathers declared, that the decree of the holy congregation *de propaganda fide,* passed the 12th of September 1645, according to what is there made out in the doubts, is in full force, and not in the least invalidated by the decree of the sacred congregation of the holy inquisition, passed the 23rd day of March 1656, but ought to be fully observed as it lies, according to the questions, circumstances, and all things mentioned in the said doubts.[138]

Navarrete, in reporting this decree, regards it as a decisive rebuff to the Jesuits who had claimed that the 1656 decision superseded that of 1645. In fact, it was obviously a continuation of the policy observed hitherto. 'The questions, circumstances, and all things mentioned' in the submissions of both Morales and Martini were questions of fact which could be determined only on the spot.

It was at this very time, 1669, that a thoroughgoing attempt was made to reach agreement amongst the missionaries in China itself. The occasion for the conference of missionaries that met in Canton at the end of 1667 was not a happy one. They were, in fact, forcibly gathered in Canton due to a violent wave of anti-Christian sentiment sparked off by one Yang Kuang-hsien. Yang had had a chequered political career[139] and in 1659 joined with some disgruntled Muslim astronomers who were jealous of the European astronomers in an attack on Christianity and Western astronomy and calendrical calculation. Till the death of the Shun-chih Emperor, who was closely attached to Adam Schall, these attacks proved fruitless. But after the accession of the infant K'ang-hsi Emperor in 1661, Yang found receptive ears at court, especially those of one at least of the Regents, and the Manchu President of the Board of Rites, Engedder. Yang's *Pu-te-I,*[140] 'I could not do otherwise', sent to the Board of Rites in September 1664, resulted in the arrest and imprisonment of Schall, Ferdinand Verbiest who was the assistant to the aging and ailing astronomer, Luigi Buglio and Gabriel de Magalhaes. Verbiest conducted a vigorous defence, and the Jesuits'

138. Navarrete, *Account,* 354.

139. For a biography of Yang Kuang-hsien, see Hummel, *Eminent Chinese,* 889–92; and (significantly coupled with Adam Schall and Ferdinand Verbiest) in the *Ch'ing shih kao, lieh chüan,* 59; see also JD Young, *Confucianism and Christianity,* chapter V, 77–85.

140. Reprinted in the *T'ien-chu-chiao tung-ch'uan wen-hsien hsü-pien,* III, 1069–1332.

astronomy was vindicated by a successful prediction of an eclipse which was miscalculated by the Muslims, but Schall and his Chinese collaborators were condemned to death. An earthquake, which was interpreted as an omen, saved Adam Schall and his Jesuit colleagues from execution, and they were allowed to remain in the capital; but all the other missionaries in China, apart from three Dominicans who went into hiding in Fukien, were banished to Canton and kept under house-arrest there. It was this unfortunate circumstance that brought together Jesuits, Dominicans and Franciscans in late 1667 to analyse their successes and mistakes and hammer out a common policy on mission practices and methods.

Although the motives behind Yang's attack seem to have been largely personal'[141] and its success due mainly to political factors,[142] the *Pu-te-i* also mounted a formidable attack on the Jesuit interpretation of Confucianism. Yang was particularly incensed at a work published in 1664 by the Christian official and student of Schall, Li Tsu-po, entitled *T'ien-hsüeh ch'uan-kai.*[143] Li's is the first Chinese work I know to attempt to link early Chinese history with biblical history, and his treatment of the relationship of the Old Testament to Chinese tradition anticipates by some forty years the theories of the Jesuit Figurists.

> The first Chinese (he writes) really descended from the men of Judea who had come to the East from the West, and the Teaching of Heaven is therefore what they recalled. When they produced and reared their children and grandchildren, they taught their households the traditions of the family, and this is the time when this teaching came to China.[144]

141. Dunne, *Generation of Giants,* 360, denies this, but all he succeeds in demonstrating is that his motive was not to succeed Schall in the Bureau of Astronomy. John D Young argues the case for orthodox Confucian motivation in 'An Early Confucian Attack on Christianity: Yang Kuang-hsien and his *Pu-te-I*', in *Journal of the Chinese University of Hong Kong,* III/1 (1975): 155–86, and his *Confucianism and Christianity.* It is, however, difficult to explain his vehemence and persistence without an element of personal animosity and the *Pu-te-i* is directed quite specifically against Li Tsu-po and Schall, with fatal results for the former and near-fatal for the latter.

142. See Hummel's biographies of Kang-hsi (Hsuan-yeh), and Oboi (*Eminent Chinese,* 328, 600).

143. 'Summary of the Propagation of the Teaching of Heaven'. See the text in the *T'ien-chu-chiao tung-ch'uan wen-hsien hsü-pien,* II, 1043–1068.

144. *T'ien-hsueh ch'uan-kai,* 1058.

It is difficult to establish whether this view of the origin of Chinese traditions was Li's own invention, or had become the common teaching of the Jesuits, but in many respects it was a logical consequence of current views on biblical chronology. If the biblical Deluge was universal as was commonly believed, the beginnings of Chinese civilisation must postdate the Deluge, and, if Chinese history was very ancient, it must date from close after the flood itself. Hence the founder of the Chinese Empire, usually taken to be Fu Hsi, must have been an immediate descendant of Noah.

Yang refutes Li Tsu-po by claiming that Fu Hsi was not the first Chinese Emperor, since the histories give a whole series of previous rulers including Pan Ku, the Three Emperors, and the Heavenly Emperor (*T'ien-huang*). In fact, he says, if we calculate the period from *T'ien-huang* to the third year of Ming T'ien-ch'i (1623 AD) we find that 19,379,460 years have elapsed.[145]

But Li Tsu-po, as we have seen, claimed more than that the Chinese people postdated the Deluge. What makes him a proto-Figurist is his claim that the Chinese classics embody the same primitive revelation as the Christian classics (i.e. the Bible). Yang trenchantly remarks:

> Formerly Li Ma-Iou used the Chinese sacred classics and commentaries of the sages as texts to adorn his heterodox teachings. Today [Li] Tsu-po cites the Chinese sacred classics and commentaries of the sages as passages from the scriptures of the heterodox teaching itself. Tsu-po's crime deserves the greater punishment.[146]

It is unlikely that Li Tsu-po would have presented these views to the public independently of the Jesuits. Yang Kuang-hsien, in his memorial to the Board of Rites, states that T'ang Jo-wang (Adam Schall) had inspired the work and Li Tsai-k'o (Luigi Buglio)[147] had asked Hsü Chih-chien to write the preface.[148] It has even been claimed that it was, in fact, written by Buglio and Magalhaes and simply put into good Chinese by Li.[149] But, whatever the true story of the authorship of the work, its reception by Yang Kuang-hsien

145. *Pu-te-i,* 1085. See also Fu Lo-shu, *Documentary Chronicle,* I, 35.
146. *Pu-te-i,* 1087.
147. Tsai-k'o was Buglio's *hao.* He was usually known as Li Lei-ssu.
148. Fu, *Documentary Chronicle,* I, 35.
149. Fu, *Documentary Chronicle,* II, 447, n 27.

apparently persuaded the Jesuits to avoid this line of argument in the future, at least in their Chinese books. Luigi Buglio in his reply to Yang, the *Pu-te-i-pien,*[150] conspicuously fails to take up this section of the argument of the *Pu-te-i.* In works intended for a European audience, however, the Jesuits frequently advanced arguments aimed at reconciling Chinese and biblical chronology. Even here, it was only slowly, and against considerable opposition, that the argument for vestiges of the primitive revelation in the Chinese classics began to appear. And perhaps the strongest of all the counter-arguments was the simple appeal to the effect of such a claim on Chinese scholars if they came to hear of it. It always remained much more an attempt to resolve essentially European problems—the difficulty of a revelation outside Christendom and the scandal of the antiquity of China—than part of a program of accommodation to Chinese culture.

Most of the *Pu-te-i* is devoted to what by now was the common currency of anti-Christian literature. The Jesuits have misinterpreted Confucianism by regarding *Shang-ti* as a personal God, rather than as identical with the Neo-Confucian *li.*[151] Their 'Lord of Heaven', Jesus, was a common criminal, 'a plotter against the state',[152] and his portrait, as given by Adam Schall in one of his works, is that of a man executed by crucifixion.[153] The Jesuits have misled the Chinese by compiling erroneous maps of the world.[154] The last half of the *Pu-te-i* is devoted to an attack on the Jesuits' astronomical calculations, an attack which was to prove Yang's undoing. He was forced to accept the post of Director of the Astronomical Bureau in place of Schall, and he and his assistants made so many errors in compiling the calendar that the Western method of calculation was restored, and Ferdinand Verbiest appointed Associate Director in April 1669. Yang died on his way into exile and Schall was posthumously[155] restored to his titles and ranks.[156]

150. *T'ien-chu-chiao tung-ch'uan wen-hsien,* 225–332.
151. The third and fourth essays, the *P'i-hsieh lun-shang* and *P'i-hsieh lun chung, Pu-te-i,* 1103–1120.
152. *Pu-te-i,* 1137.
153. *Pu-te-i,* 1129–1134.
154. *Pu-te-i,* 1129–1134.
155. He had died on 15 August 1666.
156. For a contemporary account of the vindication of the Jesuits see *Innocentia Victrix sive Sententia Comitiorum Imperii Sinici pro Innocentia Christianae Religionis late juridice per annum 1669,* Canton, 1671. Lawrence Kessler, *K'ang-hsi,* 61–64, demonstrates that political factors were more important than the Jesuit version suggests.

In the memorial condemning Yang Kuang-hsien, the Prince of K'ang (Giyesu) and the other officials suggested that Yang should be executed and his family banished. They add,

> Concerning their (the Westerners') worship of the Lord of Heaven, they only follow the old custom of their own country. So far they have demonstrated no trace of evil-doing. Therefore their old sentences must be removed.[157]

It is interesting to note that the Emperor,[158] while approving the main provisions of the memorial, did not follow the suggestion that the Western missionaries in exile in Canton should be summoned back to Peking.

> The twenty-five missionaries, including Li An-tang (Antonio de Santa Maria) and others, should not be summoned back to the capital. Only Nan Huai-jen (Verbiest) and the other (Europeans in the capital) may practice Catholicism as before, However, we fear that in the provinces (the Europeans) may again set up churches and convert people to their religion; therefore, we order that this practice be strictly prohibited.[159]

In fact, in the years that followed, the Jesuit and other missionaries did return to their churches in the provinces and the next serious persecution, in 1691, resulted in an edict of religious toleration.[160] But, in late 1669, the situation of Christianity in China must have looked decidedly grim.

Two years earlier, when the Canton Conference opened, the future must have seemed even more dubious. On 18 December 1667, twenty-three missionaries gathered in Canton to discuss a uniform policy for the whole of the China mission. Their submissions and decisions, as well as the subsequent correspondence with Rome, and the renewed controversy in Europe, cover a wide range of subjects. Some points dealing with administration of the sacraments of the church, liturgy and ecclesiastical discipline need not concern us. Others relate to the

---

157. Fu, Lo-shu, *Documentary Chronicle,* I, 45 (from the *Ta-ch'ing Sheng-tsu Jen Huang-ti Shih-lu,* chapter 31, 5a.)
158. After the imprisonment of Oboi in June 1669, K'ang-hsi reigned in fact as well as name. (v Hummel, *Eminent Chinese,* 328)
159. 159 Fu Lo-shu, *Documentary Chronicle,* I, 46.
160. See Fu Lo-shu, *Documentary Chronicle,* I, 104–106.

Rites controversy in the broadest sense— questions of ecclesiastical jurisdiction, canon law etc—which are better left for discussion in the next chapter. For the present, I shall confine myself to comments on the questions relating to Confucianism and the Jesuit interpretation of Confucianism.

The gathering at Canton in 1668–1669 was hardly representative of the whole mission in China, given the preponderance of Jesuits. But it must have been the first occasion in the history of the mission when a majority of the missionaries, even of the Jesuits, had been able to gather in one place. And the strongest critics of the Jesuits—Navarrete and Antonio de Santa Maria—were participants in the discussions. According to one of those present, Franeesco de Ferrariis SJ, the initiative for a formal conference came from the Dominicans.

> Given the opportunity, when we were all here, with time on our hands, and at the insistence of the Fathers, especially those of St Dominic, Father Provincial, with the consent of all our Fathers, resolved to hold a sort of Synod, in which we would discuss all together the matters in dispute between us and the other Religious, and strive for a uniformity necessary for the preaching of the Holy Gospel. Father Domingo Navarrete several times told me and others of our Fathers that he had orders to this effect from his superiors.[161]

It was; then, a perfect sounding board for all shades of opinion on the mission.

We do not have a full record of the discussions, but, as we shall see, the decisions, in 41 articles,[162] are recorded in a document entitled *Praxes quaedam discussae in pleno coetu 23 Patrum, quorum nomina in fine describuntur, statutae et directae ad servandum inter nos in Sinica Missione Uniformitatem* of which several copies are extant. It is dated 26 January 1668, presumably the terminal date of the Conference proper.

161. De Ferrariis to the Jesuit General, Oliva, Canton, 5 October 1668 (ARSJ: JS *162*, 210r).

162. There are two versions of this document, one in 41 points, and another revised version in 42 points, in which Nos 20 and 21 are expanded into Nos 20, 21 and 22. The sections changed are not substantial—they deal with the question of saying mass and attending mass with head uncovered—and were probably amended in response to the objections of the Visitor in Macao, Luis da Gama. The 41 point version seems to be that approved and signed by the assembly. I have used the copy in ARSJ: JS *162*, ff. 253–58.

The two items of greatest interest are those dealing with funerals, and rites for Confucius and the ancestors. On funerals, it is agreed that the greatest possible ceremony is to be observed, both the customary Christian funeral liturgy and those practices sanctioned by local custom. As for the latter, 'no certain law can be given; but it is left to the prudence (of the minister) taking into account the place, circumstances and people involved'.[163] On the other rites, the decree of 1656 is invoked:

> Regarding the ceremonies by which the Chinese honour their master Confucius, and the dead, the replies of the Holy Congregation of the Universal Inquisition approved by His Holiness Alexander VII in the year of Our Lord *1656*, are to be followed in all respects, since they are founded on a very probable opinion, to which no contrary evidence can be found. By invoking this probability, the door of salvation is not closed to the innumerable Chinese who would be excluded from the Christian religion if they were prohibited from doing these things which licitly and in good faith they can do, and which they could only with the greatest difficulty be persuaded to give up.[164]

The Jesuits, as we would expect, all agreed to these propositions. So, too, did the members of other orders, except for Navarrete and Antonio de Santa Maria. It is worth examining the responses of the non-Jesuits in order to uncover the grounds for their disagreement with the Jesuit view, as also the cases and reasons where they agreed with the majority view.

Domenico Sarpetri, a Dominican, adhered to the Jesuit view, as a series of letters and treatises, written at the same time, demonstrate.[165] According to a later Jesuit account[166] he had been specially deputed

163. ARSJ: JS *162*, 261 r (No 34).
164. ARSJ: JS *162*, 26lv (No 41).
165. They were reprinted later at the height of the Rites Controversy in the *Apologia pro Decreto S.D.N. Alexandri VII et praxi Jesuitarum circa Ceremonias, quibus Sinae Confucium et Progenitores mortuos colunt, ex Patrum Dominicanorum et Franciscanorum scriptis concinnata*, Louvain, 1700; and in a xylographed work produced in Peking in 1704, reproduced in facsimile in CR Boxer, *A Proposito dum Livrinho Xilografico dos Jesuitas da Pequim (Seculo XVIII)* (Macao, 1947). For other printed versions, see the Bibliography.
166. *Apologia pro Decreto*, Praefatio.

by the Dominican Provincial of the Philippines to study the rites question, and in a document dated 9 May 1667, that is before the Canton Conference, he gave his wholehearted approval to Ricci's *T'ien-chu shih-i.*[167] It is not surprising, then, to find him approving the decisions of the Canton Conference which follow logically from Ricci's basic interpretation of Confucianism. He followed up his signature to the Conference decrees with a document[168] in which he attested that after eight years of study of the rites, he was convinced that the Jesuit practice was 'not only safe . . . but also if we examine the principles of the chief sects (of China) more probable than the opposite opinion, and very useful, not to say necessary, for opening the door of the Gospel to the local people'. Confucius did not adore any God 'except the living Heaven, whatever that may be'.[169] In a letter to the Congregation of Propaganda, he attacks Antonio de Santa Maria for reviving the old argument about the rites and terms, but interestingly on Longobardo's old grounds that the Chinese are materialists and, therefore, incapable of adoring Confucius and their ancestors.[170]

Finally, in a long *Treatise,*[171] dated 30 September 1670, he defends his position with a series of arguments that show a keen and discriminating mind. He points out that the 'sacrifices' in the Chinese classics, especially in the *Shu Ching,* are offered to such a wide variety of beings and on such a variety of occasions, that it is ridiculous to lump them together. The crucial point is not the form of the ritual, but its object: *Shang-ti,* the inferior spirits, or the ancestors? As offered to Confucius and the ancestors, in a special context, they are not a religious cult.[172] On the other hand, the sacrifices described in the *Li Chi* as offered to *Shang-ti* and to 'certain spirits *(genii)* and kings whom the Chinese once regarded as saints', are, of course, religious.[173]

---

167. *Apologia pro Decreto,* 1–2. Dr Cummins implies in his discussion of Sarpetri that his adherence to the Jesuit position was unexpected and probably influenced by his uncle, the Jesuit Brancati. *(Travels and Controversies,* II, 415) This document indicates that his 'conversion' was not so sudden.
168. Dated Canton, 4 August 1668, and printed in *Apologia pro Decreto,* 3–7.
169. *Apologia pro Decreto,* 4.
170. *Apologia pro Decreto,* 12–19 (letter dated 12 November 1668).
171. *Apologia pro Decreto,* 21–68.
172. *Apologia pro Decreto,* 29.
173. *Apologia pro Decreto,* 51.

He does not dogmatically hold the distinction between the two kinds of rites as absolute. Some Chinese do seek favours from the dead, just as some Jews adored false gods, some Englishmen are not heretics, and some Christians are superstitious.[174] Commentators differ on the significance of these ceremonies, and the Chinese themselves give different interpretations on them. The point is whether a favourable face can be put on them, and a probable opinion arrived at.[175]

From this sensible and soundly based argument, showing a discrimination and common sense all too *often* absent in the Apologias of the Jesuits and their opponents, we may turn to the objections of Antonio de Santa Maria OFM. I shall not attempt here to deal adequately with this active missionary and prolific writer.[176] It is to some extent misleading to deal with a few of his ideas in isolation from his whole career and experience. But even the most superficial examination of his writings reveals a basic orientation diverging from that of the Jesuits; and his opposition to the Canton program is both predictable and symptomatic.

Antonio's specific objections to the decrees were directed to Articles 6, 20, 22 and 41. Article 6 dealt with the problem of 'fasters', that is Chinese who had taken a vow to observe Buddhists fasts. Antonio was totally opposed to allowing such people who became Christians to continue their fasts, and in this he was supported by some of the Jesuits.[177] He was opposed, too, to any accommodation with Chinese practice by covering the head at mass. His arguments on this subject, were supported by the Jesuit Visitor in Macao, Luis da Gama,[178] and he may have been right in claiming that the Jesuits had

174. *Apologia pro Decreto,* 49–50, 52.

175. *Apologia pro Decreto,* 52–55.

176. See the bibliography in *Sinica Franciscana,* II, 332–344.

177. De Ferrariis in his letter to the General of 6 November 1668 (ARSJ: JS *162,* 213–4) notes that Fathers Valat and Greslon had written a treatise against the practice and that the assembly finally decided to allow it only 'in certain extraordinary circumstances where there will be no scandal and it is otherwise agreed that there is a right intention in fasting'. (213r)

178. See the letter of Francois de Rougemont SJ to the Jesuit General, Oliva, dated Canton, 18 December 1668 (ARSJ: JS *162,* 249–250). De Rougemont wrote that da Gama 'wanted to lay down the law in an arbitrary manner on matters of which he had neither experience nor knowledge'; and he adds, scornfully, that 'the Father Visitor did not even hesitate to say that to pray to God with head covered was neither Catholic nor religious' (249v)

different practices in different parts of the mission.[179] But his reasons were supported by a most revealing appeal to 'experience'. The Jesuits tell us, he says, that we must always pay attention to Chinese sensibilities. On the contrary, as we have shown by promulgating and implementing the positive law of the Church in China, it does no harm to insist on conformity to European customs. Experience has shown that since we published it in 1633, Christianity has greatly grown and augmented, flourishing intensively and extensively, much more than before, and this has been my whole experience from the year 1633 to the present day.[180] This is a very strange argument indeed to advance in 1668, with Christianity proscribed, the missionaries under house-arrest or in hiding, and the very fate of the Church in China in the balance.

It was, however, consistent with Antonio de Santa Maria's attitude since he first entered China. His initial experience, 1633–1636, had ended with his trip to Manila to present the Manila theologians and the superiors of his order with his *Informaciones* against the Jesuit practices. He does not seem to have been motivated by jealousy or inter-order rivalry. And his experience on his return to China in 1649 brought him into close and friendly contact with the Jesuits. He wrote to his Provincial on 6 December 1655 that he could not have survived in Tsinan, his mission in Shantung Province, without financial help from Schall and Francesco de Ferariis.[181] But these close relations did not prevent him from taking a strong stand against the Jesuit methods. A brief account of the history of the China mission which he wrote in 1662[182] is full of a spirit of opposition to Chinese customs and beliefs. The Chinese, he says, have the 'gigantic presumption' to

179. This was his argument in a letter to the Jesuit General, Oliva, dated from Canton, 14 November 1668 (ARSJ: JS *162,* 232r-v). On the other hand, Francesco de Ferrariis in a letter written a few days earlier, 8 November 1668, claims that all the older fathers he had consulted— with the exception of Schall who was unable to speak after his stroke— agreed that the ancient practice of the mission was to cover the head at mass (ARSJ: JS *162,* 227–79).

180. ARSJ: JS *162,* 232r.

181. *Sinica Franciscana,* II, 433.

182. *Brevis Relatio de Ingressu Societatis Jesu Aliorumque Religiosorum in Sinicam Missionem ac de aliquibus vestigiis nostrae Sanctae Fidei antiquis, quae inventa fuerunt in Sinis,* edited after the ms in ARSJ: JS *112,* 1–12, by A Väth SJ, 'P.F. Antonio Caballero de Santa Maria über die Mission der Jesuiten und anderer Orden in China', in *Archivum Historicum Societatis Jesu,* I (1932): 291–302.

regard their sciences and 'their (so absurd) philosophy' as the only ones in the world.[183] And the Jesuits have supported them in their prejudices.

> So, the Fathers of the Society have gone to great pains to hide their errors under the cloak and guise of words with a heavenly tinge, whereas in reality beneath is concealed the pallor of hell.[184]

On the other hand, the Dominicans have remained true to their vocation.

> The Fathers and the sons of the Holy Order of Preachers, kindling with their speech a torch with which they turn the shadows of the world into light by burning heretics and extirpating heresies, have always had a great affection for the conversion of the gentiles.[185]

Antonio de Santa Maria, then takes the part of the Dominicans in their quarrel with the Jesuits over accommodation to Chinese customs. In a long treatise addressed to the Jesuit Visitor, Luis da Gama, he protested against the Jesuit interpretation of Confucianism and of Confucian ceremonies.[186] The Jesuits draw a distinction between Confucius and 'the two other idols' of China, Fo (Buddha) and the Old Man (Lao-tzu). But in reality, they are all adored as gods, and in the end are all demons.[187] The Confucian *miao* is a 'temple' not a 'hall', and the ceremonies performed there true sacrifices.

All this is supported by a wealth of descriptive detail, but the centrepiece of the argument is linguistic. Invoking a naive, but not

183. Väth, 'P.F. Antonio Caballero de Santa Maria über die Mission der Jesuiten und anderer Orden in China', 294, 295.
184. Väth, 'P.F. Antonio Caballero de Santa Maria über die Mission der Jesuiten und anderer Orden in China', 295.
185. Väth, 'P.F. Antonio Caballero de Santa Maria über die Mission der Jesuiten und anderer Orden in China', 297.
186. The original treatise, *Tratado sobre algunos punctos tocantes a esta mission de la gran China* is, according to A. van den Wyngaert, *Sinica Franciscana,* II, 343, in the archives of the Congregation de Propaganda Fide, Rome, *Scritture originali,* 1677. I have used the French translation published in 1701 in the *Anciens Traitez de Divers Auteurs sur les Cérémonies de la Chine.*
187. *Traité, 5.*

un-Chinese theory of language, he argues that all ceremonies which share the same name are essentially the same, hence the Confucian ceremonies are 'sacrifices' in the same way as the Buddhist and Taoist rites.[188] The Jesuits claim that Confucius is not 'invoked', that no prayers are directed to him. But is it possible that young Chinese can be taught such reverence for the Master and his words without acquiring 'a desire and a habit of invoking Confucius'?[189]

This is not the place to examine in detail the ceremonies discussed by Antonio de Santa Maria. One may readily concede that they were ambiguous in nature, that there were regional and local variations, and that the standard Jesuit exposition of them suppressed many overt 'religious' features in order to emphasise their civil character. One must also add, however, that it seems to have been Jesuit practice to prohibit Christians attending the solemn twice-yearly ceremonies to Confucius because of the superstitious concomitants and 'religious' honours described by the Franciscan. What is most significant, to my mind, in Antonio's treatment of the rites question, is the basic attitude to Chinese culture that underlies his arguments. Where the Jesuits looked for points of resemblance, for continuities and analogies, in order to build on them a Chinese Christian theology, he regards them as *prima facie* evidence of religious rivalry and a threat to the uniqueness of Christianity.

> Their veneration for this Philosopher goes so far, that they are accustomed to say to us missionaries, that Confucius and his teaching greatly resembles Jesus Christ and his morality; the latter dogmatises in Europe, as the former does in China; that the two legislators and their laws are the same, or at least similar. You can judge from that what ideas not only the pagan Chinese but also the Neophytes attach to this cult, and to these sacrifices, under the name of respect and civility. I have heard with my own ears what I have told you. What, then, will the future hold, if we tolerate and authorise this cult, as a simple sign of some vague sort of affection or recognition?[190]

188. *Traité*, 9–10.
189. *Traité*, 13.
190. *Traité*, 15.

Even in his description of the rites, moreover, Antonio de Santa Maria is guilty of question-begging. This is particularly the case in his treatment of 'the solemn cult of the ancestors'. He claims to have observed this in detail in Fukien together with Juan-Baptista de Morales OP, 'and having seen it in one place, is to have seen it everywhere in China'.[191] What he presents, however, is not a neutral description of what he observed. In the beginning he commits just the error he castigates in the Jesuit accounts by translating *t'ang* as 'the *chapel* of the ancestors'.[192] The participants are 'three Ministers, or, as we would say, a Priest, Deacon and Sub-deacon', together with 'acolytes'.[193] The hymns they offer are prayers to the ancestors, the rewards they expect come from their ancestors.[194]

A similar persistently Western interpretation pervades his description of domestic ancestor ceremonies[195] and funeral rites. The Chinese make offerings before the corpse, which is clearly superstitious. Admittedly in Spain and Portugal offerings are made at funerals; these, however, 'are addressed directly to God for the salvation of their soul . . . but this cannot occur in the case of Gentiles for whom Christianity does not permit either prayers or offerings'.[196] In other words, the question of facts takes second place to dogmatic theological judgements.

Apart from his 'Europeanising' bias, Antonio de Santa Maria's *Treatise* reveals a persistent misunderstanding of the Jesuit interpretation of Confucianism. He accepts, for example, Longobardo's strictures on the use of terms such as *shang-ti,* but he misunderstands Longobardo's evidence and his conclusions. Longobardo has, he says, demonstrated that Chinese philosophers are materialists and reduce

191. *Traité,* 33. The reason he advances for this highly dubious assertion is that 'the same Ritual is observed throughout the Kingdom'—by analogy, no doubt, with the *Rituale Romanum.* Two pages further on he undercuts this whole argument by criticising those who presided at the ceremony he observed for departing from the Ritual *(Traite,* 35, on the offering of wine).

192. *Traité,* 33. Its normal translation is 'hall', 'reception room', 'meeting-place', 'court of justice' (*Matthews' Chinese English Dictionary,* No 6107; and FS Couvreur, *Dictionnaire Classique de la Langue Chinoise,* 3 ème edition (Ho Kien Fou, 1911), 786.

193. *Traité,* 35.

194. *Traité,* 35–36.

195. *Traité,* 37–38.

196. *Traité,* 45–46.

everything to *Li* or 'invisible matter',[197] a curious term indeed, and certainly not Longobardo's. The Chinese, then, sacrifice to and adore this *li* whom all believe 'conducts and governs all and responds to their appeals'.[198] Antonio does not seem to have thought this a strange activity for atheists.

Again, a lot of his difficulty over the Jesuit policy appears to stem from a naive correspondence theory of language. The Jesuit approach to the terms question, from Ricci on, had been to employ *t'ien-chu* as a name for 'God' and to use *shang-ti* for apologetic purposes, equating this conception of early Confucianism with a developed Christian concept, and selecting passages from the classics that appeared to confirm their reading. For Antonio de Santa Maria, terms and their corresponding referrents had an invariable relationship. Unless one was absolutely certain that *Shang-ti* was the Christian God, the term must be avoided for fear of 'preaching the creature in place of the Creator'.[199] Ironically, one of his own works in Chinese, the *T'ien Ju yin*[200] of 1664, was later condemned for its use of *t'ien* and *shang-ti.*[201] It seems that Antonio's practice was not altogether consistent with his theory and that the exigenciesof his pastoral work had led him to an approach that, on later reflection, he disavowed.

It should be noted that although the *T'ien Ju yin* cites many passages from the Four Books, they are used in a different way from their common use in the Jesuits' works in Chinese. Instead of commenting on the usual Jesuit proof-passages, Santa Maria argues from the moral teachings of Confucians to the necessity of a *tien-chu* for their full implementation. In other words, he is not interested

197. *Traité,* 62–63.
198. *Traité,* 77.
199. *Traité,* 101–102.
200. Published in *Tien-chu-chiao tung-ch'uan wen-hsien hsü-pien,* II, 981–1042. An analysis of this work is given by David Mungello in 'Sinological Torque', in *Philosophy East and West,* 28/2 (1978): 123–41.
201. See Carlo Castorano OFM, 'Parva Elucubratio super quosdam Libros Sinenses', Rome, 1739 (ms in B Vat: *Borg Lai 530*), 2–3. Castorano condemns the work, but not its author, a fellow Franciscan, to whom he attributes 'a good intention'. He does, however, praise another work of Antonio's, the *Cheng-hsüeh liu-shih,* for its 'religiously motivated attacks on the Chinese *literati* and the Fathers of the Society of Jesus'. Castorano's annotated copy of the latter, now in the Vatican Library (Borgia Cinese 247.3), is reproduced in *T'ien-chu-chiao tung-ch'uan wen-hsien san-pien* (Taipei, 1972), 1, 89–266.

in Confucianism as such, but in demonstrating the superiority of Christianity. This, he avows in his *Treatise*, is what he sees to be the role of Christian missions.

> What does it matter to our mission whether the ancient Chinese knew God, or didn't know him; whether they named him in one way, or in another? The question is completely indifferent. We have come here to announce the Holy Gospel, and not to be apostles of Confucius.[202]

Such was clearly his honest conviction. Christianity, he says in the conclusion to the work, must be preached in its (Western) purity, without concessions. The grosser superstitions of Confucians—and amongst them he numbers 'the cult of Confucius and the ancestors—must be totally opposed and others allowed to die out gradually. And, again, he points to the great flowering of Christianity he had observed since the promulgation of Church Law in 1662. Admittedly a secret judgement of God had led to apparent disaster in the few years since then but it should be clear to all that only the purity of the gospel will prevail. One must admire the indomitable spirit of the old man even if one does not share his principles.

I must admit to feelings far from admiration for the other chief opponent of the Canton decisions, Domingo Navarrete. Despite the eulogies of the editor of the recent edition of his *Travels*,[203] and in contrast to what I have said about Antonio de Santa Maria, I cannot

---

202. *Traité*, 104.

203. JS Cummins editor, *The Travels and Controversies of Friar Domingo Navarrete*, 1618–1686 (Cambridge [Hakluyt Society, 2nd s, Nos CXVIII and CXIX] 1962). Most of the Introduction (volume I) and the Appendices (volume II) are devoted to an elaborate defence of Navarrete against his detractors. Much of it is, I think, justified, but the comments on 'The Controversy over the Chinese Rites' (Introduction, chapter II) are often misplaced. His description of Neo-Confucianism as 'looking-glass language lifted into the sphere of metaphysics' (lxv) and his agreement with Navarrete's views that 'their philosophy [was] mostly rhetoric and *belles-lettres*' (lxvi) is a travesty that no sinologist would accept. His linking of the Jesuit converts with the *San chiao* movement is belied by all the extant Chinese Christian works, and Cummins dismisses Verbiest's objections with the remark that 'he could not have denied the Chinese tendency to syncretism' (lxix). What was at issue was whether any Chinese *Christian* had, in writing, argued for syncretism. Cummins has, I think, been misled by Navarrete, whose cumulation of argument has, at times, an almost hypnotic effect.

regard his role in the Rites controversy as merely that of an honest attempt to right what he saw as evils. The best proof of this would be an impartial examination of the full texts of his *Tratados historicos, politicos, ethicos y religiosos de la monarchia de China* published in Madrid in 1676, and the rare suppressed *Controversias antiguas y modernas de la Mission de la gran China,* partly printed in Madrid in 1679 and partly in manuscript. I shall not examine the latter[204] in detail and to discuss adequately even the *Tratados* demands much more space than I have at my disposal. Once more, I have compromised by isolating a few issues, those relating to Confucianism and the Jesuit policies in regard to it, as presented in the *Tratados,*[205] and attempting to analyse the grounds for his opposition to the Jesuit line. I will not discuss the vexed question of whether or not, and for what reasons, he may eventually have signed the Canton 'concords', nor whether he was justified in secretly leaving Canton for Europe. I will, however, give some reasons for casting doubts on his objectivity and credibility.

What is in question here is not Navarrete's character so much as his accuracy and reliability in describing the facts of Chinese beliefs and customs; not his personal integrity nor his theology, but his sinology. Unfortunately none of Navarrete's Chinese works have survived, so it is impossible to assess his proficiency in Chinese. However, he spent only eleven years in China, six of these in confinement, and our knowledge of the length of time it took the Jesuits to master the language suggests that his Chinese could not have been very good. This did not, however, inhibit him from making such sweeping statements as:

> It is most certain that nation has not attained to the knowledge of any other God or nobler object, than the material heavens. What others have writ, though some persist obstinately in it to this day, is not so much as probable.[206]

---

204. I have used the copy (minus conclusions) in the Jesuit Archives (ARSJ: FG *728* n 1) and there are numerous extracts in two works by CR Boxer, his *A proposito dum Livrinho Xilografico,* and his 'Portuguese and Spanish Rivalry in the Far East during the 17th Century', in *Journal of the Royal Asiatic Society* (1946): 150–64, and (1947): 91–105.
205. To be precise, in the English translation, *An Account of China,* and, for Book VI, Cummins' edition.
206. *Account,* 20 (Book I, chapter IX).

No attempt is made to demonstrate this, and similar assertions, from Chinese sources, apart from a general appeal to 'the masters and teachers of their sciences (who) understand their own books incomparably better than we do'.[207]

It is clear that in general he is following Longobardo's interpretation of Confucianism. He includes the whole of Longobardo's *Treatise* in Book V of the *Tratados* and cites him frequently. In this way, Confucius becomes 'an absolute atheist'[208] who, very curiously, is 'worshipped' by his 'down-right atheist' followers.[209] This apparent contradiction is carried over into his discussion of Chinese Rites. They are superstitious and idolatrous, even though those who perform them are atheists. When considering the question of whether the Chinese, 'being as they are really atheists, and having no knowledge of God, angels, rational soul, reward or punishment in the life to come, are capable of oaths or the like', he decides that they are, on the grounds that they 'sacrifice, pray to and beg of heaven, the sun, moon etc.', that they 'honour, reverence, and fear them' and hence may take an oath by them.[210]

Despite the muddle-headedness of this argument, which is due to some extent to an attempt to mate Longobardo's materialist interpretation of Neo-Confucianism with the logically contrary interpretation of Chinese rites as idolatrous and superstitious, it would be possible to regard Navarrete's opinions as honest but confused. What inclines me to reject this, in favour of the stronger judgement that a good deal of sheer malice entered into his presentation of China, is my examination of the last part of his *Tratados.* In this section Navarrete lists the *Doubts* that he presented to the Roman Inquisition in 1674, together with the replies. A sample of these will, I believe, indicate the extent to which prejudice has overtaken facts.

Among his twenty-five doubts about Chinese mandarins, he argues that since 'the Chinese unanimously agree that the Tartar now reigning is a tyrant', no Christian official or soldier may serve him[211] (a principle which apart from its very dubious basis in fact, could be applied with equal force to almost any monarchy of Europe). The

207. *Account,* 85 (Book II, chapter XIII).
208. *Account,* 113 (Book III, chapter I).
209. *Account,* and *Account,* 74 (Book II, chapter IX).
210. *Account,* 201–2 (Book V, Prelude 17).
211. *Account,* 355 (Book VII, Doubt No 4).

Inquisition, I am happy to note, rejected this argument; but they did, according to Navarrete, agree that no Christian might lawfully accept the office of mandarin,[212] presumably in the light of his presentation of the ceremonies that would be incumbent upon him.[213] To his displeasure, they refused absolutely to prohibit Christians from holding the position of 'masters in public schools, who are vulgarly called HIO KUON',[214] on the grounds that it was not clear whether the ceremonies to Confucius were 'political' or 'religious'[215] and on similar grounds, refused to give judgement on funeral rites.[216] To his twenty-second Doubt, the Inquisition replied that Christians were obliged publicly to pull down any official notices which 'defame our faith'.[217] It does not require much imagination, nor much knowledge of Chinese political institutions, to envisage the fate of a Chinese Christian Church re-organised on the model proposed to the Inquisition by Navarrete. It would be drawn entirely from the non-official class, politically suspect, unprotected and alien, a European transplant with absolutely no future.

On the 'Worship given to Confucius',[218] Navarrete is evasive. Clearly the Congregation did not give him the answers he expected; as he notes in one place, 'I could have wished the answer had been plainer, and suitable to the reasons I proposed for making the doubt'.[219] But he must have been fully satisfied with their last reply under this head:

> 21. The missioners of the society have an order for their mission, which expressly forbids them by any means to affirm, that our holy law agrees with the sect of Confucians in the whole, or in any part: the holy congregation may, if it pleases, order the same upon this point. For such an order is very material for the honour of the evangelical law.

---

212. *Account*, 357 (Doubt No 12).
213. *Account*, 356–57 (Doubts Nos 6–9, as well as his explanation of No 12).
214. HIO KUON is presumably *hsüeh-kuan*, the Director of Schools at the *hsien* or district level (v. S Couvreur, *Dictionnaire Classique de la Langue Chinoise*, 218).
215. *Account*, 357 (Doubt No 13).
216. *Account*, 358–59 (Doubt No 20).
217. *Account*, 359.
218. *Account*, 360–63.
219. *Account*, 362 (Doubt No 12).

> Answer to the 21. All missioners are obliged to say the same concerning the law of Confucius, that was prescribed by the Jesuits, as is instanced by the holy congregation.[220]

Leaving aside the facts that there is no evidence of such a decision anywhere else than in the pages of Navarrete, and that it is contradicted by nearly every Jesuit work in Chinese that has survived, it is difficult to read this answer, as Navarrete does, as evidence that it was the Inquisition itself which had issued it in the first place. It is also at variance with the other decisions in this section which seem to indicate a desire on the part of the Congregation, as in the 1669 decisions, to keep the options open.

A similar caution is shown in the replies to Navarrete's 'Twenty-five Doubts concerning the Worship the Chinese give to their dead'.[221] The Congregation is prepared to assert theological propositions about the salvation of Gentiles[222] and to support tautologous propositions which assume the idolatrous or superstitious nature of the custom.[223] But when he confronted them at the end with the demand that they revoke the 1656 decree, the Congregation evaded the issue:

> I desired a fuller answer, but it was not given me; they are governed at Rome by more elevated causes, and I do not question but they are just and righteous, though neither I nor some others comprehend them.[224]

Nothing daunted, he goes on to beg the question by arguing that the Pope and the Congregations can do no wrong, and that therefore his opponents must have misunderstood the decree of 1656.

> As for Confucius's ceremonies, some are of opinion they are good, politically; others, that they are bad. These last said, the holy congregation did not approve of them, because an approbation must be a good thing; but that it tolerated them though bad, as the civil government tolerates lewd women.[225]

220. *Account,* 362
221. *Account,* 365–70
222. *Account,* 369 (Doubt No 21).
223. For example, Nos II (on ancestor rites), No 14 (on ancestor tablets), and No 16 (on sacrifices to the spirits of the place).
224. *Account,* 371.
225. *Account,* 371.

From this point on, Navarrete's tone becomes even more heated. The Jesuits 'think to govern the world'.[226] They should be condemned for building sumptuous churches, wearing costly apparel, giving presents etc.[227] Christian merchants may in no circumstances carry arms, and may not teach 'infidels' the arts of war.[228] And suddenly, in mid-flight, come the signatures of the consultors of the Inquisition, followed by a note from Navarrete to the effect that he stopped presenting his doubts at this point 'because I would not be too troublesome to those most reverend fathers, and because I was myself indisposed'.[229]

A complete disentangling of fact from prejudice in the writings of Domingo Navarrete would be a near-impossible task. A very high proportion of the *Tratados* is devoted to hearsay—what Father X said to him on such and such an occasion. Perhaps, as Verbiest suggests, the over-serious Navarrete failed to appreciate a joke at times.[230] One, at least, of the persons quoted in the *Tratados* was later to indignantly deny that he made the statements attributed to him—indeed to deny that he was in Macao at the time the conversation was alleged to have taken place there.[231] This too may be explained away on grounds of haste in writing and faulty recollection. I am prepared, also, to make allowance for his European prejudices,[232] his irritating text-chopping,[233] and his tendentious translations.[234] But, the overall impression made by his *Account* is that of an anti-Jesuit tirade in which every possible argument is marshalled to smite the enemy with little regard for logic, consistency, or above all, for Chinese reality. On some issues, the Jesuits, too, were guilty of highly selective use

226. *Account*, 371.
227. *Account*, 374.
228. *Account*, 326, 377.
229. *Account*, 377.
230. *Correspondence*, 316.
231. Dom Vasco Barbosa de Mello in his *Exemplar Attestationis*, dated 16 December 1680, in Boxer, *A Proposito dum Livrinho Xilogrdfico*, 12a–14a; translated in Boxer, 'Portuguese Spanish Rivalry . . .', 102–104.
232. See, for example, his dismissal of Chinese painting in *Account*, 53 (Book II, chapter I) as 'very mean'.
233. For example, He quotes St Anthony as an authority on Chinese moral philosophy (*Account*, 111, Book III, chapter I).
234. Compare, for example, his summary of Yang Kuang-hsien's *Pu-te-i*, in *Account*, 253–56 (Book VI, chapter XV) with the original text in the *T'ien-chu-chiao tung-ch'uan wen-hsien hsü-pien*, III, 1069–1332.

of Chinese evidence, and part of Navarrete's annoyance no doubt sprang from his realisation that the facts were more complex than they admitted. 'There are some', he wrote in the *Controversias,* 'who are so taken up with excusing the Literary Sect of China of idolatry, that they seem to me to prefer losing their lives to changing their opinions . . . I say that the Chinese from the beginning have held to idolatry and in their deceit, have conserved it to the present day'.[235] Neither attitude was a promising basis for a real and lasting religious encounter. It would be absurd to demand of a seventeenth century missionary the objectivity and outlook expected of a twentieth century sinologist, but one can surely demand a respect for facts and the avoidance of purely polemical positions. Whatever his later relations with the Jesuits[236] or his personal motives, Navarrete was largely responsible for the increasingly bitter tone of the controversy and the shifting of the grounds of debate from questions of Chinese fact to wider grounds of theology and ecclesiastical polity.[237]

Lull in the storm

While the departure of Navarrete for Rome after the Canton Conference transferred the focus of the Rites controversy to Europe, in China a period of peace and expansion once more ensued. A number of documents from this period suggest that the Canton agreement was generally observed, and that a series of practical rules were promulgated for the mission, embodying safeguards against superstition and misinterpretation.

A Chinese work entitled, 'Regulations for the Holy Church' *(Shêng-chiao kuei-ch'eng),* dating probably from this period,[238] gives detailed instructions on many aspects of religious observance.

235. Quoted in Boxer, *A Proposito dum Livrinho Xilogrdfico,* 14.

236. See Cummins' Introduction to the *Travels and Controversies,* lxxviti–lxxxiii, on Navarrete's good relations with the Jesuits of San Domingo when he became Archbishop of the island diocese.

237. One is tempted to regard Navarrete's meeting in Madagascar with François Pallu, the newly appointed Vicar Apostolic of Tonking, as a handing over of the mantle of chief scourge of the Jesuits of China. See Cummins' Appendix II, 'Navarrete and Pallu', *Travels and Controversies,* II, 425–432.

238. It was edited and translated into French by H Verhaeren CM, in *Monumenta Serica,* IV (1939–40): 451–57, under the title of 'Ordonnances de la Sainte Eglise', after the original manuscript in the Pei-t'ang Library, Peking.

These regulations show the development of specifically Christian customs on a traditional base. The Buddhist *Fo-kan* or niche for the Buddha image is to be replaced in each home by a *mu-k'an*, or wooden shrine for the image of Christ.[239] Ancestor tablets may be retained but the reference to the 'spirit' *(shén* or *ling)* of the deceased should be avoided.[240] Funeral ceremonies for parents should follow 'the ancient ceremonies' with the exception of burning paper money and goods and the participation of Buddhist or Taoist priests.[241] All should attend church on feast-days, but men and women should attend separately?[242] Non-Christians should be persuaded to become Christians by good example and prudent instruction, but there is no need to publicly flaunt one's faith.[243] It is better to proceed cautiously, talking to people about 'the great Father and Mother' *(ta fu-mu)* of all things, and proceeding to explain the nature of God, of the soul, of heaven and hell, than to begin by attacking the gods and Buddhas.[244]

The forty-fifth, and last, regulation is a kind of encapsulation of the developed Jesuit interpretation of Chinese tradition, and is worth quoting in full.

> To instruct the ignorant and to form the younger generation according to the way of the sages is the greatest of virtuous tasks. Before the Three Dynasties, men acted in accordance with the teachings of their nature and their true natures prevailed. But since the burning of the books in the Chin dynasty, Buddhism and Taoism have wrongly been admitted, Neo-Confucianisrn *(Ii hsüeh)* has confused matters, and since people cannot purify the source, and are further confused by talk of 'principle' *(Ii)*, 'matter' *(chi)* and 'nature (*hsing*), the tradition has been corrupted. Orthodox and enlightened scholars must make clear distinctions in order to disabuse later generations. If they help Christian youth understand the natural law, they will not only be rewarded by God, but will have done a great service to the morals or our time.[245]

239. 'Ordonnances', No 1, 453.
240. 'Ordonnance', No XXVII, 460.
241. 'Ordonnances', No XXVIII, 461.
242. 'Ordonnances', Nos II and XXXIII, 454, 463.
243. For example, the name of Jesus should be honoured within the family, but there is no need to post it up on the doorposts (No IX, 455).
244. 'Ordonnances', No XVI, 457.
245. Translated from the text on page 476 of the 'Ordonnances', with reference to Verhaeren's translation on 466–77.

The *Regulations for the Holy Church* might be taken as marking a high-point of the Jesuit interpretation of Confucianism, a blueprint for a truly Chinese Christian church. It is difficult to determine to what extent it remained a Jesuit blueprint, and to what extent its approach was accepted by members of other orders. There is evidence that other Dominicans besides Sarpetri supported the general position of the Jesuits. Juan de Paz OP, an eminent Dominican theologian, lecturer in theology and later chancellor of the University of Santo Tomé in Manila, wrote in 1679 a reply to some queries from Dominican missionaries in China on the rites question. His position is substantially that of the *Regulations;* and the *preguntos* or questions he is replying to, are clearly based on current Jesuit practice, perhaps on the *Regulations* themselves. Ancestor tablets, amended to avoid any implication that the souls of the dead actually reside there, are permissible. The replies of the Inquisition to Polanco and Navarrete were based on the assumption that the Chinese really believe the souls are present. If this is not so, as the 'better informed *literati*' are alleged to hold, then they are licit.[246] Similarly, candles and incense may be used before the tablets, although Christians should not associate themselves with those who may be guilty of superstition in this regard.[247] De Paz is less liberal in regard to offering of food and drink to the dead. Although Alexander VII allowed it, 'provided there is no superstition involved', it seems impossible to avoid all danger of idolatry and the replies of the Inquisition to Navarrete are to be followed in this matter.[248] On the ceremonies for Confucius, however, de Paz again adopts the Jesuit position. The solemn rites are to be avoided by Christians because of the superstitious concomitants and the sacrificial ritual, but genuflections, candles and other signs of respect for Confucius as a master' are certainly licit.[249]

In the last section of his *Treatise,* in which he replies to some difficulties proposed by Andreas Lopez OP, Juan de Paz makes two points which appear perfectly obvious to the outsider, but were commonly confused by disputants in the Rites controversy. It is very strange that 'the infidel *literati* of China', whom all missionaries assert to be atheists, should be accused of offering 'divine' honours and

246. ARSJ: JS *163,* 78r *(Pregunto)* and 79r-v (de Paz's reply).
247. ARSJ: JS *163,* 78v and 80r–81r.
248. ARSJ: JS *163,* 78r-v and 79v-80v.
249. ARSJ: JS *163,* 78r-v and 79v-80v.

genuine sacrifices to him. If he is really regarded as a god, why have the missionaries been allowed freely to deny his divinity for a century? It is also strange that it is commonly the newly arrived missionaries who question 'the ancient Fathers' of the mission. They may not always be right and where conscience demands, or a clear evil exists, their practices should be challenged, but there is a presumption in their favour.[250] If these sound methodological principles had been observed by all the missionaries of China, there might have been no Rites Controversy.

The most prominent Dominican to support, in general terms, the Jesuit position on Chinese Rites, was the Chinese friar, later Bishop, Gregory Lopez (Lo Wen-tsao). My knowledge of Lo's views is derived solely from a number of letters and excerpts from his works published by the Jesuits in 1700.[251] They may be unrepresentative[252] and were certainly carefully selected as part of the defence of the Jesuit position in the Rites Controversy, but they indicate clearly that, on some key issues at least, the only native Christian prelate of the seventeenth and eighteenth centuries agreed with the Jesuit interpretation.

The earliest of these letters recount Lo's conflict with members of his own order over the rites issues.[253] When the Bishop-elect visited Manila in 1684, he found the Dominican Provincial, Antonio Calderon, so opposed to his 'Jesuit opinions' that, as he wrote to Pope Innocent XI, 'he virtually put me in confinement in one of the convents of my order', and threatened to deprive him of the habit and recall all Dominicans from China.[254] Another letter, to the Cardinals of Propaganda,[255] recounts his trials at the hands both of the Portuguese of Macao, who were opposed to his consecration which they held to be in breach of the Portuguese *padroado,* and of

250. ARSJ: JS *163,* 82–87.

251. In the *Apologia pro Decreto S.D.N. Alexandri VII. . .,* Louvain, *1700; and Anciens Mémoires de la Chine touchant les honneurs que les Chinois rendent à Confucius et aux morts* (Paris, 1700). I refer throughout to the text in the *Apologia.* For cross-references to other editions, see the Bibliography.

252. They are, however, the only works of Gregory Lo included in the standard Dominican bibliography, *Scriptores Ordinis Praedicatorum,* edited by J Quétif and J Echard, II, 709.

253. Letter to Philippe Couplet SJ, 10 November 1682 and to the Dominican Master General (undated), *Apologia,* 1–6.

254. Letter from Manila, 10 June 1684, in *Apologia,* 7–8.

255. Manila, 'III Idus Junii', 1684, *Apologia,* 9–16.

his fellow Dominicans in the Philippines. Although the latter claimed to be objecting to his acceptance of the episcopacy without consulting them, the real difficulty was that

> I am inclined to the Fathers of the Society of Jesus in China, and agree with certain opinions and judgements of these Fathers regarding the controversies about the cults, the behaviour, the religion and the idolatry, of the Sects of the *Literati*.[256]

In the end, he writes, he was forced to place himself under the protection of the Spanish authorities who found him a place in the convent of the Augustinians.

I do not presume, without examining the Dominican records of the period, to make any but a tentative judgement on the truth of these charges. I see no reason, however, to question Lo's account. He was quite familiar with the Spanish language and with Manila, having studied and worked there for several years, so there is no reason to suspect mutual misunderstanding.[257] His consecration as Bishop was certainly delayed till 1685, when he returned to Canton, despite the patents he had received from Rome in late 1683[258] appointing him Bishop of Basilea and Vicar-Apostolic of Nanking. By 1684, Navarrete's *Tratados,* and probably the contents at least of his *Controversias,* must have been widely known in Manila. Although Navarrete took credit for Lo's appointment,[259] Lo's views, it now appeared, were diametrically opposed to his; and it is not surprising that the Dominicans of the Province of the Holy Rosary should fear that his appointment would prove ammunition for their opponents. The later use made of Lo's letters proves that their fears were well placed.

The fullest statement of Lo's views in the documents I have consulted is a treatise, dated 18 August 1686, from which the Jesuit editor has selected five propositions for comment. Even if they are taken out of context, they seem to establish beyond question Gregory

256. *Apologia,* 12.
257. See the brief note in Pfister, *Notices,* 361–2; and AC Moule, 'Gregory Lopez, Bishop', in *New China Review,* I (1919): 481–82.
258. 16 December 1683. See *Apologia,* 9. Latourette *A History of Christian Mission in China,* 123, discusses the details of the delays over the consecration.
259. *Travels and Controversies,* II, 371.

Lo's adherence to the central thesis of the Jesuits regarding the rites, their essentially civil and social character. With abundant citations from the classics, the Confucian Four Books and such works as the *Chia Li* of Chu Hsi, Lo attempts to establish that the term 'ci' *(chi)* does not necessarily mean 'sacrifice', that a *miao* is not always a 'temple', that 'xing' *(shêng)* refers to the wisdom, not the sanctity, of the person thus labelled. The customary offerings to Confucius and the dead are also made to the living who are highly respected; and the dead are not prayed to in the hope of receiving favours.[260] This is a reading of Chinese practices by the most eminent Chinese Christian of his day, in precisely the same terms as Ricci a century before.

There are indications that Gregory Lo's views were not completely in accord with those of all the Jesuits. A letter of the Jesuit Francesco Saverio Filipucci, dated 20 February 1686,[261] complains of a recent instruction of the Bishop of Basilea on the amendment of the inscriptions on the ancestor tablets. Lo appears to want to prohibit the use of the expressions *shêng chu* and *ling wei* which do not mean 'seat of the soul' but respectively 'he, in whose honour or on whose behalf the dead are recalled' and 'the epitaph, memorial, representation, or substitute for the dead'[262] However, Filipucci's reading of these characters is rather eccentric and, as we have seen, Article 27 of the *Regulations for the Holy Church* had earlier prohibited such inscriptions on prudential grounds. On this head, it seems to be Lo rather than Filipucci who was presenting the agreed view on the tablets.

The position taken up by Gregory Lo raises once more the question of fact or prejudice as the determining element in the Rites Controversy. There is a very revealing passage in the standard bibliography of Dominican writers, published in 1721, which draws a distinction between Lo's expertise in Chinese affairs and in theology.

> As to his contention in his letter to the Master of the Order that as a Chinaman he knew more about the language and rites of the Chinese than his Brothers could do; even if it is allowed it proves nothing. For he ought at the same time to have shown that he was more skilled than they were in Holy

260. *Apologia,* 17–35.
261. ARSJ: JS *163,* 325–28, to Alessandro Ciceri SJ.
262. ARSJ: JS *163,* 326r.

> Scripture, tradition, the Canons, history, sacred and profane, and theology, and one who after a comparison of all the points involved would be able to see and decide more easily than the others what should be tolerated and what forbidden. But that assuredly no one thought of him, so that at best he could claim to describe the Chinese rites, and so too his little effusion was regarded as of small weight.[263]

This seems to me to be a perfect example of pre-judgment and a closed mind. The Jesuit interpretation of Chinese Rites involved prejudice, too, to some extent, in the sense of a bias towards the legitimacy of the practices. But at least the Jesuits regarded the question of fact as central. To dismiss it as irrelevant, as proving nothing, is to claim that European theologians should pronounce *a priori* on Chinese realities. The Rites Controversy was the triumph, in principle, of prejudice over facts.

Confucius Sinarum Philosophus

Despite the publication of Navarrete's work and the controversy it aroused, the 1670s and 1680s were marked, for the China mission, by consolidation and expansion.[264] The uneasy compromise of the 1669 decrees of the Inquisition and the *de facto* partition of the mission, with the different orders working according to their own methods in separate areas, prevented the rites question from becoming explosive. When Prospero Intorcetta reported to the Congregation de Propaganda Fide in 1672, he presented a picture of a flourishing church recovering from persecution.[265]

---

263. Quetif and Echard, *Scriptores Ordinis Praedicatorum,* II, 709, translated by AC Moule in *New China Review,* I (1919): 486.
264. A manuscript catalogue of 1663, signed by the Visitor, Luis da Gama, gives a total of 110,000 Christians, and 34 churches (see Havret, *La Stele Chrétienne de Si-Ngan-Fou,* II, 99–100, n 1. By the 1690s, according to Le Comte, there were close to 300,000 (*Nouveaux Mémoires,* II, 181).
265. *Compendiosa Narratione dello stato della missione Cinese cominciando dell'anno 1581 fino al 1669,* Rome, 1672. See also Philippe Couplet, *Relatio de statu et qualitate missionis Sinicae post reditum Patrum e Cantoniensi exilio sub annum 1671* in the Bollandists' *Propylaeum ad Acta Sanctorum* Maii, Antwerp, 1685, 126 ff.

Intorcetta was sent to Rome in 1668 as Procurator for the Vice-Province of China, hut his concern was not, as in the case of Martini before him, with the Chinese Rites issue, but rather with domestic affairs of the mission. One of the by-products of his trip was the publication of his translation of the *Doctrine of the Mean* which was partly printed in Canton in 1667 and augmented in Goa in 1669. This work, the *Sinarum Scientia Politico-Moralis,* was not widely circulated,[266] but it received some notice in Europe through its republication in Thévenot's *Relations de divers Voyages curieux*[267] thus becoming the first translation of a Chinese work to appear in Europe.

It was not, however, the first translation of a Confucian work to be published in a Western language. This honour belongs to an earlier translation by Intorcetta and Ignacio da Costa, the *Sapientia Sinica,* published in Chien-ch'ang in Kiangsi, in 1662, which included parts of the *Analects* of Confucius and the *Great Learning.* These in turn were probably based in part on the manuscript translation by Ricci and Trigault which had circulated in the mission and been used in the language training of newly arrived missionaries.

The most important and most influential of the translations of the seventeenth century was undoubtedly the *Confucius Sinarum Philosophus* published in Paris in 1687. This, like Intorcetta's earlier translation, was a product both of the Canton Conference which brought together the collaborators and of a visit to Europe. It was published, and probably edited by Phillipe Couplet, who was elected as Procurator of the mission in 1679 and left Macao for Europe in late 1681. It incorporated, in revised form, the two earlier published translations, thus presenting three of the Four Books to the European learned world. The fourth, the *Mencius,* did not appear in translation till 1711 in François Noël's *Sinensis Imperii Libri Classici Sex.*[268] However, perhaps because it appeared in Prague rather than in Paris,

266. On the rarity of this work, and of the earlier *Sapientia Sinica,* see CR Boxer, 'Some Sino-European Xylographic Works 1622–1718', in *Journal of the Royal Asiatic Society* (1947): 199, 200, 202; and H Cordier, *Essai d'une Bibliographic des ouvrages publics en Chine par les Europeens au XVIIe et au XVIIIe siecles,* (Paris, 1883): 13–16.

267. Part 4 (Paris, 1676).

268. The six works translated by Noel were the Four Books *(Analects, Doctrine of the Mean, Great Learning* and *Mencius),* the *Hsiao Ching* ('Classic of Filial Piety') and the *Hsiao hsueh,* a kind of primer.

the intellectual capital of the world of the time, Noël's work never supplanted the *Confucius Sinarum Philosophus.* For over a century, when European scholars and publicists referred to Confucius, as they frequently did, they were referring to 'Confucius, the Philosopher of China' as presented in this work or in one of its many translations.[269]

As far as the Jesuit interpretation of Confucianism to Europe goes, then, the *Confucius Sinarum Philosophus* is the key work. It represents the cumulative and collaborative fruit of more than a century of Jesuit investigation of Confucianism. And it also marks an important source for that extraordinary vogue for things Chinese that left such a deep mark on eighteenth century art and thought. Couplet's visit to Paris in 1684 with a young Chinese companion[270] aroused enormous interest. He was presented to Louis XIV and from this contact arose the project of sending 'mathématiciens du roi' to the court of K'ang-hsi. But he also introduced to many Frenchmen for the first time, Confucius, the Chinese Sage. The *Mercure Galant* for September 1684 carried the account by 'the learned M. Comiers, Parisian' of a visit to the Jesuit Maison Saint Louis where he met Couplet and 'the young Chinese' and saw 'the Portrait of Doctor Confucius with his great black Moustaches, who is to the Chinese what Aristotle was for the Greeks.[271] The publication of *Confucius Sinarum Philosophus* a few years later confirmed the reputation of Confucius.

What, then, were the lineaments of this Jesuit Confucius? The portrait engraved specially for the work[272] stands as a significant symbol of the whole. It is a Confucius, in Chinese dress certainly, but with European features. The books on the shelves of the library in the background are a curious compromise between Chinese sewn and boxed books and European leather-bound volumes, and the titles appear in Chinese and Latin. K'ung-tzu has become Confucius.

---

269. For example, in *La Morale de Confucius, Philosophe de la Chine,* Amsterdam, 1688, reprinted Paris, 1783 (the title-page of the British Museum copy of the 1783 edition has 'Londres', but bibliographers usually attribute it to Valande in Paris); and its English translation, *The Morals of Confucius, A Chinese Philosopher* (London, 1691). This work was essentially a popular abridgement rather than a translation of the *Confucius Sinarum Philosophus.*
270. (Michael) Shen Fu-tsung.
271. Quoted in J Dehergne, 'Voyageurs Chinois venues à Paris au Temps de la Marine à Voiles . . .', in *Monumenta Serica,* XXIII (1964): 376.
272. On page cxvi, opposite the beginning of the Life of Confucius.

Couplet's *Proémialis Declaratio*[273] presents a recapitulation of the Jesuit interpretation of Chinese religion and philosophy in general, and Confucianism in particular, up to this point. He expounds the reasons for the Jesuit adoption of the guise of *literati,* their attempt to 'complement and perfect' Confucius, and its success, and adds his hopes that this ancient and sound politico-moral doctrine will prove of value to Europe too.[274] Then in successive paragraphs he outlines the contents and authority of the Chinese classics and the teachings of the Taoists and Buddhists. The latter are atheists as well as idolaters[275] and the teachings of the Buddha, who was born in India in 1026 BC, eventually in the Han period reached China and infected the country. In later times, the teaching of the ancient sages was lost or misinterpreted, and the 'new interpreters' of the Sung, basing themselves on the mysterious diagrams of the *I Ching* which only a Confucius could explain, got lost in the 'gloomy and useless exercise or labyrinth' of the hexagrams.

The explanation of Neo-Confucianism which follows is the fullest and most accurate hitherto published. In place of the vague statements and misleading terminology of Longobardo, Couplet traces the characteristic *li-hsüeh* principles back to their source in the commentaries on the *I Ching.* He invokes scholastic philosophical terminology but as an explanatory device or familiar standard against which the statements of Chinese philosophers about *t'ai-chi* and *Ii* can be measured, not as an end to inquiry. By this means he discovers some passages that appear to imply pure materialism, but others that seem to involve the Western concept of 'spirit'. And he concludes that we should be very cautious in applying labels such as 'Atheism' to systems in which the Western philosophical categories and distinctions are unknown.[276] It was the very confusion and multiplicity of interpretations of Confucianism that gave Matteo Ricci the opportunity to introduce his Christian interpretation based firmly on the texts themselves.

---

273. The full title is, 'Operis et Scopus nec-non Sinensium Librorum, Interpretum, Sectarum, et Philosophiae, quam Naturalem vocant, Proemialis Declaratio', and it occupies pages ix–cxiv of the work.

274. 'Operis et Scopus nec-non Sinensium Librorum', ix–xiv.

275. Couplet solves the dilemma of the atheist/idolator combination by claiming that there are two doctrines, the exoteric or 'exterior' which is a popular idolatry and the esoteric or 'interior' which is an atheistic philosophy (xxx–xxxiii).

276. See especially pages lvii–lviii.

Couplet's introduction to the *Confucius Sinarum Philosophus* also raises what were to become much debated questions amongst European scholars. He asserts that despite a superficial similarity between Egyptian hieroglyphics and Chinese characters, there is no evidence of influence from Egypt, Assyria or anywhere else on Chinese customs or society. Chinese history goes back very close to the date of the biblical Deluge and Fu Hsi, the founder of the Chinese Empire, is alleged to have reigned some 200 years after the date of the Deluge according to the Septuagint computation. Hence, the ancient Chinese must have been near contemporaries and descendants of the sons of Noah and, like Noah, have had knowledge of the true God, and worshipped him.

This last point established, Couplet proceeds to expound under several heads the primitive Chinese notion of God as found in the classics. The modern *atheopotitici* have misinterpreted the clear statements of the ancient books, and it is extraordinary that certain European missionaries should prefer their interpretation of the classics to 'the beautiful light shed by the author of nature on the Chinese of the Golden Age', especially since the use of the classics has been so successful in opening up China to the Gospel.[277] The last point, with its clear reference to Navarrete and his ilk, reminds us that Couplet's work, no less than any other Jesuit writing of the seventeenth century, is not a work of pure scholarship, but part of a continuing missionary program. However, the time of publication of the *Confucius Sinarum Philosophus* was a kind of lull in the Rites Controversy storm, and it is not dominated, as many later works were, by apologetic aims.

The most important part of *Confucius Sinarum Philosophus* is, of course, the translation itself. I can do no more here, than comment on the method and general presentation, with a few examples to illustrate these. Unfortunately, Couplet did not succeed in printing an accompanying Chinese text as he announced was his intention.[278] In the First Book, the *Ta hsüeh* or Great Learning', and in part of the third, he used a system of numbers to indicate the characters translated, but this was not followed in the rest of the work, thus suggesting the abandonment of his plans for a Chinese text. It was, in fact, not till the 1740s, when Etienne Fourmont had a special fount of Chinese characters made for his grammar and projected dictionary, that such work was possible in Europe.

277. Page xcvii.

278. Liber Primus, page 1.

Couplet's method is to give a translation of the text—or rather, as we shall see, paraphrase, or expansion of it—followed, where necessary, by the 'explanation of the Interpreters' and some comments of his own. The 'Interpreters' he follows are, he says, 'especially Cham the Colao and Royal Master' that is, as Knud Lundbaek has demonstrated, the late Ming scholar, royal tutor and chief minister, Chang Chu-cheng.[279]

The translation of the very first sentence of the First Book will serve as an example of the method. I give first the fairly literal translation of the passage by James Legge:

> What the Great Learning teaches is—to illustrate illustrious virtue; to renovate the people; and to rest in the highest excellence.[280]

This is already a slight expansion of the original sixteen characters, but it follows closely the structure as well as the sense of the original. Compare it, however, with what Couplet calls a literal *(ad litteram)* version.

> Magnum adeoque virorum Principium, sciendi institutum consistit in expoliendo, seu excolendo rationalem naturam a coelo inditam; ut scilicet haec, seu limpidissimum speculum, abstersis pravorum appetitum maculis, ad pristinam claritatem suam redirc possit. Consistit deinde in renovando seu reparando populum, suo ipsius scilicet exemplo et adhortatione. Consistit demum in sistendo firmiter, seu perseverando in summo bono.[281]

279. Lundback has rightly corrected my earlier assumption that this reference was to Ch'eng I v. 'The First Translation from a Confucian Classic in Europe', in *China Mission Studies (1550–1800) Bulletin,* I (1979) 9, n 29; and 'Chief Grand Secretary Chang Chu-cheng and the Early China Jesuits', in *China Mission Studies (1550–1800) Bulletin,* III (1981): 2–11.

280. *The Chinese Classics,* I, 356.

281. *Confucius Sinarum Philosophus,* 'Scientiae Sinicae' Liber Primus, 1 (each of the three books is separately paginated). This may be compared with the first sentence (corresponding to the first eight characters) of the da Costa-Intorcetta 1662 version: '*Magnum* virorum *sciendi institutum consistit* in *illuminando* virtutibus *spiritualem potentiam* a coelo inditam, nempe animam, ut haec redire possit ad originalem claritatem, quem appetitus animalis obnubilaverunt'. (*Sapientia Sinica,* 1.) The italics are in the original to distinguish the literal translation from the amplification. The filiation of the texts as well as the greater prolixity of the later version are clear.

(Or, to translate the translation)

> The great purpose, especially of men of princely rank, in knowing, consists in refining or cultivating the rational nature granted them by heaven; so that it, like the clearest of mirrors, wiped clean of the stains of depraved appetites, can return to its pristine clarity. It consists, next, in renewing or restoring the people,[282] through his own example and encouragement. And, finally, it consists in standing firm or persevering in the highest good.

What we have here is not at all a literal translation of the text. It is an amplification of the original, partly derived from Chu Hsi's commentary, but mainly drawn from European moral philosophy. The 'mirror' metaphor, for example, although common in Chinese philosophy, is not employed in the Ch'eng-Chu commentary, and may have found its way here via the European 'Mirror of the Soul' devotional literature. 'Depraved appetites' is a reference to Aristotelean ethics which has few points of contact with Chinese moral philosophy; while 'the highest good' *(summum bonum)* is a Thomistic concept with theistic overtones out of place here.

Couplet (or the Jesuit translator, whoever he was) concludes the passage with two comments. He sums up the meaning of the passage, according to the 'Interpreters' as 'the greatest conformity of all actions with right reason'; and he adds that the passage is a kind of summary of the whole book. Both comments are found almost *verbatim* in Chu Hsi's commentary.[283] And to these he adds a textual note explaining that the ninth character is normally read as *cin (ch'in)* which literally means 'love of neighbour or relatives', but that the commentators agree in reading it here as *sin (hsin)* 'to renew'.[284]

282. Note that Couplet follows the Ch'eng I/Chu Hsi amendment of *ch'in* (love) to *hsin* (renew) that is he follows the standard text and interpretation. Antonio de Santa Maria in the *T'ien-ju yin* had appealed to the older reading in support of Christian 'charity' (*Tien-chu-chiao tung-ch'uan wen-hsien hsü pien,* II, 994) *cf* commentary in Mungello, 'Sinological Torque', 128–89.

283. See Chu Hsi, *Ssû-shu chi-chu* (Hong Kong, 1968 edition), 1.

284. The editor has, I think, misunderstood Ch'eng-tzu's note. Couplet (or whoever was the Jesuit commentator on this passage) presumes that it is a question of the meaning *(nomen et significatum)* of *ch'in,* whereas it is clearly a question of a textual corruption, the substitution of one character for another of similar pronunciation and appearance.

My overall impression of this passage and the commentary is one of cultural transposition. The Jesuit authors have gone far beyond what a modern sinologist would regard as the bounds of translator's licence. Confucius[285] speaks not only in the language, but also with the thoughts of the medieval scholastic philosophers and theologians. There is some relation to the Chinese text, but only the reader who already knew enough Chinese to read it for himself, would be capable of judging the extent to which K'ung-tzu has been transformed in becoming Confucius.

For a second example, we might look at a passage from the *Doctrine of the Mean,* which figured prominently in the Rites Controversy, in order to assess the extent to which the image of 'Confucius' was modified by the need to conform to the Jesuit party-line on the question. Once more I take Legge's translation as a control, although I think that there are grounds for modifying it slightly. Legge translates the passage, at the end of Chapter 19 of the *Chung yung* as follows:

> Thus they served the dead as they would have served them alive; they served the departed as they would have served them had they been continued among them. By the ceremonies of the sacrifices to Heaven and Earth they served God, and by the ceremonies of the ancestral temple they sacrificed to the ancestors.[286]

The Jesuit would, of course, have objected to Legge's translation of *ssû hu ch'i hsien* as '*sacrificed* to the ancestors' on grounds we have already examined. The modern sinologist would reply that the term *ssû* is used, for example, for the 'sacrifices' to the kitchen god; that its primary meaning is 'sacrifice' in the normal sense, and that it should be translated this way, then qualified if necessary. On the other hand, most sinologists would, I think, query Legge's translation of *Shang-ti* as 'God'.

---

285. Modern commentators, of course, agree that the *Ta hsüeh* which is part of the *Li Chi* or *Book of Rites* was certainly not the work of Confucius. Couplet follows the traditional attribution to Confucius ('auctore Confucio, Commentatore cemcu eiusdem secundo discipulo').

286. *The Chinese Classics,* I, 403–404 (Legge's chapter division differs slightly from that of the edition of Chu Hsi already referred to, in which this is chapter 18). *cf Confucius Sinarum Philosophus.* Lib II, 58.

The Jesuit version, however, on close examination, proves to be more an elaborate piece of *parti pris* than a translation in the usual sense of the term. They gave a quite literal translation of the first part about serving the dead, which admirably suited their purpose and was, in fact, a key text in their Chinese as well as Western language writings on the subject of rites. Lest anyone should miss the point, they added a long commentary to the effect that these ceremonies arose purely from 'natural piety and polite observance' and that despite the appearance of worship, they were precisely those observed towards parents during their lifetime.

The second part of the passage, however, could not be allowed to stand in the stark and compromising terms of the original. Instead it is embedded in an elaborate exegesis:

> Confucius, wishing to imply that the brothers King Wu and the Duke of Chou followed a very beautiful way of governing, says that he who acquits himself of the appropriate duty of piety towards Heaven first, then to his ancestors, shall rule the Empire successfully. The *chiao* was that which was offered to Heaven, on a round hill. The *she*, however, was that which was offered to the earth, in a place that was low-lying and square (they thought that the earth was square). Quite different from these were the parental rites[287] offered to the ancestors, denoted here by the two terms *ti* and *ch'ang*. *Ti* was that which the Emperor offered to his ancestors with solemn rites once every five years. The *ch'ang* were those parental rites which were performed for the same in each of the four seasons of the year. Hence Confucius says: the rites and services of sacrifice to heaven and earth were that (ceremony) in which they actually honoured the supreme Emperor of heaven and earth, who is aptly as well as literally signified by the two letters *Shang ti*. The rites and services of the royal ancestral hall were those (ceremonies) in which later kings paid their respects to their dead ancestors.[288]

The commentary which follows points out that the text clearly indicates that the sacrifice is to one supreme God, 'even though Chu

287. The term used, *parentalia*, actually refers to the Roman festival in honour of deceased parents, a not inappropriate analogy.
288. *Confucius Sinarum Philosophus*, Lib II, 58.

Hsi, the Atheopolitical commentator falsely says that the name of the god of earth[289] has been omitted for the sake of brevity'. In this respect our translator has modern commentators on his side.[290] On the other hand, it is impossible to accept his further comment that this text should be used as a guide to interpretation in other contexts where Heaven and *Shang-ti* are mentioned. The text is a *locus illustris* for Ricci and Christian commentators precisely because of its uniqueness.

Once again we find the Jesuit translators guilty of the very methodological sin they impute to the Neo-Confucian commentators, confusing the text and the commentary. The European reader had no way of knowing where text finished and commentary—Jesuit or Chinese—began. In fact the passage beginning 'Hence Confucius says . . .' is a fairly close translation of the text and the introductory remarks are reasonably accurate,[291] but text and commentary have been conflated into one synthetic statement. It was indeed 'Confucius' not the Chinese K'ung-tzu who was presented.

As my third, and last, example, I take some passages from the translation of the *Analects.* On the whole this is the most successful and most literally accurate of the three translations. The problems encountered are principally those of equivalent terminology. How, for example, to render the key Confucian concept of *jen?* The Jesuit translators, like Legge and others after them, use a range of terms—*virtus, mutua fides et amor, benevolentia,* sometimes successfully, sometimes less so. Where Legge invariably translates *chün-tzu* as 'superior man', the *Confucians Sinarum Philosophus* uses a number of different *terms—perfectus vir, probus, verus philosophus,* in my opinion more effectively. Perhaps the operative factor is simply the resources of the Latin language. It seems to me better, for example,

---

289. The Chu Hsi commentary says that the name of *Hou t'u* has been omitted after Shang-ti (*Ssü-shu ch'i-chu,* 14).

290. Chu Hsi's gloss is omitted in many modern Chinese editions. According to CTC Werner's *Dictionary of Chinese Mythology,* New York, 1961,160, sacrifices to Hou T'u, the God of Earth, were not instituted till 113 BC under Han Wu Ti. In any case, as Legge notes, this view does not affect 'the judgement of the Sage himself, that the service of one being—even of God—was designated by all these ceremonies (*Chinese Classics* 1, 404).

291. One might question whether it would be more accurate to describe the *Ti* sacrifice as that to the *Founder* of the dynasty rather than the 'ancestors' of the Emperor, and the *Ch'ang* sacrifice as specifically the Autumn sacrifice (see Legge, *Chinese Classics,* I, notes on 404 and 158).

to translate the famous passage from the beginning of Bk VII of the *Analects,* as 'Praeco sum, seu relator, et non author doctrinae,[292] rather than Legge's familiar, 'a transmitter and not a maker'.[293] And I prefer 'Coelum tumulavit me!' in XI.8,[294] to 'Heaven is destroying me!'[295] since it accurately conveys both the tense (a reference to a past event, the death of Yen Yuan) and the implications of death and burial. The conciseness and lack of articles in Latin match similar features in Chinese, as in 'Rex sit Rex', compared with 'when the prince is a prince' in XII.11.[296] And it could be argued that the elegance and dignity, some might even say stuffiness, of the Latin, matches that of the original.

On the whole, *Confucius Sinarum Philosophus* is at its best in the translation of the *Anatects.* The humanistic moral and political philosophy of this work was closer to European ethics and the Renaissance philosophy of man than were other aspects of Chinese philosophy. It makes up by far the greater part of the work; and when European thinkers wrote about the ideas of Confucius, it was usually to this Third Book of the Jesuit translation that they referred. Although Couplet and his collaborators do not seem to have realised it, the *Analects* also represented the views of the genuine historical Confucius more accurately than the textually dubious *Great Learning,* and *Doctrine of the Mean.* To this extent, then, *Confucius Sinarum Philosophus* does present the real 'Confucius, Philosopher of China'; and despite its many and obvious defects, remains a cornerstone of the edifice of sinology as well as a fitting conclusion to the first century of the Jesuit encounter with Confucianism.

292. *Confucius Sinarum Philosophus,* 36.
293. *Chinese Classics,* I, 195.
294. *Confucius Sinarum Philosophus,* 71.
295. *Chinese Classics,* I, 234.
296. *Confucius Sinarum Philosophus,* 81 *cf Chinese Classics,* I, 256.

3
Son of Heaven and Vicar of Christ: The Chinese Rites Controversy (1688–1742)

As if it was not enough to disturb our peace of soul that after seventeen centuries we still dispute over points of our religion; now, that of the Chinese has entered into our quarrels. This dispute produced no great effects, but it characterised better than any other, that active, contentious and quarrelsome spirit that reigns in our part of the world.

Voltaire[1]

Voltaire was surely right in seeing the Chinese Rites Controversy as a case of China being drawn into European religious quarrels. This is true to some extent of the events described in the previous chapter, and it is almost totally true of the Rites Controversy proper, the debate conducted in Europe from the 1690s through to 1742 and even later. Unfortunately the historian of the Jesuit mission in China and of the Jesuit interpretation of Confucianism in particular, is not thereby absolved of the task of discussing the issue. Even if, as Voltaire says, it produced no great effects in Europe, it had enormous repercussions on the mission and ultimately completely undermined the Christian-Confucian rapprochement of the Jesuits. And although it was primarily a European quanel, it affected everything the Jesuits wrote, in Chinese as well as in European languages; it diverted their energies into its narrow channels; and it forced partisans on either side into gross over-simplifications. In short, it is inescapable.

In this chapter 1 offer no more than a few marginal comments on the Rites affair, with particular attention to its effect on the Jesuits' presentation of and relationship to Confucianism. I will attempt to

1. *Le Siècle de Louis XIV*, chapter XXXIX, 'Disputes sur les cérémonies chinoises', *Oeuvres Completes de Voltaire* (Paris, 1878), t 15, 76.

disentangle from the literature of the subject the comparatively few issues genuinely relating to Confucianism. Even this is, perhaps, overly ambitious. I have merely sampled the proliferation of writings on the Rites question around 1700, and concentrated on the Jesuit and pro-Jesuit material, since it is the effect of the controversy on the Jesuit propaganda about China that is my prime concern. Father Henri Bernard-Maître SJ, who probably knew better than any other authority on the subject the extent and complexity of the documentation, describes the problems without exaggeration when he says:

> In truth, what is most liable to mislead us in this matter, is certainly not the absence of documents, but on the contrary their overabundance. The result is a lack of chronological perspective. All those who have tried, even by looking at the high points from afar, to sort out this confused mass of texts have experienced immediately a feeling of total disorientation; and in a short time have felt themselves submerged beyond saving in an ocean of contradictions. Those who have the boldness, not to say temerity, to try to cut a path through this thick jungle, can only approach the problems by following a limited and oblique approach, by concentrating on one point only all the light they can bring to bear, without seeking to master in a more general way the changes and the evolution of the ideas.[2]

My 'limited and oblique approach' is through the fate of the image of Confucius and Confucianism in the Jesuit controversial literature.

The route by which the Chinese Rites controversy 'entered into our (European) quarrels' lies by way of Paris and Rome. French Jesuits and the French missionaries of the Société des Missions Etrangères de Paris brought the Rites question to the attention of the Sorbonne where it became a pawn in the struggle between Jesuit and Jansenist, Gallican and Papalist. The newly established church hierarchy in China, especially the Vicars Apostolic, and the introduction of missionaries directly responsible to the Congregation de Propaganda Fide, provided a new direct channel to the church authorities in Rome. This in turn brought to China papal legates with instructions to implement on the spot decisions made in Rome, thus projecting into

2. 'De la Question des Termcs a la Querelle des Rites de Chine: Le Dossier Foucquet de 1711', in *Neue Zeitschrift fur Missionswissenschaft,* XIV (1958): 179.

China issues of ecclesiastical politics which the barriers of distance and the Portuguese *padroado* had hitherto kept at bay.

It has been suggested[3] that the key to the whole Chinese Rites controversy lies in Jansenist influence, even a Jansenist conspiracy, in the Congregation de Propaganda Fide. This is, I am certain, exaggerated. Jansenism may partly explain the bitterness of the French exchanges, and there is truth in Montesquieu's comment: 'The Jesuits and the Jansenists are going to transport their quarrels as far as China.'[4] Jansenists certainly used anti Jesuit material about China[5] and they must have found a certain satisfaction in the refusal by Rome to allow just such a distinction between questions of fact and questions of doctrine in the case of China, that the Jesuits had denied to them in the case of the propositions of Jansenius.[6] There are, moreover, isolated passages in Jesuit letters from China alleging Jansenist collusion with the Paris missionaries.[7] But other factors were also at work. Portuguese influence in the East was clearly in decline and a realignment of ecclesiastical as well as political spheres of influence seemed called for. Whatever the reality of the influence of Jesuit confessors over Louis XIV, the apparent predominance of the Jesuits at court naturally produced an anti-Jesuit reaction at Rome as well as in France. And there were many other theological controversies besides that over Jansenism in which the Jesuits had taken sides and made enemies.[8] In some respects the Roman discussions in the Rites

3. Principally by Malcolm Hay in *Failure in the Far East* (London, 1956).
4. *Pensees,* No 55, in *Oeuvres Completes,* edited by Masson (Paris, 1950), II, 20.
5. See, for example, Pierre Jurieu, *La Religion des Jesuites,* La Haye, 1689, which compares the 'idolatry' of the Jesuits of China with their 'idolatry' of Louis XIV (34–36).
6. The distinction between facts and doctrine is the principal argument in the pro-Jesuit *Caduceus Sinicus,* Cologne, 1713. The anti-Jesuit Pere Norbert (PC Parisot *alias* Platel) in his *Memoires Historiques . . . sur les Missions Orientales* (Lucca, 1744), II, 191–93, points out that this is the same argument as the Jansenist distinction between *fait* and *droit* which had been condemned.
7. For example Pierre de Goville to Nyel, undated but probably c 1722, in Pastor, *History of the Popes,* XXXIV, London, 1941, Appendix 16, 571–73; Joseph Suarez to the Portuguese Assistant, Peking, 9 October 1713 in ARSJ: JS *175,* 18–19; João Mourao to the Patriarch Mezzabarba, 4 December 1732, translation in ARSJ: JS *198* 318r–320r. Similar charges against the MEP missionaries in Cochinchina are made by GB Sanna SJ in letters of 1721 and 1722 in ARSJ: JS *198,* 51v–56v.
8. See E Preclin and E Jarry, *Les Luttes Politiques et Doctrinales aux XVIIe et XVIIIe Siecles* (Paris, 1955).

Controversy were the first success of the curious alliance of secular and ecclesiastical forces that eventually brought about the temporary destruction of the Society of Jesus.[9]

Malcolm Hay is on the right track, however, in looking to the personnel and policies of the Congregation de Propaganda Fide for an explanation of the shift against the Jesuit accommodation policy in China. Initially, the Congregation supported a policy identical in almost all respects with that of the Jesuits. In its well-known *Instruction* of 1659 issued to the Vicars Apostolic there is a classic statement of the principle of accommodation to local conditions.

> Do not attempt in any way to persuade these peoples to change their customs, their habits and their behaviour, as long as they are not evidently contrary to religion and morality. What could be more absurd, indeed, than to transport France, Italy or some other European country to the Chinese? Do not bring them our countries but the faith, which does not reject or harm the customs and habits of any people, so long as they are not perverse; but, on the contrary, wishes to see them preserved in their entirety.
>
> And since it is as it were written into human nature that every man, in his judgement and in his heart, puts his customs and his country above all others, there exists no more powerful motive for hatred and revulsion than changing ancestral customs, especially those that men have always practised as far back as the memories of their forefathers go, and even more so if, in place of the practices abolished, one substitutes from outside those of another country. So, never make invidious comparisons between the practices of these peoples and European practices; but rather adapt quickly to theirs.[10]

It might be objected that other directives in the *Instruction* are contrary to the Jesuit policy, such as the recommendations to refuse all gifts; to avoid all entanglements with kings, magistrates and

9. *Cf* D Van Kley, *The Jansenists and the Expulsion of the Jesuits from France 1757–1765* (New Haven: Yale University Press, 1975).

10. Translated from E Duperray, *Ambassadeurs de Dieu a la Chine* (Tournai-Paris: Casterman, 1956), 48.

powerful men;[11] and to decline all official positions.[12] Yet we find missionaries of Propaganda, like the Jesuits, eventually doing all these things which were apparently unavoidable in the Chinese context, at least at the court.

What is noticeable as an effect, or perhaps cause, of the Rites Controversy, is an abandonment by the Congregation of its central tenet of accommodation. Canon Law was rigidly enforced in the missions of the Far East. Attempts to establish a Chinese liturgy were frustrated[13] and the Chinese clergy were increasingly 'Europeanised' in their training and outlook.[14] One possible source for this change of attitude is to be found in the *Monita ad Missionarios de Propaganda Fide* of 1669, in Chapter III, 'On the Right Use of Human Means'. Bishops Pallu and Lambert de Ia Motte adopt a rigid puritanical approach to the question, rejecting not only 'purely human means' and the 'heresy' of engaging in any form of commercial transactions,[15] but the 'corrupting' influence of sciences and the arts.[16] Accommodation was hardly possible on these terms, at least in the form in which it had been developed by the Jesuits of the China mission. This rejection of 'human means' together with the centralising tendencies of the Roman Congregations had by the end of the seventeenth century betrayed the vision of a Chinese Church embodied in the 1659 *Instruction.*

The fact that the first Vicars Apostolic were members of the MEP (Missions Etrangères de Paris) was one link between China and the French religious situation. Another was the establishment of the French Jesuit Mission. The full story of the beginnings of the French mission and the conflict between French and 'Portuguese' missions,

11. Duperray, *Ambassadeurs de Dieu a la Chine,* 47.
12. Duperray, *Ambassadeurs de Dieu a la Chine,* 48.
13. See F Bontinck, *La Lutte autour de la Liturgie Chinoise,* especially chapters HI, VI, VII, VIII.
14. Bontinck, *La Lutte autour de la Liturgie Chinoise,* especially chapters X and XI.
15. *Monita ad Missionarios S. Congregationis de Propaganda Fide,* 4th edition (Rome, 1886), 32. I have assumed that this edition does not differ substantially from the original seventeenth century edition. It is, unfortunately, the earliest I have available for reference.
16. *Monita ad Missionarios S. Congregationis de Propaganda Fide,* cap Ill, art VI, 'De Ceteris Humanis Mediis', 43.

is yet to be told.[17] The very bulk of the correspondence on this subject in the Roman Archives of the Society of Jesus indicates how large the issue loomed in the eyes of the members of the mission. It created disagreement at a time when unity was particularly important, and at one point the General had to write to admonish them that while they were bickering amongst themselves, in Rome the very fate of the mission was being decided.[18] The French Jesuits brought to the mission a peculiarly French approach, a French intellectual formation, a sense of the superiority of all things French, even French cuisine.[19] Reaction from the Jesuits of other nationalities was only to be expected. Some of the Jesuits of the old mission resented the French Jesuits concentrating on the intellectual apostolate instead of manning the mission stations in the provinces, a complaint that Matteo Ricci would hardly have approved. Until the French mission was formally separated from the Vice-Province of China in November 1700, there was constant conflict over their relations with the superiors of the mission in Macao and the interior. Above all, their arrival in China in French ships, avoiding Portuguese ports, represented an affront to the *padroado* which had been the lifeline of the mission for so long.

The reasons for the establishment of the French mission are partly to be sought in the general French expansionism of the period. Colbert and his successor, Louvois, had seen possible commercial advantages in having French missionaries at the courts of Siam and China; Couplet's visit to Paris had stimulated Louis XIV and the French Jesuits to revive the project; and Louis' Jesuit confessor, Père

17. A beginning has been made by John Witek SJ in chapter II of his 1973 Georgetown University doctoral thesis, 'An Eighteenth Century Frenchman at the Court of the K'ang Hsi Emperor'.
18. In a circular letter date 1700 in ARSJ: JS 767, 428–29, the General, Thyrsus Gonzalez, asks for authenticated testimony from the mission on the Rites issue, and concludes: 'Yet while the house is burning, our Fathers in China are still deep asleep, and continue to sleep, occupied with domestic dissension and national divisions which are very well known now all over Europe' (429v.).
19. One of JF Foucquet's Notebooks in B Vat: *Borg Cin 377*, has a considerable section devoted to recipes (ff 7–48). And one of the works in the Peking Library of the French Jesuits is *Le Nouveau Cuisinier royal et bourgeois, ou cuisinier moderne. Qui apprend a ordonner toute sorte de Repas en gras et tnaigre*... Par M. Massialot . . .augmented de nouveaux Ragouts par le Sieur Vincent de la Chapelle, Paris, 1739 (*Catalogue de la Bibliotheque du Pe-t'ang*, No 481, col. 130).

de Ia Chaise, had helped with the arrangements. The appointment of the six men chosen—Fontaney, Tachard, Gerbillon, Le Comte, Visdelou and Bouvet—as 'mathematicians of the King' was not just a subterfuge to avoid difficulties over the *padroado.* They were all experienced teachers of science and mathematics in the French Jesuit colleges and their subsequent correspondence with the French Academy of Science fully justified their title. There seems no question, however, that they regarded themselves primarily as missionaries, and an examination of the correspondence of Ferdinand Verbiest reveals that they did not set out completely uninvited.

Towards the end of his life Verbiest who, though no longer Vice-Provincial, was still the most important man on the mission, seems to have been obsessed with the problem of staffing an expanding mission. He had long been a staunch defender of the Portuguese *padroado* and as late as September 1678 wrote to King Alfonso VI of Portugal in fulsome praise of the support of Portugal for the Jesuits of China.[20] But a circular letter which he addressed to the Jesuits of Europe in August 1678 indicates an increasing concern about the future of the mission.[21] Learned men, especially trained mathematicians, were urgently required.[22] His letters to the new General, a fellow Belgian, Charles de Noyelle (General 1682–86), concentrated on the need for new blood and although he still professed a special concern for the Portuguese,[23] he welcomed the arrival of the French 'mathématiciens du roi'. In reply to a letter from Père de Ia Chaise introducing the six French Jesuits,[24] he promised to help in any way possible, and described his intervention with the Emperor to get permission for the five[25] who arrived in Ning-po on 24 July 1687 to proceed to the

20. *Correspondance,* No XXXII, Peking, 7 September 1678, 256–66.
21. *Correspondance,* No XXX, Peking, 15 August 1678, 230–53.
22. *Correspondance,* No XXX, Peking, 15 August 1678, 237, 241–42, 245.
23. See, for example, his boast to Noyelle of having undermined the Dutch mission for which the Jesuits acted as interpreters, in favour of the Macao connection (*Correspondance,* No LXXII, Peking, 21 September 1686).
24. Paris, 26 February 1685, in *Correspondance,* No LX, 482–6 *cf* Letter of de la Chaise to the Jesuit General on the same subject in ARSJ: *Gal. 72,* ff 141–42, dated Paris, 14 March 1685. (I am indebted to Dr A Lynn Martin for drawing my attention to this letter.)
25. Tachard had been detained in Siam.

court.[26] Both this letter and the accompanying letter to the General[27] were marked 'personal' because, as he notes, 'for certain reasons it is absolutely necessary to keep it secret'.[28] The 'certain reasons' are clearly the problems connected with the *padroado*. In the last resort, his loyalty was to what he saw as the interests of the mission rather than to Portugal.

Verbiest died ten days before the French group arrived in Peking (7 February 1688) but the wisdom of his support was soon obvious. The newcomers quickly made their mark. Jean-François Gerbillon was chosen, a few months after his arrival in Peking, to accompany Father Thomas Pereira to Siberia where they acted as interpreters and negotiators in the discussions with the Russians which resulted in the signing of the Treaty of Nerchinsk.[29] On his return, he and Joachim Bouvet began teaching geometry and philosophy to the Emperor, whom they saw twice daily for two hours at a time.[30] The other three Frenchmen were dispersed to different provinces, but after some four years Jean de Fontaney and Claude de Visdelou were recalled to Peking, where in 1693 they won fresh favour by a gift of quinine which cured K'ang-hsi's fever.

Their services were at least partly responsible for two important marks of favour from the Emperor. In 1692 K'ang-hsi issued an edict of toleration of Christianity and in 1693 granted the French mission permission to build a house within the walls of the Forbidden City. It must have seemed in early 1693, that the mission was at last reaping the rewards of a century of effort, and that Christianity was about to become a respectable native religion. It was precisely at this juncture that the Rites Controversy flared up once more.

Ching t'ien—'Adore Heaven'?

On 26 March 1693, Mgr Charles Maigrot MEP, Vicar Apostolic of Fukien, issued an *Instruction* to all the missionaries of his Vicariate,

26. *Correspondance.* No LXXV, Peking, 1 October 1687, 537–41.
27. *Correspondence,* No LXXVI, 541–44.
28. *Correspondence,* 540.
29. See J Sebes, *The Jesuits and the Sino-Russian Treaty* of Nerchinsk (1689), (Rome: Institutum Historicum, 1961).
30. Pfister, *Notices,* 434, 445–46.

ordering them 'until the Holy See shall decide otherwise,[31] to observe the following seven provisions: 1. To use *t'ien-chu* for 'God' and in no circumstances *t'ien* or *shang-ti.* 2. Not to use tablets *(tabellae)* in churches with the characters (*t'ien* and *shang-ti,* and especially *ching t'ien,* 'to adore Heaven', since 'we are of the opinion that these tablets, and especially those which contain the two words *ching t'ien* cannot be excused of idolatry; and even if the matter is not so certain as it appears, the mere suspicion of danger of evangelical workers placing the abomination of desolation in the holy place, ought turn us away from the use of the inscriptions'. 3. The decisions of Pope Alexander VII were given in response to an untrue representation of the facts and hence cannot be invoked to permit the cult of Confucius and the ancestors. 4. Christians are strictly forbidden to perform or even be present at the semi-annual solemn sacrifices to Confucius and the ancestors which 'we declare to be imbued with superstition'. 5. 'We praise most highly those missionaries who . . . have had the zeal to abolish the usage of tablets exposed in private houses in honour of the dead, and we exhort them to continue in future to follow the same practice.' If tablets must be retained, such terms as 'xin chu', 'xin goei' and 'ling goei'[32] must be removed, and a declaration in due form posted nearby 'in large characters' asserting the Christian belief about the dead and filial piety towards them.

These provisions taken in themselves, and neglecting the tone and cumulative effect, were not radical divergences from the developed Jesuit practice. In the last two provisions, however, Maigrot launched a direct attack on the whole Jesuit Interpretation of Confucianism. On the basis of six years' experience in China, and what later proved to be a very slight acquaintance with the language, be declared 'false, temerarious and scandalous', 'leading the simple into error and opening the way to superstition', the following propositions, some of which were pillars of the Jesuit interpretation:

31. I follow the text of the *Magnum Bullarium Romanum,* X, Rome, 1735 (1965 photographic reprint), 129–30. A French text, after the *Decret de Nostre S.P. le Pape Clément XI sur la grande affaire de la Chine,* 1709, is given in Etiemble, *Les Jésuites en Chine,* 103–106.

32. Presumably the terms *shên chu, shên kuei* and *ling kuei,* referring to the 'spirits'.

> —that the philosophy that the Chinese profess, if properly understood, has nothing in it contrary to the Christian law;
> —that by the term *t'ai-chi* the wisest of the ancients wished to define a God who was the First Cause of all things;
> —that the cult which Confucius rendered to spirits was civil rather than religious;
> —that the book which the Chinese call the *I Ching* is a summary of an excellent system of physics and morality.

These and 'other similar propositions' were not to be published by word or writing in his Vicariate. And, as his seventh and final prohibition, Maigrot issued a special warning against the 'atheism' and 'superstition' in the Chinese books, 'in the text as much as in their commentaries'.

It is not surprising that these instructions immediately divided the mission. Some of the Vicars Apostolic approved them for their own Vicariates, others opposed[33] or tried to remain neutral; and the religious superiors, too, were divided. Maigrot dispatched Nicholas Charmot MEP to Rome, and as the affair proceeded other parties to the dispute sent their representatives, the Jesuits finally sending Francois Noël and Gaspard Castner in 1702. The debate over the specific provisions of Maigrot's *Mandatum* soon became enmeshed with others over the extent of the jurisdiction of Maigrot and the Vicars Apostolic; over Maigrot's denial of faculties to administer the sacraments to those who opposed him; over charges of high-handedness and arrogance laid against Maigrot himself, and of encouraging physical violence to Maigrot laid against the Jesuits. All these issues we must, reluctantly, put aside; reluctantly, because they greatly aggravated the controversy and made agreement on the main issues less and less likely.

In Rome in 1697, the Consultors and Cardinals of the Holy Office began to investigate Maigrot's claims, and were later assisted by the Vicar Apostolic of Hukwang, Giovanni Francisco Nicolai a Leonessa, who drew up a report on the facts of the case.[34] Leonessa's account of Chinese practices was on the whole accurate but he was faced with the necessity of providing translations and equivalents for the Roman theologians which involved committing himself for or against the

33. See Rosso, *Apostolic Legations,* 132–33.
34. See *Magnum Bullarium Romanum,* X, 130–36.

Jesuits. He seems to have chosen, in the end, the latter course. *T'ien* means 'the material and visible Heaven or at most a certain power belonging to Heaven'.[35] Confucius is commonly called a 'saint' *(shêng)* not a 'master'.[36] The building dedicated to him in each city is called a *miao* which is a 'chapel' rather than a 'school' or 'hall'.[37] The Chinese deny the existence of spirits, since they are atheists and rationalists, but the dead are regarded as continuing to exist in some way.[38]

The Commission was divided[39] but, with the election of a new Pope, Clement Xl, finally reached agreement.[40] A papal legate should be sent to China to inquire into some of the matters and to settle the question. Charles Maillard de Tournon was chosen, consecrated Patriarch of Antioch, and on 4 July 1702, he set out for the East. More than two years after his departure, in November 1704 Clement XI signed the decree, *Cum Deus Optimus,* condemning the Chinese rites; but withheld publication in Europe, presumably to allow de Tournon greater freedom of action. The decree, following the *Responsa* of the Commission,[41] confirmed Maigrot's instructions with a few interpretative comments which, following Leonessa, identified the Confucian 'building' as a 'temple', and denied that the rites could be described as 'civil and political' rather than 'religious'.[42] The vital last two articles, however, were left to be settled by de Tournon on the spot.

It was during the course of the deliberations of the papal commission in Rome, and of the theologians of the Sorbonne in 1700, that Europe was flooded with writings for and against the Jesuit position. Most of these were republications, or first publications in the case of material hitherto in manuscript, rehearsing all the old arguments, attacking the integrity and questioning the motives and behaviour cf all parties to the dispute. Very few throw any new

35. *Magnum Bullarium Romanum,* X, 131.
36. *Magnum Bullarium Romanum,* X, 132.
37. *Magnum Bullarium Romanum,* X, 132.
38. *Magnum Bullarium Romanum,* X, 134. Leonessa, like Navarrete and Maigrot, does not seem to have been concerned with the logical incompatibilities of atheism and idolatry, materialism and praying to spirits.
39. See Rosso, *Apostolic Legations,* 135.
40. Rosso, *Apostolic Legations,* 149, 154.
41. For the *Responsa* and the Decree, see *Magnum Bullarium Romanum,* X, 136–38.
42. *Magnum Bullarium Romanum,* X, 137.

light on the subject, but are content to make points of logic, such as Jean Dez's argument that the Chinese cannot be, as Maigrot claims, simultaneously atheists and idolaters;[43] or to score personal points by contrasting Maigrot's behaviour with his words,[44] or citing Dominican against Dominican.[45] Most conspicuous is the absence of testimony from the Chinese themselves; the whole debate consisted of Europeans telling the Chinese what they really believe.[46]

The Jesuits in Peking when they, at last, realised the seriousness of the situation, conceived a master stroke. Why not get the Emperor himself to issue an authoritative statement on the meaning of the rites? They did not, at the time, see the corresponding danger that the Pope might declare the Emperor to be wrong with very embarrassing results for the mission.

The declaration of K'ang-hsi[47] of 30 November 1700 fulfilled all their expectations. He approved of their statements that Confucius was honoured as a teacher; that 'performance of the ceremony of sacrifice to the dead is a means of showing sincere affection for members of the family and thankful devotion to ancestors of the clan'; that the tablets of deceased ancestors were honoured as a remembrance of the dead rather than as the actual residence of their souls; that *t'ien* and *shang-ti* are not identified with the physical sky but are 'the ruler and the lord of heaven, earth and all things'; and that *ching t'ien* in the inscription bestowed on the Jesuit church meant 'revere Heaven' in this sense.

43. *Ad virum nobilem de cultu Confucii philosophi, et progenitorum apud Sinas,* Dillingen, 1700, especially 24.
44. For example (Lallement), *Réponse aux Nouveaux Ecrits,* 1–15 (second pagination). For example *Apologia pro Decreto S.D.N. Alexandri VII . . . ex Patrum Dominicanorum et Franciscanorum scriptis concinnata* (Louvain, 1700).
45. There is, in the Jesuit Archives in Rome, a large collection of manuscript treatises on the rites by Chinese Christians.
46. I follow the translation from the original Manchu by George Kennedy, given by Rosso in his *Apostolic Legations,* 138–43. I have also examined the very rare xylographically printed *Brevis Relatio eorum quae spectant as Declarationem Sinarum Imperatoris Kam Hi circa Coeli, Cumfucii, et Avorum Cultum datam anno 1700 . . .* (Peking, 1701). See also J Dehergne, 'L'exposé des Jésuites de Pekin sur le culte des ancetres presenté à L'empereur K'ang Hi en November 1700', *Actes du lle colloque international de sinologie* (Paris: Les Belles Lettres, 1980), 185–229.
47. *Apostolic Legations,* 146.

As we have seen, this Declaration did not prove of sufficient weight in Rome to swing the balance in favour of the Jesuits. And the fact that it failed to do so is highly significant. Contemporary and modern opponents of the Jesuit position on the rites have argued that the Emperor was interfering in a strictly theological matter in which, as Father Rosso puts it, he 'had usurped theological competence'.[48] But neither K'ang-hsi's comments, nor the Jesuits' memorial (in Manchu and Chinese versions), raise theological issues. They were solely concerned with questions of fact—what did the Chinese, or a peculiarly authoritative Chinese source, really believe about these ceremonies? It has been argued that the Emperor was under Jesuit influence, and that as an alien, he was not qualified to speak on these matters.[49] Both comments are incompatible with what we know of the character and competence of K'ang-hsi. He was deeply interested in and patronised classical Chinese studies,[50] was concerned with establishing norms for public morality,[51] and was most unlikely to promulgate an interpretation of traditional ceremonies in a sense that he did not believe to be orthodox. And even if K'ang-hsi's testimony could be dismissed in this way, what of the other testimony gathered by the Jesuits and sent to Europe between 1701 and 1704?[52]

It is not my task here to discuss, still less to defend, the substance of the Jesuit assessment of Chinese ritual practices. Some remarks about their method of approach are, however, necessary. As presented in the *Brevis Relatio* it consists of an examination of Chinese practices in addition to testimony from Chinese scholars. In section 6 of the document they present a detailed description of the temples of Heaven and Earth in Peking and the sacrifices performed in them,

48. *Apostolic Legations,* 146.
49. Young (*Confucianism and Christianity,* III), too, casts doubts on K'ang-His's scholarship and Confucian orthodoxy.
50. See Fang Chao-ying's biography of K'ang-hsi in Hummel, *Eminent Chinese,* 329 (under *Hsüan-yeh);* and JD Spence. *Emperor of China* (London: Random House 1974), especially chapter IV; and L Kessler, *K'ang-hsi and the Consolidation of Ch'ing Rule, 1661–1684,* chapter 6.
51. As in the 'Sacred Edict' *(Shêng-yu)* promulgated in 1670.
52. Most of this, together with the Declaration of K'ang-hsi, was published in the *Brevis Relatio* of 1701. The copy I have seen in the Jesuit Archives in Rome (Jap Sin I. 206) contains the autograph signatures of Antoine Thomas, Gerbillon, Bouvet and Grimaldi, authenticating the testimony of the various Chinese authorities cited.

that squares with other accounts.[53] Lest it be argued that this was an exclusively upper-class approach, they added a section on the 'notion of God in popular tradition' which draws on Chinese proverbs and Chinese customs. Some of this evidence was rather two-edged and, as they themselves admitted,[54] attested to superstitious and idolatrous practices. The main thrust of their argument was, nevertheless, clear. The question of Chinese rites was a question of fact and could only be resolved by long and patient investigation on the spot.

Maigrot's attitude, as that of many of the Roman theologians, was different. His answer to the Jesuit 'libels' and 'calumnies' in the *Brevis Relatio* was to stand on his dignity and authority as a bishop. The Jesuits accuse him of never having been at the court and of having no contacts with officials and scholars. He positively rejoices in this charge. 'It is true, thanks be to God, that I have never frequented the court', that 'famous Babylon, and to use the words of Fathers of the Society, centre of error, asylum of atheism and fortress of idolatry'.[55] Some Chinese Christians of Foochow have accused him of mistakes in the Chinese of official documents he signed. This may be so, he says, but he always leaves this sort of thing to his servants.[56] And he continues:

> But, in any case, I concede your condemnation of my ignorance, and, thanks to God, I do not pride myself on being an expert in anything. But what I do make much of, my reverend father, is, ignorant though I be, to show that the Jesuits uphold idolatry in China, and what is even more deplorable, that they deceive the church in upholding it by false oaths, and false statements which do not appear to me to excuse them from bad faith . . . This, my reverend father, is what the Jesuits have to answer and what is important: that

53. For a description of the temple, see A Favier, *Peking* (Lille: Societe de Saint-Augustin, 1902), 288–90. On the ceremonies see F Farjenel, 'Le Culte Imperial en Chine', in *Journal Asiatique*, ser X, t VIII, (1906): 491–516; ET Williams, 'The State Religion of China during the Manchu Dynasty', in *Journal of the North China Branch of the Royal Asiatic Society* XLIV (1913): 11–45; and C de Harlez *La Réligion et les cérémonies de la Chine moderne d'après le cérémonial et les décrets officiels* (Bruxelles, 1893–1894).
54. *Brevis Relatio*, 50a.
55. Letter to Antoine Thomas, Foochow, 22 December 1703, in ARSJ: JS *168*, 39 v.
56. Maigrot to Gerbillon, Foochow, 26 March 1705, in ARSJ: JS 768, 218r-v.

> I am ignorant, I admit, but that does not change the religion of China, and my ignorance does not justify the Jesuits in the bad faith which appears in their conduct.[57]

No wonder the Jesuits were annoyed at this refusal on the part of Maigrot to discuss the Chinese rites question on the level of fact. Maigrot's ominous reference in the same letter to the imminent arrival of Maillard de Tournon did not augur well for the level of discussion to come.

Whatever Maigrot's knowledge of Chinese, he displayed a consistent hostility to Chinese culture that was hardly conducive to a serious examination of the questions at issue. On his return to Europe he was accepted as a 'China expert' and, judging from one account at least, made a very negative contribution to the European assessment of China. Lelong, writing to Leibniz in September 1708, described his interviews with Maigrot as follows:

> M.[the Bishop] of Conon arrived in France six months ago. He has just received a new brief from the Pope ordering him to go to Rome. I have had the honour of entertaining him several times. He informed me, à propos of the little book of P. Malebranche,[58] that the Chinese are not capable of much concentration, that abstract matters are not at all within their grasp, that they have almost no idea of metaphysical truths. I believe that there is nothing much to be said of their sciences; all their erudition is reduced, even amongst the *literati,* to making from time to time some little compositions of two or three pages.[59]

So much for over two thousand years of Chinese philosophy, for the massive compilations of Ch'ing scholars and their concern with systems of thought, exegesis and commentary. If we may speak of legitimate and illegitimate prejudices in the case of Chinese rites, there is little doubt in which class we must place Maigrot's contributions to the debate.

57. A significant admission.
58. A reference to Malebranche's *Entretien d'un Philosophe Chrétien et d'un Philosophe Chinois* (Paris, 1708).
59. Quoted in *Oeuvres Complètes de Malebranche,* edited by A Robinet, t.xv, (Paris, 1958), ix, n 5.

Louis Le Comte vs. the Sorbonne

Perhaps the best illustration of the extent to which the debate about Chinese rites was a vicarious debate about European issues is the condemnation by the Sorbonne in August 1700 of propositions drawn from the work of the returned missionary, Louis Le Comte SJ. Not that the issues were not real ones, or unconnected with the Jesuit experience in China. Voltaire noted in *Le Siècle de Louis XIV* that 'the Christian brains' of the assembled Sorbonne theologians were 'shaken' by the Jesuits' praise of the Chinese.[60] And, in all truth, this was so. The Jesuits do not seem to have seen the potential effect of their presentation of China on the European debate about revealed religion. What the Jesuit interpretation of Confucianism was doing was nothing less than questioning the uniqueness of the Judaeo—Christian revelation.

This crucial debate, which was to be exploited to great effect by enemies of the Jesuits and the Church in the eighteenth century, was sparked off by the publication of Le Comte's *Nouveaux Mémoires sur l'Etat Present de la Chine,* in 1696. Le Comte had had very limited experience in China and it is doubtful whether he knew much Chinese. Jean-François Foucquet was probably correct in describing the *Nouveaux Mémoires* as based on second-hand material combined with limited personal observation, and erroneous in many details; but he was also correct in calling them 'so elegantly and so brilliantly written'.[61] Despite, or perhaps because of, the oversimplification of the contents, the vivacity of the work and its fashionable style made it extremely popular and led to several editions appearing in a short period of time.

What we have here in the *Nouveaux Mémoires* is the Jesuit interpretation of Confucianism presented boldly and without qualification in an extreme form. He contrasts the idolatry of the

60. '(L'abbé Boileau) déclama violemment contre les jésuites et les Chinois, et commenca par dire, que "l'eloge de ces peuples avait ébranlé son cerveau chretien". Les autres cerveaux de l'assemblée furent ébranlés aussi', in *Oeuvres Completes de Voltaire* (Paris, 1878), t 15, 79–chapter XXXIX of *Le Siècle de Louis XIV*.

61. BN: Fr 25670, 14. The contemporary correspondence of the Jesuits in China makes several references to errors in Le Comte's account of the state of the China mission. See, for example, Carlo Amiani to the General, 30 October 1702 (ARSJ: JS *167*, 73–74) and William van der Beken to Ignatius Diertens, 15 August 1700 (ARSJ: JS *167*, 287–92).

majority of Chinese with the purity of Confucian belief: 'a chosen people, who, adore in spirit and in truth the Lord of heaven and of earth' in the midst of 'a criminal crowd of adorers of Belial'.[62] Confucius himself is regarded as 'a Saint' by the Chinese, and indeed he seems on examination 'less a Philosopher formed by reason, than a man inspired by God for the reform of this new world'. Yet he has never been regarded by the Chinese as a divinity.[63] The pure religion of the ancient Chinese is explained if we admit that the Chinese were descended immediately from the sons of Noah after the Deluge and that their ancient writings contain 'vestiges' of the primitive revelation.[64] Despite the influence of idolatry on the *Jukiao* (that is, *Ju-chiao* or 'Confucianism'), there resulted a 'refined atheism' which never developed into a religious cult but remained purely 'political'.[65]

The questions which Le Comte raised by this crude version of the Jesuit standard apologia went beyond the issue of the legitimacy of Chinese Rites. He was, in effect, claiming for Chinese tradition an equivalence to the biblical revelation. Ricci had attempted to avoid this dilemma in typical Christian-humanist fashion by contrasting a 'natural' revelation with the definitive personal intervention of God in history. Theological developments during the seventeenth century had rendered this less tenable. Developments in the theology of grace and the prevailing fundamentalist interpretations of Scripture had made it difficult to conceive of salvation outside the pale of Christendom. Bossuet's influential *Discours sur l'Histoire Universelle* blandly assumes that the only history worth discussing is that of the Judaeo-Christian world, and dismisses China altogether from the 'universe'. Outside of Christianity all was darkness and sin.

Shortly before the Chinese Rites came to the attention of the Sorbonne, the 'Christian brains' of the Doctors of that august body had been shaken by one Jesuit attempt to escape from the consequences of the theological position, *extra Ecclesiam nulla salus.*[66] This was the theory of 'philosophical sin', namely that someone who had no knowledge of God could not offend against him, and hence was incapable of true sin, proposed by the Jesuit theologian François

62. *Nouveaux Mémoires* (Amsterdam, 1698), 1, 129.
63. *Nouveaux Mémoires,* 278–80.
64. *Nouveaux Mémoires,* II, 89.
65. *Nouveaux Mémoires,* II, 122.
66. 'No salvation outside the church'.

Musnier.[67] The so-called 'thèse de Dijon' was eventually condemned by some of the French Bishops in 1696, the very year that Le Comte's work appeared.

Le Comte's attempt to escape from the theological impasse by positing the persistence of a primitive revelation in Chinese tradition brought together the same coalition of Bossuet and the Jansenists that had secured the condemnation of 'philosophic sin'.[68] When the Faculty of Theology of the University of Paris met in July 1700, the question of Le Comte's *Nouveaux Mémoires* was introduced by an ally of the directors of the Missions Etrangères de Paris. Eight 'deputies' were elected to examine the work, at least five of whom were Jansenist in their sympathies.[69] This 'cabal' as Noel Varet, one of the Sorbonne theologians, called them,[70] took the opportunity to secure yet another Jesuit scalp, and in August the Faculty condemned five propositions allegedly contained in Le Comte's work. The propositions selected for attack all deal with the purity of the Chinese conception of God and of Chinese morals, independently of the Christian dispensation.

The question of the legitimacy of the rites was not explicitly raised in the 'Censure' of the Sorbonne but it figured prominently in the paper war that followed, and was swallowed up in the wider discussions preceding and accompanying the 1704 Roman condemnation. Le Comte himself followed up his defence of his *Nouveaux Mémoires* with a public letter to the Due du Maine on the ceremonies of China,[71] which some of his Jesuit confreres thought conceded too much.[72] In this exchange, too, questions of theology predominated over

67. See Etiemble, *Les Jésuites en Chine,* 231–33; and V Pinot, *La Chine et la Formation de l'Esprit Philosophique en France* (*1640–1740*) (Paris: Librairie orientaliste Paul Geuthne, 1932), 94–95, 302–304.

68. See Pinot, *La Chine,* 99.

69. See J Davy, 'La Condemnation en Sorbonne des "Nouveaux Mémoires sur la Chine" du P. Le Comte', in *Recherches de Science Religieuse,* XXXVII (1950): 370–372.

70. See extracts from Varet's journal, originally published by A Gazier in the *Bulletin Philologique et Historique* of the Comité des Travaux Historiques et Scientifiques, for 1916, in Etiemble, *Les Jesuites en Chine,* 59–63.

71. *Lettre du R. Père Louis Le Comte de la Compagnie de Jésus à Monseigneur le Due du Maine sur les Cérémonies de la Chine* (Paris, 1700). At the same time he wrote a long letter to the Jesuit General which contained a full defence of Jesuit practices re the Rites (ARSJ: JS *166,* 342–46, dated Versailles, 13 July 1699).

72. A letter of Jean de Fontaney written from Port-Louis on 9 August 1700, on the eve of his return to China, complains bitterly of 'la dernière folie' of P Le Comte in claiming that the Chinese do regard Confucius as an idol (ARSJ: JS 167, 285 v).

questions of fact. Louis de Cicé MEP, Vicar Apostolic of Siam and Japan, in a published *Letter* objecting to the Jesuits having cited him in their defence, makes a typical statement when he says:

> You (Jesuits) want . . . to lead us back to questions of words and to leave the area of knowledge, that is, of healthy and pure Theology, where you have been recalled despite yourselves.[73]

But this was precisely the question. Was the Rites issue one of 'theology' or 'words'? of *a priori* judgements or of facts about China? There was much truth in Voltaire's characterisation of the Rites Controversy as 'the most noteworthy example of abuse of words'.[74]

The Le Comte episode, however, reminds us that there were serious questions of theology involved. In his *Eclaircissement,* which concentrated on the theological issues in the dispute, he pointed out that the condemnation of his propositions was two-edged. While it might prevent the deists[75] from taking comfort, it would encourage the 'free-thinkers and atheists'.

> Would it not be much more dangerous to condemn the line taken in my book, by saying that the ancient Chinese, as those of the present day, are atheists. For will not the Freethinkers take advantage of what is presented to them, that in an empire so vast, so enlightened, established so solidly, and so flourishing, whether in the number of its inhabitants, or in the invention of almost all the arts, the Divinity has never been acknowledged. What, then, will become of the-reasoning of the Fathers of the Church who, to prove the existence of God, have drawn on the agreement of all peoples, arguing that Nature has impressed the idea on them so deeply that nothing can efface it?[76]

---

73. *Lettre . . . aux RR. PP. Jésuites sur les Idolatries et sur les Superstitions de la Chine* (Paris, 1700), 33.
74. Article 'Abus des Mots' in his *Dictionnaire Philosophique,* Oeuvres (Paris, 1878), t 17, 50.
75. Some of the Doctors of the Sorbonne had founded their objections to Le Comte on these grounds. See the *Lettre d'un Docteur sur ce qui se passe dans les assemblées de la faculté de théologie de Paris,* Cologne, 1700, as cited in Pinot, *La Chine,* 306, n 66.
76. *Eclaircissement,* 14, quoted in Pinot, *La Chine,* 307.

He cites many theological precedents for arguing that vestiges of revelation were contained in the ancient books of all nations[77] and, indeed, one might argue that this was the dominant theological tradition in late seventeenth century France.[78] Its rejection by the Sorbonne and the insistence of the 'Maigrotiens' on the atheism of the Chinese was fatally to undermine the argument for God's existence from universal consent, as thinkers like Pierre Bayle were quick to note. On the other hand, deists like Voltaire drew on the Jesuit reports for evidence for their position.[79] Each party created an image of 'Confucius' and of 'China' according to its favoured model, and the K'ung-tzu of history and of Chinese tradition was forgotten in the ensuing argument.

The papal legates

The decisions of the Sorbonne in 1700 and of Rome in 1704 might not necessarily have proved fatal to the Jesuit interpretation of Confucianism. They were limited in scope and their practical provisions were not much stricter than the evolved Jesuit policy. They could to some extent be tempered by decisions of the local Bishops and Vicars Apostolic, and as long as the general accommodation to Confucianism was retained, the accepted image of the *t'ien-chu chiao* would not be greatly affected. The two papal legations of the Patriarch (later Cardinal) Charles Maillard de Tournon and the Patriarch Carlo Ambrogio Mezzabarba, and the subsequent papal bulls of 1710, 1715 and 1742, destroyed any hope of this. Whether they were also responsible for the destruction of the mission is a further question we must consider, but there can be no doubt that they proved the final blow to the Confucian-Christian symbiosis developed by the Jesuits from Matteo Ricci through the seventeenth century.

The de Tournon mission (1705–1710) was certainly the most crucial episode in the negotiations between the Church authorities in Rome and the China mission. Since the declaration of K'ang-hsi in

77. See Davy, 'La Condemnation . . .', 387–78.
78. v A Dupront, *Pierre Daniel Huet et l'exégèse comparatiste au XVIIe Siède* (Paris: Droz, 1930).
79. See, for example, Chapter II of the *Essai sur les Moeurs;* chapter XVIII of *La Philosophie d'Histoire;* and the articles on 'Catechisme Chinois', 'Chine' and 'Philosophie' in the *Dictionnaire Philosophique.*

1700, the confrontation was necessarily now one between the pope, through his representative, and the Emperor; between the head of the Lord of Heaven Religion and the Son of Heaven. Hence, the personal qualities of the Legate became an important factor in the situation, and to fully understand the course of events a detailed study of the Legate's personality and actions are essential. Once more I must excuse myself from that task, and restrict myself to a few comments on the attitude of the Legate to Confucianism and to the Jesuits. When Father Francis Rouleau's long-awaited study of the de Tournon mission is published, it may be possible to arrive at a just appreciation of his tragic role in the history of the Jesuit mission in China.[80] Meanwhile, his actions, his relations with the Jesuits and other missionaries, even the bare chronology of events, remain shadowy, not because of lack of material, but because of their very abundance and mutual contradictions. Rather than follow Rosso's procedure of compiling a consistent narrative from a pastiche of sources, I prefer to postpone final judgement until it is possible to collate fully all the sources and subject them to critical analysis.

It is, however, possible to make a few general comments about de Tournon's behaviour without examining the detailed charges and counter-charges. Even before he arrived in China, he had left behind him in India and Manila a trail of excommunications which suggests at the least, an undiplomatic temperament; and the same mode of procedure continued during his mission to China and his final sojourn in Macao. He was subject to continual illness, described by Rosso as 'partial paralysis and convulsion',[81] which may explain but does not make less significant his constant irritation, suspiciousness and reversals of judgement. Whatever his private instructions, Innocent XI's anti-Rites decree cannot have reached him by the time he arrived in China, yet he acted as if the matter was decided. He was young, with no experience of missionary work, no knowledge of the language, and surrounded by a large retinue of curial officials and interpreters who

80. Meanwhile, we have, as a starting point, Father Rouleau's long article, 'Maillard de Tournon: Papal Legate at the Court of Peking: The First Imperial Audience', in *Archivum Historicum Societatis Jesu,* XXXI (1962): 264–323. See also Rosso, *Apostolic Legations* chapter VII and Documents 3–8; Pastor, *History of the Popes,* XXXIII, chapter VII; and Archbishop Lo-kuang's *Chiao-ting yu Chung-kuo shih chieh shih,* chapters 4 and 5.

81. *Apostolic Legations,* 157.

shielded him from unpleasant Chinese realities. The result was that what should have been a fact-finding mission and an act of conciliation, became an exercise in *Romanità* and ecclesiastical politics.

That the question was closed as far as de Tournon is concerned is shown in his exchange with Alvaro Benavente OSA, the Vicar Apostolic of Kiangsi, in Canton in mid-1705, that is a few months after his arrival and before news of the *Cur Deus Optimus* decree can have reached China. Benavente had presented the Legate with a treatise on the rites, defending the Jesuit practices. De Tournon replied that he intended to condemn the use of *t'ien* and *shang-ti* and at least the solemn cult of Confucius and the ancestors, although he had powers to suspend such a decision if he thought it best.[82] Benavente returned to Kiangsi hopeful that 'new reasons' might persuade de Tournon to change his mind.[83] He would have been disturbed to read, in a letter written by de Tournon shortly after the interview, that the Legate thought him 'little resigned to evident reason in the matter', and was grateful to him mainly for providing ammunition to use against the Jesuits.[84] I do not know at what time the Legate reached the conclusion that 'the China mission will have to be destroyed before it can be reformed',[85] but it seems likely that it was quite early in his visitation.

It must have been at this period that de Tournon met Claude de Visdelou SJ, who is the only Jesuit known to have taken an anti-Rites position at the time. The Legate made much of Visdelou, later securing his consecration as Bishop of Claudiopolis and Vicar Apostolic of Kweichow. Certainly, Visdelou was the most able sinologist amongst the missionaries in China to adopt Maigrot's position on the Rites, as his published and unpublished translations and treatises attest. Even his most severe critics admitted his expertise in Chinese. None of his extant works deal directly with the Rites question, but his translations suggest that he took his stand, as Longobardo had done earlier, on the Neo-Confucian commentaries. Unlike Longobardo, however, he

82. Benavente to Thomas, 20 July 1705 (ARSJ: JS *168*, 270r-v).
83. Benavente to Thomas, 20 July 1705 (ARSJ: JS *168*, f 270r-v).
84. Dc Tournon to the Abbe San Giorgio (di Biandrate), Canton, 20 August 1705 (ARSJ: JS *168*, 287r).
85. Onorato Ferrario, who had been sent to China to pave the way for the mission of the second Legate, Mezzabarba, wrote to Foucquet of the 'prophetic saying' of de Tournon that 'Sinensis Missio, prius destruetur antequam reformetur' (B Vat: *Borg Cin 468* [H]).

claimed that the Chinese did believe in spirits. Hence, although they were atheists, their ceremonies were often superstitious. And since their rituals were originally idolatrous, rather than part of the worship of a pure supreme being, they should be forbidden to all Christians.

Visdelou initially, like other missionaries, accepted and defended the Jesuit interpretation of Chinese Rites. There was even question of him going to Rome in 1701 with Noël to represent the views of the mission;[86] but he seems already to have been questioning some aspects of the customs approved by the Jesuits. By 1704—that is, before de Tournon's arrival—he was regarded by his fellow-Jesuits as committed to the anti-Rites position.[87] Despite an appeal for loyalty from the Jesuit Bishop, and former Visitor, Carlo Turcotti, on 9 May 1705,[88] he declared himself to the Legate as opposed to the Jesuit interpretation of Chinese Rites, and seems to have been one of de Tournon's chief sources of information. He was rewarded with a bishopric but was never able to take up his vicariate in Kweichow, owing to his refusal to accept the imperial *p'iao*, and ended his life in exile in Pondichery in India, studying and writing on Chinese history, and still maintaining his views on the Rites question. Visdelou's adherence to the opposition must have been a severe blow to the Jesuits.

Amongst the Foucquet Papers in the Vatican Library there is a collection of letters written in 1705–1706 by various French Jesuits in Peking to their colleague, Jean-François Foucquet, in the south.[89] They were private letters, obviously not intended for publication but for the information of their absent confrere, and the picture they present of de Tournon's activities between December 1705 and December 1706 is all the more valuable for that. They cover the Imperial audiences of 31 December 1705 and 29–30 June 1706; Maigrot's audience with the Emperor on 26 July 1706; and the protracted negotiations preceding the Legate's departure for the South in August, relating to K'ang-hsi's

86. See Foucquet's letter to le Gobien, 6 December 1701, in PRO: SP. 9/239, 51.

87. See, for example, the letters of Pierre Jartoux, to the General, 20 August 1704 (ARSJ: JS *168*, 123v) which suggests his recall; and of Bouvet, Peking, 27 October 1704 (BN: *Fr. 17240*, 261r) which describes him as 'guère elloigné du sentiment de nos adversaires'.

88. Copy (sent to the Jesuit General) in ARSJ: JS *168*, 227–78.

89. 'Nouvelles ecrites de Pekin', B Vat: *Vat Lai 543*. Neither Rosso nor Rouleau seem to have been aware of the existence of this most valuable contemporary evidence for events in Peking, and I know of no writer on the subject who has used them.

projected embassy to the pope. I shall draw on these in the account that follows to illustrate some of the factors that made the de Tournon mission a disastrous failure, not just from the point of view of the Jesuit approach to Confucianism, but also in relation to the future of the Catholic Church in China.

The very first exchange between the Legate and the representatives of the Emperor in Peking was an indication of the fundamental dilemma of the legation. De Tournon was unable to state frankly the purpose of his mission, and the Chinese officials would not accept his claim that he was in Peking merely to thank the Emperor for his favours to Christianity. When he was pressed he added two other reasons—that he was also to examine the lives and behaviour of the missionaries, and to obtain permission for a representative of the pope to reside in Peking to keep the Pope informed of the health of the Emperor etc. and to act as Superior General of all the missionaries.[90] The mandarins in turn questioned de Tournon about his views on the Emperor's Declaration of 1700 on the Rites, thus suggesting that K'ang-hsi well understood the real purpose of the visit.[91] Over the next few days, the Emperor continued to question de Tournon through the officials about the purpose of his visit, and said that the matters raised were mere bagatelles'.[92] He also proposed that one of the experienced Jesuits be appointed to the new post of papal representative and was apparently annoyed at the Legate's negative reaction.

This was the background to the audience of 31 December 1705, which produced little result beyond the Emperor's agreement to send gifts to the pope—and even this was to serve as grounds for dispute when de Tournon insisted on his Auditor, Sabino Mariani, bearing the gifts rather than the Jesuit, Joachim Bouvet, nominated by the Emperor himself. De Tournon was convinced that the Jesuits were intriguing against him, and that K'ang-hsi would have granted his request for a permanent papal representative in Peking, if they had not persuaded him to refuse. Certainly the Jesuits were hostile

90. 'Nouvelles . . .', 10 (Letter of Regis, dated 21 January 1706).

91. 'Nouvelles . . .', 7 and 10. Régis also notes that the Manchu officials claimed de Tournon complained that the Jesuits should not have asked the Emperor for such a Declaration, but that de Tournon and his interpreter Appiani denied having said this.

92. 'Nouvelles . . .', 13. Régis gives the Emperor's Chinese expression as 'ouan y' *(wan-i)*, a 'toy' or 'trifle'.

to the scheme and Regis, in his letter to Foucquet, makes some tart comments to the effect that the Legate 'has nothing in mind except *his dear Italians,* and he regards their establishment as his major business'.[93] But, whatever the Jesuit's role in the affair, it is highly unlikely that any Chinese Emperor could have agreed to the unprecedented recognition of a permanent diplomatic mission in Peking. Kilian Stumpf SJ in his *Acta Pekinensia* which purports to give a full verbatim account of all the events of the legation, puts these words into the mouth of K'ang-hsi:

> China has no common business with Europe. I tolerate you on account of your religion; you should care about nothing besides your souls and your doctrine. Although you come here from different countries, you all have one religion, and so any European living here is capable of writing and receiving the papal letters you talk about. As for a 'confidential agent' I don't know what you are talking about. In China we have nothing of the sort. There are some people who are close to my Throne, some at a middle distance, and others far away. If I entrust some business to any one of them, will they not carry it out faithfully?[94]

The attitude expressed here is absolutely consistent with 'the Chinese view of their place in the world'[95] and, on these premises, de Tournon's plan for a permanent papal representative was doomed to failure.

During the early months of 1706, negotiations dragged on over such minor matters as a house in Peking for the Propaganda missionaries. In private, however, the Legate continued his investigations into the behaviour of the missionaries and their converts. It was at this time, apparently, that de Tournon and his suite began to take action on the Rites issue, presumably after receiving news of the decision of the papal commission. In a letter of 12 March 1706, the French Superior in Peking described for Foucquet a confrontation between de Tournon and a deputation of Peking Christians. They accused two missionaries, Appiani, the Legate's interpreter, and Antonio de

93. 'Nouvelles . . .', 25—the emphasis is Régis's own.

94. Rouleau, 'Maillard de Tournon . . .', 318.

95. See CP Fitzgerald's Chatham House Essay, *The Chinese View of their Place in the World* (London, 1964); and JK Fairbank, editor, *The Chinese World Order* (Cambridge, Mass: Harvard University Press, 1968).

Frossinone, of having ordered them to destroy their ancestral tablets,[96] which was a breach of the Ch'ing law code,[97] and threatened to report the matter to the Emperor. Soon after,[98] the Emperor questioned Gerbillon on the subject, and Gerbillon reported the Emperor's suspicion to de Tournon who, once again, accused the Jesuits of having prejudiced the Emperor against him, and denied that he had condemned the ancestral tablets. A few days later, however, he angrily refused a petition on the subject, tearing it up and stamping on it, to the indignation of the Chinese Christians who had presented it.[99]

At the audience of 29 June, which was the second and last formal audience,[100] the Emperor warned de Tournon to tell the pope 'that the Doctrine of Confucius was the teaching of the empire, and it could not be touched if one wished that the missionaries remain in China'.[101] De Tournon objected that there were some aspects of Confucius' teaching that contradicted Christianity, and cited, as an example, revenge. K'ang-hsi replied that Confucius did not allow private revenge, but only the processes of justice. It was at this point that de Tournon made a serious error.

> Monsignor replied that vindicative justice was a virtue rather than a vice, and according to what the Emperor had told him, that those who had made him believe that revenge was approved by Confucius, had deceived him. He had never read Chinese books, and so he could not judge this teaching, but that he had ordered a European Doctor from Fukien, called Yen (i.e. Yen T'ang, Charles Maigrot) to come. He was a clever man, who knew how to write (Chinese) and understood Chinese books.[102]

96. In ARSJ: JS *168*, 188.
97. They showed de Tournon, according to this account ('Nouvelles', 42) a passage in the 'Tai Tsing Liu' *(Ta-Ch'ing lu)* 'where it is said that violation of the tablets merits death' (presumably a reference to the section on 'lack of filial piety, the seventh of the "ten abominations"' v G Boulais, *Manuel du Code Chinois* [Shanghai, 1924], 29).
98. 16 April v 'Nouvelles . . .', 49.
99. 'Nouvelles . . .', 51.
100. On 30 June the Emperor entertained the Legate at a solemn reception in the Ch'ang-ch'un-yuan outside Peking.
101. 'Nouvelles . . .', 59. This letter is dated 'Peking 6 Aoust 1718'. Clearly it dates from 1706, and the '1718' is a slip of the pen indicating, presumably, the year when Foucquet copied these letters into his notebook.
102. 'Nouvelles . . .', 60–61.

The Emperor immediately ordered that Maigrot should be sent to him in his summer residence when he arrived.

The interrogation of Maigrot, who arrived in Peking on the very day of the second audience, was a turning point in the whole affair. It is doubtful whether the Emperor, up to this time, knew of Maigrot's role in the controversies. Now de Tournon had thrust him into the centre of the stage. The 'Nouvelles Ecrits' give many examples of Maigrot's failure to live up to de Tournon's high praise of his knowledge of Chinese both during his interrogation by the mandarins and at his audience in Manchuria.[103] Even if these are discounted as Jesuit propaganda, which I believe unlikely in view of the private nature of the Foucquet correspondence, the results of Maigrot's appearance in Peking were decisive. To quote Maigrot's modern defender, Antonio Sisto Rosso, 'The Emperor, disgusted with the Bishop's ignorance of language and obstinate views on the rites, issued a decree of blame and reprimand against Maigrot, on August 2, and addressed a stern communication of the proceedings to the Legate on August 3'.[104] On 17 December, Maigrot and two other missionaries were expelled from China, and all missionaries were ordered to receive a *p'iao*, or certificate, authorising them to remain in the country on condition that they accepted 'the prescriptions of Matteo Ricci'.[105] Those who did not were to be expelled immediately. During the Imperial tour of inspection of the South in early 1707, K'ang-hsi through his son Prince Chih, personally examined many of the missionaries, 'granted certificates to some, and ordered others expelled.'[106]

Meanwhile, de Tournon, on his way back to Macao, issued in Nanking on 21 January 1707, a decree against the Rites. It was a direct reply to the Emperor's decrees about the *p'iao,* and instructed the missionaries how they were to reply to the questions asked in

103. See 'Nouvelles . . .', 61–70, 73–76, 79.

104. *Apostolic Legations,* 169.

105. *Li Ma-tou te kuei-chü.* I have not seen a Chinese text of the original decree, but the expression is used in the decree of 19 April 1707 which reiterated the Emperor's instructions (No 4 in Ch'en Yiian's *K'ang-hsi yü Lo-ma,* and translated as Document 5 in Rosso's *Apostolic Legations,* 242–4). Rosso translates *Kuei-chü* as 'customs', but it has a stronger normative sense, as is evident from its literal meaning, 'compass and square'.

106. See Rosso, *Apostolic Legations,* 172–78.

connection with the certificate.[107] The instructions purport to be in accordance with the recent degree of Pope Clement XI, but a close examination shows that they go decisively beyond both Maigrot's original decree and the decisions of Rome in 1704. They are bold and unqualified, condemning all 'sacrifices' to Confucius and the ancestors, all use of ancestor tablets, and all claims of correspondence between *T'ien* and *Shang-ti* and the Christian God. And they are to be defended by appealing to 'the infallible rule of Christians in matters of faith', the Holy See. Finally, all discussion is ruled out by a clause forbidding any 'interpretation' of the Mandate, under pain of excommunication.

If de Tournon thought to silence all discussion by this means, he was mistaken. The missionaries were, in effect, placed in the dilemma of having to choose between expulsion and accepting the *p'iao* on conditions which appeared contrary to the 1704 papal constitution. Many of them chose the latter course, and defended themselves in different ways. As yet the constitution itself had not been published either in China or Europe and there seemed reasons to doubt whether its scope was as wide as de Tournon claimed. Some pinned their hopes on the mission of the Jesuits, Antonio de Barros and Antoine Beauvollier, sent to the pope by K'ang-hsi in late 1706, and of Guiseppe Provana and Jose de Arxo, sent after them in 1707. Others, especially the Portuguese Jesuits, denied the validity of de Tournon's acts, which were held to be in breach of the Portuguese *padroado.* Yet others questioned whether there had been a papal decree at all, or argued that it was a counsel of prudence rather than a doctrinal statement.

Gradually, however, it became clear that de Tournon's actions were sanctioned by Rome. In January 1710 a ship arrived in Macao from Manila, bringing a group of Italian missionaries conveying the Cardinal's red hat to be presented to de Tournon, who lay sick and under house arrest by the Portuguese authorities, in that city.[108] On

107. I follow the Latin text given in Dunyn-Szpot, *Collectanea Historiae Sinensis,* II, 476v-477r (ARSJ: JS *105,* 11). For a French translation, see Etiemble, *Les Jésuites en Chine,* 111–15.

108. On de Tournon's conflict with the Portuguese in Macao, an excellent source is the 'Colecçao de Varias Factos acontecidos nesta mai nobre cidade de Macao pelo decurso dos annos', published by JM Braga in *A Voz do Passado* (Macao, 1964). See, especially, the entries under the years 1705–1710.

15 September 1710, Clement XI confirmed de Tournon's Mandate of 1707, and on 19 March 1715, he issued the constitution *Ex illa die* which seemed definitively to condemn the Jesuit position. Not only did it reiterate the previous prohibitions, but it prescribed an oath to be taken by all on the mission, to obey the prohibitions. its language was strong and unequivocal.

> All the above responses are to be observed with everything contained in them, exactly, completely, absolutely, inviolably and undisturbed, And let them take care and procure as far as they can, that they are similarly observed by those of whom they have charge. Nor may they dare or presume to contravene them, or anything expressed in them, whether on any grounds, reason, occasion, colour or pretext whatsoever.[109]

In fact, this was not the end of the Rites Controversy. A second papal legate, Carlo Ambrogio Mezzabarba, Patriarch of Alexandria, was sent in 1720, apparently to tie up the loose ends and implement the decree. He avoided some of de Tournon's problems by gaining approval of the King of Portugal, João V, and sailing by way of Lisbon on a Portuguese ship. He seems, too, to have behaved much more diplomatically during the series of audiences he had with the Emperor in December 1720, and January and February 1721. However, he was no more successful than de Tournon in convincing K'ang-hsi to allow Chinese Christians to follow the papal decrees on the Rites. Despite the constant complaints in the record of the embassy by Viani, the Legate's confessor, that the mission was frustrated by the intrigues of various Jesuits at the court—Thomas Pereira, João Mourão and the Chinese Jesuits Louis Fan (Shou-i) are particularly mentioned—it is clear from Viani's own report of the interviews with the Emperor, that the differences between Rome and K'ang-hsi were fundamental and irreconcilable.

At the second and private audience of 3 January 1721, K'ang-hsi asked how the Pope could judge Chinese affairs when he (the Emperor) does not judge European affairs.[110] Mezzabarba replied that

109. Text in *Magnum Bullarium Romanum,* XI, 49–53; this section (paragraph 5) on page 51. JJ Heeren's version of the Chinese text of the decree in his article, 'Father Bouvet's Picture of Emperor K'ang Hsi', *Asia Major,* VII (1932) Appendix A, 367–570, suggests that it was even stronger in tone, if not contents, than the Latin text.

110. S Viani, *Istoria delle cose operate nella China da Monsignor Gio. Ambrogio Mezzabarba,* 2nd edition (Cologne, 1740), 107.

the Pope was assisted by the Holy Spirit[111] and that he did not judge Chinese affairs, but only those regarding religion.[112] At a later interview (10 January 1721) K'ang-hsi again objected that the Chinese Rites could only be judged by someone with a perfect knowledge of the Chinese language and Chinese beliefs.[113] 'This great struggle which has arisen amongst Europeans about our praiseworthy rites, is not a controversy about religion, but a quarrel instigated by vile, rebellious men . . . the constitution issued by your Pope is not a prohibition belonging to your Holy Law, but a pure vendetta against the Fathers of the Society.'[114] Mezzabarba's retinue seems to have interpreted this as evidence that the Jesuits, especially Louis Fan, had persuaded the Emperor that Maigrot and others had been engaged in an anti-Jesuit conspiracy.[115] They should, however, have been disabused by the audience of 14 January.

This fifth audience is undoubtedly the key incident in the Mezzabarba legation. Although the accounts of Viani[116] and of the Jesuits[117] vary somewhat, they agree that the Emperor specifically defended the practices of Matteo Ricci, including the use of ancestral tablets, and of the terms *t'ien* and *shang-ti.* According to the 'Mandarins' Diary', Chia Lo (Mezzabarba) denied that he had come 'to argue about the doctrine of China' and begged pardon for Maigrot and others who had sent to Rome false reports about the Jesuits.[118] Viani, and the Jesuits' Latin version of the 'Diary' agree that the Emperor then made some remarks which appeared to approve the promulgation of *Ex illa die* in China, but the Jesuits took them as ironical, while Mezzabarba and his suite took them literally.[119]

111. K'ang-hsi, at a later audience, shrewdly remarked that Maigrot must be the Holy Spirit of the Christians (Viani, Istoria, 158–59).
112. Viani, *Istoria,* 108.
113. Viani, *Istoria,* 116–119.
114. Viani, *Istoria,* 117–118.
115. See Mezzabarba's additions ('aggiunte') to Viani's narration, especially No 4, Viani, *Istoria,* 111–12.
116. Viani, *Istoria,* 122 ff.
117. As presented in the 'Mandarins' Diary', Document 23 in Rosso, *Apostolic Legations,* 357–60. A considerable portion has also been translated by Dun J Li, in his *China in Transition,* 1517–1911 (New York, 1970), Document 9, 20–22.
118. v Rosso, *Apostolic Legations,* 359.
119. Viani, *Istoria,* 129 *cf Diarium,* quoted in Rosso, *Apostolic Legations,* 360, n 21. According to Régis, who was present, the Emperor remarked 'with a sardonic laugh' that these were minor matters that should be dealt with by the mandarins (ARSJ: JS *198,* 239v). De Mailla, who was also present, blamed Pedrini and Ripa for mistranslating (ARSJ: JS *198,* 255r).

If the Emperor did approve, he certainly changed his mind a few days later, when he read the Chinese text of the papal decree. There can be no question of K'ang-hsi's reaction, because the original vermilion endorsement in the Emperor's own hand has been preserved.

> On reading this proclamation, I can only conclude that the Westerners are small minded. How can they talk about the great ideas of China? No Westerner understands Chinese books, and when they discuss them, our people find many of their remarks ridiculous. Now I have seen the Legate's proclamation, and it is just the same as Buddhist and Taoist heresies and superstitions. I have never seen such nonsense as this. Henceforth no Westerner may propagate his religion in China. It should be prohibited in order to avoid more trouble.[120]

The threat was unmistakable.

At this point Mezzabarba agreed to promulgate eight 'Permissions' which he claimed to have received from the church authorities in Rome[121] and which mitigated the force of the decrees to some extent. They represented a return to Maigrot's regulations, before de Tournon's blanket prohibitions.[122] For example, modified ancestor tablets were permitted; funeral ceremonies, and those in honour of

---

120. My translation after the facsimile text at the conclusion of Ch'en Yiian's *K'ang-hsi yü Lo-ma cf.* translations in Rosso, *Apostolic Legations,* 376, and (the slightly different version in the 'Mandarins' Diary') in Li, *China in Transition;* 22, Rosso, *Apostolic Legations,* 364; and Heeren, 'Father Bouvet's Picture', 569–570.
121. It was later claimed that Mezzabarba had exceeded his powers by promulgating the 'Eight Permissions' but several references in Viani (for example 68, 71–72, 160) and the 'Mandarins' Diary' indicate that he had announced their existence from the beginning of his mission. The mystery has been partly cleared up by a letter recently discovered in the Archives of Propaganda, in which Mezzabarba explains that the 'Eight Permissions' were the replies to certain 'doubts' proposed to Rome by some of the Vicars Apostolic, and which he had received in Lisbon before his departure (see artictle 'Mezzabarba' by N Kowalski in the *Enciclopedia Cattolica,* VIII, cols 924–255). It is clear, however, that their proclamation was to be at Mezzabarba's discretion, and K'ang-hsi may have been correct in thinking that the Pope had, in effect, given Mezzabarba 'two different versions of the Breve and Constitution, directing (him) to submit them to the throne upon arrival in China, according to circumstances.'—'Mandarins' Diary', 350–3511.
122. See Etiemble, *Les Jesuites en Chine,* 137–78, for a translation of the 'Eight Permissions'.

Confucius were allowed, provided they did not include superstitious practices; while prostrations, incense, even offerings of food, were permitted in certain circumstances. When Mezzabarba departed on 3 March, it must have seemed that the situation regarding the Rites was largely as it had been before de Tournon's arrival.

The two missions had certainly soured K'ang-hsi's relations with the missionaries, or at least with the official hierarchy of the church. What is remarkable in the circumstances is his continued toleration and goodwill rather than his occasional outbursts of impatience. When we consider the amount of time and energy he devoted to the domestic affairs of one of the smallest of Chinese sects, it is evident how highly he must have valued the services of the small group of missionaries at court. Their precise role as cultural brokers and foreign experts, even perhaps as personal friends and advisers to K'ang-hsi, has never been fully evaluated,[123] and probably never will, since it belongs to that area of inner court affairs that escaped the surveillance and recording brush of official historians. But the tantalising glimpses we get of that relationship in Jesuit and official Chinese documents, leaves no doubt as to its importance.

Scarcely had Mezzabarba departed, however, than the intriguing began again. Some of the missionaries opposed to the Jesuits, wrote to Rome urging the repeal of the 'Eight Permissions'.[124] Mezzabarha himself adopted an increasingly hostile attitude to the Jesuits, and just before his departure from Macao, issued a Pastoral Letter, accusing the Jesuits of seeking to evade the papal constitutions by giving up missionary activity altogether. And in Rome the Congregation of Propaganda Fide adopted an ever more hostile attitude to the Jesuits of the China Mission. The charges multiplied and became more detailed in a way that suggests an organised campaign against the Jesuits with correspondents in China feeding information to Rome. The Jesuit General replied in 1725 with a Memorial and a collection of documents demonstrating the good faith and correct behaviour of the

123. See CW Allan, *Jesuits at the Court of Peking* (Shanghai, nd); and TE Treutlin, 'Jesuit Missions in China during the last Years of K'ang-his', in *Pacific Historical Review*, X (1941): 435–46.

124. See the letter of Ignatius Kogler SJ to the Portuguese Assistant, Peking, 13 November 1721, in ARSJ: JS *198*, 311v-316r.

Jesuits in China',[125] which seems to have staved off the attack for the time being. Propaganda, however, continued to gather information from anti-Jesuit sources, such as the ex-Jesuits, Visdelou in Pondichery, and Foucquet in Rome; from Matteo Ripa in Naples; and from Carlo Castorano OFM, Vicar General of the Diocese of Peking.

The last named produced for the benefit of the Congregation, on his return after thirty-three years in China, a detailed study of some of the Chinese books in the Library of the College of Propaganda Fide.[126] It was presented to Cardinal Gentili in 1739 and must certainly have influenced the deliberations then going on in the Congregation. Its conclusions were definite and unqualified. The modern Chinese are atheists; the ancient Chinese were idolaters; the Chinese classics and most of the Chinese works of the Jesuits and their converts teach doctrines contrary to Christian faith. Ancestor rites are illicit because they were originally sacrifices to the spirits of the ancestors, hence idolatrous, and even in the light of the modern materialistic interpretation, involve superstitious beliefs about the *ch'i* or material part of the souls of the departed.[127] Confucius is regarded and worshipped as a saint whereas in reality he was a public idolater and private atheist.[128]

In the light of such advice, it is not surprising to find that the Holy See decided finally against the Rites. The decree 'Ex Quo Singulari' of 1742, not only reconfirmed the decrees of 1704, 1710 and 1715, but revoked Mezzabarba's 'Eight Permissions' as the product of 'obsessions and anxieties' and permitting practices 'totally superstitious'. All missionaries not prepared to follow the prohibitions were to be recalled, and all must take an oath to observe all the precepts, including a condemnation of the practices permitted by Mezzabarba.[129]

Roma locuta est; causa finita est.

125. The 'Memorial' and the 'Summario di diverse lettere e documenti dall' anno 1706 fino al 1722, per giustificare la sollecita, e sincera condotto del P. Gle. della Comp. di Gesu . . .' are found in ARSJ: JS *198*, 4–344. Many of the letters cited in the preceding pages come from this collection.

126. The 'Parva Elucubratio super quosdam Libras Sinenses ab Illmo et R.^{mo} D. Archepiscopo Myrensi de Nicolais relictos', *ms* in B Vat: *Borg Lot 538.*

127. See 'Parva Elucubratio', 102–23.

128. See 'Parva Elucubratio', 422–507.

129. See the text in the *Magnum Bullarium Romanum,* Benedict XIV, Tom I, 188–204.

The aftermath of the Rites

All writers on the Chinese missions are agreed that the early eighteenth century was a period of marked decline for the Catholic Church in China. Not all, however, agree that it was the Rites Controversy that caused the decline, either wholly or mainly. I will not attempt a definitive answer to this question which depends to a large extent on a comparative assessment of the policies of the three Emperors whose rule spans the eighteenth century, K'ang-hsi, Yung-cheng and Ch'ien-lung. It seems, however, that the period immediately following the de Tournon mission and the early 1720s were the crucial turning points. The first of these can be attributed to the Rites issue, the second hardly at all.

There are no reliable statistics for church membership, baptisms etc. for any period of the old Jesuit mission. One is forced, therefore, to rely on general impressions derived from the reports of as large a number of mission stations as possible. The task has been somewhat simplified for us, although in an admittedly polemic context, by the collection of documents produced by the Jesuit General, Tamburini, for the Congregation of Propaganda Fide, in 1725. One section of this collection[130] is devoted to evidence of defections and difficulties caused by the Rites decision. It adds up to a rather pessimistic picture, especially regarding the upper-class converts for whom Confucian and domestic rituals were of central importance. Even the Jesuits of the Court betray a new tone of pessimism in their letters. The arch-optimist, Joachim Bouvet, whose *Portrait Historique de l'Empereur de la Chine* of 1697 is a high-water mark in enthusiasm for China and its ruler, adopted a much more cautious tone on his return to China in 1699.[131] By the time of Ch'ien-lung, the Jesuits at Court were writing of the Emperor without bothering to disguise their disillusionment.[132] But their very presence indicates that they had not given up hope.

In his last years, apart from his objections to the papal decrees on the Rites, K'ang-hsi was also beginning to become suspicious

130. Section 5, f 73 ff of ARSJ: JS *198*.
131. See Rouleau, 'Maillard de Tournon', 270, n 10.
132. See, especially, the letter of Amiot, dated 17 October 1794, published in the 1811 edition of the *Lettres Edifiantes,* t 23.

of the western maritime activity in the south. His southern tours had alerted him to the constant and illegal trading and smuggling activities of the people of the coastal provinces as well as the arrival in increased numbers of ships of new Western powers. In 1716, he issued a warning to his high officials:

> After hundreds of years, We are afraid that the Middle Kingdom will suffer injury from the overseas countries, for example, from the European countries. This is only a prediction . . . We have reigned in the Empire so many years and found the Chinese very difficult to deal with because their hearts are divided. Now our country has long enjoyed peace and order, We must not forget danger.[133]

The next year, Ch'en Mao, a military commander in Kwangtung, memorialised against Christianity, not on the familiar grounds of heterodoxy, but on suspicion of collusion with Western powers.

> Catholicism originated in Europe; now the Westerners have set up churches in various provinces which attract bandits and rascals. The hearts of these Westerners are inconceivable. At present they have established many churches both within and without the city of Canton. Moreover, their foreign ships also throng in the harbour of Canton. How can we guarantee that the missionaries and Western merchants do not communicate with each other and cause trouble?[134]

The Emperor agreed with the Board of War that the old prohibitions against the preaching of Christianity in the provinces should be revived.[135]

The beginning of the reign of Yung-cheng, in 1723, saw the introduction of a much harsher policy. Yung-cheng seems to have been suspicious by nature and the circumstances of his accession led

---

133. Fu, *Documentary Chronicle,* 123. Decree of 9 December 1716 *cf* J Spence, *Emperor of China* (London: Random House, 1974), 82.
134. Fu, *Documentary Chronicle,* 123–24.
135. Decree of 24 May 1717, Fu, *Documentary Chronicle,* 124 *cf* Spence, *Emperor of China,* 82–83.

him consciously to reverse many of his father's policies.[136] A year after his accession, he agreed to a memorial of the Board of Rites expelling all missionaries to Macao,[137] which was later modified to permit missionary scientists and other useful Westerners to remain in Peking[138] and the others to reside in Canton.[139] In 1732 those in Canton were finally expelled, leaving only twenty-three missionaries in Peking, and a few in hiding in the provinces.[140] Yung-cheng's actions against the Portuguese Jesuit João Mourão[141] and the Manchu Christian Sourniama family[142] may be explained as politically motivated. But his objections also appear to have been doctrinal.[143] In a reply to the

---

136. v Hummel, *Eminent Chinese,* 915–920 (Fang Chao-ying's biography of 'Yin-chen'); Wang Chung-han, 'Ch'ing Shih-tsung to-ti k'ao-shih', in *Yen-ching hsueh-pao,* XXXVI/62 (1949): 205–261; and Meng Sen, 'Shih-tsung ju-ch'eng ta-t'ung k'ao-shih', in his *Ch'ing-tai shih* (Taipei, 1960), 470–510. The most complete survey in English of the controversy about the legitimacy of his accession, together with a somewhat partisan account of his reign is Pei Huang's *Autocracy at Work* (Bloomington: Indiana University Press, 1974). Equally partisan and to my mind ultimately unconvincing, is the account of the accession given by Silas Wu in *Passage to Power* (Cambridge, Mass: Harvard University Press, 1979. Both Huang and Wu, however, fully document the precariousness of Yung-cheng's position and his resolution to end the factionalism of his father's last days. See also, Tom Fisher 'New Light on the Accession of the Yung-cheng Emperor', *Papers on Far Eastern History,* 17 (1978): 103–136.
137. Decree of 12 January 1724, in Fu, *Documentary Chronicle,* 138.
138. 14 December 1724, in Fu, *Documentary Chronicle,* 139. For a list of those in Peking in October 1727, see A Gaubil, *Correspondance de Ptkin, 1722–1759* (Geneva, 1970), 180–181.
139. 3 February 1725, in Fu, *Documentary Chronicle,* 139–40. For a full account of the 1724 decrees and their effect, see de Mailla's letter in *Lettres Edifiantes,* XVII (1726): 163–284.
140. See *Lettres Edifiantes,* XXI (1734): viii (du Halde's 'Epistre'); and Porquet's letter of 11 December 1732 in *Lettres Edifiantes,* XXI (1734): 217–278.
141. See the decree of 2 July 1726 in Fu, *Documentary Chronicle,* 146–147, and the full discussion in D'Elia, *Il lontano . . . confino e la tragica morte del P. João Mourão S.I.* (Lisbon, 1963).
142. See Fu, *Documentary Chronicle,* 153–55 (decrees of 27 March and 8 June 1727); Ch'en Yuan, 'Yung-cheng chien feng t'ien-chu-chiao chih tsung-shih', in *Fu-jen hsüeh-chih,* III/2 (1932): 1–36; Hummel, *Eminent Chinese,* 692–94; Parrenin's letters in *Lettres Edifiantes,* XVII, (1726): 1–62; XVIII (1728): 33–121, 248–311; XIX (1729): 1–205; XX, (1731): 1–45; XXII, (1736): 44–98; and Gaubil's letters in his *Correspondance,* 145–171.
143. It should be noted that Yung-cheng's sympathies were decidedly Buddhist. In 1733 he edited, or caused to be edited in his name, an imperial collection of

Portuguese ambassador Metello de Sousa in May 1727, Yung-cheng railed against the unreason and un-Chineseness of Christianity. A translation of the Emperor's remarks can be found in Lo-shu Fu's *Documentary Chronicle of Sino-Western Re1ations,*[144] and they are represented more ideosyncratically, although not inaccurately, in Ezra Pound's sixty-first *Canto:*

> And he put out Xtianity
> chinese found it so immoral
> his mandarins found this sect so immoral
> 'The head of a sect' runs the law 'who deceives folk
> 'by pretending religion, ought damn well to be strangled'.
> No new temples for any hochang, taoists or similars
> *sic in lege*
> False laws are that stir up revolt by pretense of virtue,
> Anyone but impertinent fakers wd have admitted
> the truth of the Emperor's answer:
> . . .
> . . . nothing personal against Gerbillon and his colleagues, but
> Xtians are disturbing good customs seeking to uproot Kung's
> laws seeking to break up Kung's teaching.[145]

Some of Yung-cheng's fulminations against Christianity specifically mention the Rites decrees as the cause of his displeasure.[146] However, I think it likely that, irrespective of the Rites controversy, under Yung-cheng and Ch'ien-lung, Christianity would have fared badly. Both Emperors seem to have been concerned with their 'image' as orthodox *Chinese* Emperors,[147] as well as following a more typically

---

Ch'an Buddhist writings, the *Yü-hsüan yü-lu* which included (chapter 12) some recorded remarks of the Emperor himself on Buddhist topics. For a judicious survey of the evidence for Yung-cheng's motivation, see Pei Huang, *Autocracy at Work,* especially 48–50.

144. 155–156, after the *Shang-yü nei-ko,* chapter 14, 13a–15b.
145. *The Cantos of Ezra Pound* (London, 1954), 350–3511. See also Canto LX, 344 & 346, on K'ang-his's decree of toleration and the activities of 'the archbishop of Antioch'.
146. See, for example, the account of the audience of 18 March 1733, in Gaubil's *Correspondance,* 351–353.
147. See Hummel, *Eminent Chinese,* 917–918, and 369–32; Goodrich, *The Literary Inquisition of Ch'ien-lung* (Baltimore: Waverley Press, 1935); and HL Kahn,

sinocentric policy in government than K'ang-hsi.[148] Their apparent reversal of K'ang-hsi's policy of toleration was really a return to a more normal pattern of foreign relations.

What was really crucial, however, was the reaction of local officials. A Christianity which appeared as seeking to uproot Kung's laws, seeking to break up Kung's teaching, which had no powerful scholar-official protectors, and whose writings were totally alien in terminology and content, had little hope of survival. The few missionaries who remained in the provinces, did so only as fugitives, ministering secretly to a cowed remnant of lower-class Christians, in constant fear of delation to the magistrates.[149] Christianity had finally acquired the label of 'foreign religion' that Ricci and his successors had worked so hard to evade. It was the Rites controversy that made that label unavoidable, and, to that extent, was responsible for the fate of Christianity in China. In the nineteenth and twentieth centuries, the label was flaunted and, in new circumstances, for a time brought success; but the truly Chinese Christianity Ricci had dreamed of never fully emerged. Is it too much to see the Rites controversy and the attitudes it engendered as the root cause of the fate of Christianity in modern China?

Monarchy in the Emperor's Eyes: Image and Reality in the Ch'ien-lung Reign (Cambridge, Mass, 1971).

148. A comparison between Jonathan Spence's *Ts'ao Yin and the K'ang-hsi Emperor,* New Haven, 1966, and Huang's *Autocracy at Work,* illustrates well the swing away from the 'personal' style of administration favoured by K'ang-hsi, to a more orthodox administrative system under Yung-cheng.

149. See, for example, F Margiotti, *II cattolicismo nello Shansi dalle origini al 1738* (Rome: Edizioni Sinica Franciscana, 1958), especially chapters 20 and 21; J Krahl, *China Missions in Crisis: Bishop Laimbeckhoven and His Times, 1738–1787* (Rome, 1964); and BH Willeke, *Imperial Government and Catholic Missions in China during the Years 1784–1785* (New York: The Franciscan Institute, 1948). Perhaps most revealing of all is the diary of the Chinese priest Andre Ly, written in Latin and revealing a Europeanising mentality (*Journal d'Andre Ly, Prêtre Chinois, missionaire et notaire apostolique 1746–1963,* edited by A Launay [Paris, 1906]).

4
Moses or China? The Jesuit Figurists

(Which is the more credible of the two, Moses or China?)
It is not a question of a rough estimate, I tell you that there is
something to confuse and something to enlighten us.
With this one word I destroy all your arguments. 'But
China obscures things', you say; and I reply: 'China obscures
the issues, but the light is there to be found; look for it' . . .
For this reason we must look at it closely; we must produce the documents.

Pascal, *Pensées*[1]

This enigmatic exchange between Pascal and his sceptical *alter ego* provides a useful point of entry to a discussion of the Jesuit 'Figurists'. Pascal was writing some fifty years before some of the French Jesuits in China developed their attempt to reconcile 'Moses' and 'China', that is to reconcile the data of the Bible, with early Chinese history and religion as represented in the Confucian tradition. But he had perceived with characteristic acuity what was to become one of the most hotly contested battlegrounds between orthodox Christians and 'enlightened' thinkers. Few, if any, of his contemporaries, and certainly not the Jesuits who were the main channel of information about China, were aware of the explosive implications of their interpretation of China. What Pascal saw, and what later thinkers saw more and more clearly, was that, ultimately, the new view of the history of mankind and the variety of human experience, deriving from reports about China and other non-Western civilisations, could not be reconciled with the accepted interpretation of the Bible.

1. Fragment 593 in the Brunschwicg edition of Pascal's *Oeuvres* (Paris, 1904), XIV, 33. Translation by M Tumell in his edition of the *Pensées* (London, 1962), 229.

Pascal clearly wished to preserve the latter, well summed up in the 'Moses' of his 'Moses or China' dichotomy. 'Moses' implied the orthodox view of the Pentateuch as the work of Moses, and a literal reading of the Old Testament as an authoritative account of the early history of mankind, and the acceptance of a date for the beginning of that history some 4000 years before Christ. If the Chinese account of their own history did not square with this, then the Chinese were wrong. However, as a close reading of the passage from his notebooks reveals, Pascal was far too sensitive and honest to allow the question to rest there. How are we to explain the way the Chinese depict their beginnings as a nation and the source of their view of man's place in the universe? Perhaps we must reinterpret the ancient Chinese books in the light of the Bible? Perhaps, even, we must reinterpret the Bible to some extent in the light of the early history of China?

Virgile Pinot in his brilliant study of the impact of 'China' on European thought, argues that we should read Pascal's remarks about China in the light of his distinction between the 'fleshly' and 'figurative' meanings of Scripture; that, just as he wished to resolve apparent contradictions in the text of the Bible by distinguishing a 'literal' and a 'spiritual' sense, so, he suggests, Pascal was arguing that Chinese history may be literally false, but figuratively true.[2] I am not sure that Pinot is correct in this interpretation. The passage is far too obscure both in wording and in logical articulation for any degree of certainty as to Pascal's thought on the subject. If this interpretation is correct, however, we must regard Pascal's as the first 'figurist' interpretation of the Chinese classics. 'Moses' is to be accepted as normative and 'China' reinterpreted in the light of 'Moses'.

I have argued in the previous chapter that the decision in the Rites controversy was crucial for Christianity in China, not so much in itself, or because of the adverse reaction of the Chinese Emperor and xenophobic Chinese officials, as because it prevented the full flowering of a distinctively Chinese Christianity. Thus far, I am in agreement with John Young in rejecting the adequacy of theories about the 'failure' of Christianity in China that rely either on 'the human factor' or on alleged sinocentrism.[3] But, where Young sees the crux of the problem in an incompatibility of Neo-Confucian metaphysics

2. Pinot, *La Chine et la Formation de l'Esprit Philosophique en France,* 347–8.
3. Young, *Confucianism and Christianity,* 128.

and Christian theology,[4] I see the problem of revelation as central. Certainly, the Jesuits were slow to appreciate the potentiality of Neo-Confucianism as a basis for developing a Chinese theology and, more importantly, a Chinese spirituality, but their converts were often well ahead of them in practice.[5]

The greater problem, however, far more serious than the danger of syncretism or idolatry, was one that arose from the very heart of the Jesuit strategy regarding Confucianism—the problem of revelation. Ricci had already come up against the reaction of many Chinese scholars to his presentation of Christianity as a kind of primitive Confucianism capped or complemented by the revelation of the triune God. If Confucianism already contained within itself, at least its pristine self, a pure natural theology, was there any need to go beyond it? Feng Ts'ung-wu, an eminent late Ming intellectual, wrote in his *Discussions in the Capital (Tu-men yü-lu),* in terms that show both an acquaintance with Ricci's writings and a shrewd appreciation of his drift:

> To accept and develop the heritage of Yao and Shun and to want to follow Confucius—that is precisely the way to honour Heaven. Those people, however, put aside Yao and Shun, Confucius and Mencius, and talk exclusively of the Lord of Heaven . . . Master Chang says: 'Our way is by itself sufficient; what business do we have to search elsewhere?' I also say: 'Our way is by itself perfect; what business do *we* have to search elsewhere?'[6]

Later Jesuit writings contain echoes of the same plaint from sympathetic Chinese scholars regarded as potential converts. Their problem was not so much the incredibility of a personal and triune God (although clearly this played a part) as the necessity for a self-revelation of a Heaven already fully encompassed by the Confucian tradition.

---

4. Young, *Confucianism and Christianity, cf* 34, 58, 65, 69–70, 75, 89–91, 126–127.
5. I base this judgement largely on a preliminary survey of manuscript Chinese works, often by third-generation Christian scholars, in the Jesuit archives in Rome. Full documentation of the claim must await further work on this material.
6. Translated from the *Feng Shao-hsü chi,* chapter 15, lla-b, in H Busch, 'The Tung-lin Academy and Its Political and Philosophical Significance', in *Monumenta Serica,* XIV (1949–55): 160–61.

It was in addressing this issue that the so-called 'Figurists' made a unique and important contribution to the Jesuit encounter with Chinese civilisation. In some respects Figurism is a side-issue, a dead-end so far as the main line of development of the Jesuit interpretation of Confucianism is concerned. Their motives and concerns went largely uncomprehended and unacknowledged by their missionary confreres; their ideas were seen as at best bizarre, at worst heretical; their new tactic for the conversion of China, evolved at the height of the Chinese Rites Controversy, was regarded by their superiors as a dangerous innovation. But they alone among the Jesuits of the old China mission directly confronted the problem presented by an ancient civilisation which had apparently developed in total isolation from the Judaeo-Christian revelation.

If 'Moses' could not be found in 'China', were they not then pitted against each other as alternative readings of human history? Did not 'China' cast doubts on 'Moses'? At the very time when, as Pascal had foreseen, men like Pierre Bayle were beginning to use the data derived from new worlds, not the least from China, to cast radical doubts on the authenticity and uniqueness of the Bible, the Figurists in China were attempting to find reflections, 'figures', of the biblical patriarchs and the biblical revelation in Chinese tradition itself. Their message was as much for the *literati* of Europe as the *literati* of China, and the urgency with which they undertook the task derived from their realisation that it was a European as well as a Chinese problem. It was no accident that it was precisely the best read and most intelligent of the Jesuits of the French mission who were attracted by Figurism. They had read the signs of the time aright.

A full study of the Jesuit Figurists would involve a prolonged excursus into the religious and intellectual history of Europe in the late seventeenth century, as well as an examination of early Ch'ing textual studies and commentaries. However, here I will confine myself to a brief outline of those ideas of the Figurists which relate to the Jesuit interpretation of Confucianism, and, especially, to the preliminary task of sorting out the divergent strands that are, for convenience, linked together as making up 'Figurism'.[7]

7. There is, as yet, no satisfactory general survey of the Figurists. Arnold Rowbotham's article in the *Journal of the History of Ideas,* XVII (1956): 471–85, 'The Jesuit Figurists and Eighteenth Century Religious Thought', is based almost exclusively on published sources. John Witek's work on Foucquet, 'An Eighteenth

Some of these strands were commonplaces of earlier missionary writings from China. From the beginning there was a vague concern with the relationship of the ancient Chinese to the biblical patriarchs. Juan Gonzalez de Mendoza's *History* of 1585 had postulated the peopling of China by the nephews of Noah.[8] Ruggieri had seen 'prophecies' and 'oracles' of Christianity in Chinese beliefs.[9] Longobardo, following João Rodrigues, had identified Fu Hsi with Zoroaster.[10] Gabriel Magalhaes, in his *History of China,* had commented that the *1-ching* was regarded by the Chinese as 'the most profound, the most learned and mysterious of any (book) in the world' and attributed it to Fu Hsi, the first king of China,[11] who reigned shortly after the Deluge.[12] Louis Le Comte had even written of the 'vestiges' of the knowledge of the true God transmitted by the sons of Noah, to be found in the Chinese histories.[13] These were, however, all works intended for a European audience, for whom the problem posed by China was one of relating the antiquity of the Chinese Empire to the accepted biblical framework. And none of them gave central importance or systematic development to these comments.

As we have seen, as early as 1664 a Chinese Christian, Li Tsu-po, had linked the Chinese doctrine of Heaven *(t'ien-hsueh)* with the earlier teaching of 'the men of Judea' from whom they were descended.[14] But Li's fate at the hands of Yang Kuang-hsien had warned the Jesuits, if warning was needed, of the dangers of this line of argument. Whatever their private thoughts on the subject, they saw clearly that their major problem was the foreignness of Christianity, and it would

Century Frenchman at the Court of the K'ang-hsi Emperor: A Study of the Early Life of Jean Francois Foucquet' (unpublished PhD thesis, Georgetown University, 1973), and David Mungello's *Leibniz and Confucianism: The Search for Accord* (Honolulu, 1977) (especially chapter 3, 'Leibniz and Bouvet') have opened up important areas, but neither is primarily concerned with Figurism as such.

8. *The History of the Great and Mighty Kingdom of China* (London, 1853), (Hakluyt Society, volumes XIV and XV) 1, 12.
9. *Commentarii* (ARSJ: JS *101,* II) 310v.
10. *Traite,* 11–12.
11. *A New History of China* (London, 1688), 98.
12. *A New History of China,* 251–52.
13. *Nouveaux Memoires,* II, 89.
14. *T'ien-hsüeh ch'uan-kai,* in *T'ien-chu-chiao tung-ch'uan wen-hsien hsü-pien,* II, 1058.

simply compound their difficulty to claim that Confucianism itself was foreign in origin. It was safer to remain silent on the question of origins, or, as Ricci had done, to appeal to 'natural reason' as the source of the early Chinese notions of God and morality.

By around 1700, when the Figurist system was germinating in China, conditions had changed. K'ang-hsi's apparent interest in Christianity and his curiosity about esoteric questions of science and literature, suggested to some of the Jesuits at court that a new approach, at once scientific and based on Chinese sources, might at last produce the fulfilment of their dreams—the conversion of the Emperor. The Jesuit interpretation of Confucianism, now over a century old, seemed based on an old-fashioned and inadequate theological foundation which concentrated in scholastic fashion on the definition of concepts, rather than on their historical origins. The Rites Controversy had revealed the vulnerability of a position which asserted the equivalence of 'natural' religion to 'revealed' religion. To men who came from an intellectual milieu in which the chronology, mythology, and customs of non-European civilisations were being used to undermine traditional beliefs, Figurism must have appeared the universal solution. If they could demonstrate from the ancient books of China that the Chinese had preserved vestiges of a primitive revelation, and that their history was really a 'figurative' version of the prediluvian biblical history of mankind, they would, at one and the same time, confirm the faith of the European sceptic and convince the Chinese of the equivalence of Christianity and their own most ancient beliefs. It was this seductive vision that explains the persistence, dedication and obstinacy of the Figurists.

The Figurists and their critics

One of the most serious difficulties facing anyone seeking to give a consistent exposition of the Figurists and their views, is the divergences amongst the Figurists themselves. A close view discloses not one system of interpretation of the Chinese classics, but several. Jean Bayard, a missionary sympathetic to the group, wrote to Etienne Souciet in 1722 that it was their lack of common purpose which was leading to their undoing.

> Everything that can be done, has been done, to persuade these four fathers [Bouvet, Gollet, Foucquet and de Prémare] to mutually aid each other, and to direct their studies to one common end by the same propositions. No one has got anywhere, and I fear that the differences in their ideas will harm the common design they have to demonstrate that the mysteries of Christianity have been known since the beginning of the world.[15]

This comment seems to me to be particularly perceptive. All they did have in common was their general conviction that in the Chinese classics 'the mysteries of Christianity' could be found concealed in some fashion or other. Their methods and the object of their studies varied enormously.

The term 'Figurist' seems to have been first applied to the group by the French savant Nicholas Fréret, or at least so a reference in a letter of Antoine Gaubil to Fréret of 28 October 1733 would suggest.[16] Gaubil, in the same letter, gives a list of some of the theories of the 'Figurists' which provides a convenient starting point for our investigation, and a tentative definition of 'Figurism'. They believe, he says, that in the Chinese *Ching* or classics, there are to be found 'vestiges' of the pure ancient religion of mankind: the creation, the fall of man, the flood etc. There are also 'prophecies' of the God-man to come, the Trinity, the Eucharist etc, 'very clearly marked'. Finally, the figures of the ancient Chinese kings in the classical version of early Chinese history are regarded as concealing the 'saints of the Old Testament', and the events are transposed from China to Mesopotamia, Judea and the earthly Paradise.[17] It is apparent that only the last of these features of 'Figurism' in fact involved an emphasis on the correspondence between the 'figures' of the *Ching* and the Old Testament. The other two—the theory of 'vestiges' and the theory of 'prophecies'—were, in principle if not in fact, quite distinct.

---

15. Bayard to Souciet, 1722 (? marked recue le 28e Juin 1723), published by H Cordier, in *Revue de l'Extrême Orient,* III (1887): 55–60; this passage on 58. The original is in ASJP: Brotier 110, No 10, 16–19.
16. 'Le nom de figuristes, que vous avez donné a plusieurs de nos missionnaires extrêmement plu . . .' (Gaubil, *Correspondance,* 363). Rowbotham, 'The Jesuit Figurists and Eighteenth Century Religious Thought', 473, further derives it from the ideas of the Jansenist Abbé d'Etémare, but I find little in common between d'Etémare's millenarianism and the Jesuit Figurists in China.
17. *Correspondance,* 364.

In the writings of the Figurists we shall find all three lines of argument developed, but with a differing emphasis. Bouvet, the founder of the system, had comparatively little to say about 'figures'; the stress in his work was quite definitely on 'prophecy', and his favourite field of study was the *I-ching* or 'Book of Changes' which gave full scope to this propensity. Foucquet, on the other hand, was primarily concerned with demonstrating that the traditional version of Chinese origins, especially in the *Shu-ching* or 'Book of History', was an elaborate allegory concealing beneath its 'figures' the Old Testament history. De Prémare, the third important 'Figurist' broke with Bouvet and Foucquet over the historical character of the classics. He upheld their basic historicity but claimed to detect in them 'vestiges' of an even earlier doctrine, the primitive revelation itself. Thus, we might argue that, in the strict sense, only Foucquet was a 'figurist'. Bouvet seems to have upheld a 'figurist' position, but to have gone far beyond it to a general theory of symbolism and prophecy; while de Prémare largely abandoned the 'figurist' aspects of the system and concentrated on 'vestiges'.

On the whole, I think that 'Figurism' is a misleading term and, but for the fact that it has become accepted usage, would be better abandoned. Father Vincent du Tartre, an acerbic critic of Bouvet and his followers, coined a number of colourful but pertinent terms to describe them and their ideas: 'the sect of Père Bouvet'[18] or 'Bouvetism';[19] 'this hieroglyphic science';[20] 'the new family of Enochists';[21] 'the Fu Hsi-Enochist Fathers';[22] 'the I-chingists'.[23] All of these are accurate enough as applied to Bouvet and his followers and highlight many of the main features of Bouvet's system as seen by his contemporaries, but they are either too specific or too general to serve as labels for the movement as a whole. On the other hand, Louis Porquet, in a letter defending the group, refers to 'père Bouvet and those who with him mythologise the personnages of the Chinese

---

18. Letter of du Tartre, 25 March 1709, in ARSJ: JS *173*, 50v.
19. Letter of 12 January 1709, ARSJ: JS *173*, 3.
20. Letter of 25 March 1709, ARSJ: JS *173*, 50v.
21. Letter of 12 January 1709, ARSJ: JS *173*, 4.
22. 'Les Pp. fohienochistes', in 'Quelques reflexions en passant sur la lettre du R.P. Dentrecolles du 8 Nov. 1710', 24 January 1711, ARSJ: JS *174*, 5–32, several times repeated.
23. Letter of du Tartre, 30 October 1722, ARSJ: JS *183*, 66r.

Ching' as 'the Mythologists'.[24] This is attractive from a number of points of view. It links the group appropriately with the proponents of comparative mythology of the late seventeenth century. It emphasises their common concern with demythologising the Chinese classics and detecting their biblical origins and point of departure. It is wider in its implications than 'Figurism', allowing for their 'discovery' of prophecies and vestiges of religious concepts, as well as of transmogrified biblical personnages. It does not, perhaps, adequately characterise the preoccupation of Bouvet, and to a lesser extent de Prémare, with symbols, mathematical and 'hieroglyphic'. In modern usage, however, symbolism tends to be regarded as a central focus of the science of mythology, and the interpretation of the symbols of the Chinese classics was only possible once their general mythological status was established. Figurism was, in effect, the mythological interpretation of Confucianism.

All sources are agreed that Joachim Bouvet was the founder of Figurism. Some contemporary accounts even claim that it was conceived by him before his departure from Europe in 1685,[25] and a letter to his sister, written from Siam in June 1686, shows him adopting a typically 'figurist' approach to his first encounter with Asian religion.[26] The explanation for this clearly lies in his studies before leaving France, his imbibing of the current theories on comparative mythology, which he had deliberately cultivated as a preparation for his mission. Bouvet's interest from the beginning seems to have been concentrated on the cabbalistic and numerological aspects of these works, an interest arising no doubt from his mathematical bent, as well as from his linguistic studies.

In the 'Preliminary Discourse' to the work which gives the fullest systematic exposition of his ideas, the 'Specimen Sapientiae Hieroglyphicae', Bouvet gives an account of the development of his theories during the over thirty years he had been on the mission.

---

24. Porquet to du Tartre, nd, B Vat: *Borg Lat 515,* 245r.
25. de Mailla, for example, in a letter of 1 November [1722?], says that Bouvet claims to have conceived his 'scheme' *(dessein)* before he left Europe (ARSJ: JS *179,* 201r).
26. He describes experiencing 'une joye secrette de reconnoitre parmi toutes les fables de la Religion de ce pais, certains vestiges de la notre'—Letter to la Soeur de la Brière, 21 June 1686, cited after the Cornell ms in JC Gatty, *Voiage de Siam du Père Bouvet* (Leiden: Brill, 1963), LX.

When he first arrived in China, he says, 'I was already furnished with a most fortunate aid to my work, for I brought with me a special knowledge of the Hebrew Mosaic cabbala, and of the Pythagorean and Platonic philosophy, which are the true elements of the whole hieroglyphic wisdom of the Chinese, or rather of the Old Patriarchs'.[27] For the next ten years, he acquired a knowledge of the Chinese language and Chinese literature, and 'began to experience the utility' of such studies.[28] The next twenty years he devoted to developing the 'system' and persuading seven or eight of his fellow missionaries of the truth of his general approach. Three or four of them agreed to devote themselves to the task of demonstrating the system 'from the texts of the canonical books'; he names these helpers as Jean-François Foucquet, Jean-Alexis de Gollet and Joseph de Prémare.[29]

Bouvet's zeal for his scheme led him to some highly unorthodox actions. Despite his claim that all his adherents were willing and free agents,[30] it is clear that Bouvet used his influence at the court to secure the transfer to Peking of Foucquet in 1711[31] and to gain the services of Gollet and de Prémare as assistants in his project of commenting on the *I-ching* in 1713;[32] that this was contrary to the wishes of the superiors of the mission[33] and that, in the case of de Prémare at least, the assistance was given with reservations.[34] Bouvet justified his actions in a letter to Cyr Contancin of 18 August 1715:

27. 'Specimen Sapientiae Hieroglyphicae', ms in ARSJ: JS *IV. 5, A*, 2.
28. 'Specimen', 2.
29. 'Specimen', 3. Bouvet adds sadly that de Prémare should have been placed first, but that 'for several years he seems to speak otherwise than he really feels, God knows why'. On de Prémare's defection from the Figurist camp, and his reenlistment, see below.
30. 'Specimen', 3. Of course, technically, none of them, vowed to obedience to their superiors were free to undertake activities explicitly forbidden by those superiors.
31. v Fu, *Documentary Chronicle*, 116; Foucquet, 'Relation exacte . . .' (B Vat: *Borg Lat 566*, 149r); Gozani, 'Compendiosa Informatio eorum quae circa P™ Joachim Bouvet contingerunt mense April 1714 . . .' (ARSJ: JS *732*,440v).
32. Gozani, 'Compendiosa Informatio . . .', 440v.
33. D'Entrecolles, the superior of the French mission, seems to have approved the transfer of Foucquet but with an explicit proviso, ignored by both Bouvet and Foucquet, not to discuss matters of religion (that is the Figurist theories) with the Emperor, (v ARSJ: JS *174*, 35–37, 53–57, 65–72). The Visitor Gozani, was totally opposed to the whole project ('Compendiosa Informatio', 440v).
34. Contancin to Tamburini, 1 September 1716 (ARSJ: JS *177*, 70r); Jartoux to Tamburini, 3 September 1715 (ARSJ: JS *776*, 350r).

> Blind obedience is an admirable virtue but not on all occasions. In the matter of the *I-ching* I am no more bound to obedience than your reverences in the matter of *t'ien* and *shang.ti.*[35]

This was a palpable hit, but hardly a justification.

Bouvet's infatuation with his theories had, it would seem, led him to a position that, for a Jesuit vowed to obedience to his superiors, was, to say the least, equivocal. That he was aware of this is shown by a letter he wrote in his defence to the Jesuit General, Tamburini, on 30 October 1712. He writes, he says, to anticipate the accounts of his activities which his superiors will send. They are to be dismissed as 'contrary, lacking valid reasons, and produced by men ridden by empty fears and in this matter (if I may say so) as it were blind'. He is convinced that he has received special help from God to reveal to the Emperor the mysteries of religion concealed in the Chinese canonical books and especially the *I-ching*. But his superiors continue to block his every move.

> This work is not undertaken by me alone, but also by Fathers Foucquet, de Prémare and Gollet, who beyond all other missionaries of the Society have devoted themselves to the profitable work of studying the characters and books of the Chinese and the solidity of our system. For a long time they have been in complete agreement and favour it with all their hearts, but have not given their time because of the total opposition of the Superiors of this mission, who, conspiring together, have left and leave no stone unturned, especially in the proliferation of orders, even in virtue of Holy Obedience, which now number more than the ten commandments themselves.

In conclusion he 'dares to suggest' to the General the replacement of both the Visitor and the Superior of the French Mission, and nominates Gollet and Foucquet for the posts.[36]

I shall have more to say later about Bouvet's mental balance, and about his and Foucquet's fears and obsessions, amounting at times to a persecution complex. For the moment, it is enough to note that if Bouvet saw a conspiracy against him, other members

35. ARSJ: JS *176*, 340.
36. ARSJ: JS *174*, 266.

of the mission saw the activities of the Figurists themselves as a conspiracy, a divisive, sectarian, secret society, undermining the unity and apostolic efficiency of the mission. Their activities seemed to justify this. A notebook belonging to Foucquet, now in the Vatican Library,[37] contains copies of letters and notes from Bouvet which apparently circulated within a restricted circle of French missionaries, in the period 1707–1710.[38] They are addressed to them not by their European names, but as letters from 'Sien Seng' (that is, *hsien-sheng*, 'Master') to 'Noke' *(no-kê=* Hervieu), 'Kouei wen' *(kuei-wen* = de Mailla), and 'Long Tchu' *(lung-ch'u* = de Prémare). These names were not the common Chinese personal names, either *tzu* or *hao,* of the persons addressed, and they seem suspiciously like code-names adopted to preserve secrecy in case they were intercepted. The secrecy may have been necessary because of the de Toumon mission and the Rites controversy[39]—de Tournon had specifically condemned one of Bouvet's Chinese works which had been delated to him[40]—but it seems equally likely that it was a device to elude the attentions of their superiors, and the 'Portuguese' Jesuits.

Of the three correspondents of Bouvet in 1707—Hervieu, de Mailla and de Premare—only de Prémare remained a Figurist into the 1720s, and with some reservations. Foucquet was certainly committed to the end, and there were one or two late recruits tò the group, such as Charles Slavichek and Jean-François Noëlas. But these, as also Jean-Alexis Gollet,[41] may be passed over as marginal figures in the movement, and their ideas regarded as derivative. The key figures in the movement are Bouvet, Foucquet and de Prémare, each of whom deserves detailed discussion in his own right.

---

37. Borgia Latino, 515.
38. Most are undated, but those that can be dated appear to be from this period. One has the date 3 December 1707 (Borgia Latino, 575, 205–22), one 24 March 1708, and another 8 July 1710 (amongst four in Borgia Latino, 575, 160–63, 172–75).
39. D'Entrecolles, in a letter of 8 March 1711, warns Bouvet against circulating 'new discoveries' because 'these papers now run the risk of being surprised by our adversaries' (ARSJ: JS *774*, 37r).
40. Bouvet's *T'ien-hsüeh pen-i.* See du Tartre, 'Quelques reflexions en passant sur la lettre du R.P. Dentrecolles du 8 Nov. 1710', ARSJ: JS *174,* 11–2.
41. Gollet's reputation as a sinologist has suffered unjustly, largely from the attribution to him of 4 volumes of mss now in ASJP (Brotier, 742–142). On close examination of these I am convinced that only Brotier, 742 is his.

Perhaps we should add to this list of Figurists the K'ang-hsi Emperor himself.[42] Certainly for a considerable period he patronised Bouvet's work on the *I-ching*. We know why he withdrew his support, or at least qualified it. A deputation of missionaries in April 1716 persuaded K'ang-hsi that Bouvet's ideas were eccentric, and even dangerous,[43] and an edict was issued on 23 April 1716:

> Tell Po Chin [Bouvet] that the memorial of Chi Li-an [Kilian Stumpf] and the others was very appropriate. Bouvet may either abandon his work on the *1-ching* or continue it. If he wishes to continue, he should do it himself and not use anyone else. There is no need to hurry. When he has completely finished the work he should report again.[44]

What we do not know is the nature of K'ang-hsi's interest in the project. The memorials on the subject are enigmatic.[45] It is possible that K'ang-hsi was simply showing sympathy for his old mathematics teacher, and responding to his enthusiasm.[46] Or perhaps he saw Bouvet's work as part of the flourishing scholarly industry on the *1-ching* which he supported.[47]

There is some evidence, however, that one aspect of Bouvet's work that particularly appealed to K'ang-hsi and aroused his interest, was his claim to have discovered a system that would not only explain past

42. See Fang Hao, 'Shih-ch'i-pa shichi lai-hua Hsi-jên tui wo-kuo ching-chi chih yen-chiu' in *Fang Hao liu-shih tzu-ting kao*, I, 196–9.

43. A Latin version of this memorial, by de Premare, is to be found in ARSJ: JS *177*, 52.

44. The text (from B Vat: *Borg Cin 439* A (c) 5) is to be found, together with a translation, as Document 12 in Rosso, *Apostolic Legations*.

45. See the collection of manuscript versions of the edicts in B Vat: *Borg Cin 439*, A and B, and in *Borg Cin 317* (4).

46. K'ang-his's admiration for Bouvet's work is shown in his remark, during the Mezzabarba mission, that only Po Chin (Bouvet) knew 'something of the purport of Chinese books' (The 'Mandarins' Diary', Rosso, *Apostolic Legations, 368).*

47. In 1715 there appeared the *Yu-tsuan Chou-i che-chung* ('Imperial Collection of Commentaries on the J-ching') edited by Li Kuang-ti *(v* Hummel, Eminent Chinese, 474). Foucquet refers to it in his 'Dissertatio' (B Vat: *Borg Lat 566*, 434) as produced under the direction of K'ang-hsi by his 'leading and most learned high officials'. Stumpf claimed that one reason for the Emperor's loss of interest in Bouvet's work was that this Palace Commentary had been completed (letter to Tamburini, 9 October 1716, ARSJ: JS *177*, 115r). Hu Wei's brilliant piece of textual criticism on the diagrams of the *1-ching*, the *1-t'u ming- pien*, which 'first placed the study of the Changes on a sound historical basis' (Hummel, *Eminent Chinese*, 336) was published in 1700.

events but predict future ones. According to Cyr Contancin, K'ang-hsi, 'attracted by the strange promises of Father (Bouvet), expected him to produce things that were new, unheard of, and known to no one else, *even about the future*'.[48] Bouvet's Superior, D'Entrecolles, lists amongst the things he is specifically forbidden to discuss with the Emperor, 'to propose, as a certainty, the term of the duration of the world, fixing it e.g. on the day which will complete 10,000 years duration, claiming that the authority of the *Chings* is clear on this, and that it is, moreover, undeniable on account of revelation'.[49] And elsewhere,[50] he refers to Bouvet's interpretation of the *hsien-t'ien* ('former heaven') and *hou-t'ien* ('latter heaven') of the *I-ching* commentaries as Messianic prophecies, and prophecies of a Golden Age to come. A superficial examination of Bouvet's Chinese and Latin manuscripts, especially those dealing with the *I-ching,* confirms Bouvet's increasing preoccupation, one might fairly say obsession with these matters. If this was, indeed, the reason for K'ang-hsi's interest in Bouvet's project, his abandonment of it is further evidence of his wisdom and good judgement.

The French Superior, François-Xavier D'Entrecolles, found himself caught in the middle of the arguments raging in the mission over the theories of the Figurists. He was not himself a Figurist, nor even a sympathiser, but he had originally been chosen for the mission by Bouvet[51] and he seems to have been personally sympathetic to the old man to whom the mission was so indebted. He also felt a special duty to defend the French missionaries against their critics from the 'Portuguese' mission.[52] In fact, the most severe critic of the Figurists was a French Jesuit, Vincent du Tartre. He appears to have been a mediocre sinologist[53] but his critique of their ideas was commonsense

---

48. Contancin to Tamburini, 1 September 1716, ARSJ: JS *177,* 70v- italics added. *cf* Jartoux to Tamburini, 2–3 September 1715, ARSJ: JS *176,* 349v, which attributes the Emperor's interest to Bouvet's claim that all European sciences may be derived from the Chinese classics, and that his system can predict the future.
49. D'Entrecolles to Contancin, 23 July 1711, ARSJ: JS *174,* 56r.
50. D'Entrecolles to Bouvet, 3 May 1712, ARSJ: JS *174,* 183.
51. See Pfister, *Notices,* 539.
52. Such as Joseph Suarez who, writing to the Portuguese Assistant, on 9 October 1713, depicts Figurism as an extreme example of the evils of the 'Schisma Gallicano' (ARSJ: JS *175,* 18–19).
53. Pfister, *Notices,* 592, attributes no Chinese works to him, but notes that Régis's translation of the *I-ching* used du Tartre's commentary on the work. If, as I suspect, this is the 'In Librum Ye Kim Brevis Annotatio' (ARSJ: JS *1.223),* it proves to be a superficial and very scholastic interpretation of the work.

and quite devastating. As early as 1708, he was attacking de Prémare for interpreting the *I-ching* in a mystical rather than a mathematical sense.[54] In January 1709, he replies to someone, probably D'Entrecolles, who had urged him to be kinder to Bouvet, that he objects primarily to the excesses of the 'cabal' of the 'Enochists'. Let them adopt their figurative interpretations of the ancient kings, provided they do not deny they were also real men; and let them spread their ideas, provided they do not treat as fools those who disagree with them.[55] He objects strongly to Bouvet's method which turns all European and Chinese literature to allegory.[56] Speculations are regarded as proof, and the biblical revelation is compromised.[57] Above all he objects to the abandonment of the established Jesuit interpretation of Confucianism, thus risking the alienation of Confucian scholars, in pursuit of chimeras.[58]

Despite his protestations, there seems to have been a good deal of personal animosity on the part of du Tartre towards Bouvet and especially Foucquet. There is even a *prima facie* case for Foucquet's charge that the French mission was divided into 'Lyons' and 'Paris' factions, and that du Tartre was the leader of the 'Lyonnais'. But there was substance in their charges, and the more moderate critiques of men like Jartoux and de Mailla were formidable. Leaving aside their theological objections which were solid, and were never really faced squarely by the Figurists, their sinological arguments were unanswerable. De Mailla's attack is the most thorough from this point of view and, except for his assumption that the early 'history' of China is veridical, would be accepted by most modern authorities. Both Bouvet and Foucquet indiscriminately draw on Taoist and Confucian sources without perceiving that they belong to different systems of thought[59] Their 'hieroglyphic' interpretation of Chinese characters, independent of their conventional sense, has no justification.[60] Above all, the Figurists are so concerned with their systems and a *priori* notions, that they fail to consider the texts themselves.

54. Letter of 9 May 1708, copy in the Foucquet papers B Vat: *Borg Lat 515,* 235
55. Letter of 12 January 1709, in ARSJ: JS *173,* 3–4.
56. Letter to D'Entrecolles (?), 25 March 1709, ARSJ: JS *173,* 49–52.
57. The twin themes of his 'Quelques reflexions en passant sur la lettre du R.P. Dentrecolles du 8 Nov. 1710', ARSJ: JS *174,* 5–32
58. See du Tartre to the Visitor, Laureati, 24 May 1719 (ARSJ: JS *182,* 233). He declares himself an adherent of the 'antiqua Missionariorum Societatis systemata'.
59. De Mailla (to D'Entrecolles?), 1 November 1722, ARSJ: JS *179,* 208–209.
60. De Mailla (to D'Entrecolles?), 1 November 1722, ARSJ: JS *179,* 212.

> They have changed, transposed and so disfigured the history and the chronology of the Chinese, that the most able of their doctors would no longer recognize anything. They propose as their goal a pious thought, or one of our European chronologies, and everything that they find in Chinese books, no matter how absurd and out of context, provided it has the least value for the system that they create, are so many precious jewels that they conserve with care and which give them the right consequently to reserve everything and confuse everything. As for me, I have not looked for mysteries; I wanted to see what the Chinese think and say, independently of any system, how their histories were written, who were their authors, what weight they had in their time, and what is the way they were put together . . .[61]

This was the voice of the scientific sinologist, heard clearly for perhaps the first time in the history of the mission. The ferment over Chinese Rites and Figurism had brought the missionaries to examine the Confucian books more closely than ever, and the result was the birth of sinology.

Joachim Bouvet and the prophecies of the *I-ching*

What, then, was the system of ideas that led—one might even say seduced—Joachim Bouvet into such strange byways for a Jesuit missionary? Its germ lay in his early studies, before he came to China, in the works of the late seventeenth century mythologists, comparative theologians, and cabbalists.

From his arrival in Peking, to his death in 1730, with the exception of the years 1693–99 when he returned to Europe at K'ang-hsi's behest to recruit more missionaries, he remained at the court, ever pursuing his vision of a Chinese Emperor and Empire converted to Christianity. His first published work, the *Portrait historique de 1'Empereur de la Chine,* Paris, 1697, is imbued with this sentiment, and dedicated to Louis XIV, presumably with a view to gaining material support from the French king. In it, moreover, for the first time, but in veiled form, appear characteristic 'figurist' ideas. Fu Hsi, that extraordinary genius

61. De Mailla to Souciet, 26 October 1727, in *Revue de l'Extrême Orient,* III (1887): 72–73.

of antiquity, has invented a universal system of symbolism, which may prove the key to all sciences. Missionaries, instead of devoting their time to unavailing efforts to prove the Chinese atheists, should devote themselves to discovering the true philosophy of Fu Hsi.[62]

Bouvet received support for his interest in the interpretation of the mysterious hexagrams of the *1-ching* from no less a source than Gottfried Wilhelm von Leibniz, mathematician, philosopher, theologian and sinophile. Leibniz had long been interested in China[63] and in 1697 published at Leipzig his *Novissima Sinica,* 'News from China', which consisted of excerpts from Jesuit writings on China. Bouvet does not seem to have actually met Leibniz while he was in Europe, but two letters, of 18 October 1697 and 28 February 1698, of Bouvet to Leibniz, are known, as is the subject of their correspondence: the nature of Chinese characters and the interpretation of the *kua* or 'lines' of Fu Hsi. Leibniz had in 1697 invented a new system of mathematics, binary arithmetic, and he and Bouvet were interested in the analogies between this and the ancient Chinese system. But, even more, Leibniz, like Bouvet, was concerned with ways of unifying and harmonising the religions of mankind.[64] He thoroughly approved of the Jesuits' missionary methods in China, and was working towards the establishment of a Protestant mission on similar lines.[65] Like the Jesuits, he saw ancient Chinese religion as a pure theism, and even entertained the conceit of Chinese missionaries restoring an atheistic Europe to its doctrinal purity.[66]

---

62. *Histoire de l'empereur de la Chine* (La Haye, 1699) facsimile edition, Tientsin, 1940, 147–50.
63. On the nature of this interest, see DF Lach, 'Leibniz and China', in *Journal of the History of Ideas,* VI (1945): 436–455, and his *The Preface to Leibniz' Novissima Sinica* (Honolulu: University of Hawaii Press 1957); FR Merkel, *Leibniz und China* (Berlin: De Gruyter, 1952); O Franke, 'Leibniz und China', in *Zeitschrift der Deutschen Morgenlandischen Gesellschaft,* Bd 7, Heft 3/4, 1928 (reprinted in Franke's *Aus Kultur und Geschichte Chinas* [Peking, 1945], 313–30); O Roy, *Leibniz et la Chine* (Paris: Vrin, 1972); and especially D Mungello, *Leibniz and Confucianism: The Search for Accord* (Honolulu: University of Hawaii Press, 1977).
64. See GJ Jordan, *The Reunion of the Churches* (London: Constable, 1927); and FR Merkel, GW *Leibniz und die China-Mission* (Leipzig: De Gruyter, 1920).
65. See his letters to Bishop Burnet (18—28 May 1697, in Leibniz, *Textes inedites,* I [Paris, 1948], 204), and to Sebastien Kortholt (25 April and 20 May 1715, in Leibniz, *Epistolae ad Diversos,* edited by C Kortholt, I (Leipzig, 1734), Nos CXCVIII and CXCIX.
66. Letter to M de Remond, in Leibniz, *Opera Omnia,* edited by Dutens, IV, 174.

Leibniz's interest and enthusiasm, his belief in mathematical and linguistic codes, and his approval of the Jesuits' work, seem greatly to have stimulated Bouvet, and on his return to Peking, he reported his progress with mounting excitement. The 'métaphysique numéraire' of the *1-ching* seems to correspond to the mysterious numbers of Pythagoras, Plato, the Egyptians and the Jewish cabbala. If so, it can only be 'the previous remains of the most ancient and most excellent Philosophy, taught by the first Patriarchs of the world to their descendants, and then corrupted and almost entirely obscured by the passing of time'.[67] Its origin must be a special revelation of the Creator.[68] Soon, he is seeing in the *kua* of the *1-ching*, the Creation and the Trinity,[69] and the next step, the allegorising of early Chinese history, follows a year later.[70] He announces to Leibniz in 1702 his project for a 'Chinese Academy' to recover and proclaim the rediscovery of this ancient system which is the source of all religion and all sciences.[71]

This, then, was the origin of Figurism, and the basis for the formation of Bouvet's group of collaborators. By 15 September 1704, the system is fully articulated in his letter to the Abbé Bignon.[72] The *1-ching* is now recognised as the *locus classicus* of the 'hieroglyphic science' of the ancient worid, and, for the first time, Fu Hsi, its alleged author, is identified with the mysterious Patriarch Enoch, who 'walked with God',[73] and whose works, according to Tertullian, had been suppressed by the Jews, because they prophesied the Messiah. A month later, he applied to the Jesuit General, Thyrsus Gonzalez, for formal permission to establish an 'Apostolic Academy' in China, devoted to the advancement of his system.[74]

Bouvet's first major Chinese work, the *T'ien-hsüeh pen-i* (revised and enlarged in 1707 as the *Ku-chin Ching-t'ien chien,* was written a

67. Bouvet to Le Gobien, 8 November 1700, in Leibniz, *Opera Omnia,* edited by Dutens, IV, 147.
68. Bouvet to Le Gobien, 8 November 1700, in Leibniz, *Opera Omnia,* edited by Dutens, IV, 149
69. Bouvet to Leibniz, 4 November 1701, BN: Fr *17240,* 81–82.
70. Bouvet to Leibniz, 8 November 1702 (Leibniz, *Opera Omnia,* edited by Dutens, IV, 166.
71. Bouvet to Leibniz, 8 November 1702 (Leibniz, *Opera Omnia,* edited by Dutens, IV, 167–168
72. I have used the copy in ARSJ: FG *731.*
73. Genesis 5:21–4.
74. Letter of 28 October 1704, ARSJ: JS *168,* 154–55.

little earlier and is a contribution to the Chinese Rites controversy rather than to Figurism. It was presented to the Emperor in 1702, only to be rejected, according to a hostile witness[75] as 'undigested, disordered and full of various errors'. It was described by its author to Leibniz as 'a complete collection of all the most beautiful expressions which are found in the classical books of China relating to the divinity, arranged in the form of a catechism'.[76] The only noticeable departure from the standard Jesuit position in these works is a greater emphasis on texts from the *1-ching* which had not hitherto featured largely in the Jesuit writings, and a claim to certain knowledge of the Trinity on the part of the ancient Chinese.[77]

The last point was developed further in a Chinese work written around this time, the *T'ien-chu san-i lun*, which was sent to Europe in late 1707. In a letter of 5 November 1707, he describes this little essay as a new beginning in his studies. 'It ought suffice as an intimation of what I have promised regarding the Messiah and the Mystery of the restoration of the world. This is what we are going to work on seriously.'[78]

The last remark suggests that the beginning of Bouvet's collaboration with other missionaries should be dated from this point, late in 1707. The earliest of the dated circular letters in the Foucquet Papers, comes from 3 December 1707[79] and the notes which passed between Bouvet and Hervieu, de Mailla and de Prémare,[80] reporting on the Master's discoveries in mathematics and in the classics, appear to date between late 1708 and 1710. He outlines to his disciples the 'theology of the ancient Patriarchs of the world' as found in the

75. The Visitor, Emanuele Laurifice, who had opposed its presentation to the Emperor, v Laurifice to the Jesuit General, Gonzalez, 16 December 1702, ARSJ: JS *767*, 101.
76. BN: Fr *17240*, 83r.
77. In a letter referring to the Latin translation of the *Ku-chin ching-t'ien chien*, dated 25 October 1707, Bouvet singles out the passages on the 'san-ye' as of particular significance (ARSJ: JS *171*, 42).
78. Gatty, *Voiage de Siam du Pere Bouvet*, CX.
79. It is a comment on a letter from Leibniz describing a cabbalistic inscription on a medallion (B Vat: *Borg Lat 515*, 205–20).
80. One should perhaps add Foucquet himself to the list, but he is not mentioned in the headings. Perhaps the letters came into his possession only after arrival in Peking in 1711.

Chinese classics and other ancient literatures.[81] He examines the figure of Confucius himself and declares him 'mythological' and 'a pure figure of the Son of God'.[82] In one letter he even purports to find 'the hypostatical union of God and man in the mystery of the right angled triangle'.[83] Given such extreme 'mythologising' it is not surprising to find defections from the group even at this early stage.

The second stage in Bouvet's development of his system, after the initial discovery of the traces of the primitive revelation, is his work on the *1-ching*. This may be dated, for convenience, from 1711, when Foucquet came to Peking, but we have already seen him beginning to explore the *1-ching* at an earlier period. In 1711–1716, however, Bouvet, Foucquet and, for a time, de Prémare, were working on a series of Chinese commentaries on the *1-ching*, many of which are now in the *Borgia Cinese* collection of the Vatican Library.[84] Their method seems to have been to collect texts and commentaries which fitted the system, and to interpret them in terms of the system. These manuscripts were then circulated for comment. A note, in Bouvet's hand, on the cover of one of these works[85] gives us a clue as to the circulation and the composition of the group at this period: 'aux R.R. PP. Foucquet, de Premare, Dc Chavagnac de la Comp.^e de Jesu. Le P. De Premare ne Ia pas veue'. Hervieu and de Mailla who were mentioned in 1707 are now absent from the list; Foucquet and de Chavagnac have been added. De Chavagnac was an active missionary in far-off Kiangsi and must be regarded as a sceptical sympathiser at best; which leaves Bouvet, Foucquet and de Premare as the hard-core Figurists, or '1-chingists'.

The proliferation of texts on the *1-ching* produced by the group almost defies analysis. Most are undated—those that are dated are from 1712 and 1713—none are signed, and they are in a variety of

---

81. B Vat: *Borg Lat 515,* 178r.

82. B Vat: *Borg Lat 515,* 196v (to de Premare).

83. B Vat: *Borg Lat 515,* 199r.

84. Especially Borgia Cinese *317* (1)–(16). There is another series of Chinese works in Borgia Cinese *361* (2)–(6) which appear to be connected with this enterprise. The latter are closely associated with Foucquet's papers, and certainly contain comments in Foucquet's hand, so for convenience I have treated the Borgia Cinese *317 mss* as Bouvet's, with the exception of Borgia Cinese *317* (5) and (7) which seem more likely to be Foucquet's; and the Borgia Cinese *361 mss* as Foucquet's.

85. The *Ta-I yüan-i nei-p'ien,* Borgia Cinese *317* (9).

calligraphy. The question of their mutual relationship and of their Chinese sources is so complex that I pass over it completely and restrict myself to a brief analysis of the main arguments. Bouvet himself summarised his system of interpretation in the preface to his 'Key to the *I*' *(1-yo)* of 1712. He argues that 'the Holy teaching of the great I' is mysterious and only to be discovered by cooperation between Chinese and Western scholars.

> All the people of China and the Western regions originally came from one ancestor; they are all brothers, born of the same mother, the same great Father and Mother who produced Heaven, Earth and men. So, originally they were one family, and as one family with one heavenly Father and Mother, they submitted to the one Way, the one principle and the one teaching They had the same teachers, one and the same heavenly teaching and beliefs, and so on. When you think about the fact that China and foreign countries are both the people of one God *(t'ien-ti),* how could the ancient Chinese have the true tradition of the heavenly teachings and beliefs, and the myriad countries of the Western nations not at all? Chinese scholars, since they do not travel, and do not study the strange writings of the myriad countries, have not examined their records, and so find it difficult to penetrate foreign affairs. Western scholars have made a special study of antiquity and have travelled widely through the world; they have studied the writings of each country, read their books, examined their sources, translated them into their own language. There can be no doubt that it is of great benefit to all scholars to study and test their works, and to know them thoroughly.[86]

What we must do is to compare the scriptures and dogmas (*ta tao)* of Christianity with the ancient Chinese traditions, especially the *I-ching* and the other classics, and by combining them rediscover the heavenly teachings and beliefs of the earliest age of mankind. The *1-ching* is the most difficult of all these texts to understand, but its diagrams hold the key to these teachings.[87]

86. Borgia Cinese *317* (2).
87. *1-yo,* [ll]v-[2]v.

The rest of the *I-yo* is in two sections: an exposition of Christian doctrine beginning with the Trinity and ending with the life of Christ; and an interpretation of the hexagrams of the *1-cling* as 'proof for the preceding'. The method is simplistic in the extreme—three solid lines represent the Trinity, broken lines signify sin and the broken unity of mankind, and so on. This method is pursued in later works, which extend the search for Christian mysteries to the commentaries and diagrams illustrating the *i-ching.* A diagram from the *1-lei hsiang-t'u,* for example, which is triangular in form, is interpreted as proof of the knowledge of 'three powers' *(san-ts'ai)* and 'three supremes' *(san-chi),* that is a trinity, in the supreme being.[88] Yet another work, 'Dissertation on the Vestiges of Ancient Traditions' *(Fu ku-chuan i-chi lun)* extends the search for trinities beyond the *1-ching* to the *Tao-te-ching.*[89]

The reasons for the hostility of their fellow Jesuits to the 'Ichingists' are apparent even from this brief description. Bouvet was staking all on the validity and acceptability of an argument that postulated a break with both Western and Chinese habits of mind.

He had undergone a kind of conversion experience which left him unable to see the world except in terms of his system. And the more he pondered, the more the pieces of his mental universe were subtly re-organised to fit into the pattern. Hundreds of pieces of disconnected and inconclusive evidence added up to certainty. One can speculate about his motivation and psychological orientation. In the first place, his kind of number mysticism had a quite respectable ancestry, of which he was conscious. Augustine, Nicholas of Cusa, Marsilio Ficino, Pico della Mirandola, and Leibniz, all provide examples of a type of mind which seeks the key to 'all religion and all sciences' in numerical symbols. Bouvet's abberration, if such it was, was not a historical 'sport'. But perhaps even more important were the pressing needs of the mission, the impasse that the old Jesuit approach had arrived at. Bouvet had witnessed the furore aroused by Le Comte's *Nouveaux Mémoires* in Paris; he had lived through the disaster of the de Tournon legation. Just as Francis Xavier had been driven by a vision of souls damned because he had not reached them,

88. *I-hsüeh wai-p'ien,* Borgia Cinese 3/7(10), 2r-v.

89. Borgia Cinese *317* (7), 24v.

so Bouvet was driven by a vision of Christ recognised in places where he had not previously been sought.[90]

As the pressure from his opponents and superiors built up, Bouvet, far from retreating from his positions, became even more bold. This third stage in the development of his system centred on prophecy, and a theory about the three stages of the world. In his 'Idea Generalis Doctrinae Libri Ye Kim'[91] sent to Rome in November 1712 he announces that he is now convinced that the *1-ching* contains the idea of three 'states' of the world: a state of original perfection, a state of corruption, and a state of reformation and restoration. He has been forbidden by his superiors to speak to the Emperor about 'the supernatural mysteries of the Christian law' but he regards himself as free to develop the 'natural theology' of the *1-ching* and the Emperor has expressed his interest in the theory of the three ages and 'insinuated' his approval. Whatever the nature of this 'approbation' of the Emperor, and I have been unable to find any evidence beyond Bouvet's tendentious description, Bouvet invoked it against his superiors as licence to continue his investigations. This vague approval of the Emperor, plus reference to the precedents set by the French theologians Huet and Beurrier, are his constant defence.

When, in 1718, he received 'with stupefaction' a letter from the General ordering him not to offer any of his 'singular and exotic opinions' to the Emperor without them having been first examined and approved by his Jesuit 'revisors', his reply is to refer the General to 'an exposition which I have prepared, of the integral system of hieroglyphic wisdom of the earliest Chinese';[92] his Superiors would not, unfortunately, allow him to forward it. It appears that in 1720 and 1721 he did at last send off this treatise in several parts[93] and, if this is the work still extant in the Jesuit Archives in Rome,[94] it can

90. See the 'Tractatus de Antiquitatibus Sinarum, ad Religionem Spectantes, Praeludium', ARSJ: JS *174,* 147r, where he argues that faith in Christ is necessary for salvation, and that to deny his interpretation of the ancient Chinese books, is to deny eternal life to a vast segment of humanity.

91. ARSJ: JS. / *74,* 290–291.

92. Letter to Tamburini, 30 December 1718, ARSJ: JS *178,* 251 v.

93. See the reference in his letter to Tamburini, 24 November 1721 (ARSJ: JS *IV 5,* E, f l). The Visitor, Laureati, in a letter to D'Entrecolles of 27 July 1719, told the French Superior that he had given Bouvet and Foucquet permission to send their Latin writings to the General only, but to no one else (ARSJ: JS. *178,* 290).

94. In ARSJ: JS *IV 5,* A, F and H. and *IV 25,* 1, 3, 4 and 5.

hardly have reassured the General. At a time when the Jesuits were coming increasingly under fire, a 'mystical system of prophetic times' was scarcely what he needed to defend his hard-pressed missionaries against their critics.

Till the end of his life in 1730, Bouvet continued to work on this aspect of his system. In a series of letters to Father Souciet, published by Henri Cordier in the *Revue de I'Extrême Orient,* and dating from 1725, 1727 and 1728, he refers to a number of works which he has sent to Europe, dealing with his prophetic system. One of these, 'a work of 20 to 30 pages' sent to Père Tournemine, and dealing with 'the character of *Hou-chi* ['the Lord of Millet'] who appears a perfect type of the Saviour',[95] I have identified in the Jesuit Archives in Rome.[96] The other works on 'chronology' that is on his 'system of the prophetic times', were sent to Souciet in 1726, and inspired Souciet's refutation of 29 October 1727.

There seems little point in pursuing Bouvet through the labyrinthine ways of his 'sacred algebra, belonging to the true and ancient cabbala, and common to the ancient Hebrews and the ancient Chinese'.[97] He is convinced that the *1-ching* prophesies the age of the world as 100 cycles of 120 'sabbatical years' or 91 'solar years' each; that the *hsien-t'ien* or 'former age' covers the period from the creation to the Ascension of the Lord and the *hou-t'ien* or 'latter age' from the Ascension to the end of the world[98] but he was unable to convince either his fellow missionaries or his European correspondents. The very titles of the works would be enough to arouse the suspicions of an orthodox scripture scholar like Souciet, and Bouvet's naive belief that Souciet objected primarily to his Septuagint chronology[99] demonstrates how his world had narrowed to the walls of his Peking study.

95. *Revue de I'Extrême Orient,* III, 1887, 219–20
96. Entitled 'Expositio unius odae propheticae libri canonici xi-kim, in qua clare, distincte et veluti historice sub unico typo praenuntiata Christi Salvatoris Incarnatio, nativitas, Instantia, vita privata et publica, praedicatio, passio, mors, ejusque sacrificium tum cruentem tum incruentem pro remissione peccatorum et perpetua omnium populorum faelicitate oblatim', 24 pages (ARSJ: JS *IV* 5, F).
97. Bouvet to Souciet, 18 October 1727, in *Revue de I'Extrême Orient,* III (1887): 219.
98. See the 'Vera Temporum Propheticorum Ratio et Mensura . . . Pars Prior', ASJP: Brotier *144,* 2v-3 (4–5).
99. Bouvet to Souciet, 23 November 1728, in *Revue de l'Extrême Orient,* HI (1887): 64.

Bouvet's penchant for solitariness, which had led Bénigne Vachet MEP to describe him on his first voyage out to China as 'a solitary genius' and 'a better Carthusian than a Jesuit'[100] was still in evidence. He remained optimistic and cheerful to the last, still hoping to find 'a more palpable demonstration' of his 'divine numbers' and the 'period of the prophetic times'.[101] Even the remaining Figurists, Gollet, Foucquet and de Prémare, refused to follow him in these flights. Gollet was in exile in Macao. Foucquet, recalled from the mission, and alienated from the Society of Jesus, remained committed to Figurism but confined himself to arguing the figurative nature of early Chinese history to anyone whose ear he could catch. De Prémare continued to seek 'vestiges' in Chinese language and literature, but he also produced many works of a far more conventional nature, in Chinese, French and Latin, and was almost recalled to Europe for continuing to maintain the old Jesuit interpretation of the Rites.

It is tempting, but I think a mistake, to dismiss Joachim Bouvet as a crank of a familiar type, and his life-work as totally misguided. In many respects he was more correct than his hard-headed critics. Much of the early Chinese 'history' is now seen to be clearly mythological, and its leading figures 'culture heroes' analogous to those of other traditions. The central dilemma to which he addressed himself, the scandal of religious pluralism, was one that most Christian thinkers either passed by with averted eyes, or arrogantly talked out of existence. Bouvet's enormous, if misdirected, erudition covered many areas of Chinese studies almost totally neglected in the West till two centuries later, when the *I-ching* was rediscovered and popularised by sinologists, psychologists and cultists. Even if, as ultimately I believe we must, we regard Bouvet's system as a manifestation of a kind of intellectual pathology, it is a particularly fascinating case-study, and well worth a more thorough investigation than I have given it here.

---

100. Cited in Gatty's Introduction to the *Voiage de Siam du Père Bouvet*, XXIII, n 1.
101. I have not seen the letter to Souciet of 12 October 1729 from which this passage comes, but Gatty's long extract (No 144) proves that less than twelve months before his death Bouvet was still as committed a 'Figurist' as ever.

Jean-François Foucquet and the symbolism of the Chinese classics

Jean-François Foucquet, the next of the group after Bouvet, and perhaps the better known because he spent his later years in Rome where he became a sort of institution expounding his theories to visitors on the Grand Tour,[102] is enigmatic in a somewhat different way. It is his character, rather than his ideas, that remains opaque, despite an enormous volume of personal material. He quarrelled with his superiors and colleagues, wrote endless apologias, was finally recalled to Europe by the Jesuit General, defected to the anti-Jesuit camp, became a consultor in Rome to the Congregation *De Propaganda Fide,* and was made a bishop for his pains. If there is one thread running through this variegated and stormy career, it is his commitment to Figurism. He might even be said to be the one consistent Figurist, following neither Bouvet in his prophetic flights nor de Prémare in a fruitless search for vestiges of revelation; but concentrating on the 'figures' or symbols of the Chinese classics.

Foucquet arrived in China in mid-1699, and worked in Fukien and Kiangsi before being called to Peking by the Emperor, at Bouvet's prompting, in May 1711. Before this period he was already a member of the inner circle of Figurists,[103] and had in 1709 or 1710 produced a lengthy 'Memoir on the System of the Three Dynasties or Imperial Families that are alleged to have governed China from Yao to the Ch'in',[104] which argued that the Hsia, the Shang and the Chou dynasties were mythical and the classics should be read figuratively not literally. Although he was diverted in April 1712 to work on astronomy, he

102. v Charles (le President) de Brosses, *Lettres familières écrites d'Italie,* lettre xlvi to M de Neuilly (Dijon, 1927 edition, t 2, 200–209); Montesquieu met him in 1729 (*Le Spicilège, Oeuvres Complètes,* edited by A Masson [Paris, 1950], II, 819–20); and Joseph Spence in 1732 (*Observations, Anecdotes and Characters of Books and Men,* edited by JM Osborn [Oxford: Oxford University Press, 1966], No 1406 II, 519–520).

103. Apart from the copies in his notebooks of Bouvet's letters of 1707–1710 to other missionaries, there are several letters and notes by Foucquet in B Vat: *Borg Lat* 515, dating probably from 1707–1708, indicating his adherence to the 'I-chingists'.

104. The manuscript of the *Mémoire* in BN: Fr na *5744,* was sent Etienne Souciet in 1719, but a note at the end says that it was written in 1709 or 1710, and that he had not had time to revise it since.

was at the same time deeply involved in Bouvet's *1-ching* project. Foucquet's habit of compiling lengthy apologias for his superiors, leaves us in no doubt about this.[105] They were in daily contact and communicated their discoveries to each other. Something of the excitement of the period is captured in a note in Bouvet's hand in Foucquet's papers:

> Mon. R. Pere,
> Vers midi jay trouvé une demonstration palpable pour faire voir a l'Europe et a la Chine tout ensemble, que les *3.hoam,* les *5 ti,* les *fouhi,* les *hoamti,* ne sont autre chose qu'Enoch.
> Jay besoin do dictionnaire de furetiere.
> V.T.R.S.J. Bouvet.[106]

Several manuscripts in the Foucquet papers consisting of notes, excerpts from texts and commentaries, translations and drafts, and presumably dating from this period, illustrate this collaboration.[107] They are clearly, from their titles and contents, contributions to Bouvet's project, and it is not always certain whether they are Foucquet's own work, or his copies, with comments, of Bouvet's works. There can be no doubt, however, that Foucquet was, at this period, Bouvet's most ardent 'I-chingist' collaborator.

Most of Foucquet's Chinese and Latin manuscripts, however, do not concentrate on the *1-ching,* and I think it is possible to trace his growing divergence from Bouvet on this issue. Foucquet's interests lay much more in the evidence he thought he discerned in the Chinese classics for the transmission from the sons of Noah of a primitive revelation. The *1-ching* was for him but one source of these ideas, and the basic concepts of Chinese philosophy as found in a very wide variety of sources, ancient and modern, were drawn upon. Unlike Bouvet, who was increasingly preoccupied with prophecy and extraordinary revelations, Foucquet knew what he wanted to discover: the basic doctrines of Christianity concealed or figured in

105. See his 'Relation exacte de ce qui s'est passé a Peking par rapport a l'astronomie Européenne depuis le mois de Juin 1711, jusqu'au 1e Novembre 1716', B Vat: *Borg Lat 566,* 144–184.

106. B Vat: *Borg Lat 565,* 32. The dictionary referred to is the Jesuit *Dictionnaire Universel de Furetière,* published by the editors of the *Journal de Trevoux.*

107. For example, the *1-kuo* ('Notes on the . . .') in B Vat: *Borg Cin 317(7);* the *I-hsüeh wai p'ien* in B Vat: *Borg Cin 361,* and other items in this *fondo.*

the personages and concepts of Chinese tradition; and he devoted all his energies to unveiling them. Again unlike Bouvet, he was not concerned with system-building so much as with assembling disparate pieces of evidence to support his general theory, as the title of his major work, 'Dissertation on the True Origin of the Doctrine and Records of the Chinese . . .'[108] indicates. Whereas Bouvet eventually moved from Figurist premises via the *I-ching* to a 'universal prophetic system', Foucquet remained a Figurist in the strict sense.

Foucquet's Chinese manuscripts, by comparison with Bouvet's, are fragmentary: compilations and notes rather than drafts or finished treatises. This may be due to the fact that he was less adept in Chinese than Bouvet, but it probably also reflects his and Bouvet's disillusionment over converting K'ang-hsi. The later works of both are all in Latin and French, and aimed at convincing European scholars of the universality of revelation, rather than at converting the Chinese.[109] Another difference is the wide range of topics they cover: the interpretation of *t'ai-chi*[110] the alleged deathbed 'conversion' of Chu Hsi from his atheism;[111] the essence of the classics;[112] the nature of the 'true Lord[113] and the true Confucian scholar.[114]

Perhaps the most interesting of Foucquet's Chinese works is a treatise entitled, 'According to an examination of the Ancient Classics,

108. 'Dissertatio de Vera Origine Doctrinae et Manuscriptorum Sinensium contenta quatuor propositionibus.' On the extremely complicated state of the manuscript of this work in B Vat *Borg Cin 358* and *437,* and *Borg Lat 544* and 566, see the Bibliography.

109. Note the significant change between Foucquet's original sub-title for the 'Propylaeum Templi Veteris Sapientiae' (B Vat: *Borg Cin 566),* which is addressed solely to China missionaries—'eruditis legis evangelicae praeconibus, in vinea Sinica adlaborantibus'—and the title he later gave it in *Borgia Cinese 371* (interleaf opposite page 2), which is addressed to European scholars as well—'eruditis, Christi gloriae zelatoribus ac operariis ministris Evangelicis in vinea Sinica adlaborantibus'.

110. *Tai-chi lüeh-shuo* (B Vat: *Borg Cin* 317 [5]). I attribute this to Foucquet on grounds of calligraphy and contents, as well as his undoubted authorship of the accompanying mathematical treatise.

111. *Chu Hsi wan-nien t'ung-hui chih chu* (B Vat: *Borg Cin 357* (11) and *380* (1).

112. *Ching-i ching-yao* (B Vat: *Borg Cin 380* (2) to (4).

113. *Chen-tsai ming-chien* (B Vat: *Borg Cin 316* [18]). The author is unnamed, but it bears some notes in French in Foucquet's hand.

114. *Chêng-Ju*—a draft only with notes in French and Chinese (B Vat *Borg Lat 566,* 113–139).

the Appearance of the Heavens is not Invariable'.[115] It is presented in the form of a dialogue between a Chinese and a European about the irregular motion of the five planets. The European says that the Chinese classics contain a good example of a major and irregular change in the distinction drawn by the *1-ching* between the *hsien-t'ien* and the *hou-t'ien.* When the Chinese protests that the commentators are vague about the meaning of these terms, the European demonstrates from the *1-ching* and other classical texts that it is really a distinction between the state of innocence and the fallen state of man.

> In these various remains of the ancient Philosophers, it must be conceded that some things can be found, not it is true in their original and pure state, but, as it says in the Proverbs, gold is refined from dross. Nor should it be said that no vestige remains of the ancient and true doctrine. Certainly, there are some records, especially some of the figures of the *1-ching* which as even the modern school of Philosophers admits, have been lost to the followers of degenerate systems, and have long been hidden.[116]

So far, then, we have a restatement of Bouvet's *1-ching* theories, with the rather irrelevant variation of a starting-point in astronomy.

What follows, however, is pure Foucquet, Figurism run wild. A whole series of common Chinese characters are analysed into components which are alleged to 'figure' the Old Testament story. The character *ch'iu,* 'hillock' or mound', originally represented two people on a plain, that is, Adam and Eve in Paradise.[117] *Kuo* or 'state'[118] comes from the world and its heavenly king.[119] And so it goes on for several pages of ingeniously conceived but utterly unfounded examples. If any real Chinese, outside the pages of Foucquet's imaginary dialogue, had followed him this far, which is almost inconceivable even in the early eighteenth century when Chinese linguistics was in its infancy, I am sure the conclusion would have repelled him.

---

115. *Chü ku-ching-ch'uan k'ao t'ien-hsiang pu chun-ch'i* (B Vat: *Borg Cin 380* [6] with Latin translation–and *380* [7], text alone).
116. *Chü ku-ching-ch'uan k'ao t'ien-hsiang pu chun-ch'i* (B Vat: *Borg Cin 380* [5]). (I have translated the Latin rather than the Chinese, as representing more accurately Foucquet's mind on the subject.
117. *Chü ku-ching-ch'uan k'ao t'ien-hsiang pu chun-ch'i* (B Vat: *Borg Cin 380* [20]).
118. Foucquet argues quite speciously, but necessarily for his argument, that the common abbreviated form for this character is in fact primary.
119. *Chü ku-ching-ch'uan k'ao t'ien-hsiang pu chun-ch'i* (B Vat: *Borg Cin 380* [19]).

Foucquet's last examples were taken from basic characters dealing with nature, which figure prominently in Taoist works such as the *Tao-te-ching.* He moves on from this to argue that the traditional hostility of Confucian to Taoist was misplaced. The true Confucianism was the teaching of the *Tao-te-ching* which was not opposed to cultivation of virtues such as *jen* and *i,* 'mercy' and 'justice,[120] but fulfilled them by preaching the *shêng-jen,* the Sage, the Christian Saviour.[121] Thus the *Tao-de-ching* rather than the *I-ching* becomes the key text of Foucquet's new variant on the Jesuit interpretation of Chinese tradition.

That this is not a temporary phase in his thinking is shown by a massive work of Foucquet's sent to the Jesuit General in 1718[122] entitled *Problème Théologique.*[123] The 'Problem' is 'whether one can say, and how one can say, that in the unique true sense of the ancient Chinese books, the character *tao* signifies the God whom the Christians adore?' And the answer is affirmative. *Tao* is the Christian God, and the *shêng-jen,* 'celebrated in a thousand ways in the ancient monuments of China, is the Messiah promised by our Scriptures, the Saint par escellence'.[124] Evidence is gathered together from mainly Taoist sources—the *Tao-te-ching, Lieh-tzu, Chuang-tzu, Huai-nan-tzu,* and later Taoist commentators. But he also draws on the *I-ching* and *Shih-ching* which he describes as 'equally' sources of 'the spirituality of Tao'.[125] Thus, the Jesuit interpretation of Confucianism has become the Jesuit interpretation of Taoism!

Behind all this theorising, however, is a basic 'Figurist' premise:

> No one should, therefore, be surprised to find this subtle and sublime doctrine amongst the ancient sages of China. I would say two things about it. Firstly, that this doctrine is as ancient amongst the Chinese as it is amongst the Chaldeans and Egyptians; since the origin of all these peoples is the same,

120. *Misericordia* and *justitia.*
121. *Chü ku-ching-ch'uan k'ao t'ien-hsiang pu chun-ch'i* (B Vat: *Borg Cin 380* [29]).
122. See the accompanying letters to the General of 23 and 26 November 1718, in ARSJ: JS *182,* 66–68, and further references the following year, 19 November 1719, ARSJ: JS *182,* 240r.
123. There are identical copies, 321 pages each, in B Vat: *Borg Cin 371,* and ARSJ: JS *IV. 3.*
124. Borgia Cinese, 371, 3.
125. Borgia Cinese, 371, 46.

> their doctrine also comes from one and the same source, namely Noah and his children, Secondly, what one finds there is incomparably more pure, more inspired and more complete than in the remains which have been conserved of their Philosophy.[126]

Confucius is said to have had seventy-two disciples to whom he taught a secret or mystical doctrine, much of which was lost in the burning of the books.[127] But he who holds the key to the ancient Chinese books can read them.

Foucquet was aware that his reinterpretation of China's past required reinforcing in two directions. Firstly, he had to demonstrate that the Chinese ideas about their origins as a nation and their early history were false, or rather misinterpretations of the ancient tradition. And secondly, he had to convince European theologians that his views were orthodox. It was to this task that he devoted his last years in China, and the result is a vast collection of completed and incomplete 'propositions', variously titled, and scattered through the Foucquet papers. I shall not attempt to arrange them in definite order, but simply to report their main arguments.

The four propositions to which Foucquet addressed himself in his *Dissertatio de Vera Origine Doctrinae et Monumentorum Sinensium* may be summarised as follows.[128] 1. Adam, the first man, had knowledge not only of the mysteries of religion, including a future redeemer, but also of all arts and sciences which he was entrusted to transmit to posterity 'in graphic form', 'through the infinite multitude of symbols'. 2. Some of Adam's sons and nephews were given the key to these mystic symbols or *cabala*, especially Seth and Enoch. The 'arcane tradition' was revived by Moses, and again, after the captivity of Babylon, by Esdras. 3. The *cabala* was preserved not only orally, but in books kept secret from the common people. 4. These books were saved in Noah's Ark, and they, together with the oral tradition, were handed on through Noah's sons to all the nations of the world. The most extensive and best-preserved source of this ancient tradition is to be found in China, and by studying the ancient Chinese books the 'sacred enigmas' can be restored and the 'divine science' systematically expounded.

---

126. Borgia Cinese, 371, 69.

127. Borgia Cinese, 371, 235–236.

128. After the text in *Borgia Latino 566*, 338r-340v.

It is not surprising to find that Foucquet never completed more than a small part of this formidable programme. He did, however, produce a substantial draft of the section dealing with China (fourth proposition, second part) as well as a sketch of the whole argument in a preface. The *Preface* acknowledges his debt to the kind of thinking on comparative mythology that we have already noted to be common in the seventeenth century. He cites Kircher, Huet, scripture scholars such as Bellarmine and Cornelius a Lapide, and Pico and the cabbala.[129] There is another substantial fragment on the cabbala, in several copies, amongst the Foucquet papers,[130] which covers the same ground but adds little to the argument. The breadth of reading is impressive, especially since the Chinese rice-paper and Chinese ink indicate that it must have been produced entirely in China using the limited resources of the Jesuit libraries there; but it is hardly original.

The section on China,[131] however, is certainly original and constitutes a unique contribution to the Jesuit interpretation of Confucianism. Foucquet is attempting nothing less than a complete reinterpretation of the whole of Chinese tradition in the light of his Figurist assumptions. He rejects the traditional (and Jesuit) distinction between schools of thought in early China as irrelevant since their more profound teachings flow from a common source. By a combination of careful textual criticism and wild symbolic interpretation of characters, he demonstrates to his satisfaction that the source is the ancient Patriarchs and the teachings are the basic dogmas of Christianity, the Trinity and Incarnation, the Fall and the Redemption.

A good example of his method of working is his treatment of Confucius. With considerable erudition, and drawing on a wide variety of courses, he reconstructs the life of Confucius. He shows critical sense[132] as well as knowledge of the texts, and the general

129. *Borgia Latino 566,*327v–336v (and identical copy in ff. 612–613, 682–689).

130. *Borgia Cinese 358* (3) and (4) contains 17-[272] and *Borgia Latino 566,* ff 785–905 has 17-[260]. There are other fragments in *Borgia Latino 566,* ff 614–65 (21–129) and 690–780 (17–197).

131. This makes up the '4a Propositio, 2a Pars' of the 'Dissertatio'. It is divided into 2 chapters. The first of these is found in *Borgia Latino 566,* 359–602 and (an identical copy made in Europe and lacking characters) in *Borgia Cinese 437.* The second chapter is in *Borgia Cinese* 358 (1) and (2) and (a European copy without characters) in *Borgia Latino* 544.

132. For example, in his treatment of the *Chia Yü, Borgia Latino 566,* 370r-372v.

picture that emerges is one that would be acceptable to any Chinese scholar of his time. All this is, however, nothing but a backdrop to his main point. Confucius claims to have received his teaching from the ancients, especially from one Lao P'eng.[133] Lao P'eng is called, by Chuang-tzu, P'eng Tsu, P'eng the Ancestor, and can be no other than Adam himself.[134] Confucius got this teaching from a visit to Chou, where he met Lao Tan or Lao Tzu, keeper of the records. These records, from which both Confucius and Lao Tzu drew their ideas, were clearly the records of the early world which Noah preserved in the Ark, or copies of them', brought to China after the flood. *Chou* means 'universal' which comes from its function as repository of the universal teaching. The ancient name for China, *Chung-kuo,* is misapplied to China, but fits Judea perfectly.[135]

As time went on, this pure doctrine was distorted by the commentators. The Han commentators, after the burning of the books, fell into 'heresies', 'monstrosities' and 'errors'.[136] Chu Hsi in the Sung misinterpreted the Saint or Messiah, as a mere human sage. *T'ien-tzu,* or 'Son of Heaven', was regarded as referring to the Emperor, but when the *Li Chi* says that only the *t'ien-tzu* or *shêng-jen* can sacrifice to God, it must refer to Christ.[137] The *1-ching* has been wrongly regarded by some as 'magic, atheism, and the dregs of all superstitions'.[138] If that is so, why did Confucius wish for fifty years to be added to his life, in order to study it?'[139]

The major part of the first chapter of the fourth proposition, Part 2, over 350 pages of manuscript,[140] is devoted to proving from an indiscriminate array of texts, ancient and modern, Confucian and

133. Presumably a reference to *Analects,* VII. I: 'The Master said, "A transmitter and not a maker, believing in and loving the ancients, I venture to compare myself with our old P'ang"' (Legge translator). It would be possible, although contrary to all the commentators, to read *ch'ieh* in its original sense of 'to steal' rather than the deprecative 'my humble self, I venture', and hence to arrive at Foucquet's reading, 'I borrow my ideas from Old P'eng.'
134. *Borgia Latino 566,* 363r-v.
135. *Borgia Latino 566,* 402v-406r.
136. *Borgia Latino 566,* 406v, 408r.
137. *Borgia Latino 566,* 410r.
138. *Borgia Latino 566,* 428v.
139. *Analects,* VII. 16. On this question, see H Dubs, 'Did Confucius study the Book of Changes?', in *Toung Pao,* XXV (1927–1928): 82–92.
140. *Borgia Latino 566,* 430–602.

Taoist, that the authentic esoteric teaching of the ancient Chinese was that there was one supreme lord, infinitely wise and just; that the soul was immortal; that we should love our neighbour as ourselves; and that there was a Saint to come. This section, too, displays that peculiar mixture of erudition and misplaced ingenuity, critical sense and wild flights that characterises Foucquet's work. So often his argument turns on a verbal trick or false etymology. A passage in the Imperial Commentary on the *1-ching* which associates 'spirit' (*shên*) with 'word' *(yen)* must be a reference to *the* Word, or Christ.[141] The character *t'ien* is composed of symbols for 'two' and 'man', and must be read as a prophecy of the second Adam, Christ.[142] Yet, he is also much more aware than most of his Jesuit predecessors of the polytheistic (he calls them 'idolatrous') elements in the sacrificial rites described in the *Shu-ching* and *Li chi.*[143] Some of the roots of his future breach with his order over the Rites issue are there, not yet recognised even by Foucquet himself.[144]

The second chapter of Part 2 of the fourth proposition[145] attempts the much more difficult task of determining Confucius' role in the transmission of the 'arcane doctrine' of the Patriarchs. In this chapter, unlike the earlier account of the life and career of Confucius, he proceeds to mythologise the historical Confucius. He makes much of the fact that Confucius, like Christ, had seventy-two disciples, a clear 'sign' (*sacramentum*) of Confucius' Messianic expectations. The Confucians called themselves *Ju,* the character for which comes from *jen,* 'man', and *hsü,* to 'expect' or 'hope',[146] hence 'those Philosophers were men who were expecting or hoping'.[147] What were they hoping for? Both the ancient form of the character *hsü* and the 'canonical

141. *Borgia Latino 566,* 436r-v, citing the text of the *Chou-i che-chung,* chapter 17:15.
142. *Borgia Latino* 566, 442r.
143. See, for example, his discussion of the *chiao* and *she* rites, *Borgia Latino 566,* 438r-440v.
144. Here, as elsewhere in the Foucquet manuscripts, a later comment (recognisable by the browned European ink) draws out the implications contrary to the Rites, which remained undeveloped in the earlier text (see the note on f 441r).
145. Entitled 'De Arcana Doctrina Confucii et Monumentorum Sinensium'.
146. I can find no dictionary warrant for such an interpretation of *hsü* which normally means 'to be necessary or required'.
147. *Borgia Cinese 358* (1), 22.

definition'[148] of the *hsü* hexagram of the *I-ching* are explained as 'clouds ascending above the heavens'. Who ascended above the heavens in a cloud of glory but the Lord, Jesus Christ?[149]

To the objection that the Confucian Books contain public teachings, not a cabbalistic secret doctrine, he replies with what he obviously regarded as a devastating syllogistic argument.

> The doctrinal system is one and the same, and expressed in characters of completely the same nature, in the other canonical books as in the *I-ching*. But the doctrinal system of the *I-ching* is wholly symbolic. Therefore, it is wholly symbolic also in the other canonical books.[150]

No wonder du Tartre and the other critics of the Figurists found it impossible to pin them down. Ultimately, Figurism was an act of faith, which defied logic, or rather created an invincible closed logic of its own.

We have seen enough of Foucquet's theories to understand the hostility of his Superiors and colleagues. But Bouvet, too, perhaps even more than Foucquet, held extreme theories, and he was allowed to remain in Peking and continue his writings. Foucquet was later to claim that he was driven out of China because of his views on the Rites',[151] but his own habit of keeping documents and compiling dossiers and elaborate defences of his actions provides ample evidence to refute this. Foucquet's downfall was his refusal to obey his superiors, not only about his writings, but in countless other matters as well.[152] He saw conspiracies everywhere, listened at closed doors,[153] interpreted every action of the other Jesuits as aimed at him,

148. Actually the commentary attributed to the Duke of Chou. See Legge, The *I-ching*, Sacred Books of the East, volume XVI (Oxford, 1899), Appendix II, 272–273.

149. *Borgia Cinese* 358 (1), 25.

150. *Borgia Cinese* 358 (2), 128.

151. See the 'Notizie Breve spettante alia persona di P.[is] Fran.[ci] foucquet Gesuita francese', ARSJ: JS *177*, 426–429.

152. There are long lists of his acts of disobedience in a letter of Jartoux, 23 September 1720 (ARSJ: JS *178*, 384–385).

153. See 'Au R.P. Laureati et ses Consulteurs', in B Vat: *Borg Lat 566*, 198r and 212r, where Foucquet claims to have overheard the 'Lyons Fathers' plotting against him. There is a revealing slip in this account, because at the first mention he claims to have been passing by and to have accidentally heard du Tartre say, in a loud voice, that they would have to search his room. The second time. (212v) he says that du Tartre spoke 'in a very low voice', an admission of eavesdropping.

and sent a huge volume of complaints against his superiors to Rome.[154] As early as October 1716 he had asked to be recalled to Europe to be freed from these vexations[155] and his surprise at his eventual recall is rather ingenuous. His complaints had become so vociferous, and his personal relations with other members of the mission so strained that the Jesuit General had no choice but to recall him.

On the eve of his departure for Europe in January 1722, Foucquet left in the hands of de Goville, the mission procurator in Canton, a number of letters, one of which was for D'Entrecolles, the Superior of the French Mission. He insisted,

> This sad issue is the consequence and the result of the firm and invariable attachment that I have had to a very true doctrine of which, I am persuaded more than ever, an understanding is necessary for the salvation of this mission.[156]

His description of this doctrine makes it clear that he is referring to his Figurist views. The first three Chinese dynasties are 'chimerical' and the Christian God is the deity proclaimed by the Chinese, not only by the names *t'ien* and *shang-ti,* but also as *tao, t'ai-chi, shen* and *Ii.* But there is also a new note which I have not found in any of his writings prior to this date.

> Let us suppose, as you are pleased to have it, that the Emperor has the right idea about the supreme being, which is something that demands long and serious examination; it is, nevertheless, certain that this Prince in practice, I mean in the public cult of *shang-ti* and *tien,* namely in the sacrifices which he offers to them, often displays idolatry. He associates his

154. See especially his letter to the General, 30 October 1716 (ARSJ: JS 777, 149–153); his 'Lettre a communiquer aux RR. Peres Admoniteurs et Consulteurs du R.P Dentrecolles', 22 January 1717 (ARSJ: JS 777, 30–51; 'Au R.P. Laureati et ses Consulteurs" 18 January 1718 (B Vat: *Borg Lat 566,*185–324); and 131 pages of copies of letters dealing with the appointment and actions of Vincent du Tartre as Superior of the French Jesuit House in Peking, forwarded to the General on 26 November 1718 (ARSJ: JS *182,* 71–137). Note the ever-increasing length and complexity of the apologias. In 1718 alone, he sent no less than 300 pages of letters or copies of letters to Rome (Letter to Guibert, 26 October, 1719, ARSJ: JS *182,* 197).

155. Letter to Guibert, 31 October 1716, ARSJ: JS 777, 159v.

156. Letter, dated 13 December 1721; Foucquet's copy in B Vat: *Borg Lat 565,* 109v-110r (this passage f 110r). Another copy, by D'Entre-colles, is in ARSJ: JS *IV. 5* (E).

> ancestors to this Supreme Being, he renders them an honour like that he renders to *shang-ti*. It is a veritable apotheosis of those Princes who died in infidelity.[157]

Note that he is certainly not a 'Maigrotian'; he does not believe the Chinese are atheists—on the contrary, on the 'terms' question he is far more liberal than his confreres. Nor does he refer to the ceremonies at the heart of the Rites Controversy—those to Confucius, the recent dead, and the ancestors. But he is beginning to claim that his 'heresy' and the reason for his recall relate to the Rites issue, not primarily to Figurism, or to his behaviour.

On his way south to Canton, Foucquet had met the papal legate, Mezzabarba, who was proceeding to Peking. It is not known exactly what happened at that meeting, but some of his fellow Jesuits began to suspect that Foucquet would go over to the enemy. There were some unpleasant exchanges with de Goville over money; over his books which he regarded as his own, and his Superiors as belonging to the mission; and over a young Chinese he was bringing back to Europe. De Goville intercepted a letter Foucquet wrote from the ship to Perroni, one of the Propagandists, which seemed to confirm his suspicions.[158] When he arrived in Paris, Foucquet bypassed his Superiors and proceeded to Rome where he placed himself at the disposal of the Congregation of Propaganda Fide. In March 1725, he was consecrated Bishop of Eleutheropolis, and spent the rest of his life as a special consultant (on Chinese affairs) to the Congregation.

Many items in the Foucquet papers, dating from 1723 to his death in 1741, attest to the kind of information he gave to Propaganda in those years. On his arrival, he informed one of the Cardinals that he could prove that for two thousand years the Chinese had rendered an idolatrous cult to *t'ien* and *shang-ti*, but that these were originally terms for the true God.[159] In the 'hieroglyphics' of the Chinese classics, all the mysteries of the Christian religion were to be found. The Congregation was prepared to listen to his views on the Rites but not apparently to what was closest to his heart, his Figurist theories.[160]

157. *Borgia Latino 565*, 109v.
158. See de Goville to the General, 19 December 1722 (ARSJ: JS *779*, 239) and the copy of the intercepted letter itself in Jap Sin *179*, 156.
159. See his *Diary* for 12 September 1723 on an interview with 'Le Cardinal del giudice' (B Vat: *Borg Cin 565, 111)*.
160. Copy of a letter, undated but probably of this period, to the Cardinal Prefect (of Propaganda?) in B Vat: *Borg Cin 468* (last item).

Foucquet is described by many visitors to Rome in those years as a garrulous old man who would talk for hours about his theories.[161] In 1732 he expounded to Joseph Spence the contents of the works on Figurism he intended to publish.[162] Spence's scepticism as to whether they would see the light of day was fully justified. It is not surprising, given the theological climate of the time, that the Bishop of Eleutheropolis did not publish his magnum opus. What is more surprising is that he did not even continue his work on it. Many times he made copies of parts of the work already done in China'[163] but, apart from a short 'Preliminary Introduction to the Understanding of the *Ching*',[164] he wrote no more on the subject.

The 'Essai d'Introduction Préliminaire a l'Intelligence des Kings' itself adds very littie to the argument of the earlier works. Once more we are treated to the assertion that the *I-ching* is the key to understanding the Chinese classics',[165] and that it depicts the three states of nature, 'Anterior Heaven', 'Posterior Heaven', and a third emerging age in which Nature will be re-established in its primitive goodness.[166] The bulk of the work consists of an extreme and eccentric Figurist interpretation of Chinese characters. For example, Fu Hsi's name is broken down into the elements of the characters, and it is deduced that *fu* = 'dog' and 'man' = the Egyptian god Anubis = Hermes = Mercury Trismegistus = Enoch; and *hsi* means the 'originator of sacrifices'.[167] The Emperor Yao is really *Shang-ti* or God, since 'Yao is clearly derived from the Hebrew Yahweh'.[168]

---

161. See R Etiemble, *L'Orient Pkilosophtque,* II, 7, on the President de Brosses' encounter with Foucquet.
162. J Spence, *Observations, Anecdotes, and Characters of Books and Man,* edited by JM Osborn (Oxford: Clarendon Press, 1966), No 1406, II, 519–520.
163. These copies, amongst the Foucquet Papers in the Vatican Library, are easily distinguished by the European paper and ink, and most are in the hand of a secretary.
164. There is considerable confusion about this work which has been wrongly attributed to both Visdelou and de Premare. The title of the copy in B Vat: *Vat Lat 12870,* which is the fullest version (133 pages) is given as 'Essai d'Introduction Preliminaire a lTntelligence des Kings, c'est a dire des Monumens Antiques conserves par les Chinois' and it is subtitled, 'Sentimens de l'Eveque d'Eleutheropolis sur la Doctrine des Chinois Anciens et Modernes'.
165. B Vat: *Vat Lat 12870,* 6.
166. B Vat: *Vat Lat 12870,* 7–13.
167. B Vat: *Vat Lat 12870,* 17–20.
168. B Vat: *Vat Lat 12870,* 60.

The method is bolstered by a theory of the nature and origin of Chinese characters which might be described as the root of the Figurist misinterpretation of characters:

> Each character represents the Idea, of at least one being if the character is very simple, or the Ideas of several beings if it is composed of more parts; so that these beings are themselves Images in some fashion of their Author, or of their Restorers; it follows that each character always contains some meaning concerned with Religion, and so it signifies something Sacred. But this sacred meaning, which is fundamental, primitive, and essential, is concealed by the normal and secular meaning which is superficial and, as it were, the wrapping of the first.[169]

Needless to say, this kind of meta-linguistics has no basis in reality and, in Foucquet's case at least, seems to have been invented *post factum* to justify conclusions previously reached on other grounds. It is nonetheless important, since it spells out baldly the basis on which both Bouvet and Foucquet proceeded. Even de Premare, who was a pioneer in the scientific study of the Chinese language, ultimately concurred with the notion that Chinese characters were at least in origin 'hieroglyphics', sacred symbols rather than a conventional notation. The false analogy with Egyptian hieroglyphics, perhaps derived ultimately from Kircher, was taken by the Figurists to disastrous lengths, and by none more disastrously than Foucquet.

The only work of Foucquet to be printed during his lifetime, apart from a letter published in the *Lettres Edifiantes* for 1705,[170] was the *Chronological Table of Chinese History*,[171] published at Rome in 1729. Despite its title and subject matter, this too is a Figurist work, in the sense that it aims at demonstrating the inauthenticity of all Chinese chronology before 425 BC, and hence the mythical nature of the Hsia, Shang and Chou dynasties. The purpose of the work is clearly indicated in the original subtitle:[172] 'According to the most important

169. B Vat: *Vat Lat 12870*, 28.
170. Letter to le Duc de la Force, 26 November 1702, in *Lettres Ediftantes*, V (Paris, 1705).
171. *Tabula Chronologica Historiae Sinicae connexa cum cyclo qui vulgo Kla-tse dicitur.*
172. Found in a letter of D'Entrecolles attacking the work, the manuscript of which had been 'detained' (arrestée) by the French Provincial (D'Entrecolles to Guibert, 14 October 1713, ARSJ: JS *199*, 1, 307–308).

History, the true dating of the history of the Chinese goes back to some 400 years BC; and so the fable that the Chinese Empire was instituted many thousands of years before Christ is exposed to the ridicule of critics'. And Foucquet's 'Explanation' of the table, which circulated widely, insisted even more strongly that the early Chinese kings were 'truly chimerical men'.[173] However, as his Jesuit critics were quick to point out, Foucquet's source for this *Table* was a Chinese official, Nien Hsi-yao, whose table, following Chu Hsi's, began for convenience in 425 BC without, by any means, questioning the reliability of historical records before that date.[174] It was as if a history of Rome from the time of Julius Caesar, was produced as evidence for the unreliability of Roman history before Julius Caesar.

There is something deeply tragic about Foucquet's last years. His library of 4,000 Chinese books, which he had fought so hard to bring back from China, was appropriated by the French king. He found himself involved in the sordid scramble for ecclesiastical benefices.[175] He was heeded when he denigrated the purity of Chinese beliefs and practices, while his great idea, for which he gambled all, was ignored. And, judging from the number of extant manuscripts and letters, the Jesuit Figurists who remained in China had more influence on European scholars than he did from Rome. One wonders whether he regretted his breach with the mission and the Society of Jesus.

Joseph de Premare and the theory of 'vestiges'

The third of the trio of leading Figurists, Joseph de Prémare, provides yet another variation on the Figurist theme. He remained to the end a convinced Figurist, in that he accepted the basic premise of a primitive revelation transmitted through the Chinese classics, the 'vestiges' of which were to be found there by those who knew what to look for.

173. 'An Explanation of the New Chronological Table of the Chinese History . . .', *Philosophical Transactions,* XXXVI (1729–1730): 400.

174. See a letter of Gaubil, 20 September 1730, in his *Correspondance,* 262–263; and letters of D'Entrecolles to Guibert, 14 October 1723 (ARSJ: JS *199,* I, 307–308) and de Mailla to Souciet (ASJP: *Brotier* 123, 18–19, 22–9). There was, surprisingly, a quite favourable notice on the work in the Jesuit *Journal de Trevoux,* XXX (1730): 179–82.

175. See H Cordier, 'Correspondance du Pere Foucquet avec le Cardinal Gualterio', in *Revue de l'Extrime Orient,* I, (1882): especially 47.

He was, however, alienated from both Bouvet and Foucquet, whose behaviour he found offensive, and whose ideas exaggerated, and he appears from his writings a sounder if less spectacular sinologue. For this reason he was, in the long run, the most influential of them all.

The Superior of the French Mission, FX D'Entrecolles, in his report to the Jesuit General of 17 November 1707, summed up de Prémare in terms that well describe him as he appeared throughout his career in China:

> He is extremely talented, even, perhaps, excessively so, since his understanding is a little facile. He is adaptable to all tasks, and wonderfully suited to the Chinese sciences, and the fruits of his work match his labours; so that he deserves the crown amongst all our Fathers, and more than once put down Father Visdelou when he was boasting of his knowledge of Chinese. On the other hand, in practical matters he has little capacity on account of his excessive facility and credulity, and he cannot keep a secret, but is full of leaks.[176]

His facility, his credulity and his impracticality are all in evidence in the documents that de Premare left behind;[177] but so also is the learning and the penetration of things Chinese. None of his works was printed in his lifetime[178] They were, nevertheless, widely known, and in the nineteenth century were hailed as laying the groundwork of modem sinology.[179] And not only his linguistic and literary studies were influential; Abel Rémusat, in praising his *Notitia Linguae Sinicae,*[180] also notes favourably his theory of 'vestiges'.[181] His, too, was the only major treatise on Figurism ever to be published.[182]

Is there any basis for the nineteenth century reputation of de Prémare? and how did his views differ from those of Bouvet and

176. ARSJ: JS *171,* 115r.
177. See the (very incomplete) listing in Pfister, *Notices,* 522–529, and the Bibliography to this work.
178. Except a few unimportant letters in the *Lettres Edifiantes* series.
179. See the eulogy of de Prémare by Rémusat in his *Nouveaux Melanges Asiatiques,* II (Paris, 1829), 262 ff.
180. Published in Malacca in 1831 by the Anglo-Chinese College.
181. *Nouveaux Melanges Asiatiques,* II, 367–369.
182. 'Vestiges des principaux dogmes chretiens tires des anciens livres chinois,' trans, and edited by A Bonnetty and P Perny (Paris, 1878) (originally in the *Annates de Philosophic Chretienne,* Vie se, t VII–XIII).

Foucquet? A close examination of his works shows that he was a convinced '1-chingist' and, despite the linguistic expertise displayed in his *Notitia* and his work on the six kinds of Chinese characters,[183] as firm a believer in the hieroglyphic interpretation of Chinese characters as the other two. He was, however, much more moderate in his arguments for these views. He was no 'Enochist', preferring to argue from Chinese sources alone without invoking the cabbalistic lore that Bouvet and Foucquet were so fond of. He did not follow Bouvet in his immersion in the prophetic system of the *1-ching.* Nor did he, like Foucquet, reduce all ancient Chinese history to mythology. It was this moderation in his views, together with his mild personality, that preserved him from the more severe criticism of his colleagues on the China mission and gained him a hearing for Figurism where Bouvet and Foucquet were dismissed as cranks.

De Premare's earliest works, written within a few years of his arrival in China in late 1698, show an extraordinary ability in Chinese that fully justifies D'Entrecolles' high praise. He produced a Chinese work on the Rites question, the *Ju-chiao shih-i* or 'True Meaning of Confucianism', under the pseudonym of Wen Ku-tzu, as well as a long treatise on the same subject, now in the Vatican Archives.[184] Although the former is undated, the latter, which appears to be a reworking of the Chinese treatise in scholastic form, is dated 26 September 1705, less than seven years after his arrival.

Neither of these, nor another Chinese work of the same period, the 'Record of a Dream of Paradise' *(Meng mei-t'u chi)* show any trace of Figurist ideas. However, copies of his letters in the Foucquet Papers[185] indicate that he was one of Bouvet's collaborators as early as 1703. He, with Hervieu, translated the *T'ien-hsüeh pen-i* in 1706, and in a letter to Bouvet of 12 July 1707, he calls himself a 'disciple'.[186]

The fruits of this discipleship are revealed in a long letter to Father Grimond, Superior of the Professed House of the Society of Jesus in Paris, dated 25 October 1707.[187] Through Father Bouvet, he says, he and a number of other French Jesuits have had the good fortune to

183. *Liu-shu shih-i,* ms in B Vat: *Borg Cin 357* (10).

184. 'Tractatus de Ju Kiao', in ASV: *Albani 242,* 6–162.

185. *Borgia Latino 565,* 400–462.

186. *Borgia Latino 565,* 459r.

187. BN: *Lat na 156,* 8–21.1 have used the copy in the Foucquet Papers, B Vat: *Borg Lat 565,* 463–477.

come to understand the mystery behind the Chinese classics, which is concealed in the form of Chinese characters. He gives several examples which are no different from, and no more convincing than, those presented by Bouvet and Foucquet. He does, however, give a rationale for this kind of approach to the classics which I have not found elsewhere in the Figurist writings. Ricci's method of arguing to the existence of God from the texts of the classics is, he says, still fruitful, but it does not go far enough.

> When we come to talk to them of the Incarnation, they cry out, like the Jews, 'This is a hard saying'; and they withdraw saying, *pu hsin,* 'we cannot believe that'.[188]

In other words, for de Prémare, Figurism is not a substitute for the old Jesuit interpretation of Confucianism, but its complement, to meet the difficulty of relating the new revelation to Chinese tradition.

This missionary orientation comes out very strongly in his correspondence with Foucquet after his sudden departure from Peking. Foucquet had evidently accused him of being a turncoat, of yielding to flattery and other forms of subtle pressure from the 'Lyonnais'.[189] De Prémare replied that he still believed that the central mysteries of Christianity were to be found in the classics and other early Chinese texts. What he objected to was the theory 'that the *I-ching* and other like books, were revealed by God to some of the first antediluvian Patriarchs . . . for the truth is that for all our conjectures, neither you nor I can know anything of that. Here is the crux of the matter, for, without it, no more Systems'.[190] If this cannot be demonstrated, and at best, he says, all that Bouvet and Foucquet have demonstrated is a mere possibility, then it is useless as a method of apologetics.[191]

De Prémare's position was frequently misunderstood by both parties to the dispute. They tended to think of Figurism as a total

188. B Vat: *Borg Lat 565,* 470r-v.
189. The letters to which de Prémare is replying are, unfortunately lost, but in his 'Relation Exacte', Foucquet accuses him of yielding to 'the flattery, the caresses, the presents even' of his opponents (B Vat: *Borg Lat 566,* 165v).
190. Letter to Bouvet and Foucquet, 23 September 1717, in B Vat: *Borg Lat 565,* 627.
191. De Prémare to Foucquet, 30 December 1717, in B Vat: *Borg Lat 565,* 625; and de Prémare to Guibert, 14 September 1718, ARSJ: JS *178,* 169r.

system which one either accepted or rejected, and when de Prémare returned to the south in August 1716 the anti-Figurists rejoiced at his 'defection'[192] while Foucquet accused him of no longer being the same man.[193] In fact, he remained true to his convictions—a moderate Figurism. In a note appended to one of Bouvet's works which speaks of Bouvet as if he were dead and so must belong to the end of de Prémare's life (1730–1736) he maintains his Figurist convictions. The theories of Bouvet are not proven but 'I judge them to rest on grounds more than sufficient for apostolic men to use them safely to restore the China mission which is almost extinct'.[194]

The treatises and letters belonging to de Prémare's later years in China reveal a double concern—on the one hand, the defence and development of the established Jesuit interpretation of Confucianism, and on the other, the articulation of the theory of 'vestiges'. In the first case, there are a number of letters to Foucquet protesting at his association of Figurism with opposition to Chinese Rites,[195] as well as two documents, the circulation of which were to lead to demands for his recall. The first of these was a long letter dated 10 October 1728,[196] notable chiefly for its attempted refutation of the charge of

---

192. See, for example, Contancin to the General, 1 September 1716, ARSJ: *SS177,* 70r.
193. Foucquet to de Premare, undated, in B Vat: *Borg Lat 565,*12v-13r.
194. Note to Bouvet's 'Demonstratio aeterni et sacri mysterii' (BN: *Lat na, 1173,* 60r).
195. See, especially, his letter to Foucquet, 24 December 1725, in B Vat; *Borg Cin 468* [F], 1–7, and Foucquet's reply of 13 October 1726, in B Vat; *Borg Cin 468* [F], 7–25. De Prémare further developed his objections to Foucquet's poisition in a letter to Etienne Fourmont, 1 November 1730 (BN: *Fr 15195,* 40–45). In *Borgia Cinese 468* [D], 53–57, there are some notes by Foucquet outlining the points of agreement and disagreement between himself and de Prémare. He wrongly, I think, restricts the area of disagreement to the Rites question; wrongly, because, as I shall demonstrate, de Prémare remained sceptical about the cabbalistic aspects of Foucquet's theory, and about the non-historical nature of the first three dynasties.
196. The copy I have used is that in B Vat: *Borg Cin 361 (l) d.* It is addressed to 'monsieur . . .', and is almost certainly the 'dissertation sur l'athéisme pretendu des chinois' which de Prémare mentions in a letter to Fourmont of 10 November 1730, as having been sent to the Abbé Raguet (BN: *Fr 15195,* 46r). There are two published versions, edited by G Pauthier; part of the letter, under the title of 'Sur le non-atheeisme des Chinois', was published in the *Revue de l'Orient,* nouv ser, t V, (1857): 10–27; and the whole, including the Chinese characters, in the *Annales de Philosophie Chrétienne,* 5e ser, t Ill, (1861) (I have used the offprint, Paris, 1861).

'atheism' made against the Neo-Confucians, which cites numerous texts in support of the thesis that Chu Hsi and other Neo-Confucians acknowledged a God. Rather ingenuously, de Prémare claimed that, while the Holy See had forbidden missionaries to use *t'ien* and *shang-ti* in their evangelisation of China, that is in practice, it was not forbidden to argue that these terms were, in theory, acceptable[197] That he was wrong was shown by the reception given to a letter of his to Father de Briga, intercepted on the way to Europe, and delated to Rome. Only his ill-health and bureaucratic procrastination prevented his recall from China. The original letter has not survived, but the excerpts which caused the fuss, together with de Prémare's reply, are extant in several copies,[198] and de Prémare's 'crime' is clear. He denies that the Chinese are atheists, and he continues to believe that they can be converted by an appeal to their own classics, thus, says his delator, 'rendering the preaching of the gospel useless.'[199]

De Prémare attempted to avoid this impasse by simultaneously defending in general theological terms his right to use the method of 'citing the documents of the gentiles in favour of the Christian religion,[200] and by expounding his theory of 'vestiges'. We can trace the progress of his work in his letters to Europe, especially those to the French philologist and chronologer, Etienne Fourmont. His attention was drawn to Fourmont by a report in the Jesuit *Journal de Trévoux* of Fourmont's dissertation of 1722 to the Académie des Inscriptions et Belles-lettres, on 'Chinese Literature'.[201] In December 1725, he wrote suggesting that Fourmont might be interested in his 'system' for understanding the real meaning of Chinese characters.[202]

---

197. B Vat: *Borg Cin 361 (1) d,* 1–2.
198. 'Extrait d'une dissertation envoye de St. Malo a M. le Nonce en France . . . ou Précis d'une lettre au R.P. de Briga interprete de la bande d'Isis par le R.P. de Prémare, jesuite missionnaire en Chine' (BN: *Fr 15195,* 5–9, and *Lat na 156,* 22–51; B Vat: *Borg Cin 468 [A]* and *Borg Lat 565,* 612–613). De Prémare's 'Reponse à un Extrait envoyé, dit on, de St. Malo à Monseigneur le Nonce à Paris, 16 August 1727', is in BN: *Fr 15195,* 10–20 and B Vat: *Borg Cin 468* [B].
199. BN: *Fr 15195,* 5v.
200. See the 'Quindecim Quaestiones Doctis Viris Propositae' (BN: *Fr 12209,* 37–38, and B Vat: *Borg Cin 468* [F], 4–7) and 'Examinatur an Missionary possint, et interdum debeant citare gentium monumenta in favorem Christianae Religionis', 2 September 1727 (B Vat: *Borg Cin 468* [C], I–II, and ASJP: *Brotier* 119, 95–101r).
201. A summary of this dissertation is to be found in the *Histoire de l'Académie Royale des Inscriptions et Belles-Lettres,* V (1729): 312–319.
202. Letter of 1 December 1725 in BN: *Fr 15195,* 1–4.

Fourmont must have replied favourably, because in late 1728, de Prémare unleashed on him a flood of letters and treatises expounding his ideas.[203] He notes that Fourmont is sceptical that 'a simple dissection of characters would make much impression upon scholars',[204] and he admits that while the Chinese commonly see symbolic importance in the elements of the characters, they also distinguish in them what, in modern terms, we would call 'radical' and 'phonetic' elements.[205] However, in interpreting Chinese characters, as in interpreting Chinese texts, one constantly finds there is a mysterious element that evades analysis.

> My idea is that it is necessary to interpret the hieroglyphics in the same way as one interprets the *Ching.* One must follow what the Chinese say, as far as it is possible, and show that when they fall short or offer no satisfactory explanation, it is usually because they have lost the traditional teaching which was revealed to the patriarchs, and then to the prophets; and which the Son of God, who taught them all, came to teach us himself.[206]

Thus did de Prémare attempt to reconcile sinology and theology, and the result, although less extravagant than in the works of Bouvet and Foucquet, was equally forced and ultimately untenable.

One of the letters de Prémare sent to Fourmont in 1728, was a fifty page notice on the *1-ching,* which he described as 'some preliminaries' to the 'commentaries on the *I-ching*' that he was working on.[207] In 1731 he completed a longer (124-page) work, called 'Notes Critiques pour entrer dans l'Intelligence de l'y King', which contained, in addition to a general introduction, a chapter interpreting the first two *kua* of the

203. Ten main items are listed in his accompanying letter of 4 December 1728, including six letters to Fourmont; and a further four items, in another letter dated 10 December 1728 (BN: *Fr 15195,* 34–35, 36–37).

204. BN: *Fr 15195,* 24v-25r.

205. BN: *Fr 15195,* 25r

206. BN: *Fr 15195,* 25r.

207. The manuscript of this work is now in BN: *Fr* N.A. *4754.* A slightly earlier and related work, 'Variae Quaestiones circa libros *King,* et eorum usum proponuntur et solvuntur' dated 2 October 1727, is in the Foucquet Papers, B Vat: *Borg Cin 468* [C] 39–52. Both are ultimately descended from the 'Latina Interpretatio' (ARSJ: JS I. 22) of 1720–1721.

I-ching, as symbolic of the Incarnation.[208] Even a brief glance at these works makes it clear why they were never published. They are forced and unconvincing, as simplistic as any of the extant Figurist works.

What distinguished de Prémare from the other Figurists is his historical sense, which must have been constantly at war with his Figurist theories. This appears most clearly in his *magnum opus*, *Vestiges des principaux dogmes Chrétiens tirés des anciens livres chinois,*[209] where, together with the standard Figurist interpretation of selected texts from the *I-ching*, the *Tao-te-ching* and elsewhere, there are some quite shrewd comments on the unhistorical character of much of the accepted 'history' of early China. He abstains from judgement on the general question of historicity of the first three dynasties—'I leave the Chinese their histories'[210]—but notes the obviously mythological nature of many of the details. Are we really to believe that ancient China was divided into neat 'well-field' units of nine equal areas of land?[211] or that Kings Wen and Wu, the founders of the Chou Dynasty, behaved in such an ideal fashion?[212] Are the dragons, tortoises, unicorns and phoenixs of Chinese tradition, real or symbolic creatures? Having raised these very pertinent questions, however, he assumes that the symbolic significance of these and countless other passages is to be discovered by applying the key of *Christian* symbolism and mythology. Instead of vestiges of 'primitive' modes of thinking about the nature of the world and man's place in it, he discerned vestiges, or more correctly perhaps, presages, of his own beliefs.

208. There are two copies known, one in the Foucquet Papers, B Vat: *Borg Cin 361 (I) b,* and one described in detail by Cordier in his *Bibliotheca Sinica* (cols 1372–1373) in the Bibliotheque Nationale in Paris *(Chin* 9247)

209. The original Latin manuscript, 'Selecta Quaedam Vestigia . . .', is in the Bibliotheque Nationale, Paris *(Chin* 9248). It was published in French translation by Augustin Bonnetty and Paul Perny in the *Annales de Philosophie Chrétienne,* Vie ser, t VII–XIII, and later reprinted in a limited edition in Paris in 1878. In the Jesuit Archives in Rome *(Jap Sin II. 168)* is a 79-page Latin manuscript entitled *Antiquae Traditions Selecta Vestigia,* in four articles, with an Introduction ('Ad Tractatum Sequentem Quaestio Proemialis quo circiter tempore ponendum sit initium verae Sinarum Historiae'). This is not, as an accompanying note has it, 'probabilmente . . . il manoscritto del de Prémare: Selecta Quaedam Vestigia'. Rather, it is a summary and defence of the work, probably the one referred to in dc Premare's letters to the General, 5 December 1729, and 13 November 1730 *(Jap Sin 184,* 47–49, 54–57).

210. *Vestiges,* 173.

211. *Vestiges,* 177.

212. See the last section of the *Vestiges* on 'Ven-vang' and 'Vou-vang'.

It would be foolish to dismiss de Prémare and the other Figurists, as a mere historical dead-end. They were grappling with very real problems, which their more 'scientific' successors frequently failed to be aware of, let alone to solve. They were ahead of their time in applying the comparative method; they correctly perceived that mythology and symbolism were key elements in the interpretation of the Chinese classics; and, as Jarry notes, it was the Figurists more than any other thinkers of the time, who 'deoccidentalised' the historical and geographical bounds of European intellectual life.[213] They obeyed Pascal's injunction to 'produce the documents' and forced other thinkers, Christian and anti-Christian, to examine them. Few agreed with the Figurists in seeing Moses in the Chinese documents; but if Moses was not there, what was there? And how did China relate to Moses, to the biblical revelation? Of such questions was born the scientific study of religion, and Figurism played a significant part in its conception.

213. E Jarry, 'La Querelle des Rites', chapter XV of S Delacroix, *Histoire universelle des missions Catholiques*, II (Paris, 1957), 339.

5
The Jesuits and the Beginning of Scientific Sinology

It is, indeed, really difficult, to take the just medium between those who too highly extoll, and those who too much despise the Chinese literature.

Antoine Gaubil[1]

The attitude displayed by Antoine Gaubil in his letter to the Secretary of the Royal Society cited above, is that of the scientific sinologist, who seeks to arrive at an objective and balanced judgement about Chinese culture, and to communicate it to a non-Chinese audience. It was a position that was hardly possible for a Jesuit missionary to adopt much before the time Gaubil arrived in China (1722), at least as a basic aim. Some of Gaubil's predecessors were sinologists, as it were, in their spare time. They wrote for a European public, letters and treatises of the 'curious' as well as 'edifying' type.[2] But their orientation was necessarily missionary, and their approach to Chinese culture dominated by that missionary concern. The bulk of their time was devoted to presenting Christianity to the Chinese, and their reports

1. Letter to Dr Cromwell Mortimer, Secretary of the Royal Society, 2 November 1752, published in *Philosophical Transactions*, XLVIII, 1753 (reprinted in Gaubil, *Correspondance*, 695).
2. Already, by 1722, fifteen volumes of the *Lettres édifiantes et curieuses écrites des missions étrangères* had appeared in Paris, the first in 1703. They contained, like the earlier *Annual Letters* and the many treatises, accounts, histories, travels etc., as we have already noted in passing, much 'sinological' material, as well as propaganda on behalf of the missions. A statistical survey of the bulk of printed literature would, I believe, show that the balance between 'edifying' and 'curious' was tipped in favour of the 'curious' by the arrival in China of the French 'mathématiciens du roi' who took seriously their responsibility as corresponding members of the French Academy of Sciences.

to Europe were aimed at securing aid for their missionary work, and, as the Rites Controversy developed, defending the methods they had evolved.

During the reigns of the Yung-cheng (1723–1736) and Ch'ien-lung (1736–1796) Emperors, missionary work of a public kind almost ceased. The literary apostolate to the Chinese continued, but on a much-reduced scale, inhibited both by the defection of Chinese scholar-officials as a result of the Rites decisions and imperial sanctions against Christianity; and by the problems of church censorship and the need to avoid Confucian terminology. The missionaries who remained in Peking as Western experts of one sort or another, had the leisure that their predecessors had lacked, and freedom from the overriding missionary and propagandist pressures that had dominated the earlier mission. They no longer felt the need to 'extol' or to depreciate Chinese tradition, and could begin to attempt to present it in its own terms to an eager European public.

I do not wish to imply that the mid and late eighteenth century Jesuit sinologists were free from bias, nor that they always preserved the difficult balance that Gaubil spoke of. In some respects, it seems to me that the 'scientific' interpretation of Confucianism that resulted, precisely because it was content for the most part to present the self-image of Confucianism, the K'ung-tzu of over two thousand years of accrued legend and adulation, was less perceptive than the earlier Riccian and Figurist interpretations. Ricci and his immediate successors had perceived, dimly but surely, the 'religious' dimensions of an overtly 'secular' tradition. The Figurists, however misguided in their use and interpretation of their insight, had grasped the mythological and symbolic features of much of the Confucian 'deposit of faith'. And both earlier interpretations had been founded on a missionary optimism, the opposite of which occasionally emerges in the writings of their frustrated successors.

They certainly had reason for feeling frustrated. They had crossed the world to preach the gospel, and instead found themselves producing playthings for the amusement of the Emperor and his court. In 1714, Pierre Jartoux wrote an account of his missionary career[3] in which he laments the fact that in thirteen years on the mission he had done no real missionary work, but had been 'a mere workman' for the

3. 'Brevis Vitae Ratio P. Petri Jartoux Missionarii S.J. in Sinis . . .', Peking, 23 August 1714, in ARSJ: JS *175*, 381–386

Emperor, producing clocks, mapping the Great Wall, and teaching mathematics to one of the Emperor's sons.[4] All he had to show for so many years of toil were toys like the clockwork tiger which the Emperor used for target practice.[5] Fifty years later, Pierre-Martial Cibot bitterly described himself as a gardener in the Versailles of China.[6] Even the scientific works that the Jesuits produced were, it appears, in the Ch'ing period, restricted to court use, and not allowed to circulate amongst a wider public. Bernard-Maître argues plausibly that it was this deprivation of a wider Chinese audience that drove so many of the eighteenth century missionaries to prefer writing for a European public which would appreciate their work.[7]

On the whole, however, the Jesuits of the eighteenth century probably erred, in Gaubil's terms, by 'too highly extolling' China and things Chinese. This may partly have been self-justification for their continued presence in China; partly, too, retrospective vindication of their lost cause in the Rites dispute. The sinophilism which marked Jesuit writings about China from the beginning, reached its climax in the great French Jesuit collections—the *Lettres Edifiantes,* Du Halde's *Description . . . de In Chine,* de Mailla's *Histoire Genérale de la Chine,* and the *Mémoires concernant l'histoire, les sciences, les arts, les moeurs, les usages . . . des Chinois.* It was these works and the works of the French *savants* who corresponded with the French Jesuits in Peking, which entitle the Jesuits to be regarded as the founders of scientific sinology. And it is the 'Confucius' of this last stage in the Jesuit interpretation of Confucianism that is the subject of this chapter.

Jean Baptiste do Halde

Jean Baptiste du Halde SJ was never in China, yet his contribution to sinology was second to none. Du Halde was for nearly forty years the official editor of French Jesuit missionary material, and especially that emanating from China. He edited Volumes IX to XXVI of the *Lettres Edifiantes* (1709–1743), and brought together in his *Description*

4. ARSJ: JS *175,* 381r.
5. ARSJ: JS *175,* 381v
6. Letter to Brotier, 22 October 1767, published in *Revue de l'Extrême Orient,* III (1887) 255.
7. In 'Les adaptations chinoises d'ouvrages européens . . .', *Monumenta Serica,* X (1945): 369.

géographique, historique, chronologique, politique, et physique de l'Empire de la Chine (Paris, 1735) the most comprehensive account of China hitherto available. The latter was, as Dr Johnson advised Boswell to do,[8] 'consulted' by almost all the important mid and late eighteenth century writers—and many later—who invoked China on one or other side of their debates; and the popularity of the former is attested by the many editions of the late eighteenth and early nineteenth centuries.

The *Lettres Edifiantes,* as we have seen, contain much that is 'curious' as well as 'edifying', and amongst the 'curious' material there is occasional reference to Confucius and Confucianism. None, however, is very substantial or original. In the nineteenth collection (1729), we find an attack by de Prémare on Eusèbe Renaudot's *Anciens Relations des Indes et de Ia Chine* (1718) in which, in very guarded fashion, de Prémare introduces his views on the 'hieroglyphic' nature of Chinese writing, the derivation of Chinese religious ideas from the survivors of the Deluge,[9] and the significance of the *1-ching,*[10] as well as defending the Chinese from the charge of atheism.[11] The last point was taken up at greater length by Parrenin in the twenty-first volume (1734) in a letter to Dortous de Mairan, dated 11 August 1730, where he claims that the charge of Chinese 'atheism' is based on a one-sided examination of the Sung philosophers, and a failure to examine popular beliefs and attitudes.[12]

In general, however, the *Lettres Edifiantes* are silent on Confucianism, and the reasons are not far to seek. The first *Recueil* appeared in 1703, when de Tournon was already on his way to China, and a favourable reference to Confucianism would have drawn fire from Rome as well as the French opponents of the Society. The policy of the editors, Le Gobien, du Halde and Patouillet,[13] seems

8. Boswell asked Johnson if he should read du Halde's *China.* 'Why, yes, (said he) as one reads such a book; that is to say, consult it.'—Boswel's *Life of Johnson* (Oxford, 1934), II, 55 (under Spring 1768).
9. *Lettres Edifiantes* XIX, 1729, 461–462, and 483.
10. *Lettres Edifiantes* XIX, 1729, 476.
11. *Lettres Edifiantes* XIX, 1729, 485–491.
12. See, especially, 133–134.
13. Le Gobien edited t I–VIII, du Halde t IX–XXVI. Louis Patouillet edited at least t. XXVII, XXXI, XXXIII, and XXXIV t XXIX, XXX and XXXII have introductions signed 'MJ' which Retif suggests signifies '(Rene) Marechal, jésuite', but Patouillet may well have been responsible for these too (v Rétif, Brève Histoire. . ., 40, n 14).

to have been to select and publish material from the letters from China that contributed to a favourable picture of Chinese culture, Chinese morals and Chinese society, and thus, indirectly to refute their opponents' basic premise of a benighted atheistic China. There is considerable debate as to the extent to which du Halde and the others edited their material. Virgile Pinot in *La Chine et ía formation de I'espri philosophique en France*[14] gives several examples of cuts and rewriting of letters by du Halde, while Alexander Brou SJ claims that, on the whole, he was a faithful editor, guilty of suppressions certainly, but not, for the most part, of positive distortions of the views of the contributors.[15] Pinot cites[16] one disgruntled contributor—Foucquet—-but Foucquet is hardly a reliable authority since at the time he wrote he was a declared opponent of some of the principles which the other contributors as well as the editors shared. On the other hand, there was one case at least where two letters were spliced together, attributing a quite false statement to the author under whose name the 'letter' appeared.[17] De Prémare, in a letter to Fourmont, refers to the letter, already cited, refuting Renaudot, and points out that du Halde has made two additions and some abbreviations. He does not, however, appear very upset, and concludes: 'for the most part he has made a fairly good *précis* of what I said at much greater length'.[18] This seems to me a fair comment on du Halde's method.

Pinot is more justified, I think, in his criticism of du Halde's editing of material that appeared in the *Description.* Admittedly, du Halde does not cite his sources, except in a general acknowledgement in the preface, and the work purports to be his personal synthesis. But I agree with Pinot[19] rather than Brou[20] in this case. As Pinot shows, du Halde especially suppressed passages which referred to popular

14. Virgile Pinot, *La Chine et ía formation de I'espri philosophique en France,* 158–167.
15. v A Brou, 'Les jésuites sinologues de Pékin et leurs éditeurs de Paris', in *Revue d'histoire des missions,* XI (1934): 557–566. This, too, is Mme Thomaz de Bossierre's verdict on du Halde's editing of a letter of D'Entrecolle's (*François-Xavier Dentrecolles,* 23).
16. *La Chine,* 160 (letter of 7 November 1736).
17. See de Mailla's complaint on this matter, in a letter of 17 September 1730, published in *Revue de l'Extrême Orient,* III (1887): 651–652; and (under the date 27 September 1730) in his *Histoire Générale,* I, clxx–clxxi.
18. Prémare to Fourmont, 10 November 1730 (BN: *Fr 15195,* 51r-v).
19. See *La Chine,* 167–180.
20. See 'Les jésuites sinologues . . .', 562–563.

Chinese religious practices and superstitions, thereby exaggerating the profundity and purity of Chinese religious ideas. As a later missionary noted, 'Father du Halde is much too flattering to the Chinese in the portrait he gives of them'.[21]

Despite this, however, the *Description . . . de la Chine* is a key work in the evolution of the Jesuit interpretation of Confucianism. Precisely as a work of synthesis, it brings together a great deal of Jesuit writing on Chinese religion and on Confucianism. Despite du Halde's protestations in the preface that he writes purely as historian and avoids all matters in dispute,[22] the *Description* contains a restatement of the central Jesuit position on Confucianism. He is cautious, avoiding explicit statements which might bring down on him the wrath of the anti-Rites party,[23] but the established Jesuit interpretation is implicit in the whole work. On Chinese chronology, he accepts the traditional view and appeals to the Septuagint to avoid problems of discrepancy with the Bible.[24] He describes the *I-ching* as 'a pure enigma'[25] but he is prepared to regard Confucius as having prophesied the Messiah,[26] and he attributes the foundation of the Chinese Empire to the sons of Noah.[27] He is, however, no Figurist, since he sees the first Chinese as following 'the law of nature which they had received from their Fathers'[28] rather than as transmitters of a primitive revelation.

In the section on Chinese religion[29] he contrasts the worship of *Shang-ti* and *T'ien* by the ancient Chinese, with the Epicureanism of the Taoists[30] and the idolatry of the Buddhists.[31] The Taoists and

21. Letter of François Bourgeois SJ, 1 September 1767, in *Lettres Ediftantes,* XXIX (1773): 152.
22. *Description,* La Haye, 1736, 1, xxxi.
23. See du Halde's letter to Foucquet of 5 July 1734, cited in Pinot, *La Chine,* 172–173.
24. *Description,* I, 261.
25. *Description,* II, 345.
26. *Description,* II, 387.
27. *Description,* III, 2.
28. *Description,* III, 15.
29. Beginning t III of the Hague edition.
30. *Description,* III, 19. Du Halde includes to the Figurist theory that Lao-tzu had some knowledge of the Trinity, but he qualifies it as 'une connoissance bien grossière'.
31. *Description,* III, 23–34, contains the strongest language I have seen used in any Jesuit work, in describing the Buddha and Buddhism. For example, in describing the death of Buddha: 'ce fût alors, quand il étoit prêt de sa fin, que mettant le comble à l'impiété, il vomit de son sein tout le venim de l'athéisme'.

Buddhists are responsible for the perversion of ancestor rites into superstition.[32] But elements of the pure ancient religion remain in the practices of the *literati* and the imperial sacrifices to *Shang-ti*[33] and they are maintained in their purity by the vigilance of the 'Tribunal of Rites'.[34] Similarly, in philosophy, although 'a great number of mediocre and untalented *literati* have followed the recent Commentators on the ancient texts who have evolved 'a sort of Atheism', 'the truly learned' follow the text rather than the gloss, and believe in a supreme God, *Shang-ti* or *T'ien*.[35]

None of this is new, and most can be found verbatim in earlier Jesuit writings. The interesting thing about du Halde's *Description*, apart from its value as a *summa* of Jesuit views on China, and its undoubted influence on eighteenth century thinkers and writers, is that as late as 1735 he could uphold the old Jesuit interpretation of Confucianism. He even rehearses the old Rites controversy arguments[36] in detail, making it perfectly clear where his sympathies lie. It is very doubtful whether the church authorities in Rome can have been content with his plea that he was merely writing 'en qualité d'Historien',[37] and an examination of du Halde's third volume goes far towards explaining the severity and strict legal provisions of the 1742 decree against the Rites. Even as a historian and as a sinologue, the Jesuit editor remained attached to the basic principles of interpretation laid down by Matteo Ricci the man he eulogised as 'the Apostle of China'.[38]

Antoine Gaubil

The recent publication of the *Correspondance de Pékin* of Antoine Gaubil has, to my mind, established beyond doubt his status as the greatest sinologist of the whole period of the old Jesuit mission in China. Abel Rémusat, well over a century ago, described him as 'incontestably amongst all Europeans, the one who best knew Chinese literature, or at least, who was able to make the most useful and the

32. *Description,* II, 154.
33. *Description,* III, 6.
34. *Description,* III, 17.
35. *Description,* III, 142 ff.
36. *Description,* III, 142 ff.
37. *Description,* III, 39.
38. *Description,* III, 142.

greatest number of contributions to its study'.[39] Since Rémusat's time, of course, there have been many sinologists whose works are superior to Gaubil's in erudition and judgement. His translations have been superseded and the premises which underlie his work on Chinese chronology and astronomy—premises derived from the Chinese themselves—have been found false. But in his time, and judged by the standards of his time, he was a prodigy.

Gaubil had some advantages that many later sinologists have lacked, especially his continuous residence in Peking for thirty-seven years and his contact with Chinese scholars. We should not, however, exaggerate the value of this in the circumstances surrounding the mission in the mid-eighteenth century. Whereas Ricci and his immediate successors had contact with, and the collaboration of eminent Chinese scholars, Gaubil was reduced to hiring Chinese secretaries who, by his account, were not very helpful. Writing to Joseph Delisle, in 1752, he complained:

> Here we do not have the facilities that you have in Paris . . . Up till now I have had enough to employ a copyist; but even with the money, it is very difficult to fnd people who can obtain the books and explain what is difficult for us in them. What are called able Chinese scholars are usually people with no critical sense, little erudition, and lacking the principles of our sciences, and inwardly full of a ridiculous disdain for anything not Chinese. Furthermore, they have few scruples about deceiving us, saying, if it is in their interest, that white is black. One must be in a position to verify properly what they advance, otherwise one is subject to many errors of this sort; this has done much harm, and been the cause of many blunders and laughable misunderstandings.[40]

That this judgment was not motivated by European prejudice is shown by many passages in his letters appreciative of Chinese scholarship, and sympathetic towards the Chinese as people. It does, however, show the difficulties under which he laboured.

39. Quoted in Pfister, *Notices*, 667, from Rémusat's *Nouveaux Mélanges Asiatiques*, II, 289.
40. Gaubil, *Correspondance*, 666 (letter of 13 August 1752).

Perhaps Gaubil's greatest contribution to sinology, was not his numerous published works[41] but the influence of his manuscripts and his letters on European scholars. Gaubil was rightly critical of the failure of such scholars, clerical and lay, to appreciate the value of his work, and that of other Jesuits:

> When you have seen [the manuscripts] that M. Fréret had collected, those that P. Sonciet has left, what P. Patouillet collected etc., you would conclude that most of our Fathers have completely wasted their time and effort in sending to Paris so many memoirs and writings, of which some have been rejected as ridiculous, others split up into sections and sent in all direction, without being put all together, and others thrown away. See what has come of so much trouble taken; and the example of past experience teaches us for the future.[42]

Joseph Brucker has shown how Souciet and du Halde mutilated Gaubil's works, which they printed in their collections; and how de Guignes plagiarised his work on the Huns.[43] It was not till the nineteenth century that many of his works were appreciated and published. On the other hand, a mere glance at the list of his manuscripts now in various European collections, and even more at the addressees of his letters, demonstrates the extent of his contribution to European studies on China, and on scientific questions. He was a correspondent of leading figures in the Academies of Paris, London and St Petersburg—of Delisle, Bayer, Fréret, Dortous de Mairan, Deshauterayes, the elder de Guignes, Anquetil du Perron, Mortimer and Birch. And many of the letters, as collected in his *Correspondance,* prove to be miniature treatises on a wide variety of subjects, full of information, corrections and suggestions that were incorporated in his correspondents' works.

Unfortunately the subjects he discussed did not, except marginally, touch on Confucianism. History, chronology and astronomy were his chosen fields, and in them he saw his function as that of translator and compiler.

---

41. For a full listing of published and unpublished works, see Joseph Dehergne's 'Bibliographic des ouvrages du Père Antoine Gaubil' in the *Correspondance,* 884–910.
42. *Correspondance,* 674 (Gaubil to Delisle, 28 August 1752).
43. See J Brucker, 'La Chine et 1'Extrême Orient d'après les travaux historiques de P. Antoine Gaubil, missionaire à Peking (1723–1759)', in *Revue des questions historiques,* XXXVII (1885): 485–539 (especially 511–12 and 525–530).

> I have always been surprised [he wrote to Delisle in 1752] that the missionaries did not begin by making sure that they had faithful translations of the *ching* and the histories; I believe that this would have cut short many useless disputes. It is one thing to see some truncated fragments of the *ching* and the histories, and another to see them as a whole.[44]

His own translations included those of three of the classics; the *Shu-ching,* sent to Europe in 1739 and published after Gaubil's death by de Guignes; the *Shih-ching,* sent in 1749, but never published; and the *I-ching,* which does not appear to have been sent to Europe, nor perhaps to have been completed.[45] These do not strictly belong to the area of 'interpretation' of Confucius and Confucianism, since they remain bare translations. On the crucial question of their authorship and authority, Gaubil appears to take a quite traditional position, as he does on other textual qnestions.[46] It was not so much that he was uncritical, as that he appreciated better than other Jesuits the sheer weight of Chinese opinion behind accepted views. He preferred to follow them until there was strong evidence to the contrary, rather than reject the tradition for a *priori* and essentially European reasons. He was, as Confucius himself claimed to be, 'a transmitter and not a maker'.

Gaubil and de Mailla,[47] in their correspondence with Nicholas Fréret and others, de Prémare's letters to Etienne Fourniont,[48] and the Parrenin—Dortous de Mairan correspondence,[49] all proved important links in the growth of the scientific study of China and the Chinese. If, as is arguably the case, Western sinology could only seriously begin when the Chinese view of their own tradition had been absorbed in Europe, then to Gaubil and his colleagues, but especially to Gaubil, we must attribute the beginnings of sinology.

44. *Correspondance,* 674 (Gaubil to Delisle, 28 August 1752).
45. See *Bibliographie,* Nos 17 and 36 in *Correspondance,* 889, 897.
46. For example, his defence of the authenticity of the *Chu-shu chi-nien* against de Mailla's strictures (see *Correspondance,* 511 *cf* de Mailla's letter to Fréret, 23 May 1735, in his *Histoire generate de la Chine,* I (Paris, 1777), lxxxiii–lxxxx).
47. See especially the letters published as an introduction to the first volume of de Mailla's *Histoire générale.*
48. See the list of manuscript letters in the Bibliography to this work, and also the excerpts published by Fourmont in his *Linguae Sinarum Mandaricae, Hieroglyphicae, Grammatica Duplex* (Paris 1742).
49. See the Bibliography for manuscript and published letters of Parrenin, and Dortous de Mairan's *Lettres au R.P. Parrenin* (Paris, 1759).

Alexander de Ia Charme and the *Hsing-li chên-ch'üan*

While most of the Jesuits of the China mission in the mid-eighteenth century concentrated on sinological work for a European audience, a limited amount of writing on religious subjects was still published in Chinese. Most of these are devotional works, prayers, lives of saints, spiritual exhortations. There is, however, one outstanding exception, the work of Gaubil's near contemporary, Alexandre de Ia Charme (in China, 1728–1767). This truly major work, the *Hsing-li chên-ch'üan* ('True Explanation of Natural Philosophy'), published in 1753, is important since it represents the fullest elaboration of the standard Jesuit interpretation of Confucianism to be published in Chinese by the Jesuits of the old mission.

From the title with its clear echo of the great Neo-Confucian *sumrna*, the *Hsing-li ta-ch'üan,* we might expect that Ia Charme was attempting the last and obvious stage in the Jesuit interpretation of Confucianism, the appropriation of Neo-Confucian philosophy. Alas, despite the lengthy discussion of Neo-Confucian concepts such as *t'ai-chi*, *li* and *ch'i,* we find that, at bottom, it is a straightforward expansion of Ricci's position. It, too, is a *summa,* but one that resolutely excludes from its synthesis the 'spiritual' elements in Neo-Confucianism. It does, however, incorporate arguments from Jesuit writers after Ricci on the nature of the soul, and there is a stress on the equivalence of the Christian *ching* (that is, the Bible) with the Chinese *ching,* that may be due to Figurist influence.

The preface reasserts the old Riccian distinction between the classics and their commentaries.

> What did the earlier Confucians say? Believe in the classics and do not believe in the commentary; discuss the classics, and do not discuss the small print [of the commentary]. And what do the later Confucians say? Believe in the classics and also believe in the commentary; discuss the classics, and also discuss the small print.[50]

The modern Confucians, then, are untrue to the classics, using language not given prominence in the classics to develop doctrines unheard of in the time of Confucius. Above all, they replace the clear

50. Cited in Ch'en Shou-i, 'Ming-mo Ye-su-hui-shih te Ju-chiao-kuan chi ch'i fan-ying', in *Ming shih lun-ts'ung,* X (*Ming-tai tsung-chiao*)*,* 89.

notion of a creator, maker of all things, with vague and contradictory notions that are not true equivalents. *T'ai-chi* is associated with the creator in producing matter, but is not identical with him; *t'ai chi* must blend with *ch'i,* it cannot of itself be the origin of things.[51] Similarly, *li, ch'i, yin* and *yang,* as described by the 'later Confucians', have properties which make it impossible that they could function as equivalents to the lord and maker of things.[52]

What is more remarkable about Ia Charme's work is the positive side of his argument. It was clearly dangerous after the 1742 Rites decision simply to repeat Ricci's arguments in their original form. La Charme goes to quite extraordinary lengths at times to retain the argument from equivalence without using the terms proscribed by Rome, and without appearing to claim too much for Confucianism. He attempts to evade the terms problem by inventing yet another term, *shang-chu,* 'the lord above', which was neither classical nor Christian, but had overtones both of the classical *shang-ti* and the Christian *t'ien-chu.* Where Ricci would have used *t'ien,* Ia Charme uses *shang-chu.*[53] He cites the classics frequently, but avoids the *t'ien* and *shang-ti* passages that were the common stock of the seventeenth century Jesuit works.

On the other hand, he includes an argument that seems to come from the Figurists and implies, though does not spell out, the Figurist claim of a revealed source for the Chinese classics:

> China has its five classics, the *Songs*, History, *Changes, Rites* and *Annals;* Christianity, too has its five classics, its *Songs, History, Changes, Rites* and *Annals.* But the classical books which Christianity has, have not undergone the Ch'in

51. *Hsing-li chên-ch'üan, ch. 2,* chapter 4, 100. cited by Chu Ch'ien-chih, 'Ye-su-hui tui-yu Sung Ju li-hsüeh chih fan-ying', in *Ming shih lun-ts'ung,* X (*Ming-tai tsung-chiao*), 156.
52. See the passages cited in Chu Ch'ien-chih, 'Ye-su-hui tui-yu Sung Ju li-hsüeh chih fan-ying', 156–157.
53. Ch'ên Shou-i, 'Ming-mo Ye-su-hui-shih te Jo-chiao-kuan chi ch'i fan-ying', 90 nn 1 and 2, argues that *shang-chu* must have been introduced in the later Shanghai, 1889 edition, in place of the condemned *t'ien* used in the original 1753 edition. I have superficially examined the rare original edition (in B Vat: *Borg Cin 362)* and my recollection is that it carefully avoided all use of the condemned terms *t'ien* and *shang-ti.* It is notable that amongst the complaints of Propaganda about the work (on which, see below) this charge was not made, which it certainly would have been if La Charme's text had given any grounds for complaint.

> burning, and are complete and without *lacunae;* while the classical books which China has, have undergone the Ch'in burning, are deficient and missing characters.[54]

This passage would seem to claim for the Chinese *ching* a revealed rather than a 'natural' origin, and this appears to have been the interpretation placed on it by certain anti-Jesuit sources. The Jesuit Administrator of the Diocese of Peking, Laimbeckhoven, received a sharp letter in 1767[55] from Propaganda, informing him that 'on the testimony of certain people' it was believed that the Jesuits in China had published a work in Chinese 'in which the law of the Old Testament is compared with the ancient doctrine of Confucius and other Chinese philosophers, and this Confucius is even called a "Saint" and said to be inferior to none of the Patriarchs'.

Laimbeckhoven, in reply, forwarded the testimony of the official 'revisor', the Carmelite Joseph of St Theresa, which denied that any of these ideas were to be found in the text of the *Hsing-li chên-ch'uüan*. The scope of the work is simply 'to demonstrate in a new style, and in a philosophic way, that the true Religion is to be embraced by all, and that the Christian Religion is such'.[56] Laimbeckhoven adds his own version of the method of the work:

> The author, feigning to be a Chinese philosopher, leads Chinese *literati* to a knowledge of the true God, of the immortality of the soul, and of other principal dogmas of the True Religion, to a knowledge of which we can come by the natural light of reason alone.[57]

What is most curious is that both Joseph of St Theresa and Laimbeckhoven appear to have thought that to argue from reason and from Chinese texts was a new method invented by Ia Charme. If neither was being deliberately ingenuous—and I think it unlikely—we have striking evidence of the extent to which the Rites Controversy had disrupted the methods of the mission and undermined the Jesuit interpretation of Confucianism.

---

54. Cited in Ch'ên Shou-i, 'Ming-mo Ye-su-hui-shih te Ju-chiao-kuan chi ch'i fan-ying', 93
55. Dated 29 January 1767 (copy in ARSJ: JS *181*, 294).
56. Ms in ARSJ: JS *184*, 240r.
57. Letter of 6 August 1769, ARSJ: JS *181*, 294r.

On the whole the *Hsing-li chên-ch'uan* was a disappointing conclusion to the tradition. Despite its considerable length, it marked no real advance on its predecessors, and, in some respects, was more simplistic and unperceptive. La Charme's other literary productions reveal him as essentially a compiler rather than an original thinker; and his translation of the *Shih-ching*, admittedly an early work, has been strongly criticised by later sinologists.[58] But, original or not, it testifies to the continuing Jesuit attachment to Confucianism, and their attempt to salvage something from the debris of the post-Rites Chinese Church.

The *Mémoires concernant l'histoire . . . etc des chinois*

The last major product of the old Jesuit mission in China appeared, as it were, posthumously, since it was published after the dissolution of the Society of Jesus. It was, however, a fitting monument to the industry and sinological work of the Jesuits. The fifteen volumes of the *Memoires concernant l'histoire, les sciences, les arts, les moeurs, les usages, &c, des chinois, par les Missionaires de Pékin* appeared in Paris in 1776–1791, and brought to light much of the material that had lain gathering dust in manuscript in the libraries of French scholars and institutions. It also published the work of some of the last generation of Jesuits in China, such as Jean-Joseph-Marie Amiot, Pierre-Martial Cibot, and the two Chinese Jesuits, Kao Lei-ssu and Yang Te-wang.

The programme of the *Mémoires* was proclaimed in the first item in volume one, the 'Essay on the Antiquity of the Chinese', in the phrase, 'only China can make China known',[59] in other words, Chinese culture should be presented in its own terms. And the 'Essay' itself exemplifies this in quite brilliant fashion, dismissing extremes in European interpretations, such as the Figurist view of the *I-ching*, as the intrusion of 'systems' into a confused mythology.[60] The writer, or writers,[61] are equally harsh on the enthusiasm of Chinese *literati*

58. J Legge, *Chinese Classics*, I, v.
59. 'La Chine seul peut faire connoltre la Chine', in (*Mimoires*, I, 23).
60. *Memoires*, I, 42–43, 104.
61. The 'Essai' seems to be principally the work of Kao Lei-ssu and Cibot. Since 'Ko' is given as the author, I presume that he had the leading part. Amiot in *Memoires*, XV, 274, seems to refer to Cibot as the author, since he notes that the author of the 'Essai' died in August 1780. Cibot's Chinese name, however, was Han (Kuo-

who regard the *i-ching* as 'the philosopher's stone of the arts and sciences'. True scholars, Western and Chinese, know it for what it is: a mixture of all kinds of symbols and allegories, difficult to decipher and understand, but containing some 'important things'.[62]

On the question of Chinese chronology, the 'Essay' takes a cautious position, based, it is claimed, on the best Chinese histories. According to these, nothing authentic is known much before Yao.[63] As for Fu Hsi, beloved of the Figurists:

> Fu Hsi has been more fortunate in Europe than here. He is believed, so far away across the seas, to be the Founder of our Monarchy. In fact, our historians have been careful not to mention him, and those who have spoken of him do not allow him into our annals except by way of supplement, and simply to say something on the subject.[64]

It should be noted that the authors, or perhaps the editor,[65] assume that China was a colony, founded by the survivors of the Deluge,[66] but this Christian perspective is merely incidental. The main purpose of the work, in which it succeeds remarkably, is to present the orthodox accepted version of early Chinese history based on the best sources.

Another trace of Christian interpretation in the 'Essay on the Antiquity of the Chinese' is a general assumption that 'Religion and the Divinity'[67] are to be found in the Chinese classics, not perhaps in the overt form that the Figurists claimed, but in some form. I suspect

ying) not Ko. Joseph Dehergne in his entry on Kao in his *Repertoire* (134) notes that while the manuscript of the 'Essai (BN: *Brequigny* 106) is in Cibot's hand, an essay on an allied subject (Brequigny 22) is partly in Kao's handwriting, partly in Cibot's. Probably Cibot at least polished the style, since the work is one of the best written of all the contributions to the *Mémoires*.

62. *Mémoires,* I, 43.
63. See Article II, 149 ff.
64. *Mémoires,* I, 131.
65. Who the editor or editors were is uncertain but I suspect they were former Jesuits, that is members of the disbanded Society of Jesus, seeking literary employment. The Abbe Grosier, who edited de Mailla's *Histoire* was an ex-Jesuit. A reference in a letter of Cibot to Pere Brotier suggests that Brotier may have been one at least of the editors of the *Mémoires* (see Cibot to Brotier, 5 November 1769, in *Revue de l'Extrême Orient,* III, 1887, 262).
66. *Mémoires,* I, 250.
67. *Mémoires,* I, 43.

that this argument is Cibot's rather than his Chinese collaborator's since in other places Cibot reveals himself as something of a Figurist. He belongs rather to the line of de Prémare than that of Bouvet or Foucquet, seeing limited traces of Christian doctrines in the form of Chinese characters,[68] but accepting the historicity of Yao, Shun, Yu and the first three dynasties. He wrote to Brotier, in explanation of his position, in November 1769.

> You can put your mind at ease about my way of thinking. If I go astray, it will not be in the footsteps of Fathers Bouvet, Prémare, Gollet etc. However, I warn you in advance that the rays of Revelation shine in all the ancient monuments of China . . .[69]

What saved Cibot from excesses was his common-sense and his realisation of the limited knowledge Europeans have of China.

> China is the America of men of letters. European scholars are like the Portuguese who boast of having conquered the Indies because they discovered them and built a few little forts on their coasts.[70]

The note of humility, in itself, was a valuable contribution to sinology. There is hardly a contribution to the *Mémoires* that does not in some way touch on Confucianism, but it is in the twelfth and thirteenth volumes that we find the major works on the subject, Amiot's 'Life of Confucius' and his 'Brief Lives of the Principal Disciples of Confucius'. It is typical of these works that he refers to 'Koung-tsée, appellé vulgairement CONFUCIUS'. His aim is, indeed, to present K'ung-tzu, not Confucius; to be 'the Historian of the Historians of him whose life I write',[71] and 'to present K'ung-tzu such as he is in the eyes of his nation, and so, necessarily, to tell what the nation tells of

68. See his 'Lettre sur les caracteres chinois' in *Mémoires,* I, reprinted after the original edition, *Lettre de Pékin sur le génie de la langue chinoise,* Brussels, 1773; and the 'Essai sur la langue et les caractères des chinois: Article Second', in *Mémoires,* IX, especially 378–389.
69. *Revue de l'Extrême Orient,* III (1887): 262 (letter of 5 November 1769).
70. Letter to Brotier, 22 October 1767, in *Revue de l'Extrême Orient,* III (1887): 256–257.
71. *Mémoires,* XII, 12.

him'.[72] Unfortunately, Amiot seems to have set out to tell *all* that the nation tells of Confucius that is, to assemble from all available sources all the remarks, all the stories, all the references relating to Confucius. Rarely does he cite sources, although he frequently indicates by quotation marks that he is quoting from a Chinese source. The result is not a critical biography of Confucius but a compilation, even extending to a complete and detailed 'Table Chronologique' of his 'life'. The lives of the disciples in the thirteenth volume are similarly detailed and uncritical. The Confucian line of succession is traced, its heroes eulogised, and their places on the tablets of the Confucian sanctuary justified.

All this was far from the methods of the modern historian of Chinese philosophy. Neither the biographies nor the ideas are subjected to critical analysis. Yet it was an important stage in the European discovery of Confucianism. No longer was Confucianism presented as a *praeparatio evangelica,* seen in a historical evolutionary sequence that would end inevitably in the fullness of Christian revelation. Nor was it seen as a version of the Judaeo—Christian tradition garbled in transmission. The aim of the exercise was to present Confucius as he was seen by those who called themselves his successors and followers, and as he actively influenced the lives of living Confucians. The myth of Confucius was the logical starting-point for the scientific study of Confucianism, and Amiot's 'Life' was the first European work to present the myth in full. Thus, the last contribution of the old Jesuit mission to sinology was to present the K'ung-tzu who for nearly two centuries had been obscured by the Jesuit Confucius.

72. *Mémoires,* XII, 12, n 4.

An agenda

A survey, such as this study has been, cannot, I think, legitimately issue in a conclusion. Its logical end is rather a non-conclusion; an agenda for further investigation. In this note I would like briefly to indicate what the main items on such an agenda might be.

Firstly, I see the need for a much more thorough exploration than I have been able to give here, of the Rites Controversy and of Figurism. Both episodes in Sino-Western interpretation touched on tender spots in the European consciousness, laying bare assumptions, attitudes, systematic preconceptions, that had been ignored or misunderstood till the challenge of Chinese circumstances brought them to the surface. China acted as a catalyst, and the Jesuits, in their role of cultural middle-men, helped bring about a confrontation whose implications have yet to be fully worked out. The Jesuit interpretation of Confucianism was but one element in the European reassessment of values described variously as the 'Enlightenment', the process of 'secularisation', 'la crise de la conscience européene'[1] but it was a not unimportant one.

Secondly, there is the question, put to one side in the course of this work, of the ultimate validity of the Jesuit interpretation, or interpretations, of Confucianism. This is not a matter of a simple comparison between the Jesuit views and the accepted views of modern scholarship. It involves a reassessment not only of the Confucian tradition, but of the whole Chinese intellectual tradition, and of its Western interpretations. The Jesuits, representatives of

1. The title of Paul Hazard's masterly study of the period 1680–1715 (Paris, 1935), translated as *The European Mind*.

European values and intellectual methods, attempted, as their European successors have done, to understand Chinese intellectual life in terms of systems, and transmuted the tradition of the *Ju* or Chinese 'scholars' into an '-ism', Confucianism. They concentrated on conceptual correspondences—hence the crucial importance of 'terms' in the Rites Controversy—rather than on analogies of function and the integration of values in the social behaviour of 'Confucians'. Their European frame of reference proved inadequate to expressing Chinese reality, and they were often, at least dimly, aware of this. Modern sinologists, applying a battery of linguistic, archaeological and text-critical methods, have been able to recover, with some certainty, the historical Confucius from the Confucius of Chinese tradition but, for all their sophistication, one suspects that many of the same assumptions that vitiated or at least obfuscated the Jesuit interpretation of Confucianism have been at work. What is needed is a re-examination of the hermeneutics of sinology. In historical perspective the deficiencies of the Jesuit interpretation of Confucianism are evident, but their bias was overt and their assumptions usually quite explicit. The assumptions of more recent scholars are often far less obvious, but they are not necessarily less biased.

A third, and closely related, item on the agenda, is to determine the applicability of the secular/sacred categories to China. For the Jesuits of the China mission this was much more than an abstract or theoretical problem. It was a personal dilemma, affecting as it did their self-image and their whole lifestyle. Could one dress, act, even think as a Confucian scholar, and still be a 'religious' man? The Jesuits at court felt this tension most acutely and some, judging by their complaints, were unable to resolve it. Most, I believe, resolved it in practice, but did not, or could not, find a theology to articulate the personal harmonisation of their actual occupations and their ultimate goals. The reason was that in China, even more than in Europe, and in Confucianism more than in Buddhism or Taoism, the Western-style division of life into secular and religious areas was inapplicable. Family life, government, personal relations, were in many respects 'sacred' activities, no more and no less than various kinds of ritual. The ambiguity of the Confucian concept of *li,* at once the prescription of ethics and of polite custom, a matter of religious obligation and of social convention, illustrates this well. The Jesuits learnt to be

Confucian *chün-tzu* and to live by such a code, and they judged Chinese customs and behaviour in the light of their experience. When forced to defend themselves, however, they found it necessary to use such terms such as 'atheist', 'civil', 'political', which were incompatible with their general interpretation and, they realised, misleading. At a time when theologians, historians and phenomenologists of religion, and philosophers are engaged in renewed debate on such issues as 'secular Christianity', the nature of transcendence and the secularisation of Western society, the Jesuit experience in China may prove an enlightening paradigm.

The last, and perhaps most important, item on the agenda is a full study of Chinese Christianity from the point of view of Chinese Christians themselves. The history of Christianity in China has far too often been seen as a variety of mission history, or as part of the European expansion into China, or, in justifiable reaction by modern Chinese historians, as a side-effect of imperialism, an alien growth on the Chinese body-politic. The Chinese Christians of the past must be allowed by their supporters as much as by their critics, to speak for themselves, and this might facilitate a new dialogue between the patriotic Christians of contemporary China and their Christian compatriots, as well as with Christians outside China.

All these must remain, for the moment, mere suggestions, and a programme for possible future research. But they demonstrate the centrality and relevance of the Jesuit interpretation of Confucianism, not only to Chinese studies, but to many other areas of contemporary interest. It would surely have delighted the survivors of the Jesuit mission in China at the end of the eighteenth century to know that their work had not been completely in vain. At the blackest moment, when news of the suppression of the Society of Jesus reached Peking, Amiot wrote an inscription for the Jesuit cemetery, which remains even today a moving document:

> Stand, passerby, and
> Read;
> And think a little of the inconstancy of human affairs.
>
> Here lie the French missionaries of that,
> While it lived, most renowned Society, which everywhere
> Taught and promoted the genuine cult of the true God,
> And imitated closely Jesus, whose name it bore,

In all things, so far as human frailty allows,
And amidst toils and troubles, cultivated virtue,
Aided its neighbour, and became all things to all men,
That it might benefit all, and flourished for over two centuries,

Giving to the Church its martyrs and confessors.
We, Joseph-Marie Amiot,
And other French missionaries of the same Society,
While in Peking in the Kingdom of China, under the auspices and protection Of the Tartar-Chinese monarchy, obtained through science and the arts, Still promoting the affairs of God;

While in the imperial palace itself, amidst so many useless Sanctuaries, our French church still shines forth;
Alas! quietly waiting for our lives to end,
Have placed this monument of brotherly love

In this last resting place.
Go, passerby, congratulate the dead, Condole the living, and pray for all, wonder and Be silent.

In the year of Christ MDCCLXXIV,
On the fourteenth day of the month of October;

In the thirty-ninth year of the reign of Ch'ien-lung, On the tenth day of the ninth month.[2]

Wonder, indeed, but let us not leave them in silence, since they still have much to tell us.

2. My own translation *cf.* the original Latin in Pfister, *Notices*, 992–993; French translation in Pfister, *Notices*, 991–992; and English translation in Cary-Elwes, *China and the Cross*, 169–170.

Bibliography

Reference:

(Bernard-Maître), H. 'Les adaptations chinoises d'ouvrages européens. Bibliographie chronologique depuis la venue des Portugais à Canton jusqu'à la mission française de Pékin (1514–1688)', in *Monumenta Serica*, X (1945): 1–57, 309–88.

- 'Les adaptations chinoises d'ouvrages européens. Bibliographie chronologique. Deuxième partie: depuis la fondation de la mission française jusqu'à la mort de l'empereur K'ien-long (1689–1799)', in *Monumenta Serica*, 19 (1960): 349–83.

Berton, C. *Dictionnaire des cardinaux*, Paris, 1857 (rp. Westmead, Gregg Interational, 1969).

Braga, J. M. 'Jesuitas na Asia', in *Boletim Eclesiastico da Diocese de Macau*, 1955)-LVIII (1960) *passim* (and manuscript continuation kindly made available by Mr Braga).

Brandt, J. van den 'La bibliothèque du Pé-t'ang: notes historiques', in *Monumenta Serica*, IV (1939–1940): 616–21.

Cordier, H. *Bibliotheca Sinica*, Paris, 1904–1924 (rp. Taipei, Ch'eng-Wen, 1966)

Dehergnee, J. 'Les chrétientés de Chine de la période Ming (1581–1650)', in *Monumenta Serica*, XVI (1957): 1–136.

- 'La mission de Pékin vers 1700: étude de géographie missionnaire', in *Archivum Historicum Societatis Jesu*, XXII (1953): 314–38.

- '"Les missions du nord de la. China vers 1700: étude de géographie missionnaire', in *Archivum Historicum Societatis Jesu*, XXIV (1955): 251–294.

- 'La Chine centrale vers 1700. I. L'évêché de Nankin. Etude de géographie missionnaire', in *Archivum Historicum Societatis Jesu*, XXVIII (1959) 289–330.

- 'La Chine centrale vers. 1700. II. Les vicariats apostoliques de la côte. Etude de géographie missionnaire', in *Archivum Historicum Societatis Jesu*, XYX (1961): 307–366.

- 'La Chine centrale vers 1700. III. Les vicariats apostoliques; de l'intéieur. Etude de géographie missionnaire', *Archivum Historicum Societatis Jesu*, XXXVI (1967): 37–71, 221–246.

- 'La Chine du Sud-est. Guangxi et Guangdong. Etude de géographie missionnaire', in *Archivum Historicum Societatis Jesu*, XLV (1976): 1–55.

Répertoire des jesuttes de Chine de 1542 à 1800, Rome (Bibliotheca Instituti Historici Societatis Jesu, XXXVII), 1973.

Goodrich, L.C. Fang Chaoying editors, *Dictionary of Ming Biography, 1368–1644*, 2 volumes New York (Columbia University Press) 1976.

Hummel, A.W. *Eminent Chinese of the Ch'ing Period (1644-1912)*, Washington, 1943 (rp. Taipei, Ch'eng-wan, 1967).

Metzler, J. editor *De archivis et bibliothecis missionibus atque scientiae missionum inservientibus*, Rome (*Euntes Docete*, XXI) 1968.

Paris: Bibliothèque Nationale, Department des manuscripts. *Catalogue des livres chinois, coréens, japonais etc.* par Maurice Courant, 8 fasc. Paris (Leroux) 1900–1912.

Pelliot, P. 'Inventaire sommaire des manuscripts et imprimés chinois de la Bibliothèque Vaticane', 1922, ms. (B. Vat. Sala Cons. mss. 512)

Pfister, L. *Notices biographiques et bibliographiques sur les jésuites de l'ancienne mission de Chine, 1552–1773*, 2 volumes, Shanghai, 19321934 (rp. Nendeln/Liechenstein, Kraus, 1971).

Quetif, J. & Echard, J. *Scriptores Ordinis Praedicatorum*, Paris, 1719–1923 (rp. New York, Burt Franklin, 1959–1961).

Rule, P. 'Jesuit Sources', in *Essays on the Sources for Chinese History*, edited by D. Leslie, C. Mackerras and Wang Gungwu, (Canberra: Australian National University Press), 1973, 176–187.

Schütte, J. F. *Introductio ad Historiam Societatis Jesu in Japonia, 1549–1650*, (Rome: Institutum Historicum S.J.), 1968.

Streit, R. & Dindinger, J. editors *Bibliotheca Missionum*, volumes 1, 4, 5, 7, (Rome: Herder, 1916–1931).

Van der Sprenkel, 0. 'A Selective Annotated Bibliography of Writings on Chinese History, Thought and Institutions in Western Languages' (unpublished).

Verhaeren, H. *Catalogue de la bibliothèque du Pe-t'ang*, Peking, 1949 (rp. Paris, Les Belles Lettres, 1969).

Primary sources

Manuscript collections

ARSJ (Archivum Romanum Societatis Jesu), Borgo Santo Spirito 5, Roma.

Epp. Nn. 46.

Fondo Gesuitico (FG) 721, 722, 723, 724, 730, 731. Gal. 72.

Hist. Soc. 79. Instit. 170.

Jap. Sin. (JS) 1, 4, 5, 6, 8, 9, 10, 11, 12, 13, 14, 15, 16, 17, 18, 19, 22, 23, 38, 69, 98, 99, 100, 101, 102, 103, 104, 105, 106, 107, 109, 110, 111, 112, 113, 114, 115, 116, 116a, 117, 118, 119, 120, 121, 122, 123, 124, 125, 126, 127, 128, 131, 132, 133, 134, 142, 143 7 144 7 145, 146, 148, 149, 150, 150a, 1557 158, 161, 163, 164, 165, 166, 167, 168, 169, 171, 174, 175, 176, 177, 178, 179, 180, 181, 182, 183, 184, 185, 186, 186a, 189a, 190, 193, 194, 195, 198, 199; 1. 1–227 1. 26–447 1. 46–87 1. 57–8, 1. 116–24, 1. 126–7, 1. 131–67, 1. 170–201, 1. 205–6, 1. 223–4; 11. 15, 11. 22, 11. 54, 11. 64, 11. 66–77, 11. 87–9, 11. 91, 11. 113–68 11 172; 111 1–19 111 21 4 1 IV. 26. Regesta S.J. I-Va.

ASJP (Archives of the old Jesuit 'Province de Paris') now at Le Centre Culturel 'Les Fontaines', Chantilly. Brotier 93–94, 1037, 109–111, 119–121, 123–129, 133, 142–145, 147–148. Chine, Rites 1. Vivier 1.

ASV (Archivo Segreto Vaticano), Vatican City.

Albani 242

BL (British Library, formerly British Museum), London.

Add. Mss. 16913, 16933, 20583, 26815–16818

Dept. of Oriental Printed Books and MSS. 15215 b.8 and c. 10; 15314 e.4.

BN (Bibliothèque Nationale), Paris.

Chinois (Chin.) 7160–2.

Français (Fr.) 12209, 15195, 17239, 17240, 25670.

Français nouv, acq. (Fr. n.a.) 4754, 4755, 22167, 22435.

Latin nouv. acq. (Lat. n. a.) 155, 156.

B. Vat. (Biblioteca Apostolica Vaticana), Vatican City.

Borg. Cin. (Borgia Cinese) 91, 108–109, 154, 316, 317, 321–323, 357–358, 361, 371, 374, 376–377, 380, 437, 439, 462, 468–469, 485, 513, 535.

Borg. Lat. (Borgia Latino) 93, 508–523, 538, 542–544, 553–554, 565–567, 576, 586, 589. Estremo Oriente 30.

Vaticano Latino (Vat. Lat.) 12851–12854, 12862–12867, 12870.

PRO (Public Records Office), London.

For. Corr. XVI/Ith. cent., China.

Documentary collections

Boxer, C.R. editor *South China in the Sixteenth Century*, (London: Hakluyt Society, 1953).

Cartas que os padres e irmaos da Companhia de Jesus escreverão dos Reynos de Japão & China aos da mesma Companhia da India & Europa des do anno de 1549 ate o de 1580, 2 volumes (Evora: Manoel de Lyra, 1598).

Coedès, G. editor *Textes d'auteurs grecs et latins relatifs à l'Extrême Orient*, (Paris: Leroux, 1910).

Cordier, H. editor 'Documents inédits pour servir à l'histoire ecclésiastique de l'Extrême-Orient', *Revue de l'Extrême- Orient*, I - III (1882–1887) *passim*.

Couvreur, S. editor *Choix de documents*, 3rd edition (Ho-kien-fou: Imprimerie Catholique, 1901).

Dawson, C. editor *The Mongol Mission* (New York: Sheed & Ward, 1955).

Duperray, E. editor *Ambassadeurs de Dieu à la Chine* (Tournai: Casterman, 1956).

Etiemble, R. editor *Les jésuites en Chine: la querelle des rites* (Paris: Julliard, 1966).

Fu, Lo-shu editor *A Documentary Chronicle of Sino-Western Relations (1644–1820)*, 2 volumes (Tucson: Association for Asian Studies, 1966).

Guerreiro, F. *Relação Anual das Coisas que fizeram os Padres da Companhia de Jesus nas suas missões do Japão, China, Cataio . . . nos anos de 1600 a 1609 . . .* (Evora/Lisbon, 1603–1611) (rp. Coimbra/Lisbon: Scriptores Rerum Lusitanorum, serie A, 1930–1942, 3 volumes).

Legge, J. *The Chinese Classics*, 5 volumes, 2nd edition, Oxford, 1893 (rp. Taipei, Ch'eng-wen, 1966).

Lettres édifiantes et curieuses écrites des missions étrangères, 34 volumes (Paris: Le Clerc, 1703–1776); nouv. edn, Toulouse (Sens & Gaude) 1810–1811.

Li, D.J. *China in Transition* (New York: Van Nostrand, 1969).

Magnum Bullarium Romanum, Rome, 1733–1762 (rp. Graz, Akademische Druck. u. Verlagsanstalt, 1964).

Mémoires concernant l'histoire, les sciences, les arts, les mouers, les usages, etc, des chinois, par les missionnaires de Pékin, 16 volumes (Paris: Nyen; Treuttel & Würtz, 1776–1791, 1814).

Monumenta Xaveriana ex autographis vel ex antiquioribus exemplis collecta, Madrid, 2 volumes, 1899–1900, 1912.

Pinot, V. editor *Documents inédits relatifs à la connaissance de la Chine en France du 1685 à 1740* (Paris: Geuthner, 1932).

Propylaeurn ad acta sanctorum Maii (Antwerp: Michael Kobbarus, 1685).

Purchas, S. *Haklytus Posthumus, or Purchas his Pilgrimes*, volume III of original edition, volume XII of Glascow, 1906 edition, pages 239–311, 'Generall Collection and Historical Representation of the Jesuites Entrance into Japan and China'.

Ramusio, G.B. *Delle Navigationi et Viaggi*, 3rd edition (Venice: Giunti, 1563–1574).

Rosso, A.S. *Apostolic Legations to China of the Eighteenth Century* (South Pasadena: P.D. & Ione Perkins, 1948).

Schütte, J.F. editor *Monumenta Historica Japoniae*, 1, 'Textus Catalogorum Japoniae', Rome (Monumenta Historica S.J., 111), 1975.

Teng, S.Y. & Fairbank, J.K. editors *China's Response to the West* (New York: Atheneum, 1963).

Vincentiis, G. de editor *Documenti e titoli sul . . . Matteo Ripa* (Naples: Salvati, Melfi & Joeli, 1904).

Wicki, J. editor *Documenta Indica*, volumes VII, XI, XII, XIII, XIV (Monumenta Historica S.J. 89, 103, 105, 113, 118) Rome (Institutum Historicum S.J.) 1962–1979.

Wyngaert, A. van den *et al.* editors, *Sinica Franciscana*, Quaracchi . . . Firenze/ Roma, 1929–1975, 8 volumes.

Visschers, P. *Onuitgegeven Brieven van Eenige Paters der Societeit van Jesus, Missionarissen in China, van de XVII de en XVIII de Eeuw met Aanteekeningen* (Arnhem: Josue Witz, 1857).

Individual authors

(All items are listed as far as possible in chronological order. For the sake of completeness Chinese works of Jesuit authors are listed here; for the Chinese characters of the titles see the section on Chinese works under the Chinese name of the author.)

Acosta, J. de 'Paracer sobre la guerra de la China' (Mexico, 15 March 1587) and 'Respuesta a los fondamentos que justifican la guerra contra la China' (23 March 1587) in F. Mateos editor, *Obras del P. Jose de Acosta* (Madrid: Biblioteca de Autores Espafioles LXXIII, 1954), 331–345.

-'De promulgatione evangelii apud barbaros, sive de procuranda Indorum salute', (Salamanca, 1589); Spanish translation in *Obras*, 387–608.

- 'Historia natural y moral de la Indias' (Seville, 1590), in *Obras*, 1–247; English translation, *The Natural and Moral History of the Indies*, 2 volumes (London: Hakluyt Society, 1880).

Aduarte, D. *Historia de la Provincia dal Santo Rosario de la Orden de Predicadores en Philippinas, Japon y China* (Manila, 1640), translated in E.H. Blair and J.A. Robertson, eds. *The Philippine Islands, 1493–1803*, volumes 30–32.

Aleni, Giulio (Ai Ju-lio) *Hsi hsüeh fan* ('A General View of Western Learning') Hangchow, 1623; rp. in Li Chih-tsao, ed. *T'ien-hsüeh ch'u-han* (Taipei, 1965 edition, 1, 9–59).

- *San-shan lun hsüeh-chi* ('Dialogues of the Three Mountains'), Hangchow, 1625; rp. in *T'ien-chu-chiao tung-ch'uan wen-hsien*, Taipei, 1966, 419–493.

- *T'ien-chu sheng-chiao ssu-tzu ching-wen* ('The Christian Four Character Classic'), Peking, 1642.

- *Hsi-fang ta-wen* ('Questions and Answers regarding the West'), text (from B.Vat: Borg. Cin. 324 (17)) and translation by J.L. Mish in *Monumenta Serica*, XXIII (1964): 1–87.

- *Ta-hsi Li Hsien-sheng Ma-tou chuan* ('Biography of Mr Li Ma-tou of the Great West'), trans. L. Desbuquois, in *Revue d'histoire des missions*, 1 (1924): 52–70.

- *T`ien-chu chiang-sheng yin-i*, 'Questions sur l'Incarnation', Chinese text and French translated by H. Otto in *Collectanea Commissionis Synodalis* (Peking), VII (1939): 230–239, 366–371, 489–497, 566–578.

Amiot, J.M. 'L'antiquité, des chinois prouvée par les monumens', in *Mémoires concernant l'histoire . . . etc. des chinois*, II, Paris, 1777.

- 'Vie de Koung-tsée, appellé vulgairement Confucius' in *Mémoires*, XII, Paris, 1786.

- 'Abrégé de la vie des principaux d'entre les disciples de Koung-tsée', in *Mémoires*, XIII, Paris, 1786.

Anciens Mémoires de la Chine touchant les honneurs que les chinois rendent à Confucius & aux morts, (Paris: Nicolas Pepié, 1700).

Apologia pro decreto S. N. D. Alexandri VII et praxi Jesuitarum circa caerimonias, quibus sinae Confucium & progenitores mortuos colunt, ex patrum Dominicanorum & Franciscanorum scriptis concinnata (Louvain: Aegidius Denique, 1700).

Arriaga, P.J. de *Extirpaci6n de la Idolatria del Peru*, Lima, 1621, translated L.K. Keating, *The Extirpation of Idolatry in Peru*, (Lexington: University of Kentucky Press, 1968).

Avril, P. *Voyage en divers etats d'Europe et dAsie, entrepris pour decouvrir un nouveau chemin à la Chine* (Paris: Barbin, 1692).

Bayle, P. *Historical and Critical Dictionary: Selections*, translated R.H. (Popkins: Indianapolis, Bobbs-Merrill, 1965).

Beurrier, P. *Speculum Christianae religionis in triplici lege, naturali, mosaica et evangelica* (1633), 2 volumes (Paris: Langlois, 1666).

Bouvet, J. (Po Chin) *Voiage de Siam du Pere Bouvet*, edited J.C. Gatty (Leiden: Brill, 1963).

- *Histoire de l'empereur de la Chine presentée au roi* (Paris, 1697), La Haye (Meyndert Uytwerf) 1699 (facs. edn Tientsin, 1940); and amplified Chinese edition, *Ch'ing K'ang Ch'ien liang ti yü t'ien-chu-chiao ch'uan-chiao shih*, Taichung, 1966.

- *T'ien-hsüeh pen-i* ('The Original Teaching of the Doctrine of Heaven'), 1703 (ms. in B. Vat: Borg. Cin. 317 (15); and BN: Chin. 7160).

- *Ku-chin ching-t'ien chien* ('Examination of the Ancient and Modern Cult of Heaven'), author's preface of 1707 (ms. in B. Vat.: Borg. Cin. 316 (14); BN: Chin. 7161, 7162).

- 'De cultu coelesti Sinarum veterum. et modernorum' (Latin translation of preceding, by Hervieu and de Prémare), 1706, ms. in BN: Lat. n. a. 155.

- *I-yo* ('Key to the *I-ching*'), ms. in B.Vat: Borg. Cin. 317 (16); and under the title *Ching-t'ien chien yin: fa-ming t'ien-hsüeh pen-i* ('Introduction to the *Ching-t'ien chien*: clarification of the *T'ien-hsüeh pen-i*') ms. in B. Vat: Borg. Cin. 357 (9) *ff* 35–74.

- *Shih ken-pen chen-tsai ming-chien* ('Knowledge of the original true Lord clearly demonstrated'), ms. in ARSJJS IV.5, C.

- *T'ien-chu san-i lun* ('Discourse on the Lord of Heaven, Three and One') ms. in ARSJJS IV.5, C.

- *Chou-i yuan-chih-t'an mu-lu* ('An Index to the *Chou-i yuan-chih-t'an*') ms. in B. Vat: Borg. Cin. 361 (3).

- *I-yo* ('Key to the *I-ching*'), 1712, ms. in B. Vat: Borg. Cin. 317 (2); same title but different contents to above.

- *I-ching tsung-lun* ('A General Discussion of the *I-ching*'), ms. in B. Vat.: Borg. Cin. 317 (3).

- *I-k'ao* ('Investigations into the *I-ching*') ms. in B. Vat: Borg. Cin. 317 (4).

- *I yin yuan-kao* ('A Draft Introduction to the *I-ching*'), ms. in B. Vat: Borg. Cin. 317 (6).

- *Fu ku-ch'uan i-chi lun* ('Dissertation on the Vestiges of Ancient Traditions'), ms. in B. Vat: Borg. Cin. 317 (7).

- *I-hsüeh wai-p'ien* ('A Study of the *I-ching*: Second Part'), ms. in B. Vat.: Borg. Cin. 317 (8).

- *I-hsüeh tsung-shuo* ('General Discussion of the Teaching of the *Iching*'), ms. in B. Vat: Borg. Cin. 317 (8).

- *Ta-i yuan-i nei-p'ien* ('The original meaning of the great *I-ching*'), ms. in B. Vat: Borg. Cin. 317 (9).

- *I-hsüeh wai-p'ien* ('A Study of the *I-ching*: Second Part'), ms. in B. Vat: Borg. Cin. 317 (10), different to above.

- *Shih hsien-t'ien wei-p'ien, shih-chung chih lei, yu t'ien-tsun ti-pi t'u erh sheng* ('Explanation of the Former Heaven, unchanging from beginning to end, according to the *t'ien-tsun ti-pi t'u*), ms. in B. Vat: Borg. Cin. 317 (11), 1713.

- *Tsung-lun pu-lieh lei lo-shu teng fang-t'u fa* ('An Introduction to Methods of Arranging the *Lo Shu* Magic Square diagrams'), ms. in B. Vat.: Borg. Cin. 317 (12).

- "Tractatus de antiquatibus Sinarum ad religionern spectantibus, Praeludium', ms. in ARSJ: JS 174, 147–148.

- 'Idea generalis doctrinae libri Ye Kim sive expositio brevis totius sytematis, sapientiae jeroglyphicae in antiquissimis Sinarurn libris contentae facta Rdo. Pri. Joanni Paulo Gozani Visitatori hanc exigenti', 1712, ms. in ARSJ: JS 174, 290–291, and BN: Fr. 17239, 35–38.

- 'Examen examinis, seu responsum ad scripturn censoris anonymi, sub hoc titulo, examen propositionurn ad R.P. Superiorem Pp. Gallorum', 1715, ms. in ARSJ: JS 177, 240–60, and JS IV.5, B.

- 'Tabula figuratorum et mysticorum numerorum, quibus signantur praecipui characteres temporum chronopaae systematis Ye Kim', ms. in ARSJ: JS IV.25 (1).

- 'Sapientia Hieroglyphica seu theologia symbolica. priscorum Sinarum, cuius expositione sacrum legis naturalis systema, et propheticum veritatis evangelicae mysterium, sub parabolarum et enigmaticurn cortice pluribus annorurn millibus sepulturn, incipit in lucem prodiri. Proemium. (1720?) ms. in ARSJ: JS IV.5, H.

- 'Specimen sapientiae hieroglyphicae seu theologiae symbolicae priscorum Sinarum, proponendum omnibus viris apostolicis, & caeteris nationum orientalium conversationem ardentibus desiderantibus. Discursus Praeliminarius: De arcana priscorum Sinarum doctrina in genere et de via a nobis inita ad secretiora eius mysteria retegenda' (1721?) ms. in ARSJ: JS IV.5, A.

- 'Specimen sapientiae hieroglyphicae priscorum patriarchorum, reconditae in vetustis Sinarum monumentis. Pars posterior: De sacris mundi fastis, seu mystico temporurn propheticorurn systemate, eruto ex dictis monumentis.' (1721?) ms. in ARSJ: JS IV.5, H (another variant in ARSJ: is IV.25 (3)).

- 'Synopsis genuinae systematis chronologicae priscorum sapientum Sinarum', in quo, cum perfecta praecisione & cohaerentia, elucet tota chronici Sacri temporum Series; et cuius mirus ac multiplex computus, aperit viam omnino planam, ad perfecte conciliandas inter se celebriores christianorum chronologorum, opiniones, quantumvis inter se dissentientes.' ms. in ARSJ: JS IV. 25, 5 (2).

- 'Expositio analytica plurimarum figurarum magicarum unde prodeunt omnes numeri mystici, quibus nititur totum systema temporum libri mutationum *ye kim*, cum caeteris canonicis Sinarum libris, totaque ipsorum Sapientia jeroglyphica connexum, nec a genuino sacri chronici temporum Systemate ullatenus diversum', ms. in ARSJ: JS IV.25, 5(l).

- 'Quaedam propositiones de religione Sinarum seu Sinensium a primis temporibus. Cognitio veri Dei eis nota fuit etc.' (1725?) ms. in ARSJ: JS 180, 174–175.

- 'Expositio unius odae propheticae libri canonici xi-kim, in qua clare, distincte et veluti historice sub unico typo praenuntiata Christi Salvatoris Incamato, nativitas, instantia, vita privata et publica, praedicatio, passio, mors, ejusque sacrificium tum cruentem pro remissione peccatorum et perpetua omnium populorum faelicitate oblatum.' ms. in ARSJ: JS IV. 5, F.

- 'Nova expositio periodi consummationis saeculi seu systernatis temporum propheticorum olim SS. Patriarchis et Prophetis distincte revelati, subinde permultis saeculis alta oblivione sepulti, ac demum recens faeliciter detecti in Jeroglyphicis Sinarum monumentis', ms. in ASJP: Brotier 143, 1–56.

- 'Brevis synopsis sytematis temporum propheticorum faeliciter detecti in vetustis Sinarum monumentis', ms. in ASJP: Brotier 143.

- 'Vera temporum propheticorum ratio et mensura ab annis 15. et ultra faeliciter detecta, in Jeroglyphicis Sinarum monumentis. Pars Prior complectens seriem tum saeculorum, tum generationum ab ipso mundi primordio, usque ad Messiam Redemptorem nostrum complectum', ms. in ASJP: Brotier 144, 1–9.

- 'Mystici temporum propheticorum numeri, in vetustissimis & Jeroglyphicis Sinarum monumentis, pluribus abhinc annis faeliciter detecti; iidem nuper cum simili faelicitate et evidentia observati, in antiquioribus ponderum et mensuram tabulis, ex primaeva, ut videtur, SS Patriarchorum traditione, per munus Aegyptiorum, ad Graecos et Romanos traductis', ms. in ASJP: Brotier, 144, 10–17r.

- 'Confirmatio systematis temporum propheticorum petita ex magica constructione et mysticis figurae Uei ki pan tu, seu abaci majorum latrunculorum, a diluvii tempore, usque ad praesentem aetatem, in hieroglyphica Sinarum traditione servatae', ms. in ASJP: Brotier 144, 18–28.

- 'Confirmatio majorum periodorum & notabiliorum epocharum prophetici temporum systematis, detecti in Sinarum monumentis, petita ex pluribus ac diversis figuris magicis, ab omni aevo toto orbe dispersis', ms. in ASJP: Brotier, 144, 29–46, and figures (47–52).

- 'Specimen elementorum arithmeticae formalis et symbolicae, in vetustiori Sinarum traditione faeliciter detectae; ex cujus principiis generantur plurimae ac diversae numerorum propheticorum characteres, et celebriores, ne dicam omnes epochae sacrae', 1724. ms. in ASJP: Brotier 145, 53–124.

- 'Supplementum explicationis speculi astronomici Sinensis', ms. in ASJP: Brotier 145, 125v–140.

- 'Pro expositione figurae sephiroticae kabalae Hebraeorum, & generatim demonstranda mira conformitate, primaevae Sinarum sapientiae hieroglyphicae, cum antiquiore et sincera Hebraeorum kabala, ab ipso mundi primordio, per sanctos patriarchos et prophetas successive propagata', ms. in ASJP: Brotier 145, 141–161.

- 'Traditiones propheticae Sinarum', file of papers in BN: n.a. Lat. 1173.

Boym, M. *Briefve Relation de la Chine et de la notable conversion des persones royales et de l'estat de la religion chrestienne en la Chine* (Paris: Sebastien Cramoisy, 1654). Reprinted in N.M. Thevenot, editor, *Relations de divers voyages curieux*, Paris (Langlois) 1664, Pt. 2.

Buglio, L. (Li Lei-ssu) *Pu-te-i pien* ('Refutation of the Pu-te-I'), 1665, in *T'ien-chu-chiao tung-ch'uan wen-hsien*, Taipei, 1965, 225–332.

Brevis relatio eorum quae spectant ad declarationem Sinarum Imperatoris Kam Hi, circa coeli, Cumfucii et avorum cultum datam anno 1700. Accedunt primatumdoctissimorumque virorurn et antiquissimae traditionis testimonia. Opera Patrum Soc. Jesu Pekini pro evangelii propagatione laborantium, Peking, 1701.

Buzomi, F. 'Trattato delle nome Thienchu scritto italice Thienchiu idest Signor del cielo fatto dal P. Franc.º Buzomi', (1622?), ms. in ARSJ:JS150a.

Caduceus Sinicus, modernorum decretorum explanatio theologica, apostolicae sedis judicio subjecta, Cologne (Edmond) 1713.

Castorano, C.O. 'Parva elucubratio super quosdam libros sinenses ab Ill.mo et R.mo D. Archiepiscopo Myrensi de Nicolais relicto', Rome, 1739, ms. in B. Vat: Borg. Lat. 538; and BL: Add. ms. 26815.

- 'Vita Confusii Philosophi', Rome, 1739, ms. in B. Vat: Borg. Lat. 538, 422–507.

Caussin, N. *De symbolica Aegyptiorum sapientia*, (Paris: R. de Beauvais, 1618).

Cibot, P.M. 'Essai sur l'antiquité des chinois' in *Mémoires concernant l'histoire . . . etc. des chinois*, 1, Paris, 1776, 1–272. (With Kao Lei-ssu).

- Lettre de Pékin sur le génie de la langue chinoise et la nature de leur écriture symbolique comparée avec celle des anciens Egyptiens, Brussels (De Boubers) 1773. Reprinted in *Mémoires*, 1.

Cicé, L.de *Lettre aux Rr. Pp. Jesuites sur les idolatries et sur les superstitions de la Chine*, s. l., n.d. (Letter dated Paris, 15 August 1700).

Clement XI, Pope *Ex illa Die*, 19 August 1715, translation of Chinese version by J.J. Heeren in *Asia Major*, VII (1932) 567–70.

Constitutiones Societatis Jesu (Monumenta Historica Societatis Jesu, vol.65) Rome, 1938.

Costa, 1. da, & Intorcetta, P. *Sapientia Sinica, exponente P. Ignacio a Costa Lusitano Soc. Jesu a P. Prospero Intorcetta Siculo eiusd. Soc. orbi proposita*, Kiem cham in urbe Sinarum Provinciae Kiam Si, 1662.

Couplet, P. 'Relatio de statu et qualitate missionis sinicae post reditum Patrum e Cantoniensi exilio sub annum 1671', in *Propylaeum ad Acta Sanctorum Maii . . . Paralipomena* (part of the Bollandists' *Acta Sanctorum* series), Antwerp, 1685.

- *Tabula chronologica monarchiae sinicae juxta cyclos annorum LX ab anno ante Christum 2952 ad annum post Christum 1683*, Paris, 1687 (usually appended to the following).

- *Confucius Sinarum Philosophus*, (Paris: Horthemels, 1687).

D'Entrecolles, F.-X. 'Animadversions sur l'ode de heou tu et sur les mystères incomprehensibles qu'on dit qu'elle contient', ms. in ARSJ:JS IV.5, G.

[Dez, J.] *Ad virum nobilem de cultu Confucii philosophi, et progenitorum apud Sinas*, Dillingen (Bencard) 1700.

'Diarium Mandarinorum', 1720–1721, ms. in ARSJ: JS 193, 347–359.

Diaz, Manoel (the Younger) *Ching-chiao liu-hsing chung-kuo pei-sung cheng-ch'iian* ('Commentary on the Inscription celebrating the introduction of Nestorianism into China'), 1638, in *T'ien-chu-chiao tung-ch'uan wen-hsien hsü-pien*, 11, 653–754.

- *T'ien-wen lüeh* ('Treatise on Astronomy'), Peking, 1615, in *T`ien-hsüeh ch'u-han*, rp. Taipei, 1965, V, 2639–2718.

Dortous de Mairan, J.J. *Lettres au R.P. Parrenin, Jésuite, missionnaire à Pékin* (Paris: Imprimerie Royale, 1770).

Dunyn-Szpot, T.I. 'Collectanea historiae Sinensis ab anno 1641 ad annum 1700', 1710, ms. in ARSJ: JS 104, 105.

- 'Historia Sinarum Imperii', ms. in ARSJ: JS 102, 103. 'Collectanea pro Historia Sinica', ms. in ARSJ: JS 109–111.

Escalante, B.de *Discurso de la navigacion que los Portugueses hazen a los reinos y provincias del oriente, y de la noticia que se tiene de las grandezas del reino de la China*, Seville, 1577 (facsimile edition by C. Sanz, *Primera historia de China*, Madrid, Siarez, 1958). English translation by John Frampton, *A Discourse of the Navigation which the Portugales doe make*. . . . London, 1579 (facsimile edn, Amsterdam/New York, Theatrum Orbis Terrarum/Da Capo, 1973).

Fenicio, J. *Livro da Seita dos Indios Orientais*, edited by J. Charpentier, Uppsala (Arbeten utgivra med understöd av Vilhelm Ekmans Universitetsfond, 40)1933.

Filippucci, F.S. *De Sinensium Ritibus Politicis Acta* (Paris: Pepié, 1700).

Fontaney, J. de *Relation de ce qui s'est passé à la Chine en 1697, 1698, & 1699, à l'occasion d'un établissement que M. l'abbé de Lyonne a fait à Nien-Tcheou, Ville de la Province de Tche-Kiang (Liege: Daniel Mournal, 1700).*

[Foucher, S.] *Lettre sur la morale de Confucius, philosophe de la Chine*, Paris (Daniel Horthemels) 1688.

Foucquet, J.F. (Fu Sheng-tse).

Notebooks:

'Dissertationes de variis philosophicis sententiis Sinarum', B.Vat: Borg.Cin. 321.

'Discussiones de nomine Dei', B. Vat: Borg. Cin. 322.

'Dissertationes de historia rerum trium dynastiarum Fâng, Yü et Hia', B. Vat: Borg. Cin. 323.

'Nouvelles ecrites de Pekim' (letter-book covering 10 Dec. 1705 to 29 Dec. 1706), B. Vat: Borg. Lat. 543.

Journal 18 May 1721 to 15 August 1738, B. Vat: Borg. Lat. 565.

Other notebooks: ARSJ: JS 11. 155; B. Vat: Borg. Cin. 357, 361, 374, 376, 377, 380, 462, 523; Borg. Lat. 508, 509, 510, 511, 512, 513, 514, 516, 517, 518, 519, 520, 521, 522, 567, 576, 586, 589; BL: add. ms. 20583, 26816–26818.

Letters:

Letter to Duc de la Force, Nanchang, 26 Nov. 1702, in *Lettres Edifiantes*, V, 1705.

'Relation exacte de ce qui s'est passé à Pékin par rapport A l'astronomie européen depuis le mois de Juin 1711 jusqu'au 10 novembre 1716' (includes extracts of many letters), B. Vat: Borg. Lat. 56, 144–184, and ARSJ: JS 11.154 (transcript as an appendix to J. Witek, 'An Eighteenth

Century Frenchman at the court of the K'ang-hsi emperor . . .', 453–678).
'Correspondance du Père Foucquet avec le cardinal Gualterio', edited by H. Cordier in *Revue de l'Extrême Orient*, 1 (1882): 16–51.

Treatises:

'Factum congeries quibus probatur voce et littera (*t'ien*), item vocibus et litteris (*shang-ti*) bene significari Deum apud Sinas', B. Vat: Borg. Lat. 515, 9–19.

'Mémoire sur le système des trois dynasties ou familles imperiales que l'on pretend avoir gouverné la Chine depuis Yao jusqu'aux Tcin', 1709 or 1710, BN: Fr.n.a. 4755.

Memorial to the K'ang-hsi emperor, 4th month 1713, B. Vat: Borg. Cin. 439, A.

I-kao ('Notes on the I-ching'), 1711?, B. Vat: Borg. Cin. 317 (7).

Chou-i i-li ('Outline of the Chou-i'), B. Vat: Borg. Cin. 361 (2).

Chou-i li-shu ('Computation of the arrangement of the *Chou-i*'), B. Vat: Borg. Cin. 361 (4).

I-ching chu-chia chieh-shuo ('Explanations of the I-ching drawn from all schools'), B. Vat: Borg. Cin. 361 (5).

I-hsüeh wai-p'ien yuan-kao ('A Draft of the *I-hsüeh wai-p'ien*'), B. Vat: Borg. Cin. 361 (6).

I-hsüeh wai-p'ien ('Additional commentaries on the *I-ching*'), B. Vat: Borg. Cin. 361 (now at end of 361, originally at 361 (5); a copy of chapters 9 to 12 of 361 (6)).

T'ai-chi lüeh shuo ('A Brief Discourse on t'ai-chi'), B. Vat: Borg. Cin. 317 (5).

Chu Hsi wan-nien t'ung-hui chih chü ('The Evidence for Chu Hsi's Final Repentance'), B. Vat: Borg. Cin. 357 (11) and 380 (1).

- *Ching-i ching-yao* ('The Essence of the Classics'), B. Vat: Borg. Cin. 380 (2)-(4).

- *Chen-tsai ming-chien* ('Examination of the True Lord'), B. Vat: Borg. Cin. 316(13).

- 'Cheng Ju, le veritable philosophe. Sur d'ouvrages pour les chinois' (draft), B. Vat: Borg. Lat. 566, 113–39.

- *Chü ku-ching-ch'uan k'ao t'ien-hsiang pu chun-ch'i* ('According to an examination of the ancient classics, the appearance of the heavens is not invariable'), B. Vat: Borg. Cin. 380 (6) & (7). 380 (6) has an interleaved Latin translation entitled 'Dialogus Sinarum inter et Europaeum'.

- 'Problème théologique', c. 1718, B. Vat: Borg. Cin. 371; ARSJ: JS IV.3; B. Vat: Borg. Lat. 565, 523–44v (incomplete).

- 'Dissertatio de vera origine doctrinae et monumentorum Sinensium contenta quatuor propositionibus', 1720. The text is found in fragments in B. Vat: Borg. Cin. 358, 437; Borg. Lat. 544, 566; and ARSJ: JS IVA, as follows:

Preface: Borg. Lat. 566, 327r–36v, 612–13, 682–689v; JS IV. 4, fasc. 1, pp. 1–20, and fasc. 3.

4 Propositiones: Borg. Lat. 566, 388r–40r; JS IVA, fasc. 1, pp. 23–25, and fasc. 3; and summary in Borg. Cin. 437, 34 and Borg. Lat. 566, 361.

Idea . . . totius operis: Borg. Lat. 566, 341r–43v; JS IV. 4, fasc. 3.

4a Propositio (Cap. 1um?): Borg. Lat. 566, 359–602; JS IV. 4, fasc. 2; and Borg. Cin. 437 (copy without Chinese characters).

4a Propositio, 2a Pars, Cap. 2um: Borg. Cin. 358(l) and (2); JS IV. 4, fasc. 2; and Borg. Lat. 544 (copy without Chinese characters, incomplete, and with sub-title, 'De Arcana Doctrina Confucii et Monumentorum Sinsensium').

- 'Propylaeum templi veteris sapientiae seu aditus ad antiqua monumenta Sinensium', Borg. Cin. 358 (3) and (4) pages 17–272: Borg. Lat. 566, 614–65 pages 21–129; 690–780 pages 17–197; 785–906 pages 17–260.

- 'Notizie breve spettante alla Persona di P. Jis Franc.ci Foucquet Gesuita Francese-di se medmo. allo Sacra Cong. Ne', 1724?, ARSJ: JS 178, 426–429.

-'Judicium de quibusdam funeribus honoribus Sinensium', B. Vat: Borg. Lat. 542, 1–6; BN: Fr. 12209, 69–80v.

- 'Giudizio sopra alcuni onori funebri dei cinesi', B. Vat: Borg. Lat. 542, 91–101 (Italian version of above).

- 'De funeribus Sinensium disquisitio prolusoria', 1724, B. Vat: Borg. Lat. 542, 11–74. The work of the same title in BN: Fr. 12209, appears to correspond to the 'Disquisitionis Prolusoriae de funeribus Sinensium synopsis' in B. Vat: Borg. Lat. 542, 7–8.

- 'Clausula disputationum de caerimoniis sinensibus', 1724, BN: Fr. 12209. 81–98. Version entitled 'Quaestio Sinico Theologica' in BL: add. ms. 26816 1–104.

- 'Responsum Episcopi Eleutheropolitani ad quaestionem hanc gravissimam: "an potissimum id temporis dum ferret apud Sinas generalis contra christianam fidem persecutio, ad sacerdotium promovere nativos Sinenses expediat"', 1728, B. Vat: Borg. Lat. 544; BL: add. ms. 26818.

- 'Réponse aux questions regardant la bibliothèque historique et critique des geographes et des voyageurs', 1727, BN: Fr. 25670, 1–83.

- 'Discours de l'empereur regnant aujourd'hui dans la Chine fait à ses grands le 28 mai 1727 après une audience qu'il avoit donné à l'ambassadeur de Portugal', BN: Fr. 12209, 99–103.

- 'Rituale domesticum Sinensium ad litteram ex sinico latine versum cum notis', B. Vat: Vat. Lat. 12851.

- 'Essai d'introduction preliminaire à l'intelligence des Kings, c'est à dire des monumens antiques conservés par les chinois' or 'Sentimens de I'Eveque d'Eleutheropolis sur la doctrine des chinois anciens et modernes'. Both titles are given in the fullest version, B. Vat: Vat. Lat. 12870, thus establishing Foucquet (Bishop of Eleutheropolis) as its author, rather than Visdelou to whom it is often attributed. There are also extracts in BN: Fr. 12209, 1–36; and B. Vat: Borg. Cin. 468, 57–71; and BVE: FG 1257.31.

Printed Works:

'Catalogus omnium missionariorum qui Sinarum Imperium ad haec usque tempora ad praedicandum Jesu Xti Evangelium ingressi sunt', published by H. Cordier after the ms. in BL: add. ms. 26818, 159–176, in *Revue de l'Extrême Orient*, II (1883): 58–71.

'Catalogue des livres apportés de la Chine par le Père Foucquet, jésuite, en l'année 1722', in H. A. Omont, *Missions archéologiques françaises en orient aux XVIIe et XVIIIe siècles*, Paris (Imprimerie Nationale) 1902, Appendix XXVIII (after BN: Lat. 17175, 93–117).

'Récit fidèle de ce qui regarde le chinois nommé Jean Hou que le P. Foucquet Jésuite amena de la Chine en France dans l'année 1722 sur le Prince de Conti, vaisseau appartenant à la compagnie des Indes', edited by H. Cordier, in *Revue de l'Extrême Orient*, 1 (1882): 381–422, 523–571.

Tabula chronologica historiae Sinicae connexa cum cyclo qui vulgo kia-tsé dicitur, Rome, 1729.

'An explanation of the new chronological table of the CHINESE HISTORY, translated into Latin from the original Chinese, by Father Johannes Franciscus Foucquet . . .' in *Philosophical Transactions*, XXXVI (1729–1730): 397–424.

Frois, L. *Die Geschichte Japans (1549–1578)*, edited by G. Schurhammer & E. A. Varetzsch, (Leipzig: Verlag Asia Major, 1926).

- 'Tratado em que se contem muito susinta e abreviadmente algumas contradições e diferenças de custumes entre a gente de Europa e este Provincia de Japão', edited by J.F. Schütte as *Kulturgegensätze Europa–Japan (1585)*, Tokyo (Monumenta Nipponica Monographs, 15) 1955.

Furtado, F. 'Informaçao p.a Sua Santidade de estado desta Missam da China', 5 Nov. 1639, ARSJ: JS 161. H, 221–233 and (with Latin version) in JS 123, 69–78.

- *Informatio antiquissima de praxi missionariorum Sinensium Societatis Jesu, circa ritus Sinenses, data in China, jam ab annis 1636 et 1640 . . ..* Paris (Pepié) 1700.

Gaubil, A. *Correspondance de Pékin*, 1722–1759, edited by R. Simon, Geneva (Droz) 1970.

- 'Manuscrit inédit du Père A. Gaubil S.J.', edited by H. Cordier, in *T'oung Pao*, n.s. XVI (1915): 515–561.

- *Histoire de Gentchiscan et de toute la dynastie des Mongous ses successeurs, conquirants de la Chine* (Paris: Briasson et Piget, 1739).

- 'The Journal of Anthony Gaubil, Jesuit, from Kanton to Peking, in 1722', in J Green, editor, *A New General Collection of Voyages and Travels*, III (London: Thomas Astley, 1746), 581–584.

-'Voyage du Père Antoine Gaubil, missionnaire jésuite, depuis Canton jusqu'à Peking', in *Histoire générale des voyages*, nouv. edn, ed. A. Prévost d'Exiles, VII, La Flaye (Pierre de Hardt) 1749, chapter XIV, 322–327.

- 'L'abrégé de l'histoire chinoise de la grande dynastie Tang', in *Mémoires concernant l'histoire . . . etc. des chinois*, XV & XV1, Paris, 1791 & 1814.

- *Traité de la chronologie chinoise, divisé en trois parties; composé par le Père Gaubil, missionnaire de la Chine, et publié pour servir de suite aux mémoires concernant les chinois, par M. Silvestre de Sacy*, Paris, 1814.

- 'Histoire de l'astronomie chinoise', in *Lettres edifiantes*, nouv. edn, Toulouse, 1811, XXV1, 55–236.

- 'Le Chou-king, livre sacré de la Chine, traduit en français par le P. Gaubil; revu soigneusement sur le texte chinois, et augmenté d'un grand nombre de notes par M. G. Pauthier', in G. Pauthier, editor, *Les livres sacrés de l'orient* (Paris: Panthéon Littéraire, 1843), 1–136.

Giampriamo, N S.J. 'Testimonianza giurata dal P. Giampriamo sopra la versione fatta da Mon.e Patriarca dell'Atti Imperiali', ARSJ: JS 198, 293v296v.

Gollet, J.-A. 'De vera Sinarum origine quorum Imperii Conditor extitit Jectan 2dus Heberis filius', ASJP: Brotier 142, 6–17.

- 'De origine Sinarum illorumque chronologia abhinc ipso diluvio ad nostra haec tempora dissertatio', 1725, ASJP: Brotier 142, 18–26.

- 'Cyclus Sinensis sexeganarius', ASJP: Brotier 142, 27–9.

- 'Quaestio problematica. An sciri probabiliter possit, quodnam sit illud nomen Domini, cuius fit in Gen. mentio c. 4. 26?', ASJP: Brotier 142, 30–35.

- 'Remarques sur l'observation astronomique des 4 points cardin.x faite sous Yao 1.r Emp.r de Chine', ASJP: Brotier 142, 54–55.

- 'Notes et prevues sur les nombres penetrées du plan proposé', ASJP: Brotier 142, 56–57.

- 'Abregé de remarques sur le livre classique Tchun Tsieou', ASJP: Brotier 142, 58–61.

- 'Catalogue des 36 eclipses au livre Tchun Tsieou', ASJP: Brotier 142, 62–64.

- Remarques sur un extrait du calcul que les R.d, PP. Gaubil et Schlaviceck ont fait de quelques eclipses du Tchun Tsieou raportées cy dessus', ASJP: Brotier 142, 65.

- 'Reponse du p.e Gollet aux notes critiques du Père Gaubil', ASJP: Brotier 142, 66–70r.

- 'De chronologia Sinarum abhinc ipso diluvio ad nostra haec tempora', ASJP: Brotier 142, 71–83.

-'Dissertation sur la chronologie chinoise', ASJP: Brotier 142, 84–90.

- 'Dissertation critique sur l'eclipse de soleil, dont parle le Chu King sous Tchong Cong', ASJP: Brotier 142, 91–95.

- 'Recueil de citations de divers autheurs sur les pretendus *san hoang ou ti*', ASJP: Brotier 142, 96–97r.

- 'Synopsis ou abregé, d'un traité plus ample de la tradition chinoise sur un point des temps du Messie; sçavoir à quelle année du monde à quelle saison et à quel mois de l'an, et à quel jour, et à quelle heure le Messie a du mourir', ASJP: Brotier 142, 99–100.

- 'Réponse:10. Super notis in dissertatione de origine Sinarum illorumque chronologia a deluvio ad nostra usque tempora. 20. Sur la chronologie des chinois depuis le déluge', ASJP: Brotier 142, 110.

- 'Productio universi: res omnes suam docunt originem a T'ien', ARSJ: JS IV.5, D.

Gonzalez, Thyrsus (Jesuit General) 'Informatio ad PP. Missionarios Sinicos pro maximis controversiis et litigiis quae nunc Romae, et in tota Europa maxime turbant et inquietant Societatem', 1700, ARSJ: JS 167, 428–429.

Gonzalez de Mendoza, J. *Historia de las cosas mas notables, ritos y costumbres del gran reino de la China* (Rome, 1585), edited by F. Garcia, Madrid (España Misionera 11) 1944. English translation *The History of the Great and Mighty Kingdom of China* (1588), edited by Sir George Staunton (London: Hakluyt Society, 1853–1854), volumes 14, 15.

Gouvea, A. de 'Reposta do P. Antonio de Gouvea V. Provincial da China dada a nome de V. Provincia a estes dous papeis do R.P. Praesidente [Navarrete]', 3 Oct. 1669; Latin trans. in C.R. Boxer, *A propósito dum livrinho xilográfico dos Jesuitas de Pequim (seculo XVIII)*, Macao, 1947, 5r–8r.

- 'Progressus et incrementurn fidei et christianae religionis apud Sinas: seu prosecutio annalium Sinensium Societatis Jesu Rev. Patris Nicolai Trigautii, a morte R.P. Matthaei Riccii ad nostra usque tempora concinnata maxime ex commentariis R.P. Antonii de Gouvea eiusdem Societatis Jesu', ARSJ:JS 107.

- 'Asia Extrema: entra nella a fé promulgasse a ley de Deos pollos Padres da Compagnia de Jesu', ARSJ: JS 129; and Ajuda, Lisbon, Jesuitas na Asia 49–V-1 & 2.

Guzman, L.de *Historia de las Misiones de la Compaflia de Jesus en la India Oriental, en la China y Japon desde 1540 hasta 1600* (Alcala, 1601) Bilboa (El Mesajero del Corazon de Jesus) 1891.

Halde, J.B. du *Description géographique, historique, chronologique, politique, et physique de l'empire de la Chine* (Paris, 1735), La Haye (Henri Scheurler) 1736. English translation *The General History of China containing a geographical, historical, chronological, political and physical description of the Empire of China . . .*, 4 volumes, (London: J. Watts, 1741).

Huet, P.D. *Demonstratio evangelica* (Paris: S. Michallet, 1679).

'In librum Ye Kim brevis annotatio', ARSJ: JS 1.223.

Innocentia Victrix sive sententia comitiorum Imperii Sinici pro innocentia Christianae Religionis late juridice per annum 1669 & jussu R.P. Antonii de Gouvea Soc.is Jesu, ibidem V. Provincialis Sinico-Latine exposita, Canton, 1671.

Intorcetta, P. 'Confirmationes postulatorum, et quaesita missa a V.e Prov.a Sinensi per Procuratorem Patrem Prosperum Intorcetta, anno 1668', ARSJ: JS 124, 59r–69v.

-*Sinarum Scientia Politico-moralis*, Canton, 1667.

- *Compendiosa Narratione dello stato delle missione cinese cominciando dell'anno 1581 fino al 1669*, Rome (Francesco Tizzoni) 1672; and extracts in M.Guglielminetti ed., (Classici Italiani, t.7), Torino (Unione Tipografico-Editrice Torinese) 1967, 557–563.

Jurieu, P. *La religion des jésuites, ou reflexions sur les inscriptions du Père Menestrier, et sur les escrits du Père le Tellier pour les nouveaux Chrestiens de la Chine et des Indes, contre la dixneuvième observation de l'esprit de M.e Arnaud* (La Haye: Abraham Trouel, 1689).

Ko, Aloys, (Kao Lei-ssu) 'Essai sur l'antiquité des chinois', in *Mémoires concernant l'histoire... etc, des chinois*, 1, Paris, 1776, 1–272. (With Cibot).

Kircher, A. *Oedipus Aegytiacus, hoc est universalis hieroglyphicae veterum doctrinae temporum iniuria abolitae instauratio*, 3 volumes, Rome (V. Mascardi) 1652–1654.

- *Arithmologia sive de abditis numerorum mysteriis qua origo, antiquitas, et fabrica numerorum exponitur; abditae eorundem proprietates demonstrantur; denique post Cabalistarum, Arabum, Gnosticorum, aliorumque magicas impietates detectas, vera et licita numerorum mystica significatio ostenditur* (Rome: Varese, 1665).

- *China monumentis qua sacris qua profanis . . . illustrata*, Amsterdam, 1667; rp. Frankfurt/Main (Minerva) 1966.

- *La Chine illustrée de plusieurs monuments tant sacrés que profanes* (Amsterdam: Jean Jansson A Waesberge, 1670).

- *Arca Noe, in tres libros digesta* (Amsterdam: Jansson) 1675).

- *Sphinx Mystagoga sive diatribe hieroglyphica qua mumiae, ex Memphiticis Pyramidum adytis erutae . . . plena fide & exacta exhibetur interpretatio* (Amsterdam: Jansson, 1676).

- *Turris Babel, sive archontologia qua primo priscorum post diluvium hominum vita, mores rerumque gestarum magnitudo, secundo turris fabrica civitatumque exstructio... explicatur* (Amsterdam: Jansson, 1679).

La Charme, A. de (Chang Te-chao) *Hsing-li chen-chüan*, Peking, 1753.

- *Confucii Chi-king sive liber carminum ex latina P. de la Charme interpretatione*, ed. J. Mohl, Stuttgart (Cottae) 1830.

[Lallement, J.P.] *Réponse aux nouveaux écrits de Messieurs des missions etrangères contre les jésuites*, Paris, 1702.

Le Comte, L. *Nouveaux Mémoires sur l'état présent de la Chine* (Paris, 1696) (Amsterdam: Desbordes & Schelte, 1698), 2 volumes.

Le Gobien, C. *Istoria dell'editto dell'Imperatore della Cina in favore della religione Cristiana, coll'aggiunta d'alcune notizie intorno gli honori che i cinesi rendono a Confusio & a defonti* (Torino: Zappata, 1699).

Leibniz, G.W. *The Preface to Leibniz' Novissima Sinica*, edited & translated by D.F. Lach (Honolulu: University of Hawaii Press, 1957).

-'Explication de l'arithmétique binaire qui se sert des seuls caractères, 0 et 1, avec des remarques sur son utilité et sur ce qu'elle donne le sens des anciens figures chinoises de Fohy', in *Mémoires de mathématique & de physique de l'Académie Royale des sciences*, année 1703, Amsterdam, 1707, 105–111.

- *Epistolae ad diversos*, ed. C. Korholt, 4 volumes (Leipzig: Breitkopf, 1734–1742).

- *Opera Omnia*, edited by L. Dutens, IV. Pt. l- 'continet Philosophiam. in genere, et opuscula sinenses attigentia', Geneva (de Tournes) 1768.

Longobardo, N. (Lung Hua-min) 'Traité sur quelques points de la religion des chinois', Paris (Josse) 1701 (published together with Antonio de Santa Maria's Traité under general title of *Anciens Traitez de divers auteurs sur les ceremonies de la Chine*); reprinted with annotations by Leibniz in Leibniz's *Opera Omnia*, edited by L. Dutens, IV, 89–144.

- *Ling-hun tao-t'i shuo* ('On the substance of the soul')

Lu Hsi-yen 'An account of Macao by the Chinese Jesuit Lu Hsi-yen about 1680–90', translated by E.H. Pritchard and Kwan-wai So, in *Symposium on Chinese Studies commemorating the Golden Jubilee of the University of Hong Kong, 1911–1961*, III (Hong Kong: University of Hong Kong, 1968), 110–122.

Ly, A. *Journal d'André Ly, prêtre chinois, missionnarie et notaire apostolique, 1746–1763*, edited by A Launay (Paris: Picard, 1906).

Macartney, G. (Earl) *An Embassy to China*, edited by J.L. Cranmer-Byng (London: Longman, 1962).

Maffei, G.P. *Historiarum Indicarum libri XVI. selectarum, item, ex India epistolarum, eodem interprete, libri IV* . . . (Firenze, 1588), Cologne (Birckmann) 1593.

Magaillans, Gabriel (Gabriel de Magalhdes) *A New History of China* (London: Thomas Newborough, 1688).

Mailla, J.-M.-A. de (Feng Ping-cheng) *Sheng shih ch'u jao* ('Blessings for the poor') 1733, rp. in *T'ien-chu-chiao tung-ch'uan wen-hsien hsü-pien*, II, 1413–1700.

- *Histoire générale de la Chine, ou annales de cet empire; traduites du Tong-Kien-Kang-Mou*, . . . publiées par M. I'Abbé Grosier, (Paris: Pierres, 1777–1785), 13 volumes.

Marini, G. F. de 'Elogio di Confucio' (from his *Istorie e relazione del Tunkino e del Giappone*, 1663) in M.Guglielminetti, editor (Torino: Viaggiatori del Seicento, 1967), 428–481.

Mendez Pinto, F. *Peregrinaçam de Fernam Mendez Pinto em que da conta de muytas e muyto estranhas cousas que vio e ouvio no reyno da China, no da Tartaria, no de Sornau, que vulgarmente se chama Sido, no da Calaminham, no de Pegu, no de Martardo, e em outros muytos reynos e senhorios das partes orientais* . . . (Lisbon, 1614), 2 volumes, Rio de Janeiro (Sociedade de Intercambio Cultural Luso-Brasileiro) 1952.

Monita ad missionarios S. Congregationis de Propaganda fide, 4th edition, Rome (Propaganda Fide) 1886.

Montesquieu, C. *Oeuvres complètes*, edited by A. Masson, (Paris: Nagel, 1950–1955), 3 volumes.

La Morale de Confucius, philosophe de la Chine (Amsterdam: Savouret, 1688); Londres? (Valande) 1783.

The Morals of Confucius, a Chinese Philosopher (London: Randal Taylor, 1691).

Navarrete, D.F. *An Account of the Empire of China, Historical, Political, Moral, and Religious . . .*, s.l., n.d.

- *The Travels and Controversies of Friar Domingo Navarrete, 1618–1686*, ed. J.S. Cummins, (Cambridge: Hakluyt Society 1962), 2 s., CXVIII, CXIX.

- *Controversias antiguas de la mission de la Gran China* (Madrid, 1679), copy in ARSJ: FG 728/1.

Noël, F. *Philosophia Sinica, tribus tractatibus, primo cognitionem primi entis, secundo ceremonias erga defunctos, tertio ethicam, juxta Sinarum mentem complectans* (Prague: Typis Universitatis, 1711).

- *Historica notitia rituum ac cerimoniarum Sinicarum in colendis parentibus ac benefactoribus defunctis, ex ipsis Sinensium auctorum libris desumpta* (Prague: Typis Universitatis, 1711).

- *Sinensis Imperii libri classici sex, nimirum Adultorum Schola, Immutabile Medium, Liber Sententiarum, Memcius, Filialis Observantia, Parvulorum Schola, e Sinico idiomate in latinum traducti a P. Francisco Noël Societatis Jesu missionario* (Prague: Typis Universitatis, 1711).

Norbert, Pére v. Platel, C.P.

Nunes Barreto, M. Letters from Malacca, 23 Dec. 1554; Macao, 23 Nov. 1555; Macao, 23 Nov. 1556 in *Cartas que os padres e irmaos da Companhia de Jesus escrevão dos reynos de Japao & China aos da mesma Companhia da India & Europa*, Evora, 1598. Letters from Cochin, 20 Jan. 1567 and 25 Jan. 1568 in J. Wicki ed., *Documenta Indica*, VII, Rome (Monumenta Historica Societatis Jesu, 89) 1962, 207–12, 486–94.

Pacheco, F. (Ch'eng Chi-li) *Sheng-chiao kuei-ch'eng*, 'Ordonnances de la sainte église', text and translation by H.Verhaeren, in *Monumenta Serica*, IV (1939–1940): 451–77.

Pantoia, D. de (P'ang Ti-wo) *Ch'i k'e* ('The Seven Victories'), 1624 in Li Chih-tsao, *T'ien-hsüeh ch'u-han*, Taipei, 1965 edition, II, 689–1126.

- *T'ien-chu shih-i hsü-p'ien* ('Continuation of the *T'ien-chu shih-i*') in *T'ien-chu-chiao tung-ch'uan wen-hsien hsü-pien*, Taipei, 1966, 1, 98–228.

- *Relatione dell'entrata d'alcuni Padri della Compagnia di Giesu nella China . . .*, Rome (Zannetti) 1607.

Pascal, B. *Lettres provinciales*, edited by Pléiade, Paris, 1954. *Pensées* in *Oeuvres*, edited by L. Brunschwig (Paris: Hachette, 1904), volumes XII–XIV; and English translation by M. Turnell (London: Harvill, 1962).

Paz, J.de 'Tractatus de ritibus Sinensibus', Manila, 23 October 1679, ARSJ: JS 163, 78–88; published as 'Quaesita a missionariis Tunkinensibus de cultu Confucii cum responsionibus R. Patris de Paz ex Ordine Sancti Dominici', in *Apologia pro decreto S.D.N. Alexandri VII*, Louvain, 1700, 86–94.

Platel, C. P. *Mémoires historiques presenté au souverain pontife Benoit XIV sur les missions des Indes Orientales* (Lucques: Marescandoli, 1744), 3 parts in 2 volumes.

Polo, M. *The Book of Ser Marco Polo*, translated and edited by Sir Henry Yule, 3rd edition, rev. Henri Cordier (London: Murray, 1903).

Possevino, A. *Bibliotheca selecta de ratione studiorum, ad disciplinas, & ad salutem omnium gentium procurandum; recognita novissime ab eodem et aucta*, Venice (apud Altobellum Salicatium) 1603.

Prejugez légitimes en faveur du decret de N.S.Père le Pape Alexandre VII et de la pratique des Jesuites au sujet des honneurs que les Chinois rendent à Confucius et à leurs ancestres, tirez des ecrits des Pères Dominicains, & des Pères Franciscains, missionnaires de la Chine, s.l., 1700.

Prémare, J.H. de (Ma Jo-se) 'Excerpta e variis Premari ad amicum suum Fourmontium epistolis', 1728–1731, in E. Fourmont, *Linguae Sinarum Mandaricae . . .*. (Paris: Guerin, 1742).

- *Ju-chiao shih-i* ('The True Meaning of Confucianism'), in *T'ien-chu-chiao tung-ch'uan wen-hsien hsü-pien*, III, 1333–1410.

- 'Vera idea legis dicta ju kiao [*ju chiao*] philosopho Ouën Kou Hee authore', ARSJ: FG 724/4.

- 'Tractatus de Ju Kiao [*ju chiao*]', Voutchangfou, 26 Sept. 1705, ASV: Albani 242, 6–162.

- *Meng mei-t'u chi* ('Record of a dream of Paradise'), 1707, B. Vat: Borg. Cin. 357 (9)b.

- *Liu-shu shih-i* ('The True Significance of the Six Kinds of Chinese Writing'), 1720, B. Vat: Borg. Cin. 357 (10).

-'Extrait d'une dissertation envoyé de St. Malo à M. le nonce en France en consequence des diligences faites par son ordre pour voir l'original même de la dissertation sur les caractères chinois et les livres anciens, ou Précis d'une lettre au R.P. de Briga interprete de la bande d'Isis par le R.P. de Prémare, jesuite missionnaire en Chine', B. Vat: Borg. Cin. 468 [A], Borg. Lat. 565, 612–13; BN: Fr. 15195, 5–9, Lat. n.a. 156, 22–51.

- 'Réponse à un extrait envoyé, dit on, de St. Malo A Monseigneur le Nonce A Paris', 16 Aug. 1727, BN: Fr. 15195, 10–20, B. Vat: Borg. Cin. 468 [B].

- 'Selecta Quaedam Vestigia', Canton, 21 May 1725, BN: Chin.9248.

- *Vestiges des principaux dogmes chrétiens tires des anciens livres chinois*, translated and edited by A. Bonnetty and P. Perny, Paris (Annales de philosophie chrétienne) 1878.

- *Ching-ch'uan i-chi*, 'Antiquae Traditionis Selecta Vestigia', ARSJ: JS 11.168.

- 'Circa voces seu litteras *t'ien* et *chang ti*', ARSJ: JS IV. 5, E.

- Quindecim quaestiones doctis viris propositae', BN: Fr. 12209, 37–38; B. Vat: Borg..Cin. 468.

- 'Tria opuscula Romam missa anno 1727: Examinantur an missionarii possint et interdum debent citare gentium monumenta in favorem christianae relligionis. Doctrina 12 propositionum Sinis applicatis. Variae quaestiones circa libros King et eorum usum proponuntur et solvuntur', 2 Oct. 1727, ASJP: Brotier 119, 95–123; B. Vat: Borg. Cin. 468.

- Letter to Monsieur . . ., Canton, 10 Oct. 1728, B. Vat: Borg. Cin. 361 (1)d; published by G. Pauthier as 'Lettre inédite du Père Prémare, sur le monothéisme des chinois . . .' in *Annales de philosophie chrétienne*, 5e s., 111 (1861), and as 'Sur le non athéisme des chinois . . .' in *Revue de l'orient*, n.s. V (1857): 10–27.

- *Ching-chieh: Symboli expositio*, ASJP: Brotier 120, 203v-223r. 'De tribus antiquis monumentis quae Sinae vocant san y', Canton, 29 Oct. 1730, BN: Lat. n. a. 156, 54–57.

- 'Notes critiques pour entrer dans l'intelligence de I'Y King', 1731, B.Vat: Borg. Cin. 361 (1)b.

- 'Celeberrimus locus ex motu King potest comparari cum mystica illa schala Jacob . . .', BN: Lat. n. a. 156, 6–7.

- 'Opuscula quaedam pia sinice et latine:1. Litterae sin (*hsin*) profundior sensum; 2. explicatio insignis Sacri Cordis Jesu; 3. ad orationem sequentem introductio; 4. oratio ad sacrum Cor Jesu; 5. oratio ad beatam. Virginem; 6. methodus colendi cordis Jesu.' ASJP: Brotier 119, 81–94.

- *San-i-san* ('The Three-One-Three'), ASJP: Brotier 120, 124–202.

- *Sheng Jo-se ch'uan* ('Life of St Joseph').

- 'Recherches sur les temps antérieurs à ceux dont parle le Chou-king, et sur la mythologie chinoise', in M. Pauthier, *Livres sacrés de l'orient*, 13–45.

- *Notitia linguae sinicae* (Malacca: Anglo-Chinese College, 1831).

Prière pour 1'église de la Chine, avec les raisons qui ont engage à la donner prentement, s.l., n.d.

Quaesita missionariorum Chinae, seu Sinarum, Sacrae Congregationi de Propaganda Fide exhibita, cum responsis ad ea . . ., Rome (Propaganda Fide) 1645.

[Raynaud, T.] *Missi evangelici ad Sinas, Japoniam, et Oras Confines, integri doctrinae labisque puri, nec ex admissa locutionem mente restrictorum honestatem, in foveam acti*, Antwerp (Lyons?) 1659.

Régis, J.-B. *Y-King, Antiquissimus Sinarum Liber*, edited by J. Mohl (Stuttgart: Mohl, 1834–1839), 2 volumes.

Responsa Sacrae Congregationis Universalis Inquisitionis a, SS. D.N. Alexandri VII, approbata, ad quaesita missionariorum Soc. Jesu apud Sinas anno Domini 1656, Rome (Propaganda Fide) 1669.

Ricci, M. (Li Ma-tou) *Opere Storiche*, edited by P. Tacchi Venturi, (Macerata: Giorgetti, 1911–1913), 2 volumes.

- *Fonti Ricciane*, edited by P.M. D'Elia (Rome: Libreria dello Stato, 1942–1949), 3 volumes.

- *Chiao-yu lun* ('On Friendship'), 1595; rp. in Li Chih-tsao, *T'ien-hsüeh ch'u-han*, Taipei, 1965 edition, 1, 291–320.

- '1l trattato sull'amicizia; primo libro scritto in Chinese da Matteo Ricci S.J. (1595)', edited by P.M. D'Elia, in *Studia Missionalia*, VII (1952): 425–515. 'Le "traité de l'amitié" de Matthieu Ricci', edited by Gné Yonglien and J.Dehergne, in *Bulletin de l'université I^'Aurore*, 3 s. VIII (1947): 571–619.

- *Hsi-kuo chi-fa* ('Western Memory Method'), 1595; rp. in *T'ien-chu-chiao tung-ch'uan wen-hsien*, Taipei, 1965, 1–70.

- *Hsi-chin ch'u-i pa-chang* ('Eight Songs for the Western Lute') 1601; rp. in Li chih-tsao, *T'ien-hsüeh ch'u-han*, Taipei, 1965 edition, 1, 283–290.

- *Il Mappomondo cinese del P. Matteo Ricci S.J.* (Terzia edizione, Pechino, 1602), edited by P.M. D'Elia (Vatican City: Biblioteca Apostolica Vaticana, 1938).

- *T'ien-chu shih-i* ('The True Idea of God'), 1603; rp. Taipei, 1967. Modern Chinese translation by Liu Shun-te (Taichung: Kuang-ch'i Press, 1966). French translation by Père Jacques, 'Entretiens d'un lettré chinois et d'un docteur européen sur la vraie idée de Dieu', *Lettres edifiantes*, nouv. edn, Toulouse, 1811, XXV, 143–385. Ricci's own partial Latin translation, 'Catechismus Sinicus' (1604) in Bib. Casanatense, ms. 2136.G.I.l.

- *Erh-shih-wu yen* ('The Twenty-five Sentences'), 1605, in Li Chih-tsao, *T'ien-hsüeh ch'u-han*, Taipei, 1965 edition, 1, 321–349.

- *Chi-jen shih-p'ien* ('Ten Chapters of a Strange Man'), 1608 in Li Chih-tsao, *T'ien-hsüeh ch'u-han*, Taipei, 1965 edition, 1, 93–282. Part translated as 'Sunto Poetico-Ritmico di I Dieci Paradossi di Matteo Ricci S.J', by P.M. D'Elia, *Rivista degli studi orientali*, XXVII (1952): 111–38.

-'"Transmission by Writing", presented to Master Ch'eng Yu-po' (dated 9 Jan. 1606), translated by J.J.L. Duyvendak, *T'oung Pao,* XXXV (1940): 394–397.

- *Histoire de 1'expédition chrestienne au royaume de la Chine . . . tirée des Mémoires du R. P. Matthieu Ricci de la Compagnie de Jesus, par le R. P. Nicolas Trigault Douysien de la mesme Compagnie . . . et nouvellement traduite en Français per le S.D. F. de RicquebourgTrigault* (Lille: Pierre de Hache, 1617).

- *China in the Sixteenth Century: the Journals of Matthew Ricci, 1583–1610*, translated from Trigault's Latin by L.J. Gallagher (New York: Random House, 1953).

- *Pien-hsüeh i-tu* ('Posthumous Controversies'), 1615, in Li Chih-tsao, *T'ien-hsüeh ch'u-han*, Taipei, 1965 editin, 1, 637–88.

Rodriguez, João *Historia da 1greja do Japão*, 2 volumes (Macau: Noticias de Macau, 1954).

-*This Island of Japan*, translated by M. Cooper (Tokyo: Kodansha, 1973).

Rubino, A. 'Riposta as calumnias que os padres de S. Domingo e de S. Francisco impoem aos padres da Companhia de Jesus, que se occupão na conversacão do reino da China', 1641, ARSJ: JS 155.

- *Metodo della dottrina che i padri della Companhia di Giesu insegnano a'neofiti, nelle missione della Cina*, translated by G.P. de Marini (Lyons: Boisset & Remeus, 1665).

Ruggieri, M. (Lo Ming-chien) *Tsu-ch'uan t'ien-chu shih-ch'eng* ('The Ten Commandments of God handed down by our ancestors' 1583.

- *Sheng-chiao shih-lu* ('The True Teaching of the Holy Religion'), 1584; later edition (1634–41) in *T'ien-chu-chiao tungch'uan wen-hsien hsu-pien*, 11, 755–838. French trans. in 'Notes sur la première catéchèse écrite en chinois, 1582–1584', in *Archivum Historicum Societatis Jesu*, 1 (1932).

- 'Relatione del successo della missione della Cina dal mese di Novembre 1577 sin'all año 1591 dal P. Michael Ruggieri al molto Rdo Pe Claudio Aquaviva Generale della Comp.a di Giesu nro pe, ARSJ: JS 101, 1.

- 'Commentarii', ARSJ: JS 101, 11, 296–315.

Sambiasi, F. (Pi Fang-ch'i) *Ling-yen li-shao* ('Determining the Nature of the Soul'), 1624, in Li Chih-tsao, *T'ien-hsüeh ch'u-han*, II, 1127–1268.

Sandoval, A. de *De instauranda Aethioporum Salute* (1627), edited by A. Valtierra, (Bogota: Biblioteca de la Presidencia de Colombia, 1956).

Santa Maria, A. Caballero de (Li An-tang) *Cheng-hsüeh liu-shih*, in *T'ienchu-chiao tung-ch'uan wen-hsien san-pien*, I, 89–266.

- 'Brevis relatio de ingressu Societatis Jesu aliorumque religiosorum in Sinicam missionem', 1662, edited by A. Väth as 'P. F. Antonio Caballero de Santa Maria iiber die mission der Jesuiten und anderer orden in China', in *Archivum Historicum Societatis Jesu*, 1 (1932): 291–302.

- *T'ien Ju Yin* ('On the Heaven of the Confucians'), 1664, rp. in *T`ien chu-chiao tung-ch'uan wen-hsien hsü-pien*, II, 982–1042.

- 'Traité sur quelques points importans de la mission de la Chine', in *Anciens traitez de divers auteurs sur les cérémonies de la Chine* (Paris: Josse, 1701).

Schall von Bell, J.A. *Lettres et Mémoires d'Adam Schall: Relation historique*, edited by P. Bornet (Tientsin: Hautes Etudes, 1942).

A Short Account of the Declaration given by the Chinese Emperour Kam Hi, in the year 1700, London, 1703.

'Sommario di diversi lettere e documenti dall'anno 1706 fino al 1722, per giustificare la sollecita e sincera condotta del P. Gle. della Compa di Gesit nell'ordinare, ed esiggere da suoi religiosi missionarii della Cina la dovuta esecuzione de decreti apostolici e di altri ordini della Santa Sede intorno quelle missioni e per verificare l'operato da med. missionarii per tal esecuzioni', ARSJ: JS 198, 28–344.

Souciet, E. *Observations mathématiques, astronomiques, géographiques, chronologiques, et physiques, tirées des anciens livres chinois, ou faites nouvellement aux Indes et à la Chine, par les Pères de la Compagnie de Jésus*, redigées et publiées par le P. E. Souciet de la même Compagnie (Paris: Rollin, 1729–1732), 3 volumes.

Spence, J. *Observations, Anecdotes and Characters of Books and Men*, edited by J.M. Osborn (Oxford: Clarendon Press, 1966), 2 volumes .

Status quaestionis Romae nunc temporis habitas circa honores a Sinensibus exhibitis Confucio at progenitoribus fato functis, 2nd edition, Brussels, 1701.

Thomas, A. 'Tractatus brevis de consuetudinibus ac ritibus Sinici Imperii quantum fieri potest, nunc permittendis', c. 1688, ARSJ: JS 150, 115–118r.

Trigault, N. (Chin Ni-ko) 'Annuae Sinenses de itinere et navigatione P. Trigautii et sociorum Goanum ab 1618', ARSJ: JS 121, 95–113.

- *Hsi-ju erh-mu tzu* ('The Western Scholar's Aid to Ear and Eye'), 1626, rp. Peking, 1957.

Vagnoni, A. 'Breve informação sobre o nome Xámti, e Tien em lugar di Deos p.e os sup.res', c. 1628, ARSJ:JS 161, If, 225–6.

Valignano, A. *Historia de principio y progresso de la Compañia de Jésus en las Indias Orientales (1542–1564)*, edited by J. Wicki (Rome: Instituturn Historicurn S.J., 1944).

-*Il ceremoniale per i missionarii del Giappone*, edited by J.F. Schütte (Rome: Storia e letteratura, 1946).

- *Somario de las cosas de Japón (1583)*, edited by J.L. Alvarez-Taladriz (Tokyo: Monumenta Nipponica Monographs, 9, 1954).

Verbiest, F. (Nan Huai-jen) *Correspondance de Ferdinand Verbiest de la Compagnie de Jésus (1623–1688)*, editited by H. Josson & L. Willaert (Brussels: Commission Royale d'Histoire, 1938).

- *Pu-te-i pien* ('Reply to the Pu-te-i'), 1665, in *T'ien-chu-chiao tung-ch'uan wen-hsien*, 333–469.

Viani, S. *Historia delle cose operate nella China da Monsignor Gio. Ambrogio Mezzabarba Patriarca d'Alessandria, Legato Apostolico in quell' Imperio*, 2nd edition, Cologne (Enrico Aertssens) 1740. English translation in J. Green, *A New General Collection of Voyages and Travels*, 111, (London: Thomas Astley, 1746), 584–605; French translation in A.F. Prévost d'Exiles, *Histoire générale des voyages*, V111, La Haye, 1749, 327–67.

Viera, C. and Calvo, V. 'Letters from Portuguese Captives in Canton, written in 1534 and 1536', edited by D. Ferguson, in *Indian Antiquary*, XXX (1901): 467–91; XXXI (1902): 10–32, 53–65.

Visdelou, C. 'Chou-Kim liber canonicum seu liber canonicus', B. Vat: Vat. Lat. 12854.

- 'De religione Sinarum philosophorum', B. Vat: Vat. Lat. 12863, 12864, 12865.

- 'Notes de M.r L'Evesque de Claudiopolis sur le livre chinois nommé Y-Kim ou livre canonique des changemens', 1728, BN: Fr. n.a. 22167, 1–12; printed in Livres sacrés *de l'orient*, Paris, 1843, 137–149.

Voltaire, F.M. Arouet de *Oeuvres complètes de Voltaire*, nouv. edn, edited by L. Moland, Paris (Garnier) 1877–85.

Webb, J. *The Antiquity of China or an historical essay endeavouring a probability that the language of the Empire of China is the primitive language spoken through the whole world before the confusion of Babel, wherein the customs and manners of the Chinese are presented, and ancient and modern authors consulted with* (London: Obadiah Blagrave 1678) (revised edition of *An historical essay*, London, 1669).

Xavier, F. *Epistolae S. Francisci Xaverii*, ed. G. Schurhammer and J. Wicki, 2 volumes, Rome (Monumenta Historica S.J., 67, 68) 1944–5.

Secondary sources

Western languages

Actes du colloque international de sinologie: la mission française de Pékin aux XV1le et XVIIIe siecles (Paris: Les Belles Lettres, 1976).

Actes du IIe colloque internationale de sinologie: les rapports entre la Chine et l'Europe au temps des lumières (Paris: Les Belles Lettres, 1980).

Allan, C. W. *Jesuits at the Court of Peking* (Shanghai: Kelly and Walsh, n. d.)

Attwater, R. *Adam Schall: a Jesuit at the Court of China, 1592–1666* (London: Chapman, 1963).

Baird, R.D. *Category Formation and the History of Religions* (The Hague: Mouton, 1971).

Bartoli, D. *Dell'Istoria della Compagnia di Gésù. La Cina: Terza Parte dell'Asia* (Rome, 1663), (Ancona: Aureli, 1843), 4 volumes.

Berling, J.A. *The Syncretic Religion of Lin Chao-en* (New York: Columbia University Press, 1980).

Bernard (-Maître), H. 'Whence the philosophical movement at the close of the Ming (1580–1640)', in *Bulletin of the Catholic University of Peking*, 8 (Dec. 1931): 67–73.

- *Aux portes de la Chine: les missionnaires du seizième siecle, 1514–1580* (Tientsin: Hautes Etudes, 1934).

- *Sagesse chinoise et philosophie chrétienne* (Tientsin: Cathasia, 1935).

- *Les Isles Philippines du Grand Archipel de la Chine: un essai de conquête spirituelle de I'Extrême Orient (1571–1641)* (Tientsin: Hautes Etudes, 1936).

- *Le père Matthieu Ricci et la société chinoise de son temps*, 2 vols, Tientsin (Hautes Etudes) 1937.

- 'L'Encyclopédie astronomique du Père Schall', in *Monumenta Serica*, III (1938): 35–77, 441–527.

- 'La découverte spirituelle de I'Extrême-Asie par I'humanisme Européen. III. La Découverte du Bouddhisme', in *FranceAsie*, X. 100 (1954): 1141–1153.

- 'De la question des termes à la querelle des rites de Chine: le dossier Foucquet de 1711', in *Neue Zeitschrift für Missionswissenschaft*, XIV (1958): 178–195, 267–275.

- 'The Chinese and Malabar Rites: an historicaI perspective', in *Concilium*, VII/3 (1967): 38–45.

Bettray, J. *Die Akkomodationsmethode des P. Matteo Ricci S.J. in China*, Rome (*Analecta Gregoriana* LXXVI) 1955.

Bontinck, F. *La lutte autour de la liturgie chinoise aux XVIIe et XVIIIe siècles* (Louvain: Nawrelaerts, 1962).

Boone, W.J. *Some thoughts on the proper terms to be employed to translate Elohim and Theos, into Chinese: by an American missionary in China* (Shanghai: Mission Press, 1850).

Bortone, F. *P. Matteo Ricci S.J.: il 'Saggio d'Occidente'*, 2nd edition, (Rome: Desclée, 1965).

Boulais, G. *Manuel du code chinois* (Shanghai: Variétés Sinologiques, 55, 1924).

Boxer, C.R. 'Portuguese and Spanish Rivalry in the Far East during the 17th century', in *Journal of the Royal Asiatic Society* (1946): 150–64; (1947): 91–105.

- *A propósito dum livrinho xilogrdfico dos Jesuitas de Pequim (seculo XVIII): ensaio historico* (Macao: Imprensa Nacional, 1947).

- *The Christian Century in Japan, 1549–1650* (Berkeley: University of California Press, 1951).

Braga, J.M. 'The Panegyric of Alexander Valignano S.J. (reproduced from an old Portuguese codex)', *Monumenta Nipponica*, V (1942): 523–535.

- *A Voz do Passado* (Macao: Boletim Eclesidstico, 1964).

Brodrick, J. *St. Francis Xavier (1506–1552)* (London: Burns & Oates, 1952).

Brou, A. *Saint François Xavier* (Paris: Beauchesne, 1912), 2 volumes.

- *Les Jésuites de la legende* (Paris: Retaux, 1907).

- 'Les Jésuites sinologues de Pékin et leurs éditeurs de Paris', in *Revue d'histoire des missions*, XI (1934): 551–566.

Brucker, J. 'La Chine et I'Extrême-Orient d'après les travaux historiques du P. Antoine Gaubil, missionnaire à Peking (1723–1759)', in *Revue des questions historiques* XXXVIII (1885): 485–539.

Busch, H. 'The Tung-lin Academy and its political and philosophical significance', in *Monumenta Serica*, XIV (1949–1955): 1–163.

Caraman, P. *The Lost Paradise: an account of the Jesuits in Paraguay, 1667–1768*, (London: Sidgwick & Jackson, 1975).

Cary-Elwes, C. *China and the Cross* (London: Longmans, 1957).

Chan, A. *The Glory and Fall of the Ming Dynasty* (Norman: University of Oklahoma Press, 1982).

Chang T'ien-tse, *Sino-Portuguese Trade from 1514 to 1644* (Leiden: Brill, 1934).

Chen Chih-mai, *La chiesa cattolica in Cina* (Rome: Edizioni Mediterranee, 1975).

Ch'en Yuan, *Western and Central Asians in China under the Mongols*, translated and edited by L.C. Goodrich (Los Angeles: Monumenta Serica Monographs, XV, 1966).

Ching, J. *To Acquire Wisdom: the 'Way' of Wang Yang-ming* (New York: Columbia Univesity Press, 1976).

- *Confucianism and Christianity: a comparative study* (Tokyo: Kodansha, 1977).

Chow Yih-ching, *La philosophie morale dans le neo-confucianisme* (Paris: P.U.F., 1954).

Collis, M. *The Grand Peregrination* (London: Faber, 1949).

Cooper, M. *The Southern Barbarians* (Tokyo: Kodansha, 1971).

- *Rodrigues, the Interpreter: an early Jesuit in Japan and China* (New York/ Tokyo: Weatherhill, 1974).

Cordier, H. 'Les chinois de Turgot' in *Mél anges d'histoire et de geographie orientales*, (Paris: Maisonneuve, 1920), 31–39.

Correia-Afonso, J. *Jesuit Letters and Indian History* (Bombay: Indian Historical Research Institute, 1955).

Creel, H.G. *Confucius, the Man and the Myth* (New York: Harper & Row, 1949).

- 'Was Confucius Agnostic?', in *T'oung Pao* XXIX (1932): 55–99.

Cronin, V. *The Wise Man from the West* (London: Hart-Davis, 1955).

- *A Pearl to India* (London: Hart-Davis, 1959).

Davy, J. 'La condamnation en Sorbonne des "Nouveaux Mémoires sur la Chine" du P. Le Comte', in *Recherches de science religieuse*, XXXVII (1950): 366–397.

De Bary, W.T. editor, *Self and Society in Ming Thought* (New York: Columbia University Press, 1970).

- *The Unfolding of Neo-Confucianism* (New York: Columbia University Press, 1975).

De Bary, W.T. and Bloom, I. editors, *Principle and Practicality* (New York: Columbia University Press, 1979).

De la Costa, H. *The Jesuits in the Philippines, 1581–1768* (Cambridge, Mass: Harvard University Press, 1961).

Dennerline, J. *The Chiating Loyalists: Confucian Leadership and Social Change in Seventeenth-Century China* (New Haven: Yale University Press, 1981).

Dupront, A. *Pierre Daniel Huet et l'exégèse comparatiste au XVIe siecle* (Paris: Leroux, 1930).

Dunne, G.H. *Generation of Giants* (London: Burns & Oates, 1962).

D'Elia, P.M. 'Quadro storico-sinologico, di primo libro di dottrina cristiana in cinese', in *Archivum Historicurn Societatis Jesu*, 111 (1934): 193–222.

- 'Ermeneutica Ricciana', in *Gregorianum*, XXXIV (1953): 669–679.

- 'Further Notes on Matteo Ricci's De Amicitia', in *Monumenta Serica*, XV (1956): 356–377.

- 'Prima introduzione della filosofia scolastica. in Cina (1584, 1603)' in 'Studies presented to Dr Hu Shih on his 65th birthday', *Chung-yang yen-chiu yiian: li-shih yu-yen yen-chiu-so chi-k'an* (*Bulletin of the Institute of History and Philology, Academia Sinica*, XXVIII (1956): 141–196.

- *Il lontano confino e la tragica morte del P. João Mourão S.J.*, (Lisbon: Agencia-Geral do Ultramar, 1963).

Elison, G. *Deus Destroyed: the Image of Christianity in Early Modem Japan* (Cambridge, Mass: Harvard University Press, 1973).

Etiemble, R. *L'Orient philosophique au XVIIIe siècle*, Ile Partie, Missionnaires et philosophes (Paris: Centre de documentation universitaire, 1958).

- 'Le bouddhisme chinois vu par les jésuites confucéens' in L. Lanciotti editor, *Sviluppi scientifici, prospettive religiose, movimenti rivoluzionari in Cina* (Firenze: Olschki, 1975), 103–114.

Fang Hao 'Notes on Matteo Ricci's "De Amicitia"', in *Monumenta Serica*, XIV (1949–1955), 574–583.

Fingarette, H. *Confucius - the Secular as Sacred* (New York: Harper & Row, 1972).

Fisher, T.S. 'New Light on the accession of the Yung-cheng Emperor', in *Papers on Far Eastern History* (Canberra), 17 (1978): 103–136.

Franke, O. 'Leibniz und China', in *Zeitschrift der Deutschen Morgenlandischen Gesellschaft*, VII (1982): 135–178 (reprinted in *Aus Kultur und Geschichte Chinas* (Peking: Deutschland Institut, 1945), 313–330.

- *Li Tschi und Matteo Ricci* (Berlin: Abhandlungen der Preussische Akademie der Wissenschaften, Jahrgang 1938), Phil. Hist. Klasse Nr. 5 1939.

Franke, W. 'Matteo Ricci in den Augen eines chinesischer Zeitgenossen', in *Studia Sino-Altaica: Festschrift für Erich Haenisch* (Wiesbaden: Franz Steiner, 1961), 72–75.

Fülop-Miller, R. *The Power and Secret of the Jesuits* (London: Peter Owen, 1957).

Fung Yu-lan *A History of Chinese Philosophy* (Princeton: Princeton University Press, 1973).

Gentili, O. *L'Apostolo della Cina: P. Matteo, Ricci S.J. (1522–1610)*, 2nd edition, (Macerata: Ufficio Missionario Diocesano, 1963).

Gilkey, L. *Naming the Whirlwind: the Renewal of God-language* (Indianapolis: Bobbs-Merrill, 1969).

Gernet, J. 'A propos des contacts entre la Chine et l'Europe aux XVIIe et XVIIIe siècles', in *Acta Asiatica*, 23 (1972): 78–92.

- 'La politique de conversion de Matteo Ricci et l'évolution de la vie politique et intellectuelle en Chine aux environs de 1600', in *Archives de sciences sociales de religioms*, 36 (1973): 71–89 (another version in L. Lanciotti editor *Sviluppi scieintifici, prospettive religiose, movimenti rivoluzionari in Cina* (Firenze: Olschki, 1975), 115–144.

- 'Philosophie chinoise et christianisme de la fin du XVIe au milieu du XVIIe siècle', in *Actes du colloque internationale de sinologie*, Paris, 1976, 13–25.

- 'Christian and Chinese views of the world in the sixteenth century', in *Diogenes* 105 (Spring 1979): 93–115; and *Chinese Science,* 4 (1980): 1–17.

Graham, R.B.C. *A Vanished Arcadia* (London: Heinemann, 1901).

Guy, B. *The French image of China before and after Voltaire*, Studies on Voltaire and the Eighteenth Century, XXI, 1963.

Harlez, C. de *La* réligion et les cérémonies impériales de la Chine moderne d'après le cérémonial et les décrets officiels (Bruxelles: Académie Royale de Belgique, 1893–1894.

Harris, G.L. 'The mission of Matteo Ricci, S.J.: a case study of an effort at guided cultural change in the sixteenth century', in *Monumenta Serica* XXV (1966): 1–168.

Havret, H. *La stèle chrétienne de Si-ngan-fou* (Shanghai: Variétés Sinologiques), 7, 12 and 20, 1895, 1897, 1902.

- *T'ien Tchou 'Seigneur du Ciel': à propos d'une stèle Bouddhique de Tch'eng Tou* (Shanghai: Variétés Sinologiques) 19 [1901] 2nd edition, 1909.

Hay, M. *Failure in the Far East* (London: Spearman, 1956).

- *The Prejudices of Pascal* (London: Spearman, 1962).

Huang, Pei *Autocracy at Work: a study of the Yung-cheng period, 1723–1735*, (Bloomington: Indiana University Press, 1974).

Huang, R. *1587 a year of no significance* (New Haven: Yale University Press, 1981).

Hucker, C.O. 'The Tung-lin movement of the late Ming period', in J.K. Fairbank, editor, *Chinese Thought and Institutions* (Chicago: Chicago University Press, 1957).

Hudson, G.F. *Europe and China* (London: Arnold) 1931).

Hung, Ming-shui 'Yuan Hung-tao and the late Ming literary and intellectual movement', unpublished PhD thesis, University of Wisconsin, 1974.

Kammerer, A. *La découverte de la Chine par les Portugais* (Leiden: Brill, 1944).

Kamstra, J. M. *Encounter or syncretism* (Leiden: Brill, 1967).

Kennedy, J.H. *Jesuit and savage in New France* (New Haven: Yale University Press, 1950).

Kessler, L.D. *K'ang-hsi and the consolidation of Ch'ing rule, 1661–1684* (Chicago: Chicago University Press, 1976).

Kowalski, N. Arts. 'Mezzabarba' and 'Tournon' in *Enciclopedia Cattolica* (Vatican City, 1952).

Krahl, J. *China missions in crisis: Bishop Laimbeckhoven and his times, 1738–1787*, (Rome: Gregorian University, 1964).

Lach, D.F. 'Leibniz and China', in *Journal of the History of Ideas*, VI (1945): 436–455.

- *Asia in the making of Europe* (Chicago: Chicago P.) Volume 1, Books 1 and 2, 1965; volume II, Book 1, 1970, Books 2 and 3, 1977.

Lamalle, E. 'La propagande du P. Nicolas Trigault en faveur des missions de Chine (1610)', in *Archivum Historicum Societatis Jesu*, IX (1940): 49120.

Lancashire, D. 'Buddhist Reaction to Christianity in late Ming China', in *Journal of the Oriental Society of Australia*, VI (1968–1969): 82–103.

- 'Anti-Christian Polemics in Seventeenth Century China', *Church History* XXXVIII (1969): 218–241.

Latourette, K.S. *A History of Christian Missions in China* (London, 1929) Taipei (Ch'eng-wen) 1966.

Laures, J. *Nobunaga und das Christentum* (Tokyo: Monumenta Nipponica Monographs 10, 1950).

Lawlor, R.V. *The Basic Strategy of Matthew Ricci, S.J., in the Introduction of Christianity in China* (Rome: Gregorian University, 1951).

Le Gall, S. *Le philosophe Tchou Hi, sa doctrine, son influence* (Shanghai: Variétés Sinologiques 6, 1923).

Legge, J. *Notions of the Chinese concerning God and spirits* (Hongkong: Hongkong Register, 1852).

Levenson, J.R. *Liang Ch'i-ch'ao and the mind of modern China* (Berkeley: University of California Press, 1967).

- *Confucian China and its modern fate*, volume 1 (London: Routledge and Kegan Paul, 1958).

Lundbaek, K. 'The First Translation from a Confucian Classic in Europe', in *China Mission Studies (1550–1800) Bulletin*, 1 (1979): 1–11.

'Chief Grand Secretary Chang Chü-cheng and the Early Jesuits', in *China Mission Studies (1550–1800) Bulletin*, 111 (1981): 2–11.

Lundberg, M. *Jesuitische Anthropologie und Erziehungslehre in der Friihzeit des Ordens (ca. 1540-ca. 1650)* (Uppsala: Stockholm University, 1966).

Margiotti, F. *Il cattolicismo nello Shansi dalle origini al 1738* (Rome: Edizioni 'Sinica Franciscana', 1958).

Martin. A.L. 'The Jesuit Mystique', in *The Sixteenth Century Journal*, IV (1973): 31–40.

Martin, L. *The Intellectual Conquest of Peru: the Jesuit College of San Pablo, 1568–1767* (New York: Fordham University Press, 1968).

Medhurst, W.H. *A Dissertation on the theology of the Chinese* (Shanghai: Mission Press, 1847).

Mensaert. G. 'L'Etablissement de la hierarchie catholique en Chine de 1684 à 1721', in *Archivum Franciscanum Historicum*, XLVI (1953): 369–416.

Merkel, F.R. *G.W. Leibniz und die China-Mission* (Leipzig: Heinrichs, 1920).

- 'The missionary attitude of the philosopher G.W. von Leibniz', in *International Review of Missions*, IX (1920): 399–416.

- *Leibniz und China* (Berlin: Walter de Gruyter, 1952).

Metzler, J. editor *Sacrae Congregationis de Propaganda Fide Memoria Rerum, 1622–1972* (Rome: Herder, 1971–1976), 3 volumes.

Moule, A. C. 'Gregory Lopez, Bishop', in *New China Review,* I (1919): 480–487.

- 'The First Arrival of the Jesuits at the Capital of China', in *New China Review*, IV (1922): 450–456.

- *Christians in China before the Year 1550* (London: SPCK, 1930).

- 'The Primitive Failure of Christianity in China', in *International Review of Missions*, XX (1931): 456–459.

Mungello, D.E. *Leibniz and Confucianism: the search for accord* (Honolulu: University of Hawaii Press, 1977).

- 'Sinological Torque: the influence of cultural preoccupations on seventeenth century missionary interpretations of Confucianism', in *Philosophy East and West,* 28 (1978): 123–141.

- 'The Jesuits' Use of Chang Chü-cheng's Commentary in their translation of the Confucian Four Books (1687)', in *China Mission Studies (1550–1800) Bulletin*, III (1981): 12–22.

Needham, J. *Science and Civilisation in China*, (Cambridge: Cambridge University Press, 1954, 1959; 1976), volumes II, III, V. 3.

Omont, H.A. *Missions archéologiques françaises en Orient aux XVIIe et XVIIIe siècIes* (Paris: Imprimerie Nationale, 1902).

Outerbridge, L.M. *The Lost Churches of China* (Philadelphia: Westminster, 1952).

Oxnam, R. B. *Ruling from Horseback: Manchu politics in the Oboi Regency, 1661-1669* (Chicago: Chicago University Press, 1974).

Parsons, J.B. 'Overtones of religion and superstition in the rebellion of Chang Hsien-chung', in *Sinologica*, IV (1956): 170–177.

Pastor, L. von *History of the Popes* (London: Kegan Paul, 1933–1950), volumess XXIX–XXXV.

Pinot, V. *La Chine et la formation de 1'esprit philosophique en France (1640–1740)* (Paris: Geuthner, 1933).

Preclin, E. and Jarry, E. *Les luttes politiques et doctrinales aux XVIIe et XVIIIe siècles*, Histoire de l'église, t. 19 (Paris: Bloud et Gay, 1956).

Rachewiltz, 1. de *Papal Envoys to the Great Khans* (London: Faber & Faber, 1971).

- *Prester John and Europe's Discovery of East Asia*, The 33rd George Ernest Morrison Lecture in Ethnology (Canberra: ANU Press, 1972).

Raguin, Y. 'Le sens de Dieu dans la morale de Confucius', *Documentation M. E. P.*, May 1966.

- 'Father Ricci's presentation of some fundamental theories of Buddhism', *Chinese Culture*, X (1969): 37–43.

Rajamanickam, S. *Roberto de Nobili on Indian Customs* (Palayamkottai: De Nobili Research Institute, 1972).

Rémusat, J.P. Abel *Mél anges Asiatiques* (Paris: Dandey-Dupré, 1825–1826), 2 volumes.

Rétif, A. 'Les Jésuites français en Chine d'après les Lettres Edifiantes et Curieuses', in *Neue Zeitschrift für Missionswissenschaft*, IV (1948): 175–187.

- 'Brève histoire des Lettres Edifiantes et Curieuses', in *Neue Zeitschrift für Missionswissenschaft*, VI (1951): 37–50.

- 'les missionnaires et le confucianisme', in *Bulletin des Missions*, XXVI (1952): 20–35.

Retours, R. des 'Confucianisme et Christianisme', in *Sinologica*, 1 (1947): 232–245.

Ri, J.S. *Confucius et Jésus-Christ; la première théologie chrétienne en Corée d'après l'oeuvre de Yi Piek, lettré confucéen, 1954–1786* (Paris: Beauchesne, 1979).

Richard, R. *La 'conquête spirituelle' du Mexique: essai sur l'apostolat et les méthodes missionnaires des ordres mendiants en Nouvelle-Espagne de 1523-1524 à 1572,* Travaux et Mémoires 20 (Paris: Institut d'Ethnologie, 1953).

Rocaries, A. *Roberto de Nobili S.J. ou le 'Sannyasi' chrétien* (Toulouse: Prière et Vie, 1967).

Rochemonteix, C. de *Joseph Amiot et les derniers survivants de la mission française à Pékin, 1750–1795* (Paris: Picard, 1915).

Rodrigues, F. *A Formaçao intellectuel do Jesuita* (Porto: Magalhães & Moniez, 1917).

- *A companhia de Jesus en Portugal e nas missões*, 2nd edition (Porto: Edições do Apostolado da Imprensa, 1935).

Rogers, F.M. *The Quest for Eastern Christians: travel and rumor in the Age of Discovery* (Minneapolis: University of Minnesota Press, 1962).

Roy, O. *Leibniz et la Chine* (Paris: Vrin, 1972).

Rosso, A.S. *Apostolic Legations to China of the Eighteenth Century* (S. Pasadena: P.D. & 1. Perkins, 1948).

Rouleau, F.A. 'Maillard de Tournon: Papal Legate at the court of Peking. The first imperial audience (31 December 1705)', in *Archivum Historicum Societatis Jesu*, XXXI (1962): 264–323.

- Art. 'Chinese Rites Controversy' in *The Catholic Encyclopedia* (New York: McGraw-Hill, 1967), 111, 611–617.

Rowbotham, A.H. *Missionary and Mandarin: the Jesuits at the Court of China* (Berkeley (University of California Press, 1942).

- 'The Jesuit Figurists and eighteenth century religious thought', in *Journal of the History of Ideas,* XVII (1956): 471–485.

Rule, P.A. 'Jesuit and Confucian? Chinese religion in the Journals of Matteo Ricci S.J., 1583–1610', in *Journal of Religious History*, V (1968): 105–124.

-'Jesuit Sources' in D. Leslie, C. Mackerras and Wang Gungwu editors, *Essays on the Sources for Chinese History* (Canberra: ANU Press, 1973).

- 'The Confucian Interpretation of the Jesuits', in *Papers on Far Eastern History* (Canberra), 6 (Sept. 1972): 1–61.

- 'Sacred and Secular in China' in *Australian Essays in World Religions*, edited by VC Hayes (Adelaide: AASR, 1977), 83–95.

Saeki P.Y. *The Nestorian Documents and Relics in China*, 2nd edition (Tokyo: Toho Bunkwa Gakuin, 1951).

Schurhammer, G. 'Fernao Mendez Pinto und seine "Perigrinaqam"', in *Asia Major,* 111 (1926) 71–103, 194–267 (rp. in his *Orientalia*, Lisbon-Rome, 1963, 23–103).

- *Das Kirchliche Sprachproblem in der Japanischen Jesuitmission des 16. und 17. Jahrhunderts: ein Stiik Ritenfrage in Japan* (Tokyo: Mitteilungen der Deutsche Gesellschaft für Natur-und Vö1kerkunde Ostasiens, XXIII, 1928).

- Franz Xaver: *Sein Leben und Seine Zeit* (Freiburg: Herder, 1955–1973) 4 volumes; English translation M.J. Costelloe, *Francis Xavier: his life and times*, (Rome: (Jesuit Historical Institute, 1973–1982), 4 volumes.

Schütte, J.F. *Alexandro Valignanos Ringen um die Missionsmethode in Japan Juli-Dezember 1579* (Rome: Gregorian University, 1944).

- *Valignanos Missionsgrundsätze für Japan* (Rome: Storia e Letteratura, Bd. 1, Teil 1, 1951); Teil 2, 1958.

Sebes, J. *The Jesuits and the Sino-Russian Treaty of Nerchinsk (1698)* (Rome: Jesuit Historical Institute, 1961).

Shih, J. *Le Père Ruggieri et le problème de 1'evangélisation en Chine* (Rome: Gregorian University, 1964).

Shryock, J.K. *The Origins and Development of the State Cult of Confucius* (1932*)* (New York: Paragon, 1966).

Smith, H. 'Transcendence in Traditional China', in *Religious Studies* II (1967): 185–196.

Spalatin, C.A. *Matteo Ricci's Use of Epictetus*, Waegwan, 1975.

Spence, J. *To change China: Western advisers in China, 1620–19*60 (Boston: Little, Brown, 1969).

- *Emperor of China* (London: Cape, 1974).

Stormon, E.J. 'A Modern Reappraisal of Matteo Ricci', *Milla wamilla*, I (1961): 86–91.

Sugranyes de Franch, R. *Raymond Lulle,* Schoneck-Beckenried (NZM Supplementa V) 1954.

Tacchi Venturi, P. 'II cosi detto Confucianismo del Padre Matteo Ricci', in *Atti e memorie del convegno di Geografi-Orientalisti tenuto in Macerata,* Macerata, 1911.

Teixeira, M. *Macau e a sua diocese*, volumes I–XIII, Macao, 1940–1977.

Thomaz de Bossiere, Y. de *Un Belge mandarin à la cour de la Chine aux XVIIe et XVIIIe sièles: Antoine Thomas, 1644–1709* (Paris: Belles Lettres, 1977).

- *François-Xavier Dentrecolles et l'apport de la Chine à I'Europe du XVIIIe siecle* (Paris: Belles Lettres, 1982).

Übelhör, M. 'Hsü Kuang-ch'i (1562–1633) und seine Einstellung zum Christentum-ein Beitrag zur Geister geschichte der späten Ming-zeit', in *Oriens Extremus* 15/2 (Dec. 1968): 191–257; 16/1 (June 1969): 41–74.

- 'Geistenströmungen der später Ming-zeit, die das Wirken der Jesuiten in China begüngstigen', in *Saeculum,* 23 (1972): 172–185.

Van Hee, L. 'Le Bouddha et les premiers missionnaires en Chine', in *Asia Major,* X (1935): 365–367.

-'Grands Chretiens de Chine', in *Xaveriana,* 12/140 (1930): 245–271.

Van Kley, D. *The Jansenists and the expulsion of the Jesuits from France, 1757–1765* (New Haven: Yale University Press, 1975).

Welch, H. *The Practice of Chinese Buddhism, 1900–1950* (Cambridge, Mass: Harvard University Press, 1967).

Willeke, B.H. *Imperial government and Catholic missions in China during the years 1784–1785* (New York: Franciscan Institute, 1948).

Witek, J.W. 'An Eighteenth-century Frenchman at the Court of the K'anghsi Emperor: a study of the early life of Jean-François Foucquet' (unpublished PhD thesis, Georgetown University, 1973).

- 'Jean-François Foucquet: un controversiste jesuite en Chine et en Europe', *Actes du colloque international de sinologie: la mission française de Pékin aux XVIIe et XVIIIe siècles*, Paris, 1976, 115–135.

- 'Jean-François Foucquet et les livres chinois de la Bibliothèque Royale', *Actes du IIe colloque international de sinologie: les rapports entre la Chine et I'Europe au temps des lumières*, Paris, 1980, 145–171.

Wu, S. *Passage to Power* (Cambridge, Mass: Harvard University Press 1979).

Yang, T.H. 'Three Ming Officials: Biographical Sketches', in *Journal of Oriental Studies*, VIII (1970): 380–386.

Young, J.D. 'An early Confucian attack on Christianity: Yang Kuang-hsien and his Pu-te-I', in *Journal of the Chinese University of Hong Kong*, III (1975): 155–186.

- 'Original Confucianism versus Neo-Confucianism: Matteo Ricci's Chinese Writings', in *Proceedings of the 29th International Congress of Orientalists*: Chine Ancienne, Paris, 1973, 371–7.

- 'Comparing the approaches of the Jesuit and Protestant Missionaries in China', in *Ching Feng*, XXII (1979): 107–115.

- *Confucianism and Christianity* (Hong Kong: Hong Kong University Press, 1983).

Yu, Chun-fang *The Renewal of Buddhism in China: Chu-hung and the late Ming synthesis* (New York: Columbia University Press, 1981).

Chinese Sources

Primary

Ai Ju-lio 艾儒略 (GiulioAleni S.J.)

Hsi-fang ta-wen 西方答問

San-shan lun hsüeh chi 三山論學紀

Hsi-hsüeh fan 西學凡

T'ien-chu sheng-chiao ssu-tzu ching-wen 天主聖教四子經文

Ta-hsi Li hsien-sheng Ma-tou ch'uan 大西李先生瑪竇傳

T'ien-chu chiang-sheng yin-i 天主降生引義

Chang Hsing-yao 張星耀 *T'ien-Ju t'ung-i k'ao* 天需同異考 ms. in BN: Chin.7171

Chang Ju-lin 張汝霖 & Yin Kuan-jen 印光任

Ao-man chi-lueh 澳門記略 (1752) published 1801, rp. Taipei. 1968

Chang Te-chao 張德昭 (Alexandre de la Charme S.J.)

Hsing-li chen-ch'uan 性理真詮 6 *chüan*, 1753.

Chang Wei-hua 長維華 ed. *Ming-shih Fo-lang-ch*, Lu-Sung, Ho-lan, I-to-li-ya, ssu-chuan chu-shih 明史佛郎機呂宋和蘭意大里亞四傳注釋 Peiping, 1934 rp. Taipei, 1972.

(Chao Fu-chung) 邵輔忠 Ming Ming-tzu 明明子

Tien-hsueh shuo 天學說 in *T'ien-chu-chiao tung-ch'uan wen-hsien hsü-pien*, 1, 3–18.

Ch'en Yuan 陳垣 ed. *K'ang-hsi yu Lo-ma shih-chieh kuan-hsi wen-hsu ying-yin pen* 康熙與羅馬使節關係文書影印本 Peking, 1932 rp. Taipei, 1973

Ch'eng Chi-li 成際理 (Feliciano Pacheco S.J.)

Sheng-chiao kuei-ch'eng 聖教規程

Chi-tsu yuan-i 祭祖原意 ms. in B.Vat: Borg. Cin. 316(11)

Chin Ni-ko 金尼閣 (Nicolas Trigault S.J.)

Hsi-ju erh-mu tzu 西儒耳目資1626, rp Peking, 1957.

Ch'ing-shi kao 清史稿 Manchukuo ed., 1928.

Chou Chih 周志 *Tu-i chi* 讀易記 1687, ms. in B. Vat: Borg. Cin. 357(9)c

Chu Hsi 朱熹 *Ssu-shu chi-chu* 四書集註 Hongkong, 1968 ed

Chung Shih-sheng 鐘始聲 and Ch'eng Chih-yung 程智用 *P'i-hsieh chi* 闢邪集 in

T'ien-chu-chiao tung-ch'uan wen-hsien hsü-pien, Taipei, 1966, II, 905–60.

Feng Ping-cheng 馮秉正 (Joseph de Mailla S.J.) *Sheng shih ch'u jao* 盛世芻蕘 in *T'ien-chu-chiao tung-ch'uan wen-hsien hsü-pien*, II, 1413–1700.

Fu Sheng-tse 傅聖澤 (Jean-François Foucquet S.J.)

Ching-i ching-yao 經義精要

Chu Hsi wan-nien t'ung-hui chih chü 朱熹晚年痛悔之懅

Yin-yang ta fu-mu 陰陽大父母

T'ai-chi lüehshuo 太極略說

I-kao 一稿

Chü ku-ching-ch'uan k'ao t'ien-hsiang pu chün-ch'i
據古經傳攷天象不均齊

Chou-i i-li 周易義例

Chou-i li-shu 周易理數

I-ching chu-chia chieh shuo 易經諸家解說

I-hsüeh wai-p'ien yuan-kao 易學外篇原稿

Chen-tsai ming-chien 真宰明鑒

Han Lin 韓霖 and Chang Keng 張賡, *Sheng-chiao hsin cheng* 聖教信證, 1647, published Peking 1668, rp. in *T'ien-chu-chiao tung-ch'uan wen-hsien san-pien*, Taipei, 1972, I, 267–362.

Hsi-ch'ao ch'ung-cheng chi 熙朝崇正集 in*T'ien-chu-chiao tung-ch'uan wen-hsien*, Taipei 1965, 633–691.

Hsi-ch'ao ting-an 熙朝定案 in*T'ien-chu-chiao tung-ch'uan wen-hsien hsü-pien*, Taipei, 1966, 1701–1804.

The Hsieh Chao-chih 謝著 *Wu-tsa-tsu* 五雜俎 16 ch., Shanghai, 1935.

Hsü Kuang-ch'i 徐光啟

Ling-yen li-shao 靈言蠡勺 1624, rp. in Li Chi-tsao, *T'ien-hsüehch'u-han*, Taipei, 1965 edn., II: 1127–1268.

Hsü Kuang-ch'i shou-chi 徐光啟手跡 Peking. 1962.

Pien-hsüeh shu-kao 辯學疏稿 1616, in*T'ien-chu-chiao tung-ch'uan wen-hsien hsü-pien*, Taipei, 1966, I, 19–36 (text &translation in E.C.Bridgman, 'Paul Su's apology, addrssed to the Emperor Wanlih . . .', in *Chinese Repository*, XIX (1850): 118–135)

P'i wang 闢妄, in *Chinese Repository*, XIX/II (1850): 617–651.

Hsü Kuang-ch'i chi 徐光啟集 ed. Wang Chung-min, Peking 1963, 2 volumes.

Tsao-wu-chu ch'ui-hsiang lüeh-shuo 造物主垂象略說 in*T'ien-chu-chiao tung-ch'uan wen-hsien san-pien*, Taipei 1972, II, 549–563.

Tseng-ting Hsü Wen-ting kung-chi 增訂徐文定公集. ed. Hsü Mao-hsi 徐懋禧, Taibei 1962.

Huang Tsung-hsi 黃宗羲 *Ming-Ju hsüeh-an* 明儒學案 62 ch., Ssu-pu pai-yao ed., Shanghai, 1936.

Juan Yuan 阮元 *Ch'ou-jen chuan* 疇人傳 Shanghai (Commercial Press) 1955

K'ao T'ing-chen 高廷珍 *Tung-lin shu-yuan chih* 東林書院志 22ch., 1736, rp.Taipei, 1968.

Li An-tang (Antonio de Santa Maria O.F.M.)

T'ien Ju yin 天儒印

Cheng-hsüeh liu-shih 正學鏐石

Li Chih 李贄 *Fen shu* 焚書 Tokyo, 1970

Xu fen shu 續焚書 Peking, 1959

Li Chih-tsao 李之藻 *T'ien-hsüeh ch'u-han* 天學初函 1629, rp. Taipei, 1965.

Li Lei-ssu 利類思 (Luigi Buglio S.J.) *Pu-te-i-pien*不得已辨

Li Ma-tou 李瑪竇 (Matteo Ricci S.J.)

Chiao-yu lun 交友論

Chi-jen shih-p'ien 畸人十篇

T'ien-chu shih-i 天主實義

Erh-shih-wu yen 二十五言

Hsi-ch'in ch'u-i pa-chang 西琴曲意八章

Pien-hsüeh i-tu 辨學遺牘

Hsi-kuo chi-fa 西國記法

Li Tsu-po 李祖白 *T'ien-hsüeh ch'uan-kai* 天學傳概 1664, in*T'ien-chu-chiao tung-ch'uan wen-hsien hsü-pien*, Taipei, 1966, II, 1043–1063.

Lo Ming-chien 羅明堅 (Michele Ruggieri S.J.)

Tsu-ch'uan t'ien-chu shih-ch'eng 祖傳天主十誡

Sheng-chiao shih-lu 聖教實綠

Lung Hua-min 龍華民 (Nicolo Longobardo S.J.)

Ling-hun tao-t'i 靈魂道體

Ma Jo-se 馬若瑟 (WenKu-tzu 溫古子) (Joseph de Prémare S.J.)

Ching-chieh 經解

San-i-san 三一三

Ching-ch'uan i-chi 經傳遺跡

Sheng Jose ch'uan 聖若瑟傳

Ming-hsin pao-chien 明心寶鑑

Ming Shih 明史Taipei 1962 ed. (v. also Chang Wei-hua)

Nan Huai-jen 南懷仁 (Ferdinand Verbiest S.J.)

Hsi-ch'ao ting-an 熙朝定案

Pu-te-i pien 不得已辨

Pang Ti-wo 龐迪我 (Diego de Pantoia S.J.)

Ch'i k'e 七克

T'ien-chu shih-i hsü-p'ien 天主實義續篇

Po Chin 白晉 (Joachim Bouvet S.J.)

T'ien-hsüeh pen-i 天學本義

Ku-chin ching-t'ien chien t'ien-hsüeh pen-i 古今敬天鑒天學本義

Meng mei-t'u chi 蒙美土記

T'ien-chu san-i lun 天主三一論

I k'ao 易考

Chou-i yuan-chih-t'an -lu 周易原旨探目綠

I-yao 易鑰

I-yin yuan-kao 易引原稿

I-ching tsung-lun 易經總論

Fu ku-ch'uan i-chi lun 附古傳遺跡論

I-hsüeh wai-p'ien 易學外篇

I-hsüeh tsung-shuo 易學總說

Ta-i yuan-i nei-p'ien 大易原義內篇

Shih hsien-t'ien wei-pien, shih-chung chih shu yu t'ien-tsun ti sheng-t'u erh sheng 釋先天未變始終之數由天尊地昇圖而生

Tsung-lun pu-lieh lei lo-shu teng fang-t'u fa 摠論布列類洛書等方圖法 *I-y* 啊 *o* 易鑰

Shih ken-pen chen-tsai ming-chien 識根本真宰明鑒

Ta Ch'ing li-chao shih-lu 大清歷朝實綠

T'ien-chu-chiao tung-ch'uan wen-hsien 天主教東傳文獻, Taipei, 1965.

T'ien-chu-chiao tung-ch'uan wen-hsien hsü-pien 天主教東傳文獻續編, Taipei, 1966.

T'ien-chu-chiao tung-ch'uan wen-hsien san-pien 天主教東傳文獻三編, Taipei, 1972.

T'ien-chu chiao-yao 天主教要 s.l., n.d. (ARSJ: JS 57a)

Wang Cheng 王徵 *Wei-t'ien ai-jen chi-lun* 畏天愛人極論 1628, BN: Chin. 6868

Wang Cheng i-wen ch'ao 王徵遺文抄 in *Kuo-li Pei-p'ing t'u-shu-kuan kuan-k'an* 國立北平圖書館館刊 VII/6 (1934): 21–40.

Yang Kuang-hsien 楊光先 *Pu-te-i* 不得已 In *T'ien-chu-chiao tung ch'uan wen-hsien hsü-pien*, Taipei, 1966, III, 1069–1332.

Yang Ma-no 陽瑪諾 (Emmanuel Diaz S.J.)

Ching-chiao liu-hsing chung-kuo pei-sung cheng-ch'üan 景教流行中國碑頌正詮

T'ien wen lueh 天問略

Yang T'ing-yun 楊廷筠

Tai-i p'ien 代疑篇 1621, in *T'ien-chu-chiao wen- hsien hsü-pien,* I, 39–47.

T'ien shih ming-pien 天釋明辨 in *T'ien-chu-chiao wen- hsien hsü- pien,* I, 229–417.

Hsiao luan pu ping-ming shuo 鴞鸞不并並鳴說, in *T'ien-chu-chiao wen-hsien hsü-pien,* I, 39–47.

Yen Pao-lue 嚴保祿 *Ti t'ien k'ao* 帝天考 and *Miao tz'u k'ao* 廟祠 mss. in B. Vat: *Borg.Cin.* 316(9), ff.1–14; 15–18.

Yung-cheng 雍正 *Yu-hsuan yu-lu* 御選語綠 19 ch. (1733), Taipei, 1967.

Secondary

Chang En-lung 張恩龍 *Ming-Ch'ing liang-tai lai-hua wai-jen k'ao-lueh* 明清兩代來華外人考略 in *T'u-shu kuan-hsüeh chi-k'an* 圖書館學季刊.IV (1930): 447–472.

Chang Feng-chen 張奉箴 *Fu-yin liu-ch'uan chung-kuo shih-lueh* 福音流傳中國史略 volumes. I and II.1, Taipei, 1970, 1971.

Chang Wei-hua 長維華 *Nan-ching chiao-an shih-mo* 南京教案始末 in Li Ting-i *et al*, *Chung-kuo chin-tai shih lun-ts'ung,* I.2, Taipei, 1956, 201–26.

Ch'en Shou-i 陳受頤 *Ming-mo Ye-su-hui shih te Ju-chiao kuan chi chi fan-ying* 明末耶穌會士的儒教觀及其反應 in Pao Tsu-peng, ed. *Ming-tai tsung-jiao* Taipei, 1968, 67–123.

Ch'en Yuan 陳垣 *Yung-cheng chien feng t'ien-chu-chiao chih tsung-shih* 雍正間奉天主教之宗室 in *Fu-jen hsüeh-chih* III/2 (1932): 1–36.

Ts'ung chiao-wai tien-chi so chien Ming-mo Ch'ing-ch'u chih t'ien-chu-jiao 從教外典籍所見明末清初之天主教 in *Pei-p'ing t'u-shu kuan kuan-k'an* 北平圖書館館刊 VIII/2 (1934: 1–31).

Chu Ch'ien-chih 朱謙之 *Ye-su-hui tui-yu Sung-Ju li-hsüeh chih fan-yin* 耶穌會對於宋儒理學之反響 in Pao Tsu-peng, ed, *Ming-tai tsung-chiao,* Taipei, 1968, 125–180.

Chu K'e-chen 竺可楨 *Hsü Kuang-ch'i chi-nien lun-wen chi* 徐光啟紀念論文集 Peking, 1963.

Fang Hao 方豪 *Chung-kuo t'ien-chu-chiao shih lun-ts'ung* 中國天主教史論叢 Shanghai, 1947.

Fang Hao liu-shih tzu-ting kao 方豪六十自定稿 2 v., Taipei, 1969.

Chung-hsi chiao-t'ung shih 中西交通史 5 v., Taipei, 1954–1955.

Li Chih-tsao yen-chiu 李之藻研究 Taipei, 1966.

Chung-kuo t'ien-chu-chiao shih jen-wu chuan 中國天主教史人物傳 3v, Taichung/Hong Kong, 1967–1973.

Feng Tso-ming 馮作民 *Ch'ing K'ang Ch'ien liang ti yu t'ien-chu-chiao ch'uan-chiao shih* 清康乾兩帝與天主教傳教史 Taipei, 1966.

Hou Wai-lu 侯外廬 *Chung-kuo tsao-ch'i ch'i-meng ssu-hsiang shih* 中國早期蒙思想史 Peking, 1956

*Chung-kuo ssu-hsiang t'ung-shih*中國思想通史 5 v, Peking, 1957–1963.

Hsiao I-shan 蕭一山 *Ch'ing-tai T'ung-shih* 清代通史 5 v, Taipei, 1963.

Hsü Tsung-tse 徐宗澤 *Ming Ch'ing chien Ye-su-hui-shih i-chu t'i -yao* 明清間耶穌會士譯著提要 Taipei, 1958.

Jung Chao-tsu 容肇祖 *Chia Hung chi ch'i ssu hsiang* 佳竑及其思想 in *Yen-ching Hsüeh-pao* 燕京學報 23 (June 1938): 1–45.

Ming-tai ssu-hsiang shih 明代思想史 (Shanghai, 1940), Taipei, 1962.

T'i-ch'ang san-chiao-ho-i Lin Chao-en 提倡三教合一的林兆 Peking, 1948.

Li Chih nien-p'u 李贄年譜 Peking, 1957.

Liang Ch'i-ch'ao 梁啟超 *Chung-kuo chin-san-pai-nien hsüeh-shu shih* 中國近三白年學術史 (Yin-ping-shih ho-chi, 17), Shanghai, 1936.

Liang Chia-mien 梁家勉 *Hsü Kuang-ch'i nien-p'u* 徐光啟年譜 Shanghai, 1981.

Lin Chih-p'ing 林治平 Chi-tu-chiao yu chung-kuo 基督教與中國 Taipei, 1975.

Lo Kuang 羅光 *T'ien-chu-chiao tsai hua ch'uan-chiao shih-chi* 天主教在華傳教史 Tainan, 1967.

Chiao-t'ing yu chung-kuo shih-chieh shih 教廷與中國使節史 2v, Taipei, 1966.

Hsü Kuang-ch'i chuan 徐光啟傳 Hongkong, 1963.

Li Ma-tou chuan 李瑪竇傳 2nd edition, Taipei, 1972.

Meng Sen 孟森 *Shih-tsung ju-ch'eng ta-t'ung k'ao-shih* 世宗入承大統考實 in his *Ch'ing-tai shih* 清代史 edited by Wu Hsiang-hsiang 吳相湘 Taipei, 1960, 477–510.

Pao Tsun-p'eng 包遵彭 editor, *Ming-tai tsung-chiao* 明代宗教, volume 10 of *Ming-shih lun-ts'ung* 明史論叢, Taipei, 1968.

Wang Chung-han 王鍾翰 *Ch'ing Shih-tsung to-ti k'ao-shih* 清世宗奪嫡考實 in *Yen-ching Hsüeh-pao* 燕京學報 XXXVI/62 (1949): 205–261.

Wang Chung-min 王重民 (rev Ho Chao-wu 何兆武), *Hsü Kuang-chi* 徐光啟, Shanghai, 1981.

Yang Chen-o 楊振鍔 *Yang Ch'i-yuan hsien-sheng nien-p'u* 楊淇園先生年譜 Shanghai, 1946.

Yang Shen-fu 楊參富 *Chung-kuo chi-tu-chiao shih* 中國基督教史 Taipei, 1968.

Character Index

Feng Mu-kang 馮暮岡
Feng Ts'ung-wu 馮從吾
FengYing-ching 馮應京
Fo 佛
Fo-kan 佛龕
Hai-tao 海道
Haoge 豪格
Ho-shang 和尚
Ho-t'u 河圖
Hou Chi 后稷
Hou-t'ien 後天
Hou-t'u 后土
Hsi-hsüeh shih-chieh ch'u chieh hsü 西學十誡初解序
Hsiao-jen 小人
Hsieh 邪
Hsien-sheng 先生
Hsien-t'ien 先天
Hsin (belief) 信
Hsin (renew) 新
Hsing 性
Hsing-li chen-ch'uan 性理真詮
Hsing~li ta-ch'uan 性理真詮
Hsü 需
Hsü Chih-chien 許之漸
Hsü Ju-ko 徐如珂
Hsü Kuang-chi (Hsuan-hu) 徐光啟 (玄扈)
Hsüan-hsüeh 玄學
Hsüeh-kuan 學官
Hui-liu-tao 迴六道
I 義
1-ching 易經
1-lai (-ti) 依賴(體）
1-ta-Ii-ya 意大里亞
1-tu ming-pien 易圖明辨
Jen (benevolence) 仁
Jen (person) 人
Ju 儒
Ju-chiao 儒教
Ju-tsai 如在
Kao Lei-ssu 高類思
Ko-lao 閣老
K'ou-t'ou 叩頭
Ku-chin t'u-shu chi-ch'eng 古今圖書集成
Kuan-yin p'u-sa 觀音菩薩
Kuei Wang 桂王
Kung Ting 共訂
K'ung 空
K'ung Ch'iu 孔丘
K'ung-tzu 孔子
Lao-tieh 老爹
Li (principle, reason) 理
Li (rites) 禮
Li-chi 禮記
Li Chih 李贄
Li Chih-tsao 李之藻
Li-hsüeh 理學
Li Kuang-ti 李光地
Li Ma-tou 李瑪竇
Li Ma-tou te Kuei-chu 利瑪竇的規矩
Li Ma-tou p'u-sa 利瑪竇菩薩
Li Pen-ku 李本固
Li-pien 理編
Li pu 禮部
Li T'ai-tsai 李太宰
Li Tsai-k'o (Lei-ssu) 利再可 類思
Lien Hsi-hsien 廉希憲
Ling 靈
Ling-hun 靈魂
Ling-kuei 靈鬼
Ling-wei 靈位
Lo-shu 洛書
Lo Wen-tsao 羅文藻
Lun yu 論語
Ma T'ang 馬堂
Mao Rui-cheng 茅瑞徵
Miao 廟
Ming (name) 名
Ming-i tai-fang lu 明夷待訪錄
Ming-shih 明史
Mu-k'an 木龕

T’ang Jo-wang 湯若望
Tao 道
Tao-jen 道人
Tao-li-t’ien chu 道利天主
Tao-te-ching 道德經
Ti (lord) 帝
Ti (sacrifice) 禘
Ti-pu 地部
Ti t’ien k’ao 帝天考
T’i 體
Tiao 弔
T’ien 天
T’ien-chu 天主
T’ien-chu chiang-sheng chi-lu 天主降生記綠
T’ien-chu-chiao 天主教
T’ien-chu-chiao hsüeh 天主教學
T’ien-chu-chiao yao 天主教要
Tien-chu ho? Shang Ti ye! 天主何？上帝也！
T’ien-chu-kuo (seng) 天主國（僧）
T’ien-chu Shang-ti 天主上帝
T’ien-chu (sheng-chiao) shih-Iu 天主聖教實錄
T’ien-chu shih-i 天主實義
Tien hsiao te 天曉得
T’ien-hsüeh 天學
T’ien-hsüeh ch’u-han 天學初函
Tien-huang 天皇
Tien-shen 天神
T’ien-ti 天帝
T’ien-ti chih Shang-ti 天帝之上帝
T’ien-tsun 天尊
T’ien-tzu 天子
Ting Chih-lin 丁志麟
Tou-ssu 陡斯
Tsu 祖
Tsung-ping 總兵
Tu ching-chiao pei-shu hou 讀景教碑書後
Tu-men yu-lu 都門語錄
Tung-lin shu-yuan 東林書院
Tung-lin tang 東林黨
Tzu-li (-t’i) 自立(體)
Wang Hung-hui 王宏誨
Wang P’an 王泮
Wang Tso 王佐
Wei Chung-hsien 魏忠賢
Wen-chung 問終
Wo-san-i 我三一
Wu-hsi 無錫
Wu 無
Yang Ch’i-yuan hsien-sheng ch’ao-hsing shih-chi 楊淇園先生超性事蹟
Yang Kuang-hsien 楊光先
Yang Te-wang 楊德望
Yang T’ing-yün (Ch’i-yuan) 楊庭筠 (淇園)
Yang-yeh yin-ju 陽耶陰儒
Yao 堯
Yeh Hsiang-kao 葉向高
Yeh-huo pien 野獲編
Yeh-lu Ch’u-ts’ai 耶律楚才
Yeh-su Chi’i-li-ssu-tu 耶穌契利斯督
Yen 言
Yen Tang 顏當
Yen Wen-hui 晏文輝
Yin Kuang-jen 印光任
Yin-mo 湮沒
Yo-chi 樂記
Yo-ching 樂經
Yu 有
Yü Huang 玉皇
Yü-tsuan Chou-i che-chung 御纂周易折中
Yuan 元
Yuan-chao 圓照
Yuan-chih 元質
Yuan-hsi-jen 遠西人
Yuan-li-lun 原禮論
Yüeh-chih 月氏
Yun-chi 雲棲
Yung 用

Index

C

D

E

F

G

H

I

J

K

L

M

N

S

T

U

V

W

X

Y

Z

www.ingramcontent.com/pod-product-compliance
Lightning Source LLC
Chambersburg PA
CBHW020833250525
27156CB00002B/96

* 9 7 8 1 9 2 2 5 8 2 0 8 9 *